Mathematical Modeling and Methods of Option Pricing

Mathematical Modeling and Methods of Option Pricing

Lishang Jiang
Tongji University, China

Translated by Canguo Li

World Scientific
NEW JERSEY • LONDON • SINGAPORE • BEIJING • SHANGHAI • HONG KONG • TAIPEI • CHENNAI

Published by

World Scientific Publishing Co. Pte. Ltd.
5 Toh Tuck Link, Singapore 596224
USA office: 27 Warren Street, Suite 401-402, Hackensack, NJ 07601
UK office: 57 Shelton Street, Covent Garden, London WC2H 9HE

British Library Cataloguing-in-Publication Data
A catalogue record for this book is available from the British Library.

First published in Chinese in 2003 by Higher Education Press.

MATHEMATICAL MODELING AND METHODS OF OPTION PRICING

ISBN 981-256-369-5

Printed in Singapore by World Scientific Printers (S) Pte Ltd

Preface

This text is based on the lecture notes of a graduate-level course "Mathematical Theory of Financial Derivatives", which I gave first at Department of Mathematics, University of Iowa, U.S.A., and later at Department of Applied Mathematics, Tongji University, Shanghai, China. In this course, I intended to present a systematic and in-depth introduction to the Black-Scholes-Merton's option pricing theory from the perspective of partial differential equation theory. It is the author's hope that this text may contribute to filling a gap in the existing literature.

Option is a financial derivative. Therefore its price depends on the underlying asset's price movement. In the case of the continuous time model, the movement of the underlying asset's price can be described by a stochastic differential equation. Consequently, according to the idea of Black and Scholes, the option price can be modeled as a terminal-boundary problem for a partial differential equation (PDE). Therefore it is reasonable to adopt the existing theory and methods of PDE as a fundamental approach to the study of the option pricing theory. This includes establishing the PDE models for various types of options, deriving the pricing formulas as solutions of the corresponding PDE problems, making qualitative and in-depth analysis of the structure of the option price, and designing efficient algorithms for solving option pricing problems from the viewpoint of numerical solutions of PDE problems.

As a textbook for graduate students in applied mathematics, the depth and scope of this book must be appropriate. In order to limit the prerequisites, we tried our best to make this text self-contained when topics of modern mathematics are involved. In fact, we only assume a basic knowledge of calculus, linear algebra, elementary probability theory, and mathematical physics equations. When topics of stochastic analysis, numerical methods of PDE and free boundary problems are encountered in the text, only a brief presentation of the basic concepts and results is given. That is, the conclusion is stated, the basic idea of the proof is explained, but the details are not presented, and references are provided to guide the reader for further study. Furthermore, we restrict our discussion to those financial topics whose option pricing can be formulated as a PDE problem via the Δ-hedging technique, to illustrate the basic idea of the PDE approach.

The book is organized as follows: Fundamental concepts of financial derivatives are introduced in Chapter 1, and basics of stochastic analysis are covered in Chapter 4. Chapters 2, 3, and Chapter 5 form the core of this book. In these three chapters, in addition to presenting the mathematical models, algorithms and formulas of option pricing, we expound the basic ideas behind the Black-Scholes-Merton option pricing theory from several perspectives and levels: starting from the arbitrage-free assumption, via the Δ-hedging technique, put the investors in a risk-neutral world where all risky assets have the same expected return—the risk-free interest rate, then option as a contingent claim is given a fair market price independent of the risk preference of each individual investor. In the case of the continuous time model, the pricing formula for European vanilla option is the well-known Black-Scholes formula. In Chapter 6 and §7.7, we study American option pricing problems. Since American option offers early exercise, the holder needs to select the optimal exercise strategy to get optimal returns. Mathematically, this is modeled as a free boundary problem, where the free boundary is the optimal exercise boundary of an American option. Since it is a nonlinear problem, explicit closed form solution does not exist in general, hence qualitative analysis and quantitative numerical solution play an important role. Naturally, American option pricing as free boundary problem becomes the central topic and apex of the book, where the power of the theory and methods of PDE are fully demonstrated. In Chapters 7-9, we study the models and solution methods for multi-asset options and various types of path-dependent options. New multi-dimensional PDE pricing models are introduced in those chapters, which include not only the multi-dimensional Black-Scholes equation, but also various types of terminal-boundary problems for hyperparabolic equations. In addition to studying various methods of numerical solution, we are particularly interested in the possibility of reducing a multi-dimensional problem to a one-dimensional problem. Finally, in Chapter 10, we study the inverse problem of option pricing, that is, how to recover the volatility of the underlying asset from the information of its option market. It is called the implied volatility problem. We first derive the Dupire's method from the PDE viewpoint, and then proceed to work in the optimal control framework, thus obtain a system of partial differential equations and propose a well-posed algorithm for recovering the implied volatility.

I would like to thank my colleagues and students at Financial Mathematics Group in Tongji University, who have read earlier versions of the manuscript and made helpful suggestions. My special thanks go to Mrs. Xiaoping Zhang, my editor of the original Chinese edition of this text at the Higher Education Press(Beijing), for her expertise and enthusiastic work, and to Dr. Canguo Li for his elegant and painstaking translation work. The publication of the English edition of this text would not be possible without their efforts.

Lishang Jiang
Tongji University, 2004

Contents

Chapter 1

Risk Management and Financial Derivatives

We begin with a brief and straightforward introduction to the basic concepts, properties and pricing principles of financial derivatives, and a clear statement of the main subject of the book——the valuation problem of option pricing.

1.1 Risk and Risk Management

Risk——uncertainty of the outcome.

Risk can bring unexpected gains. It can also cause unforeseen losses, even catastrophes.

Risks are common and inherent in the financial markets and commodity markets: asset risk (stocks...), interest rate risk, foreign exchange risk, credit risk, commodity risk and so on.

There are two totally different attitudes toward risks:

1. Risk aversion: quantify an identified risk and control it, i.e., to devise a plan to manage the exposed risk and convert it into a desired form. Basically, two kinds of plans are available: *a. Replace the uncertainty with a certainty* to avoid the risk of adverse outcomes even if this requires giving up the potential gaining opportunity. *b. Be willing to pay a certain price for the potential gaining opportunity, while avoiding the risk of adverse outcomes.*

2. Risk seeking: willing to take the risk with one's money, in hope of reaping risk profits from investments in risky assets out of their frequent price changes. Acting in hope of reaping risk profits from the market price changes is called **speculation**.

Financial derivatives are a kind of risk management instrument. A derivative's value depends on the price changes in some more fundamental

underlying assets.

Many forms of financial derivatives instruments exist in the financial markets. Among them, the three most fundamental financial derivatives instruments are: **forward contracts**, **futures**, and **options**. If the underlying assets are stocks, bonds, foreign exchange rates and commodities etc., then the corresponding risk management instruments are: stock futures (options), bond futures (options), currency futures (options) and commodity futures (options) etc.

In risk management of the underlying assets using financial derivatives, the basic strategy is **hedging**, i.e., the trader holds two positions of equal amounts but opposite directions, one in the underlying markets, and the other in the derivatives markets, simultaneously. This risk management strategy is based on the following reasoning: it is believed that under normal circumstances, prices of underlying assets and their derivatives change roughly in the same direction with basically the same magnitude; hence losses in the underlying assets (derivatives) markets can be offset by gains in the derivatives (underlying assets) markets; therefore losses can be prevented or reduced by combining the risks due to the price changes.

The subject of this book is pricing of financial derivatives and risk management by hedging.

1.2 Forward Contracts and Futures

Forward contract —— an agreement to buy or sell at a specified future time a certain amount of an underlying asset at a specified price.

A forward contract is an agreement to replace a risk with a certainty.

The buyer in the contract is said to hold a **long position**, and the seller is said to hold a **short position**. The specified price in the contract is called the **delivery price** and the specified time is called **maturity**.

Let K——delivery price, and T——maturity, then a forward contract's **payoff** V_T at maturity is:

$$\begin{aligned} V_T &= S_T - K, \quad \text{(long position)} \\ V_T &= K - S_T, \text{(short position)} \end{aligned}$$

where S_T denotes the price of the underlying asset at maturity $t = T$.

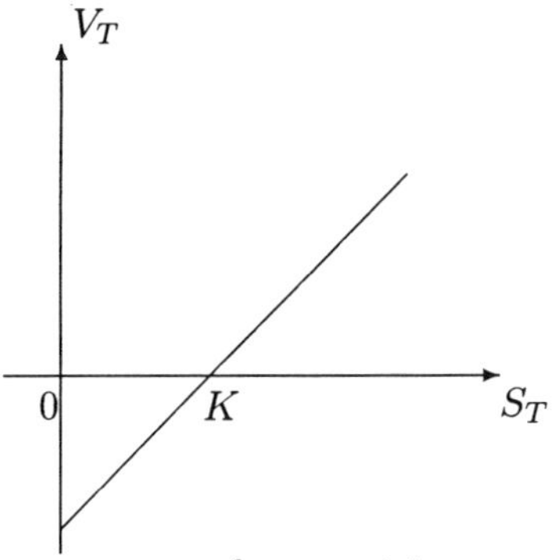

long position

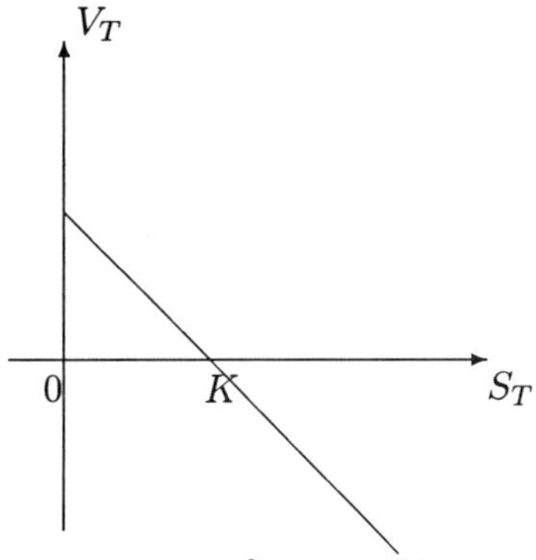

short position

Forward Contracts are generally traded OTC (over-the-counter).

Future——same as a forward contract, an agreement to buy or sell at a specified future time a certain amount of an underlying asset at a specified price. Futures have evolved from standardization of forward contracts. Futures differ from forward contracts in the following respects:

a. Futures are generally traded on an exchange.

b. A future contract contains standardized articles.

c. The delivery price on a future contract is generally determined on an exchange, and depends on the market demands.

1.3 Options

Options—— an agreement that the holder can buy from, or sell to, the seller of the option at a specified future time a certain amount of an underlying asset at a specified price. But the holder is under no obligation to exercise the contract.

The holder of an option has the right, but not the obligation, to carry out the agreement according to the terms specified in the agreement. In an options contract, the specified price is called the **exercise price** or **strike price**, the specified date is called the **expiration date**, and the action to perform the buying or selling of the asset according to the option contract is called **exercise**.

According to buying or selling an asset, options have the following types:

call option is a contract to buy at a specified future time a certain amount of an underlying asset at a specified price.

put option is a contract to sell at a specified future time a certain amount of an underlying asset at a specified price.

According to terms on exercise in the contract, options have the following types:

European options can be exercised only on the expiration date.

American options can be exercised on or prior to the expiration date.

Define K—— strike price and T—— expiration date, then an option's payoff (value) V_T at expiration date is:

$$V_T = (S_T - K)^+, \qquad \text{(call option)}$$
$$V_T = (K - S_T)^+, \qquad \text{(put option)}$$

where S_T denotes the price of the underlying asset at the expiration date $t = T$.

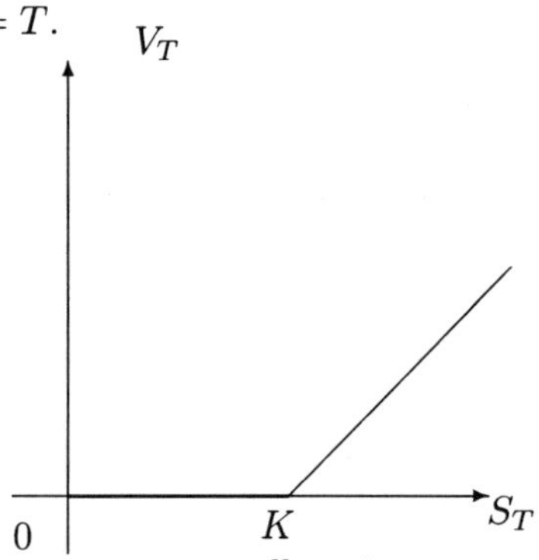

call option

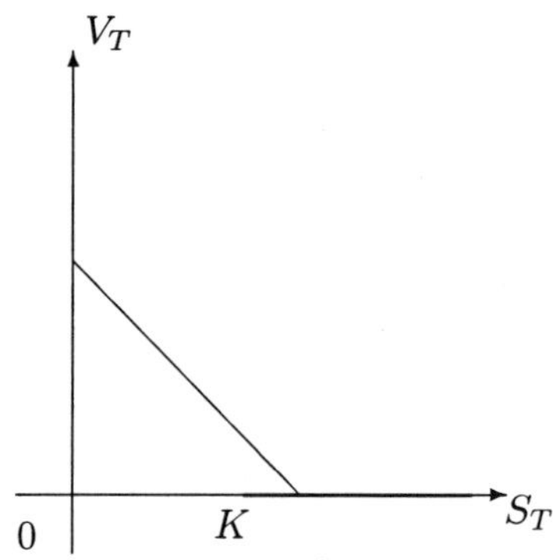

put option

Option is a contingent claim. Take a call option as example. If S_T, the underlying asset's price at expiration date, is higher than the strike price K, then the holder of the option can exercise the rights to buy the asset at the strike price K(to gain profits). Otherwise, the option is a worthless paper. Thus, to price an option is essentially to set a price to this kind of contingent claims. The significance of this fact goes well beyond the scope of derivatives pricing, and applies to many other industries such as investment and insurance etc.

The price paid for a contingent claim is called the **premium**. The needs of clients vary. Correspondingly, there exist a variety of options-the financial products developed by financial institutions. Every type of options requires pricing. Option pricing is the main subject discussed in this book. Taking into account the premium p, the total gain P_T of the option holder at its expiration date is

[Total gain] = [Gain of the option at expiration] – [Premium],

i.e.

$$P_T = (S_T - K)^+ - p, \qquad \text{(call option)}$$
$$P_T = (K - S_T)^+ - p. \qquad \text{(put option)}$$

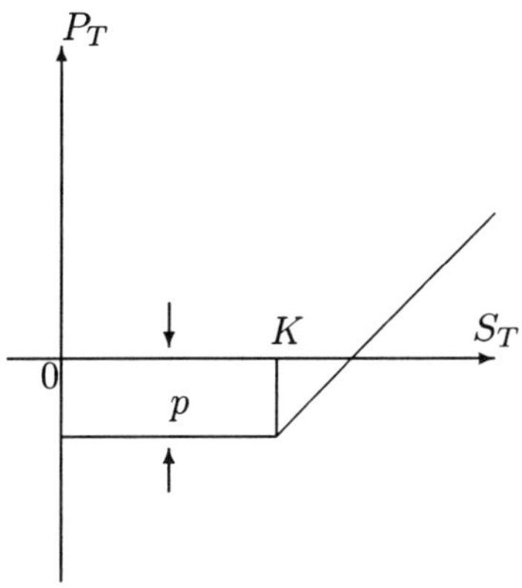

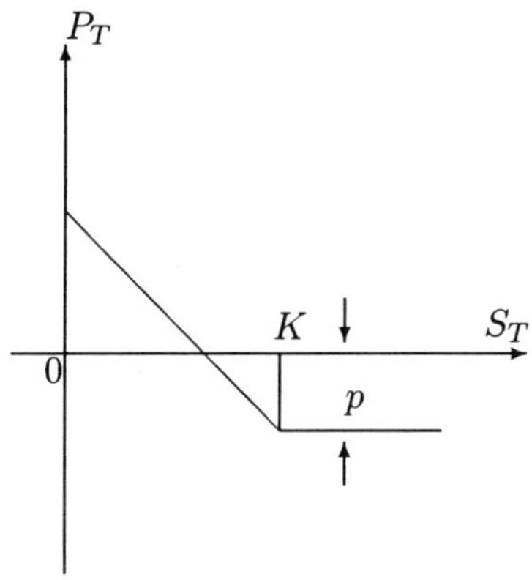

1.4 Option Pricing

As a derived security, the price of an option varies with the price of its underlying asset. *Since the underlying asset is a risky asset, its price is a random variable. Therefore the price of any option derived from it is also random. However, once the price of the underlying asset is set, the price of its derived security (option) is also determined.* i.e., if the price of an underlying asset at time t is S_t, the price of the option is V_t, then there exists a function $V(S,t)$ such that

$$V_t = V(S_t, t),$$

where$V(S,t)$is a deterministic function of two variables.*Our task is to determine this function by establishing a model of partial differential equations.*

V_T, an option's value at expiration date, is already set, which is the option's payoff:

$$V_T = \begin{cases} (S_T - K)^+, & \text{(call option)} \\ (K - S_T)^+. & \text{(put option)} \end{cases}$$

The problem of option pricing is to find $V = V(S,t), (0 \leq S < \infty, 0 \leq t \leq T)$, such that

$$V(S,T) = \begin{cases} (S-K)^+, & \text{(call option)} \\ (K-S)^+. & \text{(put option)} \end{cases}$$

In particular, if a stock's price at the option's initial date $t = 0$ is S_0, we want to know how much to pay for the premium p, i.e.

$$p = V(S_0, 0) = ?$$

The problem of option pricing is hence a **backward problem.**

1.5 Types of Traders

There are three types of derivatives traders in the security exchange markets:

1. Hedger

Hedging: *to invest on both sides to avoid loss.* Most producers and trading companies enter the derivatives markets to shift or reduce the price risks in the underlying asset markets to secure anticipated profits.

Example A US company will pay 1 million British Pound to a British supplier in 90 days. Now it faces a currency risk due to the uncertain USD/Pound exchange rates. If the Pound goes up, it will cost the company more for the payment, thus will hurt the company's profits. Suppose the exchange rate is currently 1.6 USD/Pound, and the Pound may go up, the company may consider the following hedging plans:

Plan 1 Purchase a forward contract to buy 1 million Pound with 1, 650, 000 Yuan 90 days later, and thus lock the cost of the payment in USD.

Plan 2 Purchase a call option to buy 1 million Pound with 1, 600, 000 USD 90 days later. The company pays a premium of 64, 000 USD (assuming a 4% fee) for the option.

The following table shows the results of the above risk-avoiding plans.

current rate (USD/Pound)	90 days later rate(USD/Pound)	no hedging (USD)	forward contract hedge(USD)	call option hedge(USD)
1.60	up 1.70	1, 700, 000	1, 650, 000	1, 664, 000
	down 1.55	1, 550, 000	1, 650, 000	1, 614, 000

One can see from this example: if the company adopts no hedging plan, its payment will increase if the Pound rate goes up, and thus will hurt its total profits. If the company signs a forward contract to lock the cost of the 90 days later payment, it has avoided a loss if the Pound goes up, but it has also given up the opportunity of gaining if the Pound goes down. If the company purchases a call option, it can prevent loss if the Pound goes up, and it can still gain if the Pound goes down, but it must pay a premium for the option.

2. Speculator

Speculation: an action characterized by willing to risk with one's money by frequently buying and selling derivatives (futures, options) for the prospect of gaining from the frequent price changes.

A speculator assumes the price risk, hoping to gain risky profits by holding certain positions (long or short).

Speculators are indispensable for the existence of hedging business, and they came into markets as a necessary result of the growth of the hedging business. It is speculators who take over the price risks shifted from the hedgers, and thus become the major bearers of the risks in the derivatives markets. Speculation is an indispensable lubricant in the derivatives markets. Indeed, frequent speculative transactions make hedging strategies workable.

Comparing to investing in an underlying asset, investments in its options are characterized by **high profits and high risk**, since an investment in options markets provides a much higher level of leverage than an investment in the spot markets. Such an investor invests only a small amount of money (to pay the premium) but can speculate on assets valued dozens of times higher than that of the invested money.

Example Suppose the price of a certain stock is 66.6 USD on April 30, and the stock may go up in August. The investor may consider the following investing strategies:

A. The investor spends 666, 000 USD in cash to buy 10, 000 shares on April 30.

B. The investor pays a premium of 39, 000 USD to purchase a call option to buy 10, 000 shares at the strike price 68.0 USD per share on August 22.

Now examine the investor's profits and **returns** in two scenarios (ignoring the interests).

Situation I The stock goes up to 73.0 USD on August 22.

Strategy A. The investor sells the stocks on August 22 to get 730, 000

USD in cash.

$$\text{return} = \frac{730\ 000 - 666\ 000}{666\ 000} \times 100\% = 9.6\%;$$

Strategy B. The investor exercises the option to receive a payoff:

$$\text{payoff} = 730\ 000 - 680\ 000 = 50\ 000\text{USD}$$

$$\text{return} = \frac{50\ 000 - 39\ 000}{39\ 000} \times 100\% = 28.2\%.$$

Situation II The stock goes down to 66.0 USD on August 22.

Strategy A. The investor suffers a loss:

$$\text{loss} = 666\ 000 - 660\ 000 = 6000\text{USD},$$

$$\text{return} = \frac{660\ 000 - 666\ 000}{666\ 000} \times 100\% = -0.9\%;$$

Strategy B. The investor receives a payoff:

$$\text{payoff} = (660\ 000 - 680\ 000)^{+} = 0.$$

The investor loses the entire invested 39, 000 USD, hence a loss of 100%.

3. Arbitrageur

Arbitrage: based on observations of the same kind of risky assets, taking advantage of the price differences between markets, the arbitrageur trades simultaneously at different markets to gain riskless instant profits. Arbitrage is not the same as speculation: speculation is to seek profits promised by **predictions** of the future prices, and is thus **risky**. Arbitrage is to snatch profits originated in the **reality** of the price differences between markets, and is therefore **riskless**.

An opportunity for arbitrage cannot last long. Since once an opportunity for arbitrage arises, the market prices will soon reach a new balance due to actions of the arbitrageurs and the opportunity will thus disappear. Therefore, all discussions in this book are founded on the basis that arbitrage opportunity does not exist.

Chapter 2

Arbitrage-Free Principle

"There's no such thing as a free lunch." In financial terms, *there's no such thing as an instantaneous riskless profit.* Or more precisely, *there exists no arbitrage opportunity.*

The **Arbitrage-free principle** is the foundation of the option pricing theory. Although in this chapter we cannot give quantitative answers to the derivatives pricing, because no model of the price movement of the underlying assets will be given in this chapter, yet we can deduce from the arbitrage-free principle a number of properties of option pricing, which provide in-depth qualitative description of option pricing ([32], [33]).

2.1 Financial Market and Arbitrage-Free Principle

Consider a financial market consisted of a risk-free asset B (bond) and n risky assets (stocks, options,...) $S_i (i = 1, \dots, n)$. Their prices are functions of time t, i.e. $B = B_t$ and $S_i = S_{it}, (i = 1, \dots, n)$. In time period $[t_0, t_1]$, the corresponding payoffs are $B_{t_1} - B_{t_0}$ and $S_{it_1} - S_{it_0}$, and returns are $\frac{B_{t_1} - B_{t_0}}{B_{t_0}}$ and $\frac{S_{it_1} - S_{it_0}}{S_{it_0}}, (i = 1, \dots, n)$. There is a fundamental difference between a risk-free asset and a risky asset. Suppose at $t = t_0$ we want to predict the return at a later time $t = t_1$. *For a risk-free asset, the return is certain. For a risky asset, the return is uncertain, i.e., a random variable.*

An **investment strategy** is represented by a **portfolio** Φ:

$$\Phi = \alpha B + \sum_{i=1}^{n} \phi_i S_i,$$

where $\{\alpha, \phi_1, \dots, \phi_n\} \in \mathbf{R}^{n+1}$. $\alpha, \phi_i (i = 1, \dots, n)$ are the portion invested in the corresponding asset. $\{\alpha, \phi_1, \dots, \phi_n\}$ are sometimes called the investment strategy.

In general, α, ϕ_i ($i = 1, \ldots, n$) are functions of time t, as the investor may adjust the investment strategy over the time. However, $\alpha, \phi_i, (i = 1, \ldots, n)$ are not to be changed between two adjacent transaction days $t = t_m$, $t = t_{m+1}$.

Let $V_t(\Phi)$ (or Φ_t) be the value (also known as the **wealth**) of the portfolio Φ at time t:

$$\Phi_t = V_t(\Phi) = \alpha_t B_t + \sum_{i=1}^{n} \phi_{it} S_{it}.$$

$V_{t_{m+1}}(\Phi) - V_{t_m}(\Phi)$ is the portfolio Φ's profit over time period $[t_m, t_{m+1}]$ under the investment strategy $\{\alpha_{t_m}, \phi_{1t_m}, \ldots, \phi_{nt_m}\}$:

$$V_{t_{m+1}}(\Phi) - V_{t_m}(\Phi) = \alpha_{t_m}[B_{t_{m+1}} - B_{t_m}] + \sum_{i=1}^{n} \phi_{it_m}[S_{it_{m+1}} - S_{it_m}].$$

If during the entire transaction period $[0, T]$ the investor does not add or withdraw fund, then the entire transaction process is said to be **self-financing**, or to say the investment strategy Φ is self-financing.

Definition 2.1 A self-financing investment strategy Φ is said to have arbitrage opportunity in $[0, T]$, if there exists $T^* \in [0, T)$, such that

$$V_{T^*}(\Phi) = 0$$

and

$$V_T(\Phi) \geq 0,$$

and

$$\text{Prob}\{V_T(\Phi) > 0\} > 0,$$

where Prob$\{\omega\}$ denotes the probability of event ω.

Definition 2.2 If there exists no arbitrage opportunity for any self-financing investment strategy Φ in $[0, T]$, then the market is said to be **arbitrage-free** in the time period [0, T].

Theorem 2.1 *If the market is arbitrage-free in time period* $[0, T]$, *and* Φ_1 *and* Φ_2 *are portfolios satisfying*

$$V_T(\Phi_1) \geq V_T(\Phi_2), \tag{2.1.1}$$

and

$$\text{Prob}\{V_T(\Phi_1) > V_T(\Phi_2)\} > 0, \tag{2.1.2}$$

then for any $t \in [0, T)$, *there must be*

$$V_t(\Phi_1) > V_t(\Phi_2). \tag{2.1.3}$$

Proof Suppose the conclusion is false, i.e., there exists a $t^* \in [0, T)$, such that

$$V_{t^*}(\Phi_1) \leq V_{t^*}(\Phi_2).$$

Denote

$$E = V_{t^*}(\Phi_2) - V_{t^*}(\Phi_1) \geq 0.$$

And construct a portfolio Φ_c at $t = t^*$

$$\Phi_c = \Phi_1 - \Phi_2 + \frac{E}{B_{t^*}} B,$$

where B is a risk-free bond, and $B_{t^*} = V_{t^*}(B)$. It is easy to see

$$V_{t^*}(\Phi_c) = V_{t^*}(\Phi_1) - V_{t^*}(\Phi_2) + \frac{E}{B_{t^*}} V_{t^*}(B) = 0, \tag{2.1.4}$$

and at $t = T$,

$$V_T(\Phi_c) = V_T(\Phi_1) - V_T(\Phi_2) + \frac{E}{B_{t^*}} V_T(B).$$

Let the risk-free interest rate be r, and ignore compound interests, then

$$V_T(B) = V_{t^*}(B)[1 + r(T - t^*)] = B_{t^*}[1 + r(T - t^*)].$$

Using the assumptions (2.1.1) and (2.1.2), we get

$$V_T(\Phi_c) \geq E[1 + r(T - t^*)] \geq 0, \tag{2.1.5}$$

and

$$\text{Prob}\{V_T(\Phi_c) > 0\} \geq \text{Prob}\{V_T(\Phi_1) - V_T(\Phi_2) > 0\} > 0. \tag{2.1.6}$$

With (2.1.4)—(2.1.6), and according to Definition 2.1, the portfolio Φ_c has arbitrage opportunity in $[t^*, T]$, in contradiction to the assumption that the market is arbitrage-free. Q.E.D.

Corollary 2.1 *If the market is arbitrage-free in time period $[0,T]$, and at time T*

$$V_T(\Phi_1) = V_T(\Phi_2),$$

then for arbitrary time $t \in [0,T]$ there must be

$$V_t(\Phi_1) = V_t(\Phi_2). \tag{2.1.7}$$

Proof Consider

$$\Phi_c = \Phi_1 - \Phi_2 + \epsilon B(\epsilon > 0),$$

It follows from the corollary's assumption that

$$V_T(\Phi_c) = \epsilon V_T(B) > 0.$$

Then, by Theorem 2.1, for all $t \in [0,T]$, there must be

$$V_t(\Phi_c) = V_t(\Phi_1) - V_t(\Phi_2) + \epsilon V_t(B) > 0,$$

i.e.

$$V_t(\Phi_1) > V_t(\Phi_2) - \epsilon V_t(B).$$

Let $\epsilon \to 0$, then

$$V_t(\Phi_1) \geq V_t(\Phi_2).$$

By similar argument, we can show that for all $t \in [0,T]$,

$$V_t(\Phi_1) \leq V_t(\Phi_2).$$

Therefore, for arbitrary $t \in [0,T]$, there must be

$$V_t(\Phi_1) = V_t(\Phi_2).$$

Q.E.D.

2.2 European Option Pricing and Call-Put Parity

Assumptions

1. The market is arbitrage-free.
2. All transactions are free of charge.
3. The risk-free interest rate r is a constant.
4. The underlying asset pays no dividends.

Notation

S_t——the risky asset price,
c_t——European call option price,
p_t——European put option price,
C_t——American call option price,
P_t——American put option price,
K——the option's strike price,
T——the option's expiration date,
r——the risk-free interest rate.

In the following, for convenience we assume the risky asset to be a stock.

Theorem 2.2 *For European option pricing, the following valuations are true:*

$$(S_t - Ke^{-r(T-t)})^+ < c_t < S_t, \tag{2.2.1}$$

$$(Ke^{-r(T-t)} - S_t)^+ < p_t < Ke^{-r(T-t)}. \tag{2.2.2}$$

Proof In order to prove the lower bound of c_t in (2.2.1), we consider two portfolios at $t = 0$:

Φ_1 consists of a European call option of a stock and a bank saving (or a risk-free bond) of Ke^{-rT};

Φ_2 is a stock.

For a bank saving or a risk-free bond of face value Ke^{-rT} at t=0 and interest rate r, with compound interests considered, B_t, its value at time t, satisfies the following initial value problem of the ordinary differential equation:

$$\begin{cases} \dfrac{dB_t}{dt} = rB_t, & (t \geq 0) \\ B_t|_{t=0} = Ke^{-rT}. \end{cases}$$

The solution can be expressed as

$$B_t = Ke^{-r(T-t)}.$$

Therefore,

$$\begin{aligned} V_T(\Phi_1) &= V_T(c) + V_T(Ke^{-rT}) \\ &= (S_T - K)^+ + (Ke^{-rT})e^{rT} \\ &= (S_T - K)^+ + K \\ &= \begin{cases} S_T, & S_T \geq K, \\ K, & S_T < K. \end{cases} \end{aligned}$$

Since $V_T(\Phi_2) = S_T$, therefore at $t = T$,

$$V_T(\Phi_1) \geq V_T(\Phi_2),$$

and

$$\text{Prob}\{V_T(\Phi_1) > V_T(\Phi_2)\} = \text{Prob}\{K - S_T > 0\} > 0.$$

Then according to Theorem 2.1, for all $t \in [0, T)$,

$$V_t(\Phi_1) > V_t(\Phi_2),$$

i.e.

$$c_t + Ke^{-r(T-t)} > S_t. \tag{2.2.3}$$

Now consider a European call option c. Since

$$V_T(c) = (S_T - K)^+ \geq 0,$$

but

$$\text{Prob}\{V_T(c) > 0\} = \text{Prob}\{S_T - K > 0\} > 0,$$

Therefore according to Theorem 2.1, when $t < T$,

$$V_t(c) > 0;$$

i.e.

$$c_t > 0. \tag{2.2.4}$$

By combining inequalities (2.2.3) and (2.2.4), we obtain the lower bound of c_t in (2.2.1). The rest part of (2.2.1) and (2.2.2) can be proved in a similar way and is left to the reader as an exercise.

Theorem 2.3 *Call-put parity*

$$c_t + Ke^{-r(T-t)} = p_t + S_t. \tag{2.2.5}$$

Proof Construct two portfolios at $t = 0$:

$$\Phi_1 = c + Ke^{-rT},$$
$$\Phi_2 = p + S.$$

Consider their values at $t = T$

$$\begin{aligned} V_T(\Phi_1) &= V_T(c) + V_T(Ke^{-rT}) \\ &= (S_T - K)^+ + K = \max\{K, S_T\}, \end{aligned}$$

$$\begin{aligned} V_T(\Phi_2) &= V_T(p) + V_T(S) \\ &= (K - S_T)^+ + S_T = \max\{K, S_T\}. \end{aligned}$$

Therefore

$$V_T(\Phi_1) = V_T(\Phi_2).$$

Then by Corollary 2.1, there must be

$$V_t(\Phi_1) = V_t(\Phi_2), \qquad (t < T)$$

Hence (2.2.5) is true. Q.E.D.

This theorem is very important. It shows that for a European call option and a European put option with the same expiration date and the same strike price, if the price of one option is given, the price of the other option can be deduced from (2.2.5).

2.3 American Option Pricing and Early Exercise

The holder of an American option has the right of early exercise. In what circumstance would one consider early exercising the option? Take American call option as example. If

$$C_t > (S_t - K)^+,$$

i.e., at time t, the value of the option is greater than its payoff if exercised, then obviously it is unwise to early exercise the option.

But is it possible to have $C_t < (S_t - K)^+$? The answer is negative. In fact, we have the following conclusion:

Theorem 2.4 *If the market is arbitrage-free, then for all* $t \in [0, T]$ *, there must be*

$$C_t \geq (S_t - K)^+, \tag{2.3.1}$$

$$P_t \geq (K - S_t)^+. \tag{2.3.2}$$

Proof Take American call option as example. Suppose (2.3.1) is not true, i.e., there exists a time $t \in [0, T)$ such that

$$C_t < S_t - K. \tag{2.3.3}$$

(Since $C_t > 0$, the positive part sign on the right side of (2.3.3) is omitted.) Then a trader can spend cash C_t to buy the American call option at time t, and at the same time exercise the option, i.e., to buy the stock S with cash K, and then sell the stock in the stock market to receive S_t in cash. By (2.3.3) the cash flow at time t is $S_t - C_t - K > 0$, thus the trader gains a riskless profit instantly. But this is impossible since the market is assumed to be arbitrage-free. Therefore, (2.3.1) must be true. (2.3.2) can be proved similarly. Q.E.D.

For an American option and a European option with the same expiration date T and the same strike price K, since the American option can be early exercised, its gaining opportunity must be no less than that of the European option. Therefore

$$C_t \geq c_t, \tag{2.3.4}$$

$$P_t \geq p_t. \tag{2.3.5}$$

i.e., American option's price is never less than European option's price.

Theorem 2.5 *If a stock S does not pay dividend, then*

$$C_t = c_t,$$

i.e., the "early exercise" term is of no use for American call option on a non-dividend-paying stock.

Proof By (2.3.4), (2.2.1), for any $0 \leq t < T$ there holds

$$C_t \geq c_t > (S_t - Ke^{-r(T-t)})^+ \geq (S_t - K)^+.$$

This indicates it is unwise to early exercise the option.

However, Theorem 2.5 does not hold for American put option, nor for American call option on a dividend-paying stock! In fact, for American put option, when the stock falls below a certain point, one should exercise the option immediately to avoid loss.

For example, if at time t,

$$S_t < K(1 - e^{-r(T-t)}),$$

then the holder should exercise the option immediately. In fact, the payoff at the option's expiration date will never exceed K in any case. However, if the option is exercised at time t, the immediate gain is

$$K - S_t > K - K(1 - e^{-r(T-t)}) = Ke^{-r(T-t)},$$

and by depositing the gain in a saving's account, the total payoff will exceed K at $t = T$. Similarly, for American call option on a dividend-paying stock, if the stock rises above a certain point, it is necessary to exercise the option immediately to avoid loss. In fact, if the stock is high enough at time t, when the trader exercises the option, i.e. to buy the stock at the strike price K, then comparing to exercising the option at the expiration date, the difference is that the trader must pay an extra interest $K(e^{r(T-t)} - 1)$ on the borrowed money K. However, since the dividend rate $q > 0$, if the stock price is high enough, the dividend payoff will more than offset the interest paid on the borrowed money, and therefore it is more profitable to exercise the option early.

For American options, although there exists no call-put parity like that in Theorem 2.3, there exists the following relation.

Theorem 2.6 *If C, P are non-dividend-paying American call option and put option respectively, then*

$$S_t - K < C_t - P_t \leq S_t - Ke^{-r(T-t)}. \tag{2.3.6}$$

Proof It follows from (2.3.5), (2.2.5) and Theorem 2.5, that

$$P_t \geq p_t = c_t + Ke^{-r(T-t)} - S_t = C_t + Ke^{-r(T-t)} - S_t,$$

thus the right side of the inequality (2.3.6) is proved.

In order to prove the left side of the inequality (2.3.6), we construct two portfolios at time t

$$\Phi_1 = C + K,$$

$$\Phi_2 = P + S.$$

If in period $[t, T]$ the American put option P is not early exercised, then

$$V_T(\Phi_1) = (S_T - K)^+ + Ke^{r(T-t)},$$
$$V_T(\Phi_2) = (K - S_T)^+ + S_T.$$

Therefore when $K \geq S_T$,

$$V_T(\Phi_1) = Ke^{r(T-t)} > K = V_T(\Phi_2).$$

When $K < S_T$,

$$V_T(\Phi_1) = S_T + K(e^{r(T-t)} - 1) > S_T = V_T(\Phi_2).$$

i.e.

$$\text{Prob}\{V_T(\Phi_1) > V_T(\Phi_2)\} = 1. \tag{2.3.7}$$

If the American put option P is early exercised at time $\tau (t < \tau < T)$

$$V_\tau(\Phi_1) = C_\tau + Ke^{r(\tau-t)},$$

$$V_\tau(\Phi_2) = (K - S_\tau)^+ + S_\tau.$$

Then by Theorem 2.5 and (2.2.1),

$$V_\tau(\Phi_1) > (S_\tau - K)^+ + Ke^{r(\tau-t)} \geq V_\tau(\Phi_2),$$

thus

$$\text{Prob}\{V_\tau(\Phi_1) > V_\tau(\Phi_2)\} = 1. \tag{2.3.8}$$

Therefore in any case, according to the arbitrage-free principle and Theorem 2.1, there must be

$$V_t(\Phi_1) > V_t(\Phi_2),$$

i.e.

$$C_t + K > P_t + S_t.$$

Thus the left side of the inequality (2.3.6) is proved. Q.E.D.

2.4 Dependence of Option Pricing on the Strike Price

Option pricing depends on the strike price. There exist between them important relations based on the arbitrage-free principle. For simplicity of discussion, in this section we assume the asset to be non-dividend-paying stock.

Theorem 2.7 *Let $c_t(K)$ be the price of a European call option with the strike price K. For two European call options $c(K_1)$, $c(K_2)$ with the same expiration date, if $K_1 > K_2$, we have*

$$0 \leq c_t(K_2) - c_t(K_1) \leq K_1 - K_2. \tag{2.4.1}$$

The theorem has a clear financial meaning, i.e., for two European call options with the same expiration date, the option with higher strike price leaves its holder less profit room and is therefore priced lower, but the difference between the two options shall not exceed the difference between the strike prices.

Proof We will prove the right side of the inequality (2.4.1), and leave the proof of the other side to the reader.

Construct two portfolios at t:

$$\Phi_1 = c(K_1) + K_1,$$

$$\Phi_2 = c(K_2) + K_2.$$

On the expiration date $t = T$,

$$V_T(\Phi_1) = c_T(K_1) + K_1 e^{r(T-t)} = (S_T - K_1)^+ + K_1 e^{r(T-t)},$$
$$V_T(\Phi_2) = (S_T - K_2)^+ + K_2 e^{r(T-t)}.$$

Now consider all three cases of S_T in relation to $K_1 > K_2$:

1. $S_T > K_1$:

$$\begin{aligned} V_T(\Phi_1) &= S_T + K_1(e^{r(T-t)} - 1) \\ &> S_T + K_2(e^{r(T-t)} - 1) \\ &= V_T(\Phi_2); \end{aligned}$$

2. $K_2 < S_T < K_1$:

$$V_T(\Phi_1) = K_1 e^{r(T-t)},$$
$$V_T(\Phi_2) = S_T + K_2(e^{r(T-t)} - 1),$$

thus

$$\begin{aligned} V_T(\Phi_1) - V_T(\Phi_2) &= (K_1 - K_2)e^{r(T-t)} + (K_2 - S_T) \\ &> (K_1 - K_2)(e^{r(T-t)} - 1) > 0; \end{aligned}$$

3. $S_T < K_2$:

$$V_T(\Phi_1) = K_1 e^{r(T-t)} > K_2 e^{r(T-t)} = V_T(\Phi_2).$$

Thus, at $t = T$ we have

$$V_T(\Phi_1) \geq V_T(\Phi_2),$$

and

$$\text{Prob}\{V_T(\Phi_1) > V_T(\Phi_2)\} = 1.$$

Then by Theorem 2.1, for all $t < T$ there must be

$$V_t(\Phi_1) > V_t(\Phi_2),$$

hence the right side inequality in (2.4.1) is true.

Theorem2.8 *For two European put options with the same expiration date, if $K_1 > K_2$, then*

$$0 \leq p_t(K_1) - p_t(K_2) \leq K_1 - K_2. \tag{2.4.2}$$

Theorem 2.9 *European call(put) option price $c_t(K)(p_t(K))$ is a convex function of K, i.e., for $K_1 > K_2$ and*

$$K_\lambda = \lambda K_1 + (1-\lambda)K_2, \qquad (0 \leq \lambda \leq 1) \tag{2.4.3}$$

there must be

$$c_t(K_\lambda) \leq \lambda c_t(K_1) + (1-\lambda)c_t(K_2), \tag{2.4.4}$$

$$p_t(K_\lambda) \leq \lambda p_t(K_1) + (1-\lambda)p_t(K_2). \tag{2.4.5}$$

Proof We will prove (2.4.4), and leave the proof of (2.4.5) to the reader. Construct two portfolios at $t = 0$

$$\Phi_1 = \lambda c(K_1) + (1-\lambda)c(K_2),$$

$$\Phi_2 = c(K_\lambda).$$

On the expiration date $t = T$,

$$V_T(\Phi_1) = \lambda(S_T - K_1)^+ + (1-\lambda)(S_T - K_2)^+,$$
$$V_T(\Phi_2) = (S_T - K_\lambda)^+.$$

Now consider the four cases of S_T in relation to $K_1 > K_\lambda > K_2$:

1. $S_T \geq K_1$:

$$V_T(\Phi_1) = S_T - K_\lambda = V_T(\Phi_2);$$

2. $K_\lambda \leq S_T < K_1$:

$$V_T(\Phi_1) = (1-\lambda)(S_T - K_2),$$
$$V_T(\Phi_2) = (S_T - K_\lambda) = \lambda(S_T - K_1) + (1-\lambda)(S_T - K_2),$$

thus

$$V_T(\Phi_1) > V_T(\Phi_2);$$

3. $K_2 < S_T < K_\lambda$:

$$V_T(\Phi_1) = (1-\lambda)(S_T - K_2),$$
$$V_T(\Phi_2) = 0,$$

thus

$$V_T(\Phi_1) > V_T(\Phi_2);$$

4. $S_T < K_2$:

$$V_T(\Phi_1) = V_T(\Phi_2) = 0.$$

Thus, at $t = T$ we have

$$V_T(\Phi_1) \geq V_T(\Phi_2),$$

and

$$\text{Prob}\{V_T(\Phi_1) > V_T(\Phi_2)\} = \text{Prob}\{K_2 < S_T < K_1\} > 0.$$

Then according to the arbitrage-free principle and Theorem 2.1, for any $t \in [0, T)$,

$$V_t(\Phi_1) > V_t(\Phi_2),$$

thus (2.4.4) is true.

Theorem 2.10 *European call (put) option price $c_t(p_t)$ is a linear homogeneous function of the underlying asset price S_t and the strike price K. i.e. for $\alpha > 0$,*

$$c_t(\alpha S_t, \alpha K) = \alpha c_t(S_t, K), \tag{2.4.6}$$

$$p_t(\alpha S_t, \alpha K) = \alpha p_t(S_t, K). \tag{2.4.7}$$

The financial meaning of the theorem is obvious. Consider buying α European options, with each option to purchase one share of a stock on the expiration date at strike price K; Also consider buying one European option to purchase α shares of the same stock at strike price αK on the expiration date; The money spent on the options in these two cases must be equal.

The proof of the theorem is left to the reader.

Conclusions in Theorems 2.7—2.10 also hold for American options. The proof is left to the reader.

Summary

1. The analysis made on option pricing throughout this chapter is solely based on the assumption that the market is arbitrage-free, without referring to any price model of the underlying asset.

2. By exploiting the arbitrage-free principle, we have worked backward to deduce option pricing properties in the option's lifetime. We first verify the properties of option price on the expiration date $t = T$, then infer properties over the entire lifetime $(0 \leq t < T)$ using the arbitrage-free principle. This illustrates what we pointed out in Chapter 1 that option pricing is a backward problem.

3. Without a price model of the underlying asset, only qualitative discussions on option pricing are possible. Quantitative pricing of the derivatives requires specific model on price movement of the underlying asset.

Exercises

1. Prove the upper bound in (2.2.1) and prove (2.2.2).
2. Prove Theorem 2.8.

3. Show that European put option price $p_t(K)$ is a convex function of K.

4. Prove Theorem 2.10.

5. Let $C_t(S,K), P_t(S,K)$ be prices of American call, put option with the same expiration date respectively, where S_t is the price of the underlying asset, K is the strike price. Show that for all $\alpha > 0$, there must be

(a) $C_t(S,K) \geq (S-K)^+$;

(b) $P_t(\alpha S, \alpha K) = \alpha P_t(S,K)$;

(Direct proof!)

(c) If $K_2 > K_1$,

$$0 \leq P_t(S,K_2) - P_t(S,K_1) \leq (K_2 - K_1)e^{-r(T-t)};$$

(d) If $S_1 > S_2$,

$$P_t(S_2,K) - P_t(S_1,K) \geq 0;$$

(e) For all $\lambda:\ 0 \leq \lambda \leq 1$, there must be

$$P_t(S,K_\lambda) \leq \lambda P_t(S,K_1) + (1-\lambda)P_t(S,K_2),$$

where $K_1, K_2 > 0, \qquad K_\lambda = \lambda K_1 + (1-\lambda)K_2$.

(f) For all $\lambda:\ 0 \leq \lambda \leq 1$, there must be

$$P_t(S_\lambda,K) \leq \lambda P_t(S_1,K) + (1-\lambda)P_t(S_2,K),$$

where $S_1, S_2 > 0,\ S_\lambda = \lambda S_1 + (1-\lambda)S_2$.

(Note: in fact, (b)—(f) also hold for American call options.)

6. Let c_t, p_t and C_t, P_t be prices of European call, put option and American call, put option with the same expiration date T, respectively. If the company will pay a dividend D to each share on a certain day in (T_0, T) $(T_0 > 0)$, show that following relations are true for $0 \leq t \leq T_0$:

(a) parity:

$$c_t + D + Ke^{-r(T-t)} = p_t + S_t;$$

(b) valuation:

$$S_t - D - K < C_t - P_t < S_t - Ke^{-r(T-t)};$$

(c) monotonic relation: If $D_1 > D_2$,then

$$c_t(D_1) < c_t(D_2),$$
$$p_t(D_1) > p_t(D_2),$$

and

$$C_t(D_1) < C_t(D_2),$$
$$P_t(D_1) > P_t(D_2).$$

Chapter 3

Binomial Tree Methods —— Discrete Models of Option Pricing

Suppose the price of a certain underlying asset (e.g. stock, foreign exchange rate,...) moves as a binomial tree. Our task in this chapter is to determine the option (derivative) prices for such assets according to the arbitrage-free argument and to study properties of the option price.

Essentially, the binomial tree method in option pricing puts the investors in a risk-neutral world by applying the Δ—hedging principle, and then derives the risk-neutral pricing formulas. We will illustrate this basic idea of the chapter with an example first.

3.1 An Example

Let the price of a stock be \$40 at $t = 0$, and suppose a month later ($t = T$) the stock price will be either up to \$45 or down to \$35:

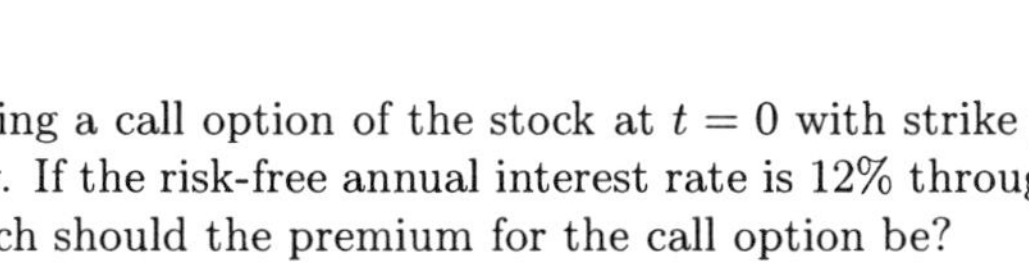

Now consider buying a call option of the stock at $t = 0$ with strike price \$40 and 1 month maturity. If the risk-free annual interest rate is 12% throughout the period $[0, T]$, how much should the premium for the call option be?

Since the payoff (value) of the call option at maturity ($t = T$) is given by

$$c_T = (S_T - K)^+,$$

the option has correspondingly two possible values at $t = T$: if S goes up, $c_T =$

$(45 - 40)^+ = \$5$; and if S goes down, $c_T = (35 - 40)^+ = \$0$.

Now construct a portfolio

$$\Phi = S - 2c$$

whose value at $t = T$ is:
if S is up,

$$V_T(\Phi) = 45 - 2 \times 5 = \$35;$$

if S is down,

$$V_T(\Phi) = 35 - 2 \times 0 = \$35.$$

No matter whether S is up or down at $t = T$, the portfolio Φ has the same definite value $V_T(\Phi) = \$35$.

Suppose the risk-free annual interest rate is 12%, then a bank deposit of $B = \frac{\$35}{1+0.01}$ made at $t = 0$ will grow to

$$V_T(B) = \frac{35}{1+0.01} \times (1 + \frac{1}{12} \times 12\%) = \$35$$

after a month, which is the same value as the investment portfolio, hence $V_T(B) = V_T(\Phi)$. Then according to the arbitrage-free principle and Corollary 2.1, we infer

$$V_0(B) = V_0(\Phi).$$

i.e.

$$S_0 - 2c_0 = B_0 = \frac{35}{1+0.01} = \$34.65$$

$$c_0 = \frac{40 - 34.65}{2} = \$2.695.$$

We conclude the investor should pay \$2.695 for the stock option.

This example reveals:

(1) The idea of hedging: it is possible to construct an investment portfolio Φ with S and c such that it is risk-free.

(2) The option price thus determined ($c_0 = \$2.695$) has nothing to do with any individual investor's expectation on the future stock price.

3.2 One-Period and Two-State Model

To study the price movement of risky assets (stock, foreign exchange rate,...), we start with the simplest model——**one-period and two-state model**. Based on this model, we study how to price the options (derivatives of the asset) in accordance with the arbitrage-free principle.

Consider a market consisting of two assets: a risky asset S and a risk-free asset B. And apply the one-period and two-state model to it.

One-period: assets are traded at the initial time $t = 0$ and the terminal time $t = T$ only, hence the term one period.

Two-state: at the terminal time $t = T$ the risky asset S has two possible values (states): S_T^u and S_T^d, with their probabilities satisfying

$$0 < \text{Prob}\{S_T = S_T^u\}, \text{Prob}\{S_T = S_T^d\} < 1,$$

and

$$\text{Prob}\{S_T = S_T^u\} + \text{Prob}\{S_T = S_T^d\} = 1.$$

Now consider this problem. Let the price of the risky asset S be S_0 at $t = 0$, and its price at $t = T$ will be either $S_T^u = S_0 u$ or $S_T^d = S_0 d$, $(u > d)$. An investor at $t = 0$ buys a European call option V at strike price K that expires on T. If the return of the risk-free asset B is the risk-free interest rate r in period $[0, T]$, i.e. $B_T = \rho B_0, \rho = 1 + rT$, ($B_0, B_T$ being the values of B at $t = 0, T$ respectively,) we want to find the option price V_0.

The asset price movements are

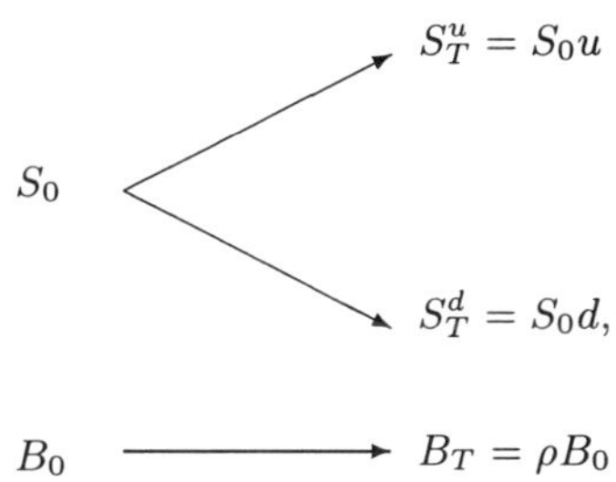

At $t = T$, the call option price is $V_T = (S_T - K)^+$, i.e.

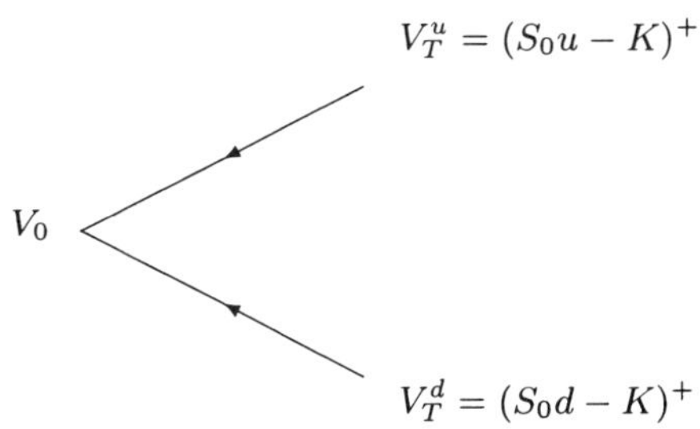

For convenience of discussion, we assume the risky asset to be a stock. Since the stock option price V_t is a random variable, the seller of the option is faced with a risk in selling it. However, the seller can manage the risk by buying certain shares (denoted as Δ) of the stocks to hedge the risk in the option. This is the idea of Δ-hedging.

Definition 3.1 **Δ-hedging**: for a given option V, trade Δ shares of the underlying asset S in the opposite direction, so that the portfolio

$$\Pi = V - \Delta S, \tag{3.2.1}$$

is risk-free.

Now we can price options using Δ-hedging strategy.
Suppose there exists a Δ, such that Π is risk-free, i.e. at $t = T$,

$$\Pi_T = V_T - \Delta S_T \tag{3.2.2}$$

is risk-free.

Being risk-free, by definition, the growth rate of the portfolio Π is the risk-free interest rate r. At $t = T$, Π grows to ρ times of its initial value, i.e.

$$\Pi_T = \rho \Pi_0, \tag{3.2.3}$$

where $\rho = (1 + rT)$ (neglecting the compound interests) is constant and definite.

Combining (3.2.2), (3.2.3), we get

$$V_T - \Delta S_T = \rho \Pi_0. \tag{3.2.4}$$

Note that (3.2.4) is a system of equations, because V_T, S_T are random variables with two possible values. Therefore (3.2.4) can be written as

$$\begin{aligned} V_T^u - \Delta S_0 u &= \rho(V_0 - \Delta S_0), \\ V_T^d - \Delta S_0 d &= \rho(V_0 - \Delta S_0), \end{aligned}$$

where Δ and V_0 are the unknowns. The solutions can be found to be

$$\Delta = \frac{V_T^u - V_T^d}{S_0(u-d)},$$

and

$$\begin{aligned} V_0 &= \frac{1}{\rho}\Pi_T + \Delta S_0 \\ &= \frac{1}{\rho}\left\{\frac{\rho - d}{u - d}V_T^u + \frac{u - \rho}{u - d}V_T^d\right\}. \end{aligned} \tag{3.2.5}$$

Suppose

$$d < \rho < u. \tag{3.2.6}$$

Define a new probability measure Q:

$$\begin{aligned} q_u &= \text{Prob}_Q\{S_T = S_T^u\} = \frac{\rho - d}{u - d}, \\ q_d &= \text{Prob}_Q\{S_T = S_T^d\} = \frac{u - \rho}{u - d}. \end{aligned} \tag{3.2.7}$$

Under the assumption (3.2.6), it is easy to see that q_u, q_d satisfy

$$0 < q_u, q_d < 1,$$

and

$$q_u + q_d = 1.$$

Thus (3.2.5) can be written as

$$V_0 = \frac{1}{\rho} E^Q(V_T), \tag{3.2.8}$$

where $E^Q(V_T)$ denotes the expectation of the random variable V_T under the probability measure Q.

Definition 3.2 Let U be a certain risky asset, and B a risk-free asset, then $\frac{U_t}{B_t}$ is called the **discounted price** (also known as the **relative price**) of the risky asset U at time t.

Since B is a risk-free asset, $B_T = \rho B_0$. Substituting ρ, and (3.2.8) can be written as

$$\frac{V_0}{B_0} = E^Q(\frac{V_T}{B_T}).$$

By now we have shown:

Theorem 3.1 *Under the probability measure Q, an option's discounted price is its expectation on the expiration date. i.e.*

$$\frac{V_0}{B_0} = \begin{cases} E^Q(\frac{(S_T-K)^+}{B_T}), & \textit{(call option)} \\ E^Q(\frac{(K-S_T)^+}{B_T}). & \textit{(put option)} \end{cases} \tag{3.2.9}$$

Remark In order to examine the meaning of the probability measure Q, consider $E^Q(\frac{S_T}{B_T})$, where S is an underlying risky asset. A simple calculation shows

$$E^Q(\frac{S_T}{B_T}) = \frac{1}{\rho B_0}(q_u S_T^u + q_d S_T^d)$$

$$= \frac{1}{\rho B_0}(\frac{\rho - d}{u - d} S_0 u + \frac{u - \rho}{u - d} S_0 d)$$

$$= \frac{S_0}{B_0} \frac{u\rho - du + ud - \rho d}{\rho(u - d)}$$

$$= \frac{S_0}{B_0},$$

i.e.

$$\frac{E^Q(S_T) - S_0}{S_0} = \frac{\frac{B_T}{B_0} S_0 - S_0}{S_0} = \frac{B_T - B_0}{B_0}.$$

This shows that under the probability measure Q, the expected return of a risky asset S at $t = T$ is the same as the return of a risk-free bond. A financial market possessing this property is called a **risk-neutral world.** *In a risk-neutral world, no investor demands any compensation for risks, and the expected return of any security is the risk-free interest rate.*

Therefore we call the probability measure Q defined by (3.2.7) a **risk-neutral measure.** The option price given under the risk-neutral measure is called the **risk-neutral price.**

Remark In this section we derived the risk-neutral option price by Δ-hedging technique. Some textbook authors use the option replication technique to derive the option valuation formula.

Definition 3.3 In a market consisted of a risky asset S and a risk-free asset B, if there exists a portfolio

$$\Phi = \alpha S + \beta B$$

(where α, β are constants) such that the value of the portfolio Φ is equal to the value of the option V at $t = T$ (note: Φ and V are both random variables), i.e.

$$\alpha S_T + \beta B_T = V_T,$$

then Φ is called a **replicating portfolio of the option** V.

If Φ is a replicating portfolio of the option V, then the option price is given by

$$V_0 = \Phi_0 = \alpha S_0 + \beta B_0.$$

The option pricing formula derived from the option replication is the same as the formula derived from the Δ-hedging technique.

In the option pricing formula (3.2.9), we can see that condition (3.2.6) plays a crucial role in defining the risk-neutral measure (3.2.7). In fact, there can be no risk-neutral measure and no risk-neutral option pricing without the condition (3.2.6).

The following theorem tells us that the condition (3.2.6) essentially states that the market is arbitrage-free.

Theorem 3.2 *In a market consisted of a risky asset S and a risk-free asset B, (3.2.6) is true if and only if the market is arbitrage-free.*

Proof First we prove that if the market is arbitrage-free, then (3.2.6) must be true.

Suppose (3.2.6) is false, e.g., $\rho \geq u$. Consider the following portfolio:

$$\Phi = -S + \frac{S_0}{B_0} B.$$

Its values at $t = 0$ and at $t = T$ are:

$$\begin{cases} \Phi_0 = -S_0 + \frac{S_0}{B_0} B_0 = 0, \\ \Phi_T = -S_T + \frac{S_0}{B_0} B_T. \end{cases} \tag{3.2.10}$$

where Φ_T is a random variable with two possible values: Φ_T^u, Φ_T^d.
If $S_T = S_T^u$,

$$\Phi_T^u = -S_0 u + \frac{S_0}{B_0} \rho B_0 = (\rho - u) S_0 \geq 0;$$

If $S_T = S_T^d$,

$$\Phi_T^d = -S_0 d + \frac{S_0}{B_0} \rho B_0 = (\rho - d) S_0 > 0.$$

Therefore Φ satisfies,

$$\Phi_T \geq 0, \tag{3.2.11}$$

and

$$\text{Prob}\{\Phi_T > 0\} \geq \text{Prob}\{S_T = S_T^d\} > 0. \tag{3.2.12}$$

(3.2.10)—(3.2.12) show that there exists arbitrage opportunity for portfolio Φ, in contradiction to the assumption that the market is arbitrage-free.

Similarly, it can be shown that $\rho \leq d$ would also contradict the arbitrage-free assumption.

Next, we show that if (3.2.6) is true, then the market must be arbitrage-free. i.e., for any given portfolio

$$\Phi = \alpha S + \beta B,$$

if

$$\Phi_0 = \alpha S_0 + \beta B_0 = 0, \tag{3.2.13}$$

and

$$\Phi_T = \alpha S_T + \beta B_T \geq 0, \tag{3.2.14}$$

then there must be

$$\Phi_T = \alpha S_T + \beta B_T = 0. \tag{3.2.15}$$

In fact, under condition (3.2.6), we can define a risk-neutral measure Q:

$$q_u = \text{Prob}_Q\{S_T = S_T^u\} = \frac{\rho - d}{u - d},$$

$$q_d = \text{Prob}_Q\{S_T = S_T^d\} = \frac{u - \rho}{u - d},$$

which satisfies

$$0 < q_u, q_d < 1,$$

and

$$q_u + q_d = 1.$$

Consider the expectation of the random variable Φ_T

$$E^Q(\Phi_T) = q_u \Phi_T^u + q_d \Phi_T^d.$$

According to the definition of the risk-neutral measure Q, and by simple calculation, and by (3.2.13), we get

$$\begin{aligned} E^Q(\Phi_T) &= \frac{\rho - d}{u - d}(\alpha S_0 u + \beta \rho B_0) + \frac{u - \rho}{u - d}(\alpha S_0 d + \beta \rho B_0) \\ &= \rho(\alpha S_0 + \beta B_0) = \rho \Phi_0 = 0. \end{aligned}$$

i.e.

$$q_u \Phi_T^u + q_d \Phi_T^d = 0. \tag{3.2.16}$$

And from (3.2.14),

$$\Phi_T^u \geq 0, \quad \Phi_T^d \geq 0. \tag{3.2.17}$$

Combining (3.2.16) and (3.2.17), we conclude

$$\Phi_T^u = \Phi_T^d = 0,$$

i.e.

$$\text{Prob}\{\Phi_T > 0\} = 0.$$

Thus (3.2.15) is true: there exists no arbitrage opportunity.

Summarizing the above, we can make a more direct statement of Theorem 3.1.

Theorem 3.2 *If the market is arbitrage-free, then there exists a risk-neutral measure Q (as defined by (3.2.7)), such that (3.2.9) is true.*

3.3 Binomial Tree Method of European Option Pricing (I) ——Non-Dividend-Paying

Divide the option lifetime $[0, T]$ into N intervals:

$$0 = t_0 < t_1 < \dots < t_N = T.$$

Suppose the price change of the underlying asset S in each interval $[t_n, t_{n+1}] (0 \leq n \leq N-1)$ can be described by the one-period & two-state model, then the random movement of S in $[0,T]$ forms a binomial tree (see the figure below).

This means that if at the initial time the price of the underlying asset is $S = S_0$, then at $t = T$, S_T will have $N+1$ possible values $\{S_0 u^{N-\alpha} d^{\alpha}\}_{\alpha=0,1,\dots,N}$. Take the call option as example, $V_T = (S_T - K)^+$, the option value at $t = T$, is also a random variable, with corresponding possible values $\{(S_0 u^{N-\alpha} d^{\alpha} - K)^+\}_{\alpha=0,1,\dots,N}$.

Denote

$$S_{\alpha}^{n} = S_0 u^{n-\alpha} d^{\alpha}, \; V_{\alpha}^{n} = V(S_{\alpha}^{n}, t_n) \quad (0 \leq n \leq N, 0 \leq \alpha \leq n), \tag{3.3.1}$$

and

$$\hat{\alpha} = \max\{\alpha | S_0 u^{N-\alpha} d^{\alpha} - K \geq 0, 0 \leq \alpha \leq N\}, \tag{3.3.2}$$

then the possible values of the option at $t = T$ are:

$$\begin{aligned} V_0^N &= S_0 u^N - K = S_0^N - K, \\ &\vdots \\ V_{\hat{\alpha}}^N &= S_0 u^{N-\hat{\alpha}} d^{\hat{\alpha}} - K = S_{\hat{\alpha}}^N - K, \\ V_{\hat{\alpha}+1}^N &= 0, \\ &\vdots \\ V_N^N &= 0. \end{aligned}$$

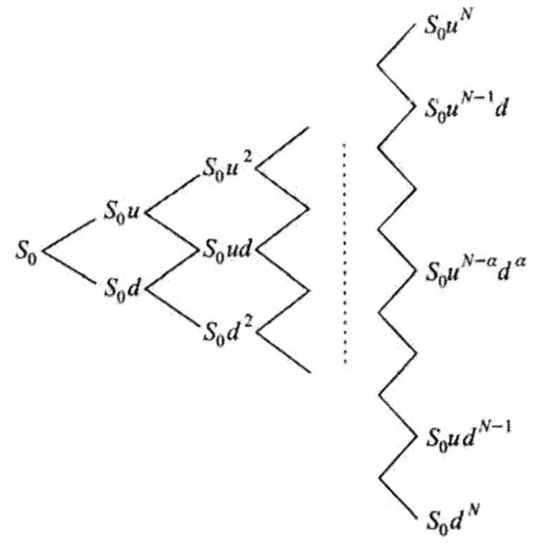

Question If $V_\alpha^N (0 \le \alpha \le N)$ are given, how can we determine $V_\alpha^{N-h} (1 \le h \le N, 0 \le \alpha \le N-h)$, in particular $V_0^0 = V(S_0, t_0)$?

With the one period and two-state model, and using backward induction, we can determine V_α^{N-h} step by step.

When $V_\alpha^N (0 \le \alpha \le N)$ are given, to find $V_\alpha^{N-1} (0 \le \alpha \le N-1)$, consider the following one period and two-state model. According to (3.3.1)

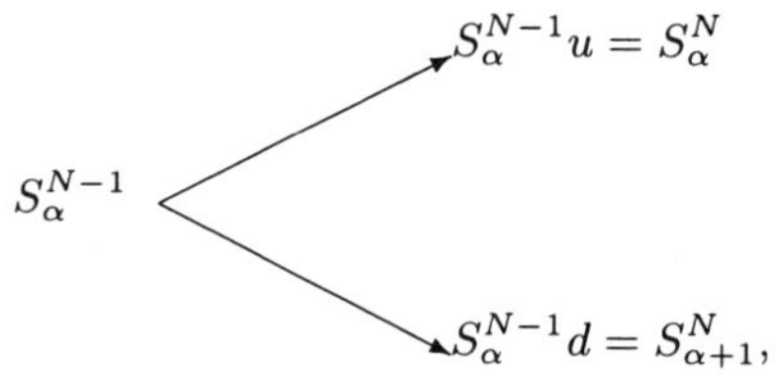

and correspondingly,

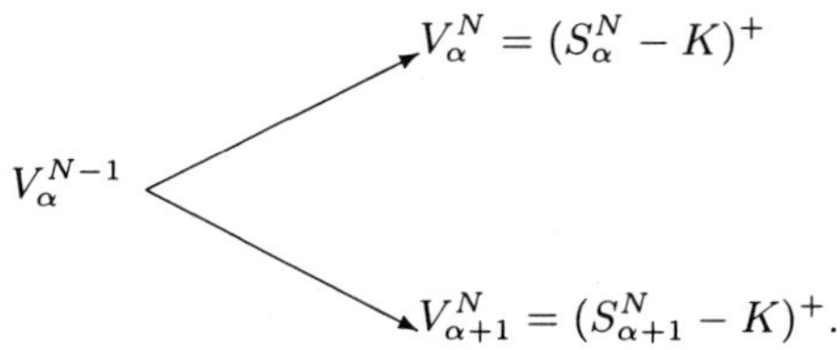

Define a risk-neutral measure Q as in (3.2.7):

$$q_u = \frac{\rho - d}{u - d} \triangleq q, \qquad q_d = \frac{u - \rho}{u - d} \triangleq 1 - q.$$

Then by (3.2.8), the option price is:

$$V_\alpha^{N-1} = \frac{1}{\rho}[qV_\alpha^N + (1-q)V_{\alpha+1}^N]. \qquad (0 \le \alpha \le N-1)$$

By backward induction, it is easy to show that for any $h (1 \le h \le N)$,

$$V_\alpha^{N-h} = \frac{1}{\rho^h} \sum_{\ell=0}^{h} \binom{h}{\ell} q^{h-\ell}(1-q)^\ell V_{\alpha+\ell}^N, \qquad (0 \le \alpha \le N-h)$$

where $\binom{h}{\ell}$ is the combination number.

According to (3.3.2), the definition of $\hat{\alpha}$,

when $\alpha \le \hat{\alpha}$,

$$V_\alpha^{N-h} = \frac{1}{\rho^h} \sum_{\ell=0}^{\hat{\alpha}-\alpha} \binom{h}{\ell} q^{h-\ell}(1-q)^\ell (S_{\alpha+\ell}^N - K); \tag{3.3.3}$$

when $\alpha > \hat{\alpha}$, $V_\alpha^{N-h} = 0$.

By (3.3.1),

$$S_{\alpha+\ell}^N = S_\alpha^{N-h} u^{h-\ell} d^\ell.$$

Denote

$$\hat{q} = \frac{uq}{\rho}.$$

Then the identity

$$qu + (1-q)d = \rho,$$

can be written as

$$\frac{d}{\rho}(1-q) = 1 - \hat{q}.$$

Then, (3.3.3) can be written as:

for $\alpha \le \hat{\alpha}$,

$$V_\alpha^{N-h} = S_\alpha^{N-h} \sum_{\ell=0}^{\hat{\alpha}-\alpha} \binom{h}{\ell} \hat{q}^{h-\ell}(1-\hat{q})^\ell - \frac{K}{\rho^h} \sum_{\ell=0}^{\hat{\alpha}-\alpha} \binom{h}{\ell} q^{h-\ell}(1-q)^\ell,$$

for $\alpha > \hat{\alpha}$,

$$V_\alpha^{N-h} = 0.$$

Define a function $(m \ge n)$

$$\Phi(n, m, p) = \sum_{\ell=0}^{n} \binom{m}{\ell} p^{m-\ell}(1-p)^\ell. \tag{3.3.4}$$

Then the **European call option valuation formula** is

$$V_\alpha^{N-h} = S_\alpha^{N-h} \Phi(\hat{\alpha} - \alpha, h, \hat{q}) - \frac{K}{\rho^h} \Phi(\hat{\alpha} - \alpha, h, q), \tag{3.3.5}$$

where

$$q = \frac{\rho - d}{u - d}, \qquad \hat{q} = \frac{uq}{\rho}.$$

In particular when $h = N,\ \alpha = 0$,

$$V(S_0, 0) = S_0 \Phi(\hat{\alpha}, N, \hat{q}) - \frac{K}{\rho^N} \Phi(\hat{\alpha}, N, q).$$

With the call—put parity (2.2.5) (Theorem 2.3) we can also derive the valuation formula for European put option.

Note that in formula (2.2.5), the factor $B_t = e^{-r(T-t)}$ is the solution of the following differential equation:

$$\begin{cases} \frac{dB_t}{dt} = rB_t, \ (0 \le t < T) \\ B_T = 1. \end{cases}$$

The financial meaning of B_t is the discount factor: to have \$1 at $t = T$ (including continuous compound interests), one needs to deposit B_t in bank at t $(t < T)$.

However, in the binomial tree method, trading occurs at discrete times $t = t_n$ $(0 \le n \le N)$ only, and therefore the compound interests should also be calculated for the discrete case. Let $B_n^\Delta (n = 0, 1, \dots, N)$ denote the discrete discount factors. They satisfy the difference equations

$$\begin{cases} B_{n+1}^\Delta - B_n^\Delta = r\Delta t B_n^\Delta, \ (0 \le n < N-1) \\ B_N^\Delta = 1. \end{cases}$$

i.e.

$$\begin{aligned} B_n^\Delta &= \frac{1}{1+r\Delta t} B_{n+1}^\Delta \\ &= \left(\frac{1}{1+r\Delta t}\right)^{N-n} B_N^\Delta \\ &= \frac{1}{\rho^{N-n}}, \end{aligned}$$

where ρ is the growth of the risk-free bond in [t, t+Δt], i.e.

$$B_{n+1}^\Delta = \rho B_n^\Delta.$$

Therefore, *for the binomial tree method, the call—put parity (in discrete form) becomes*

$$c_\alpha^{N-h} + \frac{K}{\rho^h} = p_\alpha^{N-h} + S_\alpha^{N-h}. \tag{3.3.6}$$

(The reader can also derive this formula directly, similar to the proof of Theorem 2.3).

Substituting (3.3.5) into (3.3.6), we get

$$\begin{aligned} p_\alpha^{N-h} &= c_\alpha^{N-h} + \frac{K}{\rho^h} - S_\alpha^{N-h} \\ &= S_\alpha^{N-h}(\Phi(\hat{\alpha} - \alpha, h, \hat{q}) - 1) + \frac{K}{\rho^h}(1 - \Phi(\hat{\alpha} - \alpha, h, q)). \end{aligned}$$

By (3.3.4), the definition of the function Φ ,

$$1 - \Phi(\hat{\alpha} - \alpha, h, q) = \Phi(h, h, q) - \Phi(\hat{\alpha} - \alpha, h, q)$$
$$= \Psi(\hat{\alpha} - \alpha, h, q),$$

where

$$\Psi(n, m, p) = \sum_{\ell=n+1}^{m} \binom{m}{\ell} p^{m-\ell}(1-p)^{\ell}, \qquad (m \geq n+1) \tag{3.3.7}$$

thus, the **European put option valuation formula** is

$$p_{\alpha}^{N-h} = \frac{K}{\rho^h}\Psi(\hat{\alpha} - \alpha, h, q) - S_{\alpha}^{N-h}\Psi(\hat{\alpha} - \alpha, h, \hat{q}),$$

where $0 \leq h \leq N, 0 \leq \alpha \leq N - h$.

Remark Investing in options can be compared to a gambling game. Let the initial stake be U_0. After one game, the stake becomes U_T. Since the result of gambling is subject to chance, U_T is a random variable. If the expectation $E(U_T)$ equals the initial stake U_0, i.e.

$$U_0 = E(U_T),$$

then the gamble is said to be fair. In general, let U_n be the bet at n-th game, and U_{n+1} the next bet. If, under the condition that complete information of all the previous n games are available, the expectation of U_{n+1} equals the previous stake U_n, i.e.,

$$E(U_{n+1}|\sigma(U_1, \ldots U_n)) = U_n, \tag{3.3.8}$$

then we say the gamble is fair. Here $\sigma(U_1, \ldots, U_n)$ denotes complete information of the bets $U_1, \ldots, U_n$ up to n-th game, and $E(X|Y)$ denotes the conditional expectation of X under condition Y.

In mathematics, the word "martingale" is often used to refer to a fair gamble. The bet sequence $\{U_n : 0 \leq n \leq N\}$ that satisfies condition (3.3.8), as a discrete random process, is called a **(discrete) martingale**.

As described in §3.2, under the risk-neutral measure Q, the discount prices of an underlying asset S, $\left(\frac{S}{B}\right)_{t_n}$, $(n = 0, 1, \ldots, N)$, as a discrete random process, satisfy the equation:

$$\left(\frac{S}{B}\right)_{t_n} = E^{Q}\left(\left(\frac{S}{B}\right)_{t_{n+1}}\middle|\sigma(S_0, \ldots, S_n)\right), (0 \leq n < N).$$

Hence the discount price sequence of an underlying asset is a martingale. The risk-neutral measure Q is called the **martingale measure** that is equivalent to the probability measure P.

Here "equivalence" is defined in the following sense:

Definition 3.4 Probability measure P and probability measure Q are said to be **equivalent** if and only if for any probability event (set)$\mathcal{A}$, there is

$$\mathrm{Prob}_{\mathrm{P}}(\mathcal{A}) = 0 \Leftrightarrow \mathrm{Prob}_{\mathrm{Q}}(\mathcal{A}) = 0,$$

i.e. the probability measures P and Q have the same null set.

The European option valuation formula (3.3.5), under the sense of equivalent Martingale measure Q, can be written as

$$\left(\frac{V}{B}\right)_{t_{N-h}} = E^{\mathrm{Q}}\left(\left(\frac{V}{B}\right)_{t_N} \middle| \sigma(S_0, \ldots, S_{t_{N-h}})\right);$$

or

$$V_{t_{N-h}} = \rho^{-h} E^{\mathrm{Q}}\left((S_N - K)^+ | \sigma(S_0, \ldots, S_{t_{N-h}})\right).$$

In particular

$$V_0 = \rho^{-N} E^{\mathrm{Q}}\left((S_N - K)^+\right).$$

Remark What is the relation between the arbitrage-free principle and the existence of equivalent Martingale measure?

From the discussion of BTM in §3.2–§3.3 we have already learned:

Arbitrage-free principle $\Longleftrightarrow d < \rho < u$
$\longrightarrow$ *existence of equivalent Martingale measure Q*
$\longrightarrow$ *European option pricing in a risk-neutral world*

Moreover, there is in fact an equivalence between the arbitrage-free principle and the existence of equivalent Martingale measure, known as the fundamental theorem of asset pricing.

Theorem 3.3 (the fundamental theorem of asset pricing) *If an underlying asset price moves as a binomial tree, there exists an equivalent Martingale measure if and only if the market is arbitrage-free.*

Proof In a market consisted of a risky asset S and a risk-free asset B, if the risky asset price S_t moves as a binomial tree, then by Theorem 3.2, the sufficiency part is already proved.

Now we need to prove the necessity part, i.e., if equivalent Martingale measure exists, then the market must be arbitrage-free.

For any portfolio Π, if

$$\Pi_0 = 0, \tag{3.3.9}$$

and there exists a $t^* > 0$, such that

$$\mathrm{Prob}_{\mathrm{p}}(\Pi_{t^*} \geq 0) = 1, \tag{3.3.10}$$

then what we need to prove is that there must be

$$\text{Prob}_{\text{P}}(\Pi_{t^*} > 0) = 0,$$

where P denotes an objective measure.

In fact, let Q be an equivalent Martingale measure of P, then there must be

$$\left(\frac{\Pi}{B}\right)_0 = E^{\text{Q}}\left(\left(\frac{\Pi}{B}\right)_{t^*}\right),$$

where B is a risk-free asset. Thus from (3.3.9)

$$E^{\text{Q}}\left(\Pi_{t^*}\right) = \frac{B_{t^*}}{B_0}\Pi_0 = 0. \tag{3.3.11}$$

Since measure P and measure Q are equivalent, (3.3.10) implies

$$\text{Prob}_{\text{Q}}\left(\Pi_{t^*} \geq 0\right) = 1. \tag{3.3.12}$$

From (3.3.11) and (3.3.12), we have

$$\text{Prob}_{\text{Q}}\left(\Pi_{t^*} = 0\right) = 1,$$

and therefore

$$\text{Prob}_{\text{Q}}\left(\Pi_{t^*} > 0\right) = 0.$$

Since measure P and measure Q are equivalent, this means

$$\text{Prob}_{\text{P}}\left(\Pi_{t^*} > 0\right) = 0.$$

Thus completes the proof of the necessity part. Q.E.D.

3.4 Binomial Tree Method of European Options (II) —— Dividend-Paying

An underlying asset pays dividends in two ways:

1. Pay dividends discretely at certain times in a year;
2. Pay dividends continuously at a certain rate.

In this section we discuss the BTM in European option pricing for the continuous model only, and will discuss the discrete model in Chapter 5.

But what is the practical reason for studying the continuous model?

1. Suppose the underlying asset is a foreign currency. Since the exchange rate changes randomly, the foreign currency can be regarded as a risky asset. If the foreign currency is deposited in a bank in its native country, it would accrue interests according to the local interest rate. The interest can be regarded as

the dividend of the "security". Of course, this dividend is paid continuously. Therefore, in this case, the "dividend rate" is the risk-free interest rate of the foreign currency in its native country.

2. Suppose the underlying asset is a portfolio of a large number of risky assets. Since each risky asset in the portfolio pays dividend at a certain rate at certain times, the number of dividend payments for the portfolio would be large, and we can approximate it as continuous payment (dividend rate can be time-dependent).

To illustrate the BTM for European option pricing for derivative of continuous dividend-paying assets, consider the following example:

Example A company needs to buy M Euro at time $t = T$ to pay a German company. To avoid any loss if Euro goes up, the company buys a call option of M Euro with expiration date $t = T$ at rate K. How much premium should the company pay?

Let S be the exchange rate USD/Euro. Suppose the change in the exchange rate S over $[t, t+\Delta t]$ is (one period and two-state model)

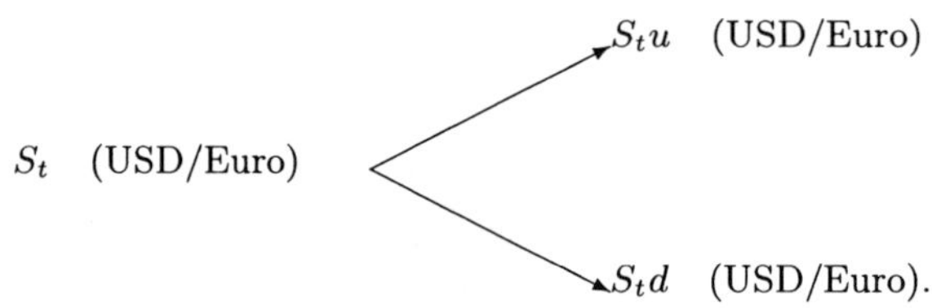

Over the same period, due to the risk-free interest ("dividend"), 1 Euro in the local bank can grow to

$$1\,(\text{Euro}) \longrightarrow \eta\,(\text{Euro}),$$

where $\eta = 1 + q\Delta t$, q is the risk-free interest rate in a German bank.

Therefore the value (dollar amount) of 1 Euro in $[t, t+\Delta t]$ changes as

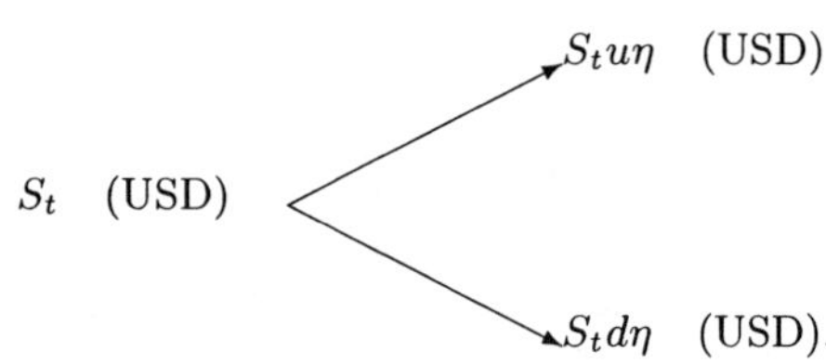

Let B be a risk-free U.S. bond. Its change in $[t, t+\Delta t]$ is

$$B_t\,(\text{USD}) \longrightarrow \rho B_t\,(\text{USD}),$$

where $\rho = 1 + r\Delta t$, and r is the risk-free interest rate in a US bank.

In each interval $[t, t + \Delta t]$, apply Δ-hedging strategy, i.e. to construct a portfolio

$$\Phi = V - \Delta S,$$

and select Δ, such that $\Phi_{t+\Delta t}$ is risk-free. Since

$$\begin{aligned}\Phi_{t+\Delta t} &= V_{t+\Delta t} - \Delta S_{t+\Delta t} \\ &= \begin{cases} V^u_{t+\Delta t} - \Delta S_t u\eta, \\ V^d_{t+\Delta t} - \Delta S_t d\eta, \end{cases}\end{aligned} \tag{3.4.1}$$

and on the other hand

$$\begin{aligned}\Phi_{t+\Delta t} &= \rho \Phi_t \\ &= \rho(V_t - \Delta S_t).\end{aligned} \tag{3.4.2}$$

Solve (3.4.1), (3.4.2) to get

$$\Delta = \frac{V^u_{t+\Delta t} - V^d_{t+\Delta t}}{\eta(u-d)S_t},$$

$$V_t = \frac{1}{\rho}\left[\hat{q}_u V^u_{t+\Delta t} + \hat{q}_d V^d_{t+\Delta t}\right],$$

where

$$\hat{q}_u = \frac{\rho/\eta - d}{u - d}, \quad \hat{q}_d = \frac{u - \rho/\eta}{u - d}.$$

We assume

$$d\eta < \rho < u\eta,$$

so that

$$0 < \hat{q}_u, \hat{q}_d < 1,$$

and

$$\hat{q}_u + \hat{q}_d = 1.$$

Since the price of the option at $t = T$ (in USD) is

$$V_T = M(S_T - K)^+ = M(S_0 u^{N-\alpha} d^\alpha - K)^+, \quad (0 \le \alpha \le N)$$

where M is the required amount of Euro, and K is the agreed exchange rate. For simplicity, let $M = 1$, and similar to what we did in §3.3, using backward induction, we can get **the pricing formula for dividend-paying European call option:**

$$\begin{aligned} V_\alpha^{N-h} &= V(S_\alpha^{N-h}, t_{N-h}) \\ &= \frac{S_\alpha^{N-h}}{\eta^h}\Phi(\hat{\alpha} - \alpha, h, \hat{q}') - \frac{K}{\rho^h}\Phi(\hat{\alpha} - \alpha, h, \hat{q}),\end{aligned}$$

where Φ is defined by (3.3.4), and

$$\hat{q} = \hat{q}_u = \frac{\rho/\eta - d}{u - d},$$

$$\hat{q}' = \frac{u\hat{q}\eta}{\rho},$$

$$\hat{\alpha} = \max\{\alpha | S_0 u^{N-\alpha} d^{\alpha} - K \geq 0,\ 0 \leq \alpha \leq N\}.$$

Similarly, we can get **the pricing formula for dividend-paying European put option:**

$$p_{\alpha}^{N-h} = \frac{K}{\rho^h}\Psi(\hat{\alpha} - \alpha, h, \hat{q}) - \frac{S_{\alpha}^{N-h}}{\eta^h}\Psi(\hat{\alpha} - \alpha, h, \hat{q}'),$$

where Ψ is defined by (3.3.7).

3.5 Binomial Tree Method of American Option Pricing

American option pricing is different from European option pricing. According to Theorem 2.4, at each node $S_{\alpha}^{N-h}(1 \leq h \leq N, 0 \leq \alpha \leq N-h)$, for American option, the price must satisfy the constraint

$$V_{\alpha}^{N-h} = V(S_{\alpha}^{N-h}, t_{N-h}) \geq (S_{\alpha}^{N-h} - K)^+; \qquad \text{(call option)}$$

$$V_{\alpha}^{N-h} \geq (K - S_{\alpha}^{N-h})^+. \qquad \text{(put option)}$$

Therefore for American option pricing (taking put option as example), its backward induction process is: at $n = N$

$$V_{\alpha}^{N} = (K - S_{\alpha}^{N})^+, \quad (0 \leq \alpha \leq N)$$

and at $n = N - 1$

$$V_{\alpha}^{N-1} = \max\{\tfrac{1}{\rho}[qV_{\alpha}^{N} + (1-q)V_{\alpha+1}^{N}], (K - S_{\alpha}^{N-1})^+\};$$
$$(0 \leq \alpha \leq N-1)$$

In general, if $V_{\alpha}^{N-h}(0 \leq \alpha \leq N-h)$ is given, then

$$V_{\alpha}^{N-h-1} = \max\{\frac{1}{\rho}[qV_{\alpha}^{N-h} + (1-q)V_{\alpha+1}^{N-h}], (K - S_{\alpha}^{N-h-1})^+\},$$

$$(0 \leq \alpha \leq N-h-1) \tag{3.5.1}$$

where

$$q = \frac{\rho - d}{u - d}.$$

I.e., in each step, after $\frac{1}{\rho}[qV_\alpha^{N-h}+(1-q)V_{\alpha+1}^{N-h}]$ is calculated, it must be compared with the payoff function $(K - S_\alpha^{N-h-1})^+$, and let V_α^{N-h-1} be the larger of the two, and so on, until V_0^0 is arrived at.

In order to see the big picture of the American option price change, we take another viewpoint to explain BTM. Suppose

$$ud = 1, \qquad \text{i.e.} \qquad d = u^{-1}.$$

Under this assumption, the underlying asset price

$$S_\alpha^n = S_0 u^{n-\alpha} d^\alpha \qquad (0 \le \alpha \le n)$$

can be written as

$$S_j = S_0 u^j. \qquad (j = n, n-2, \dots, -n+2, -n)$$

For simplicity, let $S_0 = 1$. In the plane $(S,\ t)$ we construct a grid:

$$\begin{aligned} &0 < \cdots < S_j < S_{j+1} < \dots, \\ &0 = t_0 < \cdots < t_n < \cdots < t_N = T, \end{aligned}$$

where

$$\begin{aligned} S_j &= u^j, & & j = 0, \pm 1, \dots, \\ t_n &= n\Delta t, & (\Delta t = \tfrac{T}{N}), \quad & n = 0, 1, \dots, N. \end{aligned}$$

$$V_j^n = V(S_j,\ t_n).$$

Then American put option pricing formula (3.5.1) can be written as

$$V_j^n = \max\{\frac{1}{\rho}[qV_{j+1}^{n+1} + (1-q)V_{j-1}^{n+1}],\ \varphi_j\}, \tag{3.5.2}$$

where $\qquad \varphi_j = (K - S_j)^+.$

Theorem 3.4 *If* $V_j^n \quad (n = 0, 1, \dots, N,\ j = 0, \pm 1, \dots)$ *is American put option price, then*

$$V_j^n \ge V_{j+1}^n, \tag{3.5.3}$$

$$V_j^{n-1} \ge V_j^n. \tag{3.5.4}$$

Proof We first prove the inequality (3.5.3).
When $n = N$, since

$$V_j^n = (K - S_j)^+$$

is a non-increasing function of j, thus inequality (3.5.3) is true when $n = N$.

Assuming (3.5.3) is true for $n = k+1$, now we show (3.5.3) holds for $n = k$.

In fact, due to the induction assumption

$$\begin{aligned} V_j^n &= \max\{\frac{1}{\rho}[qV_{j+1}^{n+1} + (1-q)V_{j-1}^{n+1}],\ \varphi_j\} \\ &\geq \max\{\frac{1}{\rho}[qV_{j+2}^{n+1} + (1-q)V_j^{n+1}],\ \varphi_{j+1}\} \\ &= V_{j+1}^n. \end{aligned}$$

Thus (3.5.3) is proved. It is obvious that according to the definition of American put option,

$$V_j^{N-1} \geq \varphi_j = V_j^N. \qquad (j = 0, \pm 1, \dots).$$

Thus (3.5.4) is true when $n = N$. Next we claim (3.5.4) is true in general by using backward induction process.

Theorem 3.5 *For each $t_n (0 \leq n \leq N-1)$, there exists $j = j_n$, such that*

$$V_j^n = \varphi_j, \qquad j \leq j_n, \tag{3.5.6}$$

$$V_{j_n+1}^n > \varphi_{j_n+1}, \qquad j = j_n + 1, \tag{3.5.7}$$

$$V_j^n \geq \varphi_j, \qquad j \geq j_n + 2, \tag{3.5.8}$$

and

$$j_{N-1} = -1,$$

$$j_0 \leq \cdots \leq j_k \leq j_{k+1} \leq \cdots \leq j_{N-1}.$$

Proof

Without losing generality, we assume $K = 1$ (in general, we can first make a substitution:$\hat{S} = \frac{S}{K}, \hat{V} = \frac{V}{K}$; with$\hat{S}, \hat{V}$ substituting S, V), i.e.

$$V_j^N = (1 - S_j)^+ = \varphi_j. \qquad (j = 0, \pm 1, \dots)$$

Then we have

$$\begin{aligned} V_j^N &= 0, \qquad (j \geq 0) \\ V_j^N &> 0, \qquad (j \leq -1) \end{aligned}$$

when $j \geq 0$, obviously we have

$$V_j^{N-1} \geq 0 = V_j^N, \qquad (j \geq 0)$$

where

$$V_j^{N-1} = V_j^N = 0, \qquad (j \geq 1)$$

and

$$V_0^{N-1} > 0 = V_0^N.$$

When $j \leq -1$, due to $\rho > 1$ and the identity

$$\frac{1}{\rho}[qu + (1-q)d] = 1,$$

we have

$$\begin{aligned}
V_j^{N-1} &= \max\{\frac{1}{\rho}[qV_{j+1}^N + (1-q)V_{j-1}^N],\ \varphi_j\} \\
&= \max\{\frac{1}{\rho}[q(1-S_{j+1}) + (1-q)(1-S_{j-1})],\ \varphi_j\} \\
&= \max\{\frac{1}{\rho} - S_j[\frac{qu}{\rho} + \frac{(1-q)}{\rho}d],\ \varphi_j\} \\
&= \max\{\frac{1}{\rho} - S_j, 1 - S_j\} = \varphi_j \\
&= V_j^N,
\end{aligned}$$

thus

$$V_j^{N-1} = \begin{cases} 0 & = V_j^N, & j \geq 1, \\ \text{positive} & > V_0^N, & j = 0, \\ \varphi_j & = V_j^N, & j \leq -1. \end{cases} \tag{3.5.5}$$

Thus we have

$$j_{N-1} = -1.$$

We assume the conclusion is true when $n = k$, i.e. there exists j_k, such that when $n = k$, (3.5.6), (3.5.7), (3.5.8) are true, and

$$j_k \leq j_{k+1} \cdots \leq j_{N-1}.$$

By American option pricing formula

$$V_j^{k-1} = \max\{\frac{1}{\rho}[qV_{j+1}^k + (1-q)V_{j-1}^k],\ \varphi_j\}.$$

By the backward induction assumption and the inequality (3.5.4), it is easy to obtain
as $j \leq j_k - 1$

$$V_j^{k-1} = \varphi_j,$$

and as $j \geq j_k + 1$

$$V_j^{k-1} \geq V_j^k \geq \varphi_j;$$

In particular

$$V_{j_k+1}^{k-1} \geq V_{j_k+1}^k > \varphi_{j_k+1}.$$

Since $V_j^{k-1} \geq \varphi_j$, thus for $j = j_k$ there are two possibilities:

$$V_{j_k}^{k-1} = \varphi_{j_k}, \tag{3.5.9}$$

or

$$V_{j_k}^{k-1} > \varphi_{j_k}. \tag{3.5.10}$$

If (3.5.9) is true, i.e.

$$\begin{aligned} &V_j^{k-1} = \varphi_j, && (j \leq j_k) \\ &V_{j_k+1}^{k-1} > \varphi_{j_k+1}, \\ &V_j^{k-1} \geq \varphi_j, && (j \geq j_k + 2) \end{aligned}$$

then

$$j_{k-1} = j_k.$$

If (3.5.10) is true, i.e.

$$\begin{aligned} &V_j^{k-1} = \varphi_j, && (j \leq j_k - 1) \\ &V_{j_k}^{k-1} > \varphi_{j_k}, \\ &V_j^{k-1} \geq \varphi_j, && (j \geq j_k + 1) \end{aligned}$$

then

$$j_{k-1} = j_k - 1.$$

Therefore in both cases, we have

$$j_{k-1} \leq j_k.$$

This completes the proof of Theorem 3.5 by backward induction.

On $[0, T]$, define a curve $S = S_\Delta(t)$:

$$S_\Delta(t) = \begin{cases} u^{j_n}, & t = n\Delta t, \\ \text{linear interpolation}, & n\Delta t \leq t \leq (n+1)\Delta t. \end{cases}$$

The curve $S = S_\Delta(t)$ divides $\{0 \leq S < \infty, \quad 0 \leq t \leq T\}$ into two regions: Σ_1^Δ and Σ_2^Δ.

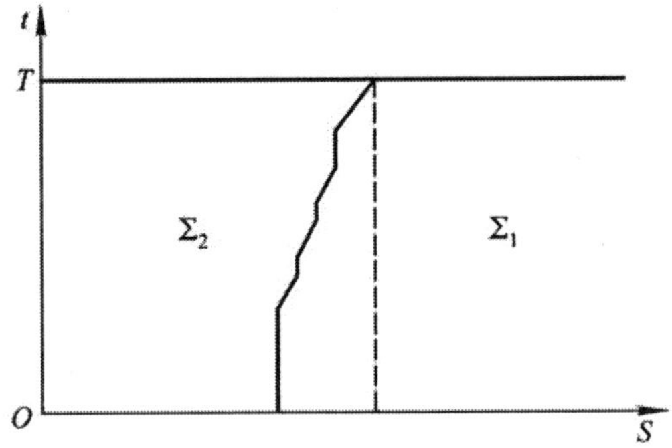

At the node $(u^j,\ t_n)$ in region Σ_1^Δ, where $j > j_n,\ 0 \le n \le N$,

$$V_j^n \ge \varphi_j.$$

And at the node close to $S = S_\Delta(t)$ (such nodes will increase with decreasing n, and will fill the entire Σ_1^Δ with $\Delta t \to 0$):

$$V_j^n > \varphi_j. \tag{3.5.11}$$

And by American option pricing formula (3.5.2), in Σ_1^Δ, there is

$$V_j^n = \frac{1}{\rho}[qV_{j+1}^{n+1} + (1-q)V_{j-1}^{n+1}]. \tag{3.5.12}$$

And the node (u^j, t_n) in region Σ_2^Δ , where $j < j_n \quad 0 \le n \le N$,

$$V_j^n = \varphi_j. \tag{3.5.13}$$

Therefore by American option pricing formula (3.5.2) and proof of (3.5.5), we can see that in Σ_2

$$V_j^n > \frac{1}{\rho}[qV_{j+1}^{n+1} + (1-q)V_{j-1}^{n+1}]. \tag{3.5.14}$$

In region Σ_1^Δ, since the option value is greater than the payoff from exercising the option, the option holder should continue to hold the contract rather than early exercising it. Therefore Σ_1^Δ is called the **continuation region.** In region Σ_2^Δ, since

$$qV_{j+1}^{n+1} + (1-q)V_{j-1}^{n+1} < \rho V_j^n,$$

which means the option's expected return is less than the risk-free interest rate, the holder should stop the contract, i.e. early exercise the option immediately. Therefore Σ_2^Δ is called the **stopping region.**

Therefore, $S = S_\Delta(t)$ is of great importance in finance, as the interface of the continuation and stopping, and is called the **optimal exercise boundary.**

Theoretically, American option holder should choose a suitable exercise strategy according to the above analysis to avoid loss.

3.6 Call-Put Symmetry

As well known, call-put parity does not hold for American options. One naturally asks whether there exists other kind of relation between American call and put options.

In order to answer this question, let us examine this problem from financial point of view.

Take stock option as example. An option as a contract gives its holder the right to exchange cash for stock (call option), or to exchange stock for cash (put option), at the strike price on the expiration date.

Here we may regard the cash as a risk-free bond earning interests according to the risk-free interest rate, and regard the stock as a risky bond earning risk-free "interests" according to the dividend rate. Then we can see a certain "symmetry" exists between the call and put options:

$$C(S,K;\rho,\eta;t) = P(K,S;\eta,\rho;t). \tag{3.6.1}$$

i.e. for options (no matter whether European or American) with the same expiration date, if the positions of S and K, and the positions of η and ρ are both swapped, the call option price and put option price should be equal.

We can prove this assertion using BTM. i.e. we assume throughout this section, American option price is determined by BTM, and under this assumption we prove that the relation (3.6.1) is true([31]).

Theorem 3.6 (call-put symmetry) *If $ud = 1$, then for American options with the same expiration date, relation (3.6.1) is true, where $t = t_n$, $(0 \leq n \leq N)$.*

To prove this theorem, we need the following results.

Lemma 3.1 *If $ud = 1$,*

$$q = \frac{\rho/\eta - d}{u - d}, \qquad q' = \frac{\eta/\rho - d}{u - d},$$

then

$$\frac{qu}{\rho} = \frac{1 - q'}{\eta},$$

$$\frac{(1-q)d}{\rho} = \frac{q'}{\eta},$$

are true.

Proof Begin with the identity

$$\eta[qu + (1-q)d] = \rho,$$

by straightforward calculation, it is easy to claim

$$\begin{aligned}\frac{qu}{\rho} &= \frac{1}{\eta} - (1-q)\frac{d}{\rho} = \frac{1}{\eta} - \frac{u-\rho/\eta}{u-d}\frac{d}{\rho} \\ &= \frac{1}{\eta}[1 - \frac{ud\eta - \rho d}{\rho(u-d)}] = \frac{1}{\eta}[1 - \frac{\eta/\rho - d}{u-d}] \\ &= \frac{1}{\eta}(1-q^{'}).\end{aligned}$$

Using the same procedure, we can prove

$$\frac{(1-q)d}{\rho} = \frac{q^{'}}{\eta}.$$

Q.E.D.

Lemma 3.2 *American option price is a linear homogeneous function of S and K, i.e. for any $\mu > 0$,*

$$V(\mu S_\alpha^{N-h}; \mu K) = \mu V(S_\alpha^{N-h}; K), \tag{3.6.2}$$

where $V = V(S;K)$ denotes the price of American option with strike price K (other nonessential parameters are omitted).

Proof Take American call option as example. Obviously when $h = 0$, (3.6.2) is true. Now we prove when $h = 1$, (3.6.2) is still true. Denote

$$V_\alpha^{N-1} = V(S_\alpha^{N-1}; K).$$

According to American call option valuation formula (3.5.1),

$$V(S_\alpha^{N-1}; K) = \max\{\frac{1}{\rho}[qV(S_\alpha^N; K) + (1-q)V(S_{\alpha+1}^N; K)], (S_\alpha^{N-1} - K)^+\},$$

where $S_\alpha^N = S_0 u^{N-\alpha} d^\alpha = S_\alpha^{N-1} u$, $S_{\alpha+1}^N = S_\alpha^{N-1} d$. Therefore

$$\begin{aligned}V(\mu S_\alpha^{N-1}; \mu K) &= \max\{\frac{1}{\rho}[qV(\mu S_\alpha^N; \mu K) + (1-q)V(\mu S_{\alpha+1}^N; \mu K)], \\ &\qquad (\mu S_\alpha^{N-1} - \mu K)^+\} \\ &= \max\{\frac{1}{\rho}[q(\mu S_\alpha^N - \mu K)^+ + (1-q)(\mu S_{\alpha+1}^N - \mu K)^+], \\ &\qquad (\mu S_\alpha^{N-1} - \mu K)^+\} \\ &= \mu V(S_\alpha^{N-1}; K).\end{aligned}$$

Using backward induction, if the lemma is true for $h = k - 1$, then by (3.5.1) it is also true for $h = k$. This completes the proof of the lemma. Q.E.D.

Proof of Theorem 3.6 Let $C(S, K; \rho, \eta; n)$ denote American call option price at $t = t_n$ $(0 \leq n \leq N)$, then by (3.5.1) (for simplicity, subscripts and superscripts are omitted, and S_α^{N-1} is thus denoted by S)

$$\begin{aligned}
C(S, K; \rho, \eta; N-1) &= \max\{\frac{1}{\rho}[q(Su - K)^+ + (1-q)(Sd - K)^+], (S - K)^+\} \\
&= \max\{\frac{1}{\rho}[qu(S - Kd)^+ + (1-q)d(S - Ku)^+], \\
&\quad (S - K)^+\} \\
&= \max\{\frac{1}{\eta}[(1-q')(S - Kd)^+ + q'(S - Ku)^+], \\
&\quad (S - K)^+\} \qquad \text{(by Lemma 3.1)} \\
&= P(K, S; \eta, \rho; N-1). \qquad (\text{ since } q' = \frac{\eta/\rho - d}{u - d})
\end{aligned}$$

Therefore when S, K are both regarded as fixed values, the theorem is true.

Using backward induction, assuming the theorem is true when $n = k + 1$, we can show that when $n = k$ the theorem is also true.

In fact, according to American call option valuation formula (3.5.1),

$$\begin{aligned}
C(S, K; \rho, \eta; k) &= \max\{\frac{1}{\rho}[qC(Su; K; k+1) + (1-q)C(Sd; K; k+1)], \\
&\quad (S - K)^+\} \\
&= \max\{\frac{1}{\rho}[quC(S; \frac{K}{u}; k+1) + (1-q)dC(S; \frac{K}{d}; k+1)], \\
&\quad (S - K)^+\} \qquad \text{(by Lemma 3.2)} \\
&= \max\{\frac{1}{\eta}[(1-q')C(S; Kd; k+1) + q'C(S; Ku; k+1)], (S - K)^+\} \\
&\quad \text{(by theorem assumption } ud = 1\text{, and Lemma 3.1)} \\
&= P(K, S; \eta, \rho; k). \qquad \text{(by induction assumption and definition of } q'\text{)}
\end{aligned}$$

This completes the proof of the Theorem. Q.E.D.

Remark Call—put symmetry (3.6.1) obviously also holds for European options.

Theorem 3.7 *For American options with the same expiration date, let $S_c(S_p)$ and $K_c(K_p)$ denote the underlying asset price and strike price for the call (put) option respectively. If*

$$\frac{K_p}{S_p} = \frac{S_c}{K_c}, \tag{3.6.3}$$

then the following relation is true

$$\frac{C(S_c, K_c; \rho, \eta; t)}{\sqrt{S_c K_c}} = \frac{P(S_p, K_p; \eta, \rho; t)}{\sqrt{S_p K_p}}, \qquad (3.6.4)$$

where $t = t_n \quad (0 \le n \le N)$.

Proof

By call-put option symmetry (3.6.1) (Theorem 3.6) and assumption (3.6.3),

$$\begin{aligned}
\frac{C(S_c, K_c; \rho, \eta; t)}{\sqrt{S_c K_c}} &= \frac{P(K_c, S_c; \eta, \rho; t)}{\sqrt{S_c K_c}} \\
&= \frac{1}{\sqrt{S_p K_p}} \frac{K_p}{S_c} P(K_c, S_c; \eta, \rho; t) \\
&= \frac{1}{\sqrt{S_p K_p}} P(\frac{K_p K_c}{S_c}, K_p; \eta, \rho; t) \\
&\qquad \text{(by Lemma 3.2)} \\
&= \frac{1}{\sqrt{S_p K_p}} P(S_p, K_p; \eta, \rho; t).
\end{aligned}$$

Q.E.D.

Corollary In particular, if $S_c = S, K_p = K_c = K$, then by (3.6.3)

$$S_p = \frac{K^2}{S}.$$

Substituting these in (3.6.4), we get **the call-put symmetry for American options with the same expiration date and strike price**

$$C(S, K; \rho, \eta; t_n) = \frac{S}{K} P(\frac{K^2}{S}, K; \eta, \rho; t_n). \qquad (0 \le n \le N) \qquad (3.6.5)$$

Summary

1. In this chapter we have introduced a discrete model——BTM to describe the underlying asset price movement, and have priced its derivatives (options) using this model.

2. Based on the arbitrage-free principle, using the Δ-hedging technique, we have introduced a risk-neutral equivalent martingale measure. The BTM of option pricing has produced a fair valuation that is independent of any individual investor's risk preference.

3. Using the BTM of American option, we have shown that there exist two regions for American put option: the continuation region and the stopping region, which are separated by the optimal exercise boundary. In the continuation region:

$$V_j^n > (K - S_j)^+,$$

$$qV_{j+1}^{n+1} + (1-q)V_{j-1}^{n+1} = V_j^n;$$

In the stopping region:

$$V_j^n = (K - S_j)^+,$$

$$qV_{j+1}^{n+1} + (1-q)V_{j-1}^{n+1} < V_j^n.$$

4. For American options, although there is no call—put parity, there exists call-put symmetry, as for European options.

Exercises

1. Let $c_\alpha^{N-h}(r,q,K), p_\alpha^{N-h}(r,q,K)$ be call and put option prices with interest rate r and dividend rate q, strike price K, where $t = (N-h)\Delta t \quad (0 \le h \le N)$, $\quad S = S_\alpha^{N-h} = S_0 u^\alpha d^{N-h-\alpha} \ (0 \le \alpha \le N-h)$. Show that:

(1) when $q_1 > q_2$,

$$c_\alpha^{N-h}(r,q_1,K) \le c_\alpha^{N-h}(r,q_2,K),$$

$$p_\alpha^{N-h}(r,q_1,K) \ge p_\alpha^{N-h}(r,q_2,K).$$

(2) when $r_1 > r_2$,

$$c_\alpha^{N-h}(r_1,q,K) \ge c_\alpha^{N-h}(r_2,q,K),$$

$$p_\alpha^{N-h}(r_1,q,K) \le p_\alpha^{N-h}(r_2,q,K).$$

(3)

$$c_\alpha^{N-h}(r,q,K_\lambda) \le \lambda c_\alpha^{N-h}(r,q,K_1) + (1-\lambda)c_\alpha^{N-h}(r,q,K_2),$$

where $K_\lambda = \lambda K_1 + (1-\lambda)K_2, 0 \le \lambda \le 1, \quad K_1, K_2 > 0$. p_α^{N-h} has the same property. It means that the option price is a convex function of the strike price.

(4)

$$c_\alpha^{N-h} \le \frac{\theta^\alpha - \theta^{\alpha_2}}{\theta^{\alpha_1} - \theta^{\alpha_2}} c_{\alpha_1}^{N-h} + \frac{\theta^{\alpha_1} - \theta^\alpha}{\theta^{\alpha_1} - \theta^{\alpha_2}} c_{\alpha_2}^{N-h},$$

where $0 \le \alpha_2 \le \alpha \le \alpha_1 \le N-h, \quad \theta = \frac{u}{d}$. p_α^{N-h} has the same property. It means that the option price is a convex function of the underlying asset's price.

(5) Let

$$\Delta_\alpha^{N-h} = \frac{c_{\alpha+1}^{N-h} - c_{\alpha-1}^{N-h}}{S_\alpha^{N-h}(\theta - \theta^{-1})},$$

then

$$\Delta_\alpha^{N-h} \ge \Delta_{\alpha-1}^{N-h},$$

where $2 \leq \alpha \leq N - h - 1$. and this is true also for put option.

2. Consider continuous dividend-paying American call option. Let V_j^n $(n = 0, 1, \ldots, N;\ j = 0, \pm 1, \pm 2, \ldots)$ be its prices, show that:

(1)

$$V_j^{n-1} \geq V_j^n,$$
$$V_j^n \leq V_{j+1}^n.$$

(2) There exist $j_n (n = 0, 1, \ldots, N)$, such that
when $j < j_n, 0 \leq n \leq N$, there are

$$V_j^n \geq \varphi_j,$$

and

$$V_j^n = \frac{1}{\rho}[q_u V_{j+1}^{n+1} + q_d V_{j-1}^{n+1}];$$

when $j > j_n, 0 \leq n \leq N$, there are

$$V_j^n = \varphi_j,$$

and

$$V_j^n > \frac{1}{\rho}[q_u V_{j+1}^{n+1} + q_d V_{j-1}^{n+1}];$$

And when $j = j_n, 0 \leq n \leq N$, there are

$$V_{j_n}^n = \phi_{j_n} = \frac{1}{\rho}[q_u V_{j_n+1}^{n+1} + q_d V_{j_n-1}^{n+1}];$$

Moreover j_n satisfies:

$$j_0 \geq j_1 \geq \cdots \geq j_N,$$

where

$$q_u = \frac{\rho/\eta - d}{u - d},$$

$$q_d = \frac{u - \rho/\eta}{u - d}.$$

3. Suppose today is 8/1, and stock price is \$75, risk-free interest rate is 4%.

(1) Suppose after 3 months, the stock price has two possible values: either goes up to \$92, or goes down to \$59. Find the up and down probability for the stock price, under the risk-neutral measure. Find the premium for a European put option with expiration date 10/31 at strike price \$75.

(2) Suppose during 3 months period, each month the stock price has two possible changes: either goes up 5% or down 5%. Find the premium for a European put option with expiration date 10/31 at strike price \$75.

(3) In addition to the assumption in question (2), suppose the contract gives the holder the right to early exercise the option at the end of each month during the lifetime of the contract. Find the premium for a put option with expiration date 10/31 at strike price \$75.

(4) If in (2) and (3), the purchased option is a call option, how much should the premium be?

4. Let $C_n(S; u, d)$ $(n = 0, 1, \ldots, N)$ be European call option prices at $t = t_n$, i.e.

$$C_n(S; u, d) = \frac{1}{\rho}[q_u C_{n+1}(Su; u, d) + q_d C_{n+1}(Sd; u, d)], \qquad (0 \leq n \leq N-1)$$

where

$$q_u = \frac{\rho - d}{u - d},$$

$$q_d = \frac{u - \rho}{u - d}.$$

Show that: when $0 < d_2 < d_1 < \rho < u_1 < u_2$,

$$C_0(S_0; u_1, d_1) < C_0(S_0; u_2, d_2),$$

where S_0 is the stock price at $t = 0$.

(Financial meaning: the higher is the volatility of the stock price, the more expensive will the premium be.)

Chapter 4

Brownian Motion and Itô Formula

The price movement of an underlying asset is a stochastic process. The French mathematician Louis Bachelier was the first to describe the stock share price movement as a Brownian motion in his 1900 doctoral thesis. In this chapter, we will give a heuristic introduction to the Brownian motion before we derive the continuous model of option pricing. In addition to giving the definition and relevant properties of the Brownian motion, we will also derive stochastic calculus based on the Brownian motion, including the Itô integral and Itô formula. To keep mathematics simple, most of the formulas are proved in the discrete case only, with the limit process briefly mentioned. All of the description and discussion in this chapter emphasize clarity rather than mathematical rigor.

4.1 Random Walk and Brownian Motion

Let us begin with a coin-tossing problem. Define a random variable $R_i(\omega), (i = 1, 2, \dots)$:

$$R_i(\omega) = \begin{cases} 1, & \omega = \text{head}, \\ -1. & \omega = \text{tail}. \end{cases}$$

It is easy to show that $R_i(\omega)$ has the following properties:

$$E(R_i) = 0, \tag{4.1.1}$$

$$Var(R_i) = 1, \tag{4.1.2}$$

$$E(R_i R_j) = 0, \qquad (i \neq j) \tag{4.1.3}$$

and

$$R_i \text{ and } R_j \text{ are independent} \quad (i \neq j) \tag{4.1.4}$$

With the random variable R_i, we can define a random variable $R_i^\Delta = \sqrt{\Delta} R_i$ and a random sequence $S_k^\Delta, (k = 0, 1, \dots)$:

$$S_0^\Delta = 0,$$

$$S_k^\Delta = \sum_{i=1}^{k} R_i^\Delta = \sum_{i=1}^{k} \sqrt{\Delta} R_i, \qquad (k = 1, 2, \ldots). \tag{4.1.5}$$

Consider a time period $0 \le t \le T$. $[0, T]$ can be divided into N equal intervals. Let $\Delta = \frac{T}{N}, t_n = n\Delta$, $(n = 0, 1, \ldots, N)$, then the partition points are

$$0 = t_0 < t_1 < \cdots < t_N = T.$$

A random walk $S^\Delta(t)$ is defined in $[0, T]$ as follows:

$$S^\Delta(t) = \begin{cases} S_k^\Delta, & t = t_k, \\ \frac{t - t_k}{\Delta} S_{k+1}^\Delta + \frac{t_{k+1} - t}{\Delta} S_k^\Delta, & t_k \le t \le t_{k+1}. \end{cases} \tag{4.1.6}$$

$S^\Delta(t)$ is called the path of the random walk.

Let us look at the distribution of the path $S^\Delta(t)$. Let $T = 1, N = 4, \Delta = \frac{1}{4}$,

$$S_0^\Delta = 0,$$

$$S_1^\Delta = \sqrt{\tfrac{1}{4}} R_1 = \{-\tfrac{1}{2}, \tfrac{1}{2}\},$$

$$S_2^\Delta = \sqrt{\tfrac{1}{4}} [R_1 + R_2] = \{-1, 0, 1\},$$

$$S_3^\Delta = \sqrt{\tfrac{1}{4}} [R_1 + R_2 + R_3] = \{-\tfrac{3}{2}, \tfrac{-1}{2}, \tfrac{1}{2}, \tfrac{3}{2}\},$$

$$S_4^\Delta = \sqrt{\tfrac{1}{4}} [R_1 + R_2 + R_3 + R_4] = \{-2, -1, 0, 1, 2\}.$$

$S^\Delta(t)$ is the path formed by linear interpolation between the above random points (see figure on the next page). For $\Delta = \frac{1}{4}$ case, there are $2^4 = 16$ paths.

$S^\Delta(t)$ has the following properties:

1. $E(S^\Delta(\hat{t}_2) - S^\Delta(\hat{t}_1)) = 0,$ (4.1.7)
2. $Var(S^\Delta(\hat{t}_2) - S^\Delta(\hat{t}_1))$
   $= E([S^\Delta(\hat{t}_2) - S^\Delta(\hat{t}_1)]^2) = |\hat{t}_2 - \hat{t}_1| + o(\Delta),$ (4.1.8)
3. $E(S^\Delta(\hat{t}_2) S^\Delta(\hat{t}_1)) = \min(\hat{t}_2, \hat{t}_1) + o(\Delta),$ (4.1.9)
4. $S^\Delta(t_k + \delta) - S^\Delta(t_k)$ and $S^\Delta(t_k)$ are independent of each other, (4.1.10)

where $t_k = k\Delta, 1 \le k \le N - 1; \delta > 0; 0 \le \hat{t}_1, \hat{t}_2 \le T$.

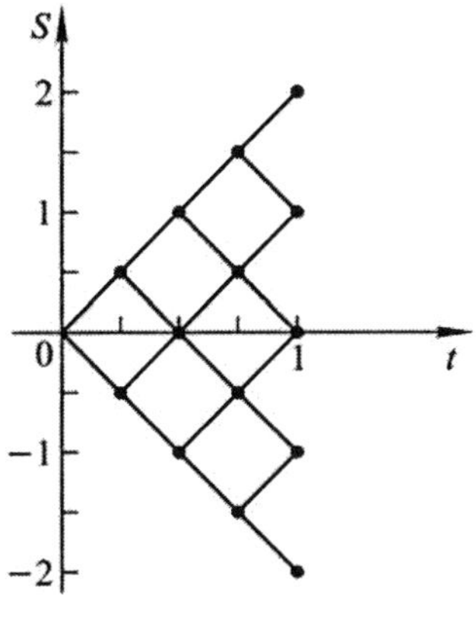

Properties (4.1.7)—(4.1.10) can be inferred directly from the properties (4.1.1)—(4.1.4) of the random variable $R_i(\omega)$.

Take (4.1.8) for example. For simplicity, let us assume $\hat{t}_2 > \hat{t}_1 = 0, t_k < \hat{t}_2 \le t_{k+1}$,

$$\begin{aligned}
&Var(S^\Delta(\hat{t}_2) - S^\Delta(\hat{t}_1)) = Var(S^\Delta(\hat{t}_2)) = E(S^\Delta(\hat{t}_2)S^\Delta(\hat{t}_2))\\
&= E([\frac{\hat{t}_2 - t_k}{\Delta} S^\Delta_{k+1} + \frac{t_{k+1} - \hat{t}_2}{\Delta} S^\Delta_k]^2)\\
&= (\frac{\hat{t}_2 - t_k}{\Delta})^2 E(S^{\Delta^2}_{k+1}) + 2(\frac{\hat{t}_2 - t_k}{\Delta})(\frac{t_{k+1} - \hat{t}_2}{\Delta}) E(S^\Delta_{k+1} S^\Delta_k)\\
&\quad + (\frac{t_{k+1} - \hat{t}_2}{\Delta})^2 E(S^{\Delta^2}_k)\\
&= (\frac{\hat{t}_2 - t_k}{\Delta})^2 (k+1)\Delta + 2k\Delta(\frac{\hat{t}_2 - t_k}{\Delta})(\frac{t_{k+1} - \hat{t}_2}{\Delta})\\
&\quad + k\Delta(\frac{t_{k+1} - \hat{t}_2}{\Delta})^2\\
&= t_k + \frac{(\hat{t}_2 - t_k)^2}{\Delta} = \hat{t}_2 + O(\Delta).
\end{aligned}$$

In order to study the limit of $S^\Delta(t)$ as $\Delta \to 0$, we need the following theorem.

The central limit theorem *For any random sequence* $\{\frac{1}{\sqrt{k}} \sum_{i=1}^{k} R_i\}$, *($R_i$ has the properties (4.1.1),(4.1.2)), as* $k \to \infty$,

$$\frac{1}{\sqrt{k}} \sum_{i=1}^{k} R_i \to X,$$

where the random variable $X \sim N(0,1)$, *i.e. the random variable* X *obeys the standard normal distribution:*

$$E(X) = 0, Var(X) = 1.$$

Let us apply the central limit theorem to find the limit of $S^{\Delta}(t)$ as $\Delta \to 0$.

For any given $t(t_k < t \leq t_{k+1})$, consider $\frac{S^{\Delta}(t)}{\sqrt{t}}$. Since $\Delta = \frac{t_k}{k}$, $(k = 1, 2, \ldots, N)$, thus for a given t,

$$\begin{aligned}
\frac{S^{\Delta}(t)}{\sqrt{t}} &= \frac{1}{\sqrt{t}}[\frac{t_{k+1}-t}{\Delta}S_k^{\Delta} + \frac{t-t_k}{\Delta}S_{k+1}^{\Delta}] \\
&= \frac{1}{\sqrt{t}}[\frac{t_{k+1}-t}{\sqrt{\Delta}}\sum_{i=1}^{k} R_i + \frac{t-t_k}{\sqrt{\Delta}}\sum_{i=1}^{k+1} R_i] \\
&= (\frac{t_{k+1}-t}{\Delta}\sqrt{\frac{t_k}{t}})\frac{1}{\sqrt{k}}\sum_{i=1}^{k} R_i + (\frac{t-t_k}{\Delta}\sqrt{\frac{t_{k+1}}{t}})\frac{1}{\sqrt{k+1}}\sum_{i=1}^{k+1} R_i \\
&\longrightarrow X_t. \qquad (\text{ as } \Delta \to 0, \text{ i.e } k \to \infty)
\end{aligned}$$

Definition 4.1 Let $W(t)$ be the limit of $S^{\Delta}(t)$, then it follows from (4.1.7)—(4.1.10) that $W(t)$ has the following properties:

1) Continuity of path: $W(0) = 0, W(t)$ is a continuous function of t.(4.1.11)

2) Normal increments: For any $t > 0$, $W(t) \sim N(0, t)$, and for $0 \leq s < t$, $W(t) - W(s)$ is normally distributed with mean 0 and variance $t - s$, i.e.,

$$W(t) - W(s) \sim N(0, t - s). \tag{4.1.12}$$

3) Independence of increments: for any choice of $t_i \in [0, T]$ with $0 < t_1 < t_2 < \cdots < t_n$, the increments $W(t_n) - W(t_{n-1}), W(t_{n-1}) - W(t_{n-2}), \ldots, W(t_2) - W(t_1)$ and $W(t_1)$ are independent. (4.1.13)

A random process $W(t)$(in short W_t) satisfying the properties 1)—3) is called a **Brownian motion** or a **Wiener process.**

Before further investigation of the properties of the Brownian motion, we give an example to illustrate the relation between the underlying asset price movement and the Brownian motion.

4.2 Continuous Models of Asset Price Movement

In the previous chapter we described the underlying asset price movement using the binomial tree method. Based on the discussion in §4.1, we can explore its limit as $\Delta \to 0$, i.e., to investigate the continuous model of the underlying asset price movement.

For this purpose we introduce the **discounted value** S_t^* of an underlying asset as follows:

$$S_t^* = \frac{S_t}{B_t}$$

For S_t^*, in time interval $[t, t + \Delta t]$, the binomial tree method can be

written as

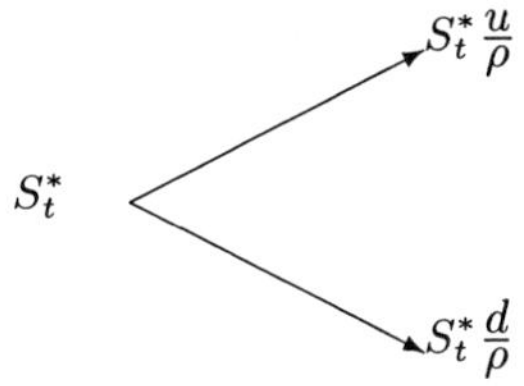

In §3.3 we proved that there exists an equivalent martingale Q such that

$$q_u = \text{Prob}\{S_{t+\Delta t} = S_t u\} = \text{Prob}\{S_{t+\Delta t}^* = S_t^* \frac{u}{\rho}\} = \frac{\rho - d}{u - d},$$

$$q_d = \text{Prob}\{S_{t+\Delta t} = S_t d\} = \text{Prob}\{S_{t+\Delta t}^* = S_t^* \frac{d}{\rho}\} = \frac{u - \rho}{u - d}.$$

Lemma 4.1 *If* $ud = 1$,

$$u = e^{\sigma\sqrt{\Delta t}}, \quad d = e^{-\sigma\sqrt{\Delta t}}, \quad \rho = e^{r\Delta t},$$

then under the martingale measure Q,

$$E^Q(\frac{S_{t+\Delta t}^* - S_t^*}{S_t^*}) = 0,$$

$$Var^Q(\frac{S_{t+\Delta t}^* - S_t^*}{S_t^*}) = \sigma^2 \Delta t + O(\Delta t^2).$$

Proof According to the definition of martingale measure Q,

$$E^Q(\frac{S_{t+\Delta t} - S_t}{S_t}) = \frac{B_{t+\Delta t} - B_t}{B_t} = \rho - 1,$$

thus by straightforward computation, we get

$$E^Q(\frac{S_{t+\Delta t}^* - S_t^*}{S_t^*}) = E^Q(\frac{S_{t+\Delta t} - \rho S_t}{S_t}) = E^Q(\frac{S_{t+\Delta t} - S_t}{S_t}) + 1 - \rho = 0.$$

Moreover, since

$$Var^Q(\frac{S_{t+\Delta t}^* - S_t^*}{S_t^*}) = E^Q((\frac{S_{t+\Delta t}^* - S_t^*}{S_t^*})^2) = q_u(\frac{u}{\rho} - 1)^2 + q_d(\frac{d}{\rho} - 1)^2,$$

by the assumption of the lemma,

$$\frac{u}{\rho} - 1 = \sigma\sqrt{\Delta t} - (r - \frac{\sigma^2}{2})\Delta t + (\Delta t^{3/2}),$$

$$\frac{d}{\rho} - 1 = -\sigma\sqrt{\Delta t} - (r - \frac{\sigma^2}{2})\Delta t + (\Delta t^{3/2}),$$

and consider that

$$q_u + q_d = 1, q_u - q_d = O(\Delta t^{1/2}),$$

thus we have

$$\mathrm{Var}^Q(\frac{S^*_{t+\Delta t} - S^*_t}{S^*_t}) = \sigma^2\Delta t + O(\Delta t^2).$$

This completes the proof of the lemma.

By the conclusion of Lemma 4.1, neglecting the higher order terms of Δt, we have

$$\frac{S^*_{t+\Delta t} - S^*_t}{S^*_t} = \sigma\sqrt{\Delta t}R_i(\omega),$$

($R_i(\omega)$ is defined in §4.1). By Taylor expansion, noticing that $\Delta S^* = S^*_{t+\Delta t} - S^*_t$ is small, hence

$$\frac{S^*_{t+\Delta t} - S^*_t}{S^*_t} = \ln(1 + \frac{S^*_{t+\Delta t} - S^*_t}{S^*_t}) + \frac{1}{2}(\frac{S^*_{t+\Delta t} - S^*_t}{S^*_t})^2 + O(|\Delta S^*|^3).$$

i.e. neglecting the higher order terms of Δt, we get

$$\ln\frac{S^*_{t+\Delta t}}{S^*_t} = \sigma\sqrt{\Delta t}R_i(\omega) - \frac{1}{2}\sigma^2\Delta t. \tag{4.2.1}$$

By definition $S^*_0 = 1$, $B_0 = 1$, therefore after partitioning $[0, T]$, at each instant $t = t_k$,

$$\ln S^*_k = \sum_{i=1}^{k}\ln\frac{S^*_i}{S^*_{i-1}} = \sigma\sum_{i=1}^{k}R^\Delta_i - \frac{1}{2}\sigma^2 t_k,$$

i.e.

$$\ln S_k = \ln S^*_k + \ln B_k = rt_k + \sigma\sum_{i=1}^{k}R^\Delta_i - \frac{1}{2}\sigma^2 t_k.$$

Let $\hat{S}^\Delta(t)$ be the "path" formed by interpolation, as we did in the previous section, then

$$\ln\hat{S}^\Delta(t) = (r - \frac{\sigma^2}{2})t + \sigma S^\Delta(t),$$

where $S^\Delta(t)$ is defined by (4.1.6). Let $\Delta t \to 0$ and let $\frac{S(t)}{S_0}$ be the limit function of $\hat{S}^\Delta(t)$, then according to the conclusion of §4.1, we have obtained the law of the underlying asset price movement under the martingale measure Q,

$$\ln \frac{S(t)}{S_0} = (r - \frac{\sigma^2}{2})t + \sigma W(t),$$

i.e.

$$S(t) = S_0 e^{(r-\frac{\sigma^2}{2})t+\sigma W(t)}, \tag{4.2.2}$$

where $S_0 = S(0)$.

This means the underlying asset price movement as a continuous stochastic process, its logarithmic function is described by the Brownian motion. The underlying asset price $S(t)$ is said to fit a **geometric Brownian motion.** This means: *Corresponding to the discrete BTM of the underlying asset price presented in the previous chapter, in a risk-neutral world (i.e. under the martingale measure), its continuous model obeys the geometric Brownian motion (4.2.2).*

4.3 Quadratic Variation Theorem

The paths of a particle following the Brownian motion are everywhere continuous, yet are nowhere differentiable.

As is well known, if $f(t) \in C^1[0,T]$, then the quadratic variation of $f(t)$ must approach to zero.

Let function $f(t)$ be given in $[0,T]$, and Π be a partition of the interval $[0,T]$:

$$0 = t_0 < t_1 < \cdots < t_N = T,$$

then corresponding to the partition Π, the **quadratic variation** of $f(t)$ is defined by

$$Q_\Pi = \sum_{k=0}^{N-1} [f(t_{k+1}) - f(t_k)]^2.$$

If $f(t) \in C^1[0,T]$, then as $\Delta = \max_{0 \le k \le N-1} |t_{k+1} - t_k| \to 0$, there must be

$$\lim_{\Delta \to 0} Q_\Pi = 0. \tag{4.3.1}$$

In fact,

$$\begin{aligned}\lim_{\Delta \to 0} Q_\Pi &= \lim_{\Delta \to 0} \sum_{k=0}^{N-1} |f'(\xi_k)|^2 (t_{k+1} - t_k)^2 \\ &\le \lim_{\Delta \to 0} \Delta \sum_{k=0}^{N-1} |f'(\xi_k)|^2 (t_{k+1} - t_k) = 0.\end{aligned}$$

Remark (4.3.1) still holds if $f(t) \in C[0,T]$ and has bounded variation on $[0,T]$.

Now let us examine the quadratic variation Q_Π of the Brownian motion under the partition Π:

$$Q_\Pi = \sum_{k=0}^{N-1} (W_{t_{k+1}} - W_{t_k})^2.$$

Theorem 4.1 *Let Π be any partition of the interval $[0,T]$, then the quadratic variation Q_Π of a Brownian motion as $\Delta \to 0$ has a limit as follows:*

$$\lim_{\Delta \to 0} Q_\Pi = T \qquad \textit{(in the sense of } L_2\textit{)}. \tag{4.3.2}$$

Before proving the theorem, let us look at its meaning.

For any $[\tau_1, \tau_2] \subset [0,T]$, let $\Pi(\tau_1, \tau_2)$ be an arbitrary partition of the interval $[\tau_1, \tau_2]$, and $Q_\Pi(\tau_1, \tau_2)$ be the quadratic variation of the Brownian motion corresponding to the partition $\Pi(\tau_1, \tau_2)$, then by Theorem 4.1,

$$\lim_{\Delta \to 0} Q_\Pi(\tau_1, \tau_2) = \tau_2 - \tau_1. \tag{4.3.3}$$

Referring to the conclusion (4.3.1) regarding the differentiable function, we have the following corollary:

The path of a Brownian motion W_t as a random walk of a particle is continuous everywhere but differentiable nowhere.

Proof of Theorem 4.1 Note that Q_Π is a random variable, thus (4.3.2) implies

$$\lim_{\Delta \to 0} E(Q_\Pi - T) = 0, \tag{4.3.4}$$

and

$$\lim_{\Delta \to 0} Var(Q_\Pi - T) = \lim_{\Delta \to 0} E((Q_\Pi - T)^2) = 0. \tag{4.3.5}$$

In fact

$$Q_\Pi - T = \sum_{k=0}^{N-1} (W_{t_{k+1}} - W_{t_k})^2 - (t_{k+1} - t_k).$$

Then by (4.1.12)

$$\begin{aligned} E(Q_\Pi - T) &= \sum_{k=0}^{N-1} E((W_{t_{k+1}} - W_{t_k})^2) - (t_{k+1} - t_k) \\ &= \sum_{k=0}^{N-1} Var(W_{t_{k+1}} - W_{t_k}) - (t_{k+1} - t_k) \\ &= 0. \end{aligned}$$

Hence (4.3.4) is true.

Now let us prove (4.3.5). Let $D_k = W_{t_{k+1}} - W_{t_k}$, $\delta_k = t_{k+1} - t_k$, then

$$\begin{aligned}
Var(Q_\Pi - T) &= E((Q_\Pi - T)^2) \\
&= \sum_{k,\ell=0}^{N-1} E((D_k^2 - \delta_k)(D_\ell^2 - \delta_\ell)) \\
&= \sum_{k=0}^{N-1} E((D_k^2 - \delta_k)^2) + \sum_{k\neq\ell} E((D_k^2 - \delta_k)(D_\ell^2 - \delta_\ell)).
\end{aligned}$$

By (4.1.13), and since $k \neq \ell$, D_k and D_ℓ are independent, therefore

$$E((D_k^2 - \delta_k)(D_\ell^2 - \delta_\ell)) = E(D_k^2 - \delta_k)E(D_\ell^2 - \delta_\ell) = 0.$$

And

$$\begin{aligned}
Var(Q_\Pi - T) &= \sum_{k=0}^{N-1} E(D_k^4) - 2\delta_k E(D_k^2) + \delta_k^2 \\
&= \sum_{k=0}^{N-1} E(D_k^4) - \delta_k^2. \qquad (4.3.6)
\end{aligned}$$

By (4.1.12), $D_k \sim N(0, t_{k+1} - t_k)$, thus $E(D_k^4)$ can be written as the following integral

$$E(D_k^4) = \int_{-\infty}^{+\infty} \alpha^4 \frac{1}{\sqrt{2\pi(t_{k+1} - t_k)}} e^{-\frac{\alpha^2}{2(t_{k+1}-t_k)}} d\alpha = 3(t_{k+1} - t_k)^2.$$

Substituting it into (4.3.6), we get

$$Var(Q_\Pi - T) = \sum_{k=0}^{N-1} 3\delta_k^2 - \delta_k^2 = 2\sum_{k=0}^{N-1} \delta_k^2.$$

Thus

$$0 \leq \lim_{\Delta\to 0} Var(Q_\Pi - T) \leq 2 \lim_{\Delta\to 0} \Delta \sum_{k=0}^{N-1} (t_{k+1} - t_k) = 0,$$

i.e. (4.3.5) is true. Thus the theorem is proved.

Remark If $dt \to 0$ (i.e. $\Delta \to 0$), let dW_t denote the limit of $D_k = W_{t_{k+1}} -$

W_{t_k}, then by Theorem 4.1, heuristically we may write

$$\begin{aligned} E(dW_t^2) &= dt, \\ Var(dW_t^2) &= E(dW_t^4) - [E(dW_t^2)]^2 \\ &= 3dt^2 - dt^2 = 2dt^2. \end{aligned}$$

Hence neglecting the higher order terms of dt, roughly speaking,

$$dW_t^2 = dt. \tag{4.3.7}$$

i.e. neglecting higher order terms, the square of the random variable dW_t is a **definitive** infinitesimal of the order of dt. This view can be helpful in our later discussion.

4.4 Itô Integral

Example A company invests in a risky asset, whose price movement is given by W_t $(0 \le t \le T)$. Let $f(t)$ be the investment strategy, with $f(t) > 0 (< 0)$ denoting the number of shares bought (sold) at time t. For a chosen investment strategy, what is the total profit at $t = T$?

Partition $[0, T]$ by: $0 = t_0 < t_1 < \cdots < t_N = T.$

If the transactions are executed at time $t = t_k (k = 1, \ldots, N)$ only, then the investment strategy can only be adjusted on trading days $t = t_k$, and the gain (loss) at $[t_k, t_{k+1})$ is

$$f(t_k)[W_{t_{k+1}} - W_{t_k}].$$

Therefore the total profit in $[0, T]$ is

$$I_\Delta(f) = \sum_{k=0}^{N-1} f(t_k)[W_{t_{k+1}} - W_{t_k}].$$

Since the investor has no information of the future price of the risky asset when selecting an investment strategy, such an investment strategy $f(t)$ is said to be non-anticipating.

Definition 4.2 If $f(t)$ is a non-anticipating stochastic process, such that the limit

$$\lim_{\Delta \to 0} I_\Delta(f) = \lim_{\Delta \to 0} \sum_{k=0}^{N-1} f(t_k)[W_{t_{k+1}} - W_{t_k}]$$

$(\Delta = \max\limits_{0 \le k \le N-1} (t_{k+1} - t_k))$ exists, and is independent of the partition, then the limit is called the **Itô integral** of $f(t)$, denoted as $\int_0^T f(t)dW_t$, i.e.

$$\int_0^T f(t)dW_t = \lim_{\Delta \to 0} \sum_{k=0}^{N-1} f(t_k)[W_{t_{k+1}} - W_{t_k}].$$

Remark We will not investigate under what conditions the Itô integral exists. But we must understand that the definition of the Itô integral is different from the definition of the Riemann integral.

$I_\Delta(f)$ can be regarded as the Riemann sum under a particular partition. However, unlike the Riemann sum as given in the calculus, here $f(t)$ is supposed to be non-anticipating, hence in $I_\Delta(f)$ the value of f must be taken at the left endpoint of the interval $[t_k, t_{k+1}]$, instead of at an arbitrary interpoint in $[t_k, t_{k+1}]$. In fact, it can be shown based on the quadratic variance Theorem 4.1 that the value of the limit of the Riemann sum of a Wiener process depends on the choice of the positions of the interpoints. i.e the limit of the Riemann sum varies with the choice of the positions of the interpoints. Therefore for a Wiener process, if the Riemann sum is calculated over **arbitrarily** chosen interpoints in $[t_k, t_{k+1}]$, then the Riemann sum of $I_\Delta(f)$ has no limit.

In order to get a better understanding of the meaning of the Itô integral, let us look at a few examples.

Example 1

$$\int_0^T W_t dW_t = \frac{1}{2}W_T^2 - \frac{T}{2}. \tag{4.4.1}$$

Proof By the definition of the Itô integral,

$$\int_0^T W_t dW_t = \lim_{\Delta \to 0} \sum_{k=0}^{N-1} W_{t_k}(W_{t_{k+1}} - W_{t_k}) = \lim_{\Delta \to 0} I_\Delta,$$

where

$$\begin{aligned} I_\Delta &= \sum_{k=0}^{N-1} W_{t_k} W_{t_{k+1}} - \sum_{k=0}^{N-1} W_{t_k}^2 \\ &= \sum_{k=1}^{N} W_{t_k} W_{t_{k-1}} - \sum_{k=1}^{N} W_{t_k}^2 + W_{t_N}^2 - W_{t_0}^2 \\ &= -\sum_{k=1}^{N} W_{t_k}(W_{t_k} - W_{t_{k-1}}) + W_T^2. \end{aligned} \tag{4.4.2}$$

I_Δ can also be written as

$$I_\Delta = \sum_{i=1}^{N} W_{t_{i-1}}(W_{t_i} - W_{t_{i-1}}). \tag{4.4.3}$$

Adding (4.4.2) and (4.4.3), we get

$$\begin{aligned} 2I_\Delta &= \sum_{i=1}^{N}(W_{t_{i-1}} - W_{t_i})(W_{t_i} - W_{t_{i-1}}) + W_T^2 \\ &= W_T^2 - Q_\Pi. \end{aligned}$$

Where Q_Π is the quadratic variation of W_t under partition Π. By Theorem 4.1, we have

$$\lim_{\Delta\to 0} I_\Delta = \frac{1}{2}W_T^2 - \frac{1}{2}\lim_{\Delta\to 0} Q_\Pi = \frac{1}{2}W_T^2 - \frac{T}{2}.$$

Thus (4.4.1) is proved.

Remark In the above proof process we can see: since the quadratic variation of a Brownian motion is nonzero, the result of an Itô integral is not the same as the result of a normal integral.

If the upper limit T is replaced by a variable t, then from (4.4.1), we get the corresponding differential formula:

$$W_t dW_t = \frac{1}{2}dW_t^2 - \frac{1}{2}dt,$$

i.e.

$$dW_t^2 = 2W_t dW_t + dt. \tag{4.4.4}$$

This indicates a corresponding change in the differentiation rule for the composite function.

4.5 Itô Formula

Let $Y_t = f(X_t, t)$, where X_t is a stochastic process. We want to know:

$$dY_t = df(X_t, t) = ?$$

This is the Itô formula to be discussed in this section. The Itô formula is the Chain Rule in stochastic calculus.

The differential of a function is the linear principal part of its increment. Due to the quadratic variation theorem of the Brownian motion, a composite function of a stochastic process will have new components in its linear principal part. Let us begin with a few examples.

Example 2

$$Y_t = f(X_t, t), \quad X_t = W_t, \qquad dY_t = ?$$

By the Taylor expansion,

$$dY_t = df(X_t, t) = \frac{\partial f}{\partial t} dt + \frac{\partial f}{\partial x} dX_t + \frac{1}{2}\frac{\partial^2 f}{\partial x^2} dX_t^2 + O(|dX_t| dt).$$

And by (4.3.7),

$$dY_t = (\frac{\partial f}{\partial t} + \frac{1}{2}\frac{\partial^2 f}{\partial x^2}) dt + \frac{\partial f}{\partial x} dW_t + o(dt).$$

Then neglecting the higher order terms, we have

$$dY_t = (\frac{\partial f}{\partial t} + \frac{1}{2}\frac{\partial^2 f}{\partial x^2}) dt + \frac{\partial f}{\partial x} dW_t. \tag{4.5.1}$$

Take $Y_t = f(X_t, t) = X_t^2$, $X_t = W_t$ for example,

$$\frac{\partial f}{\partial x} = 2x, \quad \frac{\partial^2 f}{\partial x^2} = 2, \quad \frac{\partial f}{\partial t} = 0.$$

Substituting them into (4.5.1), we get

$$dW_t^2 = dt + 2W_t dW_t,$$

which is the equation (4.4.4).

Example 3 In §4.2 we have learned: in a risk-neutral world, the price movement of a risky asset S_t can be expressed by (4.2.2),

$$S(t) = S_0 e^{(r-\frac{\sigma^2}{2})t + \sigma W_t}.$$

We want to find $dS(t)$=?

Since

$$S(t) = f(X_t, t), \qquad X_t = W_t,$$

where

$$f(x, t) = S_0 e^{(r-\frac{\sigma^2}{2})t + \sigma x}.$$

thus by (4.5.1),

$$\begin{aligned} dS(t) &= S_0[(r - \frac{\sigma^2}{2}) + \frac{1}{2}\sigma^2] e^{(r-\frac{\sigma^2}{2})t + \sigma W_t} dt \\ &\quad + S_0 \sigma e^{(r-\frac{\sigma^2}{2})t + \sigma W_t} dW_t \\ &= rS(t) dt + \sigma S(t) dW_t. \end{aligned}$$

i.e. *in a risk-neutral world, the underlying asset S_t satisfies the stochastic differential equation*

$$\frac{dS_t}{S_t} = rdt + \sigma dW_t, \tag{4.5.2}$$

where $\frac{dS_t}{S_t}$ is the return of S_t over a time interval dt, rdt is the expected growth of the return of S_t, and σdW_t is the stochastic component of the return, with variance $\sigma^2 dt$. σ is called **volatility.**

Theorem 4.2(Itô **formula)** *Denote $V_t = V(S_t, t)$. V is differentiable with respect to both variables. If the stochastic process S_t satisfies the stochastic differential equation*

$$dS_t = \mu(S_t, t)dt + \sigma(S_t, t)dW_t,$$

then

$$\begin{aligned} dV_t &= (\frac{\partial V}{\partial t} + \frac{1}{2}\sigma^2(S_t, t)\frac{\partial^2 V}{\partial S^2})dt + \frac{\partial V}{\partial S}dS_t \\ &= (\frac{\partial V}{\partial t} + \mu(S_t, t)\frac{\partial V}{\partial S} + \frac{1}{2}\sigma^2(S_t, t)\frac{\partial^2 V}{\partial S^2})dt \\ &\quad + \sigma(S_t, t)\frac{\partial V}{\partial S}dW_t. \end{aligned} \tag{4.5.3}$$

Proof By the Taylor expansion

$$dV_t = \frac{\partial V}{\partial t}dt + \frac{\partial V}{\partial S}dS_t + \frac{1}{2}\frac{\partial^2 V}{\partial S^2}(dS_t)^2 + O(dtdS_t). \tag{4.5.4}$$

Due to (4.3.7),

$$\begin{aligned} (dS_t)^2 &= (\mu(S_t, t)dt + \sigma(S_t, t)dW_t)^2 \\ &= \sigma^2(S_t, t)(dW_t)^2 + 2\mu\sigma dtdW_t + \mu^2 dt^2 \\ &= \sigma^2(S_t, t)dt + o(dt). \end{aligned}$$

Substituting it into (4.5.4), we get

$$dV_t = (\frac{\partial V}{\partial t} + \frac{1}{2}\sigma^2(S_t, t)\frac{\partial^2 V}{\partial S^2})dt + \frac{\partial V}{\partial S}[\mu(S_t, t)dt + \sigma(S_t, t)dW_t] + o(dt).$$

Thus (4.5.3) is true.

Theorem 4.3 *If X_t, Y_t are stochastic processes satisfying respectively the following stochastic differential equations*

$$dX_t = \mu_1 dt + \sigma_1 dW_t, \tag{4.5.5}$$

$$dY_t = \mu_2 dt + \sigma_2 dW_t, \tag{4.5.6}$$

then

$$d(X_tY_t) = X_t dY_t + Y_t dX_t + \sigma_1\sigma_2 dt. \tag{4.5.7}$$

Proof Since

$$d(X_tY_t) = \frac{1}{4}[d(X_t + Y_t)^2 - d(X_t - Y_t)^2]. \tag{4.5.8}$$

Thus by (4.5.5), (4.5.6) we get:

$$d(X_t + Y_t) = (\mu_1 + \mu_2)dt + (\sigma_1 + \sigma_2)dW_t,$$
$$d(X_t - Y_t) = (\mu_1 - \mu_2)dt + (\sigma_1 - \sigma_2)dW_t.$$

Therefore by the Itô formula (4.5.3),

$$d(X_t + Y_t)^2 = 2(X_t + Y_t)d(X_t + Y_t) + (\sigma_1 + \sigma_2)^2 dt,$$

$$d(X_t - Y_t)^2 = 2(X_t - Y_t)d(X_t - Y_t) + (\sigma_1 - \sigma_2)^2 dt.$$

Substituting them into (4.5.8), we get

$$\begin{aligned} d(X_tY_t) &= \frac{1}{4}[2(X_t + Y_t)d(X_t + Y_t) - 2(X_t - Y_t)d(X_t - Y_t)] \\ &\quad + \frac{1}{4}[(\sigma_1 + \sigma_2)^2 - (\sigma_1 - \sigma_2)^2]dt \\ &= X_t dY_t + Y_t dX_t + \sigma_1\sigma_2 dt. \end{aligned}$$

Thus (4.5.7) is true.

Theorem 4.4 *If X_t, Y_t are stochastic processes satisfying the stochastic equations (4.5.5),(4.5.6), then*

$$d(\frac{X_t}{Y_t}) = \frac{Y_t dX_t - X_t dY_t}{Y_t^2} + \frac{\sigma_2^2 X_t - \sigma_1\sigma_2 Y_t}{Y_t^3}dt. \tag{4.5.9}$$

Proof By the Itô formula (4.5.3)

$$\begin{aligned} d(\frac{1}{Y_t}) &= -\frac{1}{Y_t^2}dY_t + \frac{1}{Y_t^3}\sigma_2^2 dt \\ &= \frac{1}{Y_t^2}[(\sigma_2^2 Y_t^{-1} - \mu_2)dt - \sigma_2 dW_t]. \end{aligned}$$

Thus by Theorem 4.3, we have

$$\begin{aligned} d(X_t\frac{1}{Y_t}) &= X_t d(\frac{1}{Y_t}) + \frac{1}{Y_t}dX_t - \frac{\sigma_1\sigma_2}{Y_t^2}dt \\ &= \frac{Y_t dX_t - X_t dY_t}{Y_t^2} + \frac{\sigma_2^2 X_t - \sigma_1\sigma_2 Y_t}{Y_t^3}dt. \end{aligned}$$

Thus (4.5.9) is true.

Remark Theorems 4.3–4.4 tell us: due to the change in the Chain Rule for differentiating composite function of the Wiener process, the product rule and quotient rule for differentiating functions of the Wiener process are also changed. All these results remind us that stochastic calculus operations are different from the normal calculus operations!

Next let us study the **multidimensional** Itô **formula**
Let $W_j(t)$, $(j = 1, \ldots, m)$, be independent standard Brownian motions,

$$E(dW_j) = 0, \qquad (j = 1, \ldots, m)$$

$$Var(dW_j) = dt, \qquad (j = 1, \ldots, m)$$

$$Cov(dW_i dW_j) = 0, \qquad (i \neq j)$$

where Cov denotes the covariance:

$$Cov(X, Y) = E((X - E(X))(Y - E(Y)).$$

Let $X_i(t)$ $(i = 1, \ldots, n)$ be stochastic processes satisfying the following system of stochastic differential equations

$$d\begin{bmatrix} X_1(t) \\ \vdots \\ X_n(t) \end{bmatrix} = \begin{bmatrix} b_1(t) \\ \vdots \\ b_n(t) \end{bmatrix} dt + \begin{bmatrix} \sigma_{11}(t), & \ldots, & \sigma_{1m}(t) \\ \vdots & & \vdots \\ \sigma_{n1}(t), & \ldots, & \sigma_{nm}(t) \end{bmatrix} d\begin{bmatrix} W_1(t) \\ \vdots \\ W_m(t) \end{bmatrix}, \tag{4.5.10}$$

where $b_i(t), \sigma_{ij}(t)$ $(i = 1, \ldots, n;\ j = 1, \ldots, m)$ are known functions.

Theorem 4.5 *Let $V(x_1, \ldots, x_n, t)$ be a differentiable function of $n + 1$ variables, $X_i(t) (i = 1, \ldots, n)$ are stochastic processes defined by (4.5.10), then*

$$\begin{aligned} dV(X_1(t), \ldots, X_n(t), t) = {} & \left(\frac{\partial V}{\partial t} + \frac{1}{2}\sum_{i,j=1}^{n} a_{ij}\frac{\partial^2 V}{\partial x_i \partial x_j}\right)_{x_i = X_i(t)} dt \\ & + \sum_{i=1}^{n}\left(\frac{\partial V}{\partial x_i}\right)_{x_i = X_i(t)}, \ dX_i(t), \end{aligned} \tag{4.5.11}$$

$$\begin{bmatrix} a_{11} & \ldots & a_{1n} \\ \vdots & & \vdots \\ a_{n1} & \ldots & a_{nn} \end{bmatrix} = \begin{bmatrix} \sigma_{11} & \ldots & \sigma_{1m} \\ \vdots & & \vdots \\ \sigma_{n1} & \ldots & \sigma_{nm} \end{bmatrix} \begin{bmatrix} \sigma_{11} & \ldots & \sigma_{n1} \\ \vdots & & \vdots \\ \sigma_{1m} & \ldots & \sigma_{nm} \end{bmatrix}.$$

The proof of the theorem is similar to the 1-dimensional case and is left to the reader as an exercise.

Summary

1. The definition of the Brownian motion is the central concept of this chapter. Based on the quadratic variation theorem of the Brownian motion, we have established the basic rules of stochastic differential calculus operations, in particular the Chain Rule for differentiating composite function——the Itô *formula, which is the basis for modeling and pricing various types of options.*

2. By the picture of the Brownian motion, we have established the relation between the discrete model (BTM) and the continuous model (stochastic differential equation (4.5.2)) of the risky asset price movement. This sets the ground for further study of the BTM for option pricing (such as convergence proof).

Exercises

1. Partition $[0, T]$ by the points

$$0 = t_0 < t_1 < \cdots < t_N = T.$$

In each subinterval $[t_n, t_{n+1}]$ $(0 \le n \le N-1)$, for a given $\lambda \in [0,1]$, an intermediate point is given by:

$$\tau_n^\lambda = \lambda t_n + (1-\lambda) t_{n+1}.$$

For a smooth function $f(x)$, the Riemann sum $\Pi_\lambda(f)$ is:

$$\Pi_\lambda(f) = \sum_{i=0}^{N-1} f(W_{\tau_n^\lambda})(W_{t_{n+1}} - W_{t_n}),$$

where W_t is a standard Brownian motion. The integral $(\lambda)\int_0^T f(W_t)dW_t$ is defined as:

$$(\lambda)\int_0^T f(W_t)dW_t = \lim_{\Delta\to 0} \Pi_\lambda(f),$$

where $\quad \Delta = \max_{0\le n\le N-1} |t_{n+1} - t_n|.$

$\lambda = 1$ case is called the Itô integral, $\lambda = \frac{1}{2}$ case is called the Stratonovich integral, and $\lambda = 0$ case is called the backward integral. Evaluate the integral

$$(\lambda)\int_0^T W_t dW_t$$

for $\lambda = 0, \frac{1}{2}, 1$.

2. Let $S_{it} (i = 1, 2, \ldots, n)$ be n stochastic processes satisfying the stochastic differential equations:

$$\frac{dS_{it}}{S_{it}} = \mu_i dt + \sigma_i dW_i, \qquad (i = 1, \ldots, n)$$

where $W_i(i = 1, \dots, n)$ are standard Brownian motions satisfying

$$\begin{aligned}&E(dW_i) = 0,\\&Var(dW_i) = dt,\\&Cov(dW_i dW_j) = \rho_{ij} dt. \ (i \neq j)\end{aligned}$$

Find the Itô formula. i.e. if $V = V(S_{1,t}, \dots, S_{n,t}, t)$, find $dV(S_{1,t}, \dots, S_{n,t}, t)$.

3. Solve the following stochastic differential equation problem:

$$\begin{cases} \frac{dS_t}{S_t} = (r - q)dt + \sigma dW_t, \\ S_t|_{t=0} = S_0 \end{cases}$$

Where r, q, σ are parameters, and W_t is a standard Brownian motion. (Hint: find the stochastic differential equation for $\ln S_t$).

Chapter 5

European Option Pricing——Black-Scholes Formula

In this chapter, we will describe the price movement of an underlying asset by a continuous model — geometrical Brownian motion. Then we will set up a mathematical model for the option pricing (Black-Scholes partial differential equation) and find the pricing formula (Black-Scholes formula). We will also discuss how to manage risky assets using the Black-Scholes formula and hedging technique.

5.1 History

Option pricing is an old problem in finance. In 1900, Louis Bachelier published his doctoral thesis "Théorie de la Spéculation", now reckoned a milestone of the modern financial theory. In his thesis, Bachelier made the first attempt to model the stock price movement as a random walk. Option pricing problem was also addressed in his thesis.

In 1964, Paul Samuelson, a Nobel Economics Prize winner, modified Bachelier's model, using return instead of stock price in the original model. Let S_t be the stock price, then $\frac{dS_t}{S_t}$ is its return. The stochastic differential equation proprosed by P. Samuelson is:

$$\frac{dS_t}{S_t} = \mu dt + \sigma dW_t. \tag{5.1.1}$$

This correction eliminates the unrealistic negative value of stock price in the original model.

Using this model, P. Samuelson studied the call option pricing problem (Ć. Sprenkle(1965) and J. Baness(1964) also studied this problem at the same time). The result is given in the following.

Let V be the premium of a call option, S be the asset price, K be the strike price, and T the expiration date, then

$$V = e^{-\alpha_c T}[Se^{\alpha_s T}N(d_1) - KN(d_2)], \tag{5.1.2}$$

where

$$d_1 = \frac{\ln(S/K) + (\alpha_s + \frac{1}{2}\sigma^2)T}{\sigma\sqrt{T}}, \tag{5.1.3}$$

$$d_2 = d_1 - \sigma\sqrt{T}, \qquad N(x) = \frac{1}{\sqrt{2\pi}}\int_{-\infty}^{x} e^{-\frac{\alpha^2}{2}}\, d\alpha,$$

and α_s, α_c are the expected returns of the asset S_t and the option V_t, respectively, at $t = T$. Since α_s and α_c depend on the risk preference of individual investors, the pricing formula, as elegant as it looks, is not applicable in the real world trading.

In 1973, Fischer Black and Myron Scholes gave the following call option pricing formula

$$V = SN(d_1) - Ke^{-rT}N(d_2). \tag{5.1.4}$$

Comparing to (5.1.2), α_s and α_c are no longer present. Instead, the risk-free interest r enters the formula. The novelty of this formula is that it is independent of the risk preference of individual investors. It puts all investors in a risk-neutral world where the expected return equals the risk-free interest rate. The 1997 Nobel economics prize was awarded to M. Scholes and R. Merton (F. Black had died) for this brilliant formula and a series of contributions to the option pricing theory based on this formula.

In this chapter, we will derive the Black-Scholes formula and give examples of its applications.

5.2 Black-Scholes Equation

Basic assumptions

(a) The underlying asset price follows the geometrical Brownian motion:

$$\frac{dS_t}{S_t} = \mu dt + \sigma dW_t, \tag{5.2.1}$$

where

μ—— expected return rate (constant parameter),
σ—— volatility (constant parameter),
dW_t—— standard Brownian motion,

$$E(dW_t) = 0,$$

$$Var(dW_t) = dt,$$

(b) Risk-free interest rate r is a constant;
(c) Underlying asset pays no dividend;
(d) No transaction cost and no tax;
(e) The market is arbitrage-free.

Problem Let $V = V(S, t)$ denote the option price. At maturity $(t = T)$,

$$V(S,T) = \begin{cases} (S-K)^+, & \text{(call option)} \\ (K-S)^+, & \text{(put option)} \end{cases}$$

where K is the strike price. What is the option's value during its lifetime $(0 \le t < T)$?

We can derive a mathematical model of the option pricing using the Δ-hedging technique (see Definition 3.1).

Construct a portfolio

$$\Pi = V - \Delta S,$$

(Δ denotes shares of the underlying asset), choose Δ such that Π is risk-free in $(t, t+dt)$.

If portfolio Π starts at time t, and Δ remains unchanged in $(t, t+dt)$, then the requirement Π be risk-free means the return of the portfolio at $t+dt$ should be

$$\frac{\Pi_{t+dt} - \Pi_t}{\Pi_t} = r dt,$$

i.e.

$$dV_t - \Delta dS_t = r\Pi_t dt = r(V_t - \Delta S_t)dt. \tag{5.2.2}$$

Since

$$V_t = V(S_t, t),$$

where the stochastic process S_t satisfies the stochastic differential equation (5.2.1), hence by the Itô formula

$$dV_t = (\frac{\partial V}{\partial t} + \frac{1}{2}\sigma^2 S^2 \frac{\partial^2 V}{\partial S^2} + \mu S \frac{\partial V}{\partial S})dt + \sigma S \frac{\partial V}{\partial S} dW_t.$$

Substituting the above into (5.2.2), we get

$$(\frac{\partial V}{\partial t} + \frac{1}{2}\sigma^2 S^2 \frac{\partial^2 V}{\partial S^2} + \mu S \frac{\partial V}{\partial S} - \Delta \mu S)dt + (\sigma S \frac{\partial V}{\partial S} - \Delta \sigma S)dW_t$$
$$= r(V - \Delta S)dt. \tag{5.2.3}$$

Since the right hand side of the equation is risk-free, the coefficient of the random term dW_t on the left hand side must be zero. Therefore, we choose

$$\Delta = \frac{\partial V}{\partial S}. \tag{5.2.4}$$

Substituting it into (5.2.3), we get the following partial differential equation:

$$\frac{\partial V}{\partial t} + \frac{1}{2}\sigma^2 S^2 \frac{\partial^2 V}{\partial S^2} + rS \frac{\partial V}{\partial S} - rV = 0.$$

This is the **Black-Scholes equation** that describes the option price movement.

Therefore, in order to determine the option value at any time in $[0, T]$, we need to solve the following PDE problem in the domain $\Sigma : \{0 \leq S < \infty,\ 0 \leq t \leq T\}$:

$$\begin{cases} \frac{\partial V}{\partial t} + \frac{1}{2}\sigma^2 S^2 \frac{\partial^2 V}{\partial S^2} + rS\frac{\partial V}{\partial S} - rV = 0 & (\Sigma) \quad (5.2.5) \\ V\big|_{t=T} = \begin{cases} (S-K)^+, & \text{(call option)} \\ (K-S)^+, & \text{(put option)} \end{cases} & (5.2.6) \end{cases}$$

where (5.2.5), (5.2.6) is a terminal value problem for a backward parabolic equation with variable coefficients.

Remark The line segment $\{S = 0,\ 0 \leq t \leq T\}$ is also a boundary of the domain Σ. However, since the equation (5.2.5) is degenerated at $S = 0$, according to the PDE theory, there is no need to specify the boundary value at $S = 0$.

By the transformation

$$x = \ln S, \qquad \tau = T - t, \tag{5.2.7}$$

the problem (5.2.5) and(5.2.6) is reduced to a Cauchy problem of a parabolic equation with constant coefficients:

$$\begin{cases} \frac{\partial V}{\partial \tau} - \frac{1}{2}\sigma^2 \frac{\partial^2 V}{\partial x^2} - (r - \frac{\sigma^2}{2})\frac{\partial V}{\partial x} + rV = 0 & \\ \qquad (-\infty < x < \infty,\ 0 < \tau \leq T) & (5.2.8) \\ V\,|_{\tau=0} = \begin{cases} (e^x - K)^+, & \text{(call option)} \\ (K - e^x)^+, & \text{(put option)} \end{cases} & (5.2.9) \end{cases}$$

By the PDE theory, the Cauchy problem (5.2.8) and (5.2.9) is well-posed. Thus the original problem (5.2.5),(5.2.6) is also well-posed.

Remark The expected return μ of the asset, a parameter in the underlying asset model (5.2.1), does not appear in the Black-Scholes equation (5.2.5). Instead, the risk-free interest rate r appears in (5.2.5). As we have seen in the discrete model, *by the Δ—hedging technique, the Black-Scholes equation puts the investors in a risk-neutral world where pricing is independent of the risk preference of individual investors. Thus the option price arrived at by solving the Black-Scholes equation is a risk-neutral price.*

Remark Here is an interesting question:

1) Starting from the discrete option price V_j^n obtained by the binomial tree method, by interpolation, we can define a function $V_\Delta(s, t)$ on the domain $\Sigma : \{0 \leq S < \infty,\ 0 \leq t \leq T\}$;
2) If there exists a function $V(S, t)$, such that

$$\lim_{\Delta t \to 0} V_\Delta(S,t) = V(S,t), \qquad ((S,t) \in \Sigma),$$

3) and if $V(S,t) \in C^{2,1}(\Sigma)$ (i.e. V, V_x, V_{xx}, V_t are continuous in Σ),

what differential equation does $V(S,t)$ satisfy?

The answer is: $V(S,t)$ satisfies the Black-Scholes equation in Σ. I.e., if the option price from the BTM converges to a sufficiently smooth limit function as $\Delta t \to 0$, then the limit function is a solution to the Black-Scholes equation.

In the following, we explain the basic idea behind the answer (this is not a proof).

In §4.2, we arrived at a discrete model of the underlying asset price movement as described by the binomial tree process in a risk-neutral world, which is (4.2.1):

$$\ln \frac{S^*(t+\Delta t)}{S^*(t)} = \sigma\sqrt{\Delta t} R(\omega) - \frac{1}{2}\sigma^2 \Delta t,$$

where

$$S^*(t) = \frac{S(t)}{B(t)} \quad \text{——discounted price of the asset}$$

and $R(\omega)$ is the random variable in the coin-tossing problem defined as

$$R(\omega) = \begin{cases} 1, & \text{“}\omega_{\text{up}}\text{”}, \\ -1, & \text{“}\omega_{\text{down}}\text{”}. \end{cases}$$

Under the risk-neutral measure Q,

$$\text{Prob}_{\text{Q}}\{\omega_{\text{up}}\} = \text{Prob}_{\text{Q}}\{\omega_{\text{down}}\} = \frac{1}{2}.$$

Thus we have

$$S(t+\Delta t) = S(t) e^{(r-\frac{1}{2}\sigma^2)\Delta t + \sigma\sqrt{\Delta t}R(\omega)}. \tag{5.2.10}$$

In the period $[t_n, t_{n+1}]$, by the one-period & two state option pricing model (3.2.8), if the asset price S_α at $t = t_n$ is given, then by assumption 1), the option pricing formula (3.2.8) can be written as

$$V_\Delta(S_\alpha, t_n) = \frac{1}{\rho} E^{\text{Q}}(V_\Delta(S(t_{n+1}), t_{n+1}) \mid S(t_n) = S_\alpha), \tag{5.2.11}$$

where $S(t_{n+1})$ is the random variable defined by (5.2.10)

$$S(t_{n+1}) = S_\alpha e^{(r-\frac{1}{2}\sigma^2)\Delta t + \sigma\sqrt{\Delta t}R(\omega)}.$$

By assumption 2), we can substitute $V_\Delta(S,t)$ with its limit function $V(S,t)$. Neglecting the errors introduced in this process, then (5.2.11) can be written as

$$V(S_\alpha, t_n) = \frac{1}{\rho} E^{\text{Q}}([V(S(t_{n+1}), t_{n+1}) - V(S_\alpha, t_n)] \mid S(t_n) = S_\alpha) + \frac{1}{\rho} V(S_\alpha, t_n).$$

By assumption 3), we can perform the Taylor expansion to get

$$
\begin{aligned}
V(S(t_{n+1}),t_{n+1}) - V(S_\alpha,t_n) &= \frac{\partial V}{\partial t}(S_\alpha,t_n)\Delta t \\
&+\frac{\partial V}{\partial S}(S_\alpha,t_n)[S_\alpha e^{(r-\frac{1}{2}\sigma^2)\Delta t+\sigma\sqrt{\Delta t}R(\omega)} - S_\alpha] \\
&+\frac{1}{2}\frac{\partial^2 V}{\partial S^2}(S_\alpha,t_n)[S_\alpha e^{(r-\frac{1}{2}\sigma^2)\Delta t+\sigma\sqrt{\Delta t}R(\omega)} - S_\alpha]^2 \\
&+O(\Delta t^{\frac{3}{2}}) \\
&= \frac{\partial V}{\partial t}(S_\alpha,t_n)\Delta t + S_\alpha\frac{\partial V}{\partial S}(S_\alpha,t_n)\{[(r-\frac{1}{2}\sigma^2)\Delta t+\sigma\sqrt{\Delta t}R(\omega)] \\
&+\frac{1}{2}[(r-\frac{1}{2}\sigma^2)\Delta t+\sigma\sqrt{\Delta t}R(\omega)]^2\} \\
&+\frac{1}{2}S_\alpha^2\frac{\partial^2 V}{\partial S^2}(S_\alpha,t_n)[(r-\frac{1}{2}\sigma^2)\Delta t+\sigma\sqrt{\Delta t}R(\omega)]^2 \\
&+O(\Delta t^{\frac{3}{2}}) \\
&= [\frac{\partial V}{\partial t}(S_\alpha,t_n) + (r-\frac{1}{2}\sigma^2)S_\alpha\frac{\partial V}{\partial S}(S_\alpha,t_n)]\Delta t \\
&+S_\alpha\frac{\partial V}{\partial S}(S_\alpha,t_n)\sigma\sqrt{\Delta t}R(\omega) + \frac{\sigma^2}{2}[S_\alpha\frac{\partial V}{\partial S}(S_\alpha,t_n) \\
&+S_\alpha^2\frac{\partial^2 V}{\partial S^2}(S_\alpha,t_n)]R^2(\omega)\Delta t + O(\Delta t^{\frac{3}{2}}).
\end{aligned}
$$

Since

$$E^{Q}(R(\omega)) = 0,$$

$$E^{Q}(R^2(\omega)) = 1,$$

Substituting them into (5.2.12), we get

$$
\begin{aligned}
V(S_\alpha,t_n) = \frac{1}{\rho}\{[&\frac{\partial V}{\partial t}(S_\alpha,t_n) + (r-\frac{1}{2}\sigma^2)S_\alpha\frac{\partial V}{\partial S}(S_\alpha,t_n)]\Delta t \\
&+[\frac{\sigma^2}{2}S_\alpha\frac{\partial V}{\partial S}(S_\alpha,t_n) + \frac{\sigma^2}{2}S_\alpha^2\frac{\partial^2 V}{\partial S^2}(S_\alpha,t_n)]\Delta t\} + \frac{1}{\rho}V(S_\alpha,t_n) \\
&+O(\Delta t^{\frac{3}{2}}),
\end{aligned}
$$

i.e.

$$(1-\frac{1}{\rho})V(S_\alpha,t_n)=\frac{1}{\rho}[\frac{\partial V}{\partial t}+rS\frac{\partial V}{\partial S}+\frac{\sigma^2}{2}S^2\frac{\partial^2 V}{\partial S^2}]_{(S_\alpha,t_n)}\Delta t$$
$$+O(\Delta t^{\frac{3}{2}}).$$

Since $\rho = 1+r\Delta t$, where r is the risk-free interest rate, thus at the point (S_α, t_n), we have

$$\frac{\partial V}{\partial t}+rS\frac{\partial V}{\partial S}+\frac{\sigma^2}{2}S^2\frac{\partial^2 V}{\partial S^2}-rV=O(\Delta t^{\frac{1}{2}}).$$

Let $\Delta t \to 0$, and we get the Black-Scholes equation.

5.3 Black-Scholes Formula

To solve the Cauchy problem (5.2.8) and (5.2.9), set

$$V = ue^{\alpha\tau+\beta x}. \tag{5.3.1}$$

Choose constants α, β, so that equation (5.2.8) can be reduced to a heat equation. By straightforward computation, we get

$$V_\tau = e^{\alpha\tau+\beta x}[u_\tau+\alpha u],$$
$$V_x = e^{\alpha\tau+\beta x}[u_x+\beta u],$$
$$V_{xx} = e^{\alpha\tau+\beta x}[u_{xx}+2\beta u_x+\beta^2 u].$$

Substitute these into (5.2.8), eliminating $e^{\alpha\tau+\beta x}$, we get

$$u_\tau-\frac{\sigma^2}{2}u_{xx}-[\beta\sigma^2+r-\frac{\sigma^2}{2}]u_x+[r-\beta(r-\frac{\sigma^2}{2})-\frac{\sigma^2}{2}\beta^2+\alpha]u=0.$$

We choose

$$\beta=\frac{1}{2}-\frac{r}{\sigma^2},$$
$$\alpha=-r+\beta(r-\frac{\sigma^2}{2})+\frac{\sigma^2}{2}\beta^2$$
$$=-r-\frac{1}{2\sigma^2}(r-\frac{\sigma^2}{2})^2.$$

Thus by transformation (5.3.1), the equation (5.2.8) is reduced to

$$\frac{\partial u}{\partial\tau}-\frac{\sigma^2}{2}\frac{\partial^2 u}{\partial x^2}=0, \tag{5.3.2}$$

with the initial value (take call option as example)

$$u\mid_{\tau=0}=e^{-\beta x}V\mid_{\tau=0}=e^{-\beta x}(e^x-K)^+. \tag{5.3.3}$$

As we know the solution of the Cauchy problem corresponding to the heat equation (5.3.2) is given by the Poisson formula,

$$u(x,\tau)=\int_{-\infty}^{+\infty}K(x-\xi,\tau)\varphi(\xi)d\xi,$$

where $\varphi(\xi)$ is the initial value, $K(x-\xi,\tau)$ is the fundamental solution of the heat equation (5.3.2):

$$K(x-\xi,\tau)=\frac{1}{\sigma\sqrt{2\pi\tau}}e^{-\frac{(x-\xi)^2}{2\sigma^2\tau}}.$$

Thus the solution of the Cauchy problem (5.3.2),(5.3.3) can be written as

$$\begin{aligned}u(x,\tau)&=\int_{-\infty}^{+\infty}\frac{1}{\sigma\sqrt{2\pi\tau}}e^{-\frac{(x-\xi)^2}{2\sigma^2\tau}}[e^{-\beta\xi}(e^\xi-K)^+]d\xi\\&=\int_{\ln K}^{+\infty}\frac{1}{\sigma\sqrt{2\pi\tau}}e^{-\frac{(x-\xi)^2}{2\sigma^2\tau}}[e^{(1-\beta)\xi}-Ke^{-\beta\xi}]d\xi,\end{aligned}$$

where $\beta=-\frac{1}{\sigma^2}(r-\frac{\sigma^2}{2})$. Back to the original function $V(x,\tau)$,

$$\begin{aligned}V(x,\tau)&=e^{-r\tau-\frac{1}{2\sigma^2}(r-\frac{\sigma^2}{2})^2\tau-\frac{1}{\sigma^2}(r-\frac{\sigma^2}{2})x}u(x,\tau)\\&=I_1+I_2,\end{aligned}$$

where

$$\begin{aligned}I_1&=e^{-r\tau}\int_{\ln K}^{+\infty}\frac{1}{\sigma\sqrt{2\pi\tau}}\exp[-\frac{1}{2\sigma^2\tau}\{(x-\xi)^2\\&\quad+2(x-\xi)(r-\frac{\sigma^2}{2})\tau+(r-\frac{\sigma^2}{2})^2\tau^2\}+\xi]d\xi\\&=e^{-r\tau}\int_{\ln K}^{+\infty}\frac{1}{\sigma\sqrt{2\pi\tau}}\exp[-\frac{1}{2\sigma^2\tau}[x-\xi+(r-\frac{\sigma^2}{2})\tau]^2+\xi]d\xi.\end{aligned}$$

Denote

$$\eta=x-\xi+(r-\frac{\sigma^2}{2})\tau,$$

then

$$I_1=\frac{e^x}{\sigma\sqrt{2\pi\tau}}\int_{-\infty}^{x-\ln K+(r-\frac{\sigma^2}{2})\tau}e^{-\frac{(\eta+\sigma^2\tau)^2}{2\sigma^2\tau}}d\eta.$$

Denote

$$\omega = \frac{\eta + \sigma^2\tau}{\sigma\sqrt{\tau}}, \qquad N(x) = \frac{1}{\sqrt{2\pi}}\int_{-\infty}^{x} e^{-\frac{\omega^2}{2}}\,d\omega,$$

where $N(x)$ is the the cumulative probability distribution function of a standard normal distribution, then

$$I_1 = e^x N(\frac{x - \ln K + (r + \frac{\sigma^2}{2})\tau}{\sigma\sqrt{\tau}}).$$

Similarly

$$\begin{aligned} I_2 &= -e^{-r\tau}\int_{\ln K}^{\infty} \frac{K}{\sigma\sqrt{2\pi\tau}} e^{-\frac{1}{2\sigma^2\tau}[x-\xi+(r-\frac{\sigma^2}{2})\tau]^2}\,d\xi \\ &= -\frac{e^{-r\tau}K}{\sigma\sqrt{2\pi\tau}}\int_{-\infty}^{x-\ln K+(r-\frac{\sigma^2}{2})\tau} e^{-\frac{\eta^2}{2\sigma^2\tau}}\,d\eta \\ &= -Ke^{-r\tau}N(\frac{x - \ln K + (r - \frac{\sigma^2}{2})\tau}{\sigma\sqrt{\tau}}). \end{aligned}$$

Thus by the transformation (5.2.7) back to the original variable (S, t), we have

$$\begin{aligned} V(S,t) = SN(&\frac{\ln S - \ln K + (r + \frac{\sigma^2}{2})(T-t)}{\sigma\sqrt{T-t}}) \\ &-Ke^{-r(T-t)}N(\frac{\ln S - \ln K + (r - \frac{\sigma^2}{2})(T-t)}{\sigma\sqrt{T-t}}). \end{aligned}$$

Denote

$$d_1 = \frac{\ln\frac{S}{K} + (r + \frac{\sigma^2}{2})(T-t)}{\sigma\sqrt{T-t}}, \tag{5.3.4}$$

$$d_2 = d_1 - \sigma\sqrt{T-t}, \tag{5.3.5}$$

thus we have the pricing formula for a European call option,

$$V(S,t) = SN(d_1) - Ke^{-r(T-t)}N(d_2), \tag{5.3.6}$$

known as the **Black-Scholes formula**.

For the European put option, it follows from the call-put parity (2.2.5) that

$$p_t = c_t + Ke^{-r(T-t)} - S_t = Ke^{-r(T-t)}[1 - N(d_2)] - S[1 - N(d_1)].$$

With the following substituted into the above,

$$\begin{aligned} 1 - N(d_1) &= \frac{1}{\sqrt{2\pi}} \int_{d_1}^{\infty} e^{-\frac{\omega^2}{2}} d\omega \\ &= \frac{1}{\sqrt{2\pi}} \int_{-\infty}^{-d_1} e^{-\frac{\omega^2}{2}} d\omega = N(-d_1), \end{aligned}$$

we get the European put option pricing formula

$$V(S,t) = Ke^{-r(T-t)} N(-d_2) - SN(-d_1). \tag{5.3.7}$$

5.4 Generalized Black-Scholes Model (I) ——Dividend-Paying Options

To be applicable to more general cases, we modify the basic assumptions in §5.2 as follows:

(â) The underlying asset price movement satisfies the stochastic differential equation

$$\frac{dS_t}{S_t} = \mu(t)dt + \sigma(t)dW_t,$$

($\hat{b}$) Risk-free interest rate $r = r(t)$,
(ĉ) The underlying asset pays continuous dividends at rate $q(t)$,
(d) and (e) remain unchanged.

As before, we will use the Δ-hedging technique to set up a continuous model of the option pricing, and find valuation formulas.

Construct a portfolio

$$\Pi = V - \Delta S.$$

Choose Δ, so that Π is risk-neutral in $[t, t+dt]$. Analogous to the derivation in §5.2, the expected return is

$$\Pi_{t+dt} - \Pi_t = r\Pi_t dt.$$

Taking into account the dividends, the portfolio's value at Π_{t+dt} is

$$\Pi_{t+dt} = V_{t+dt} - \Delta_t S_t q_t dt - \Delta_t S_{t+dt}.$$

Therefore in place of (5.2.2), we have

$$dV_t - \Delta_t dS_t = r_t \Pi_t dt + \Delta_t S_t q_t dt.$$

Apply the Itô formula, and choose

$$\Delta_t = \frac{\partial V}{\partial S},$$

we get

$$(\frac{\partial V}{\partial t} + \frac{\sigma^2(t)}{2} S^2 \frac{\partial^2 V}{\partial S^2})dt = r(t)(V - S\frac{\partial V}{\partial S})dt + q(t)S\frac{\partial V}{\partial S}dt.$$

Thus we have a partial differential equation for V:

$$\frac{\partial V}{\partial t} + \frac{\sigma^2(t)}{2} S^2 \frac{\partial^2 V}{\partial S^2} + (r(t) - q(t))S\frac{\partial V}{\partial S} - r(t)V = 0.$$

This is the **Black-Scholes equation for dividend-paying option pricing**.

Therefore in order to price the option (take call option as example), we need to solve the following problem in Σ:

$$\begin{cases} \frac{\partial V}{\partial t} + \frac{\sigma^2(t)}{2} S^2 \frac{\partial^2 V}{\partial S^2} + (r(t) - q(t))S\frac{\partial V}{\partial S} - r(t)V = 0, & (5.4.1) \\ V \mid_{t=T} = (S-K)^+, \qquad (0 \le S < \infty). & (5.4.2) \end{cases}$$

In order to solve the initial value problem (5.4.1) and (5.4.2), set

$$u = Ve^{\beta(t)}, \tag{5.4.3}$$

$$y = Se^{\alpha(t)}. \tag{5.4.4}$$

Choose $\alpha(t)$, $\beta(t)$ to eliminate the $\frac{\partial V}{\partial S}$ and V terms in (5.4.1).

Substitute the following

$$\begin{aligned} \frac{\partial V}{\partial t} &= \frac{\partial u}{\partial t} e^{-\beta(t)} + y\frac{\partial u}{\partial y}\alpha'(t)e^{-\beta(t)} - u\beta'(t)e^{-\beta(t)}, \\ S\frac{\partial V}{\partial S} &= y\frac{\partial u}{\partial y}e^{-\beta(t)}, \\ S^2\frac{\partial^2 V}{\partial S^2} &= y^2\frac{\partial^2 u}{\partial y^2}e^{-\beta(t)}. \end{aligned}$$

into (5.4.1), we get

$$\frac{\partial u}{\partial t} + \frac{\sigma^2(t)}{2} y^2 \frac{\partial^2 u}{\partial y^2} + \{[r(t) - q(t)] + \alpha'(t)\}y\frac{\partial u}{\partial y} - [r(t) + \beta'(t)]u = 0.$$

Let $\alpha(t)$, $\beta(t)$ be the solutions to the following initial value problems of ordinary differential equations:

$$\begin{cases} \frac{d\alpha}{dt} + r(t) - q(t) = 0, \\ \frac{d\beta}{dt} + r(t) = 0, \\ \alpha(T) = \beta(T) = 0, \end{cases}$$

Solve it to get

$$\alpha(t) = \int_t^T [r(\tau) - q(\tau)]d\tau, \tag{5.4.5}$$

$$\beta(t) = \int_t^T r(\tau)d\tau. \tag{5.4.6}$$

Thus under the transformation (5.4.3),(5.4.4), the problem (5.4.1),(5.4.2) is reduced to

$$\begin{cases} \frac{\partial u}{\partial t} + \frac{\sigma^2(t)}{2} y^2 \frac{\partial^2 u}{\partial y^2} = 0, & (5.4.7) \\ u \mid_{t=T} = Ve^{\beta(t)} \mid_{t=T} = (y-K)^+. & (5.4.8) \end{cases}$$

By transformation

$$\tau = \int_0^t \sigma^2(\omega)d\omega, \tag{5.4.9}$$

(5.4.7), (5.4.8) become

$$\begin{cases} \frac{\partial u}{\partial \tau} + \frac{1}{2} y^2 \frac{\partial^2 u}{\partial y^2} = 0, \\ u \mid_{\tau=\hat{T}} = (y-K)^+, \end{cases}$$

where $\hat{T} = \int_0^T \sigma^2(t)dt.$

Applying the Black-Scholes formula (where $\sigma = 1, r = 0, T = \hat{T}, t = \tau$), we get

$$u(y,\tau) = yN(\hat{d_1}) - KN(\hat{d_2}),$$

where

$$\hat{d_1} = \frac{\ln \frac{y}{K} + \frac{1}{2}(\hat{T} - \tau)}{\sqrt{\hat{T} - \tau}},$$

$$\hat{d_2} = \hat{d_1} - \sqrt{\hat{T} - \tau}.$$

Back to the original variables, from (5.4.3)—(5.4.9), we have obtained the following **pricing formula for the European call option**

$$\begin{aligned} V(S,t) &= e^{-\beta(t)}[Se^{\alpha(t)}N(\hat{d_1}) - KN(\hat{d_2})] \\ &= Se^{-\int_t^T q(\tau)d\tau} N(\hat{d_1}) - Ke^{-\int_t^T r(\tau)d\tau} N(\hat{d_2}), \end{aligned} \tag{5.4.10}$$

where

$$\hat{d}_1 = \frac{\ln \frac{S}{K} + \int_t^T [r(\tau) - q(\tau) + \frac{\sigma^2(\tau)}{2}]d\tau}{\sqrt{\int_t^T \sigma^2(\tau)d\tau}}, \tag{5.4.11}$$

$$\hat{d}_2 = \hat{d}_1 - \sqrt{\int_t^T \sigma^2(\tau)d\tau}. \tag{5.4.12}$$

In order to derive the pricing formula for the European put option, we need to establish the call-put parity first.

Theorem 5.1 *Let $c(S,t), p(S,t)$ denote the price of a European call option and put option, respectively, with the same strike price K and expiration date T. Then the call—put parity is given by*

$$c(S,t) + Ke^{-\int_t^T r(\tau)d\tau} = p(S,t) + Se^{-\int_t^T q(\tau)d\tau}. \tag{5.4.13}$$

where $r = r(t)$ is the risk-free interest rate, $q = q(t)$ is the dividend rate, and $\sigma = \sigma(t)$ is the volatility.

Proof Consider the difference between a call and a put:

$$W(S,t) = c(S,t) - p(S,t).$$

At $t = T$,

$$W(S,T) = (S-K)^+ - (K-S)^+ = S - K.$$

W is the solution of the following problem (see (5.4.1)):

$$\begin{cases} \frac{\partial W}{\partial t} + \frac{\sigma^2(t)}{2} S^2 \frac{\partial^2 W}{\partial S^2} + [r(t) - q(t)]S\frac{\partial W}{\partial S} - r(t)W = 0, & (5.4.14) \\ W \mid_{t=T} = S - K. & (5.4.15) \end{cases}$$

Let W be of the form

$$W = a(t)S - b(t)K. \tag{5.4.16}$$

Substituting W into (5.4.14), we get

$$a'(t)S - b'(t)K + [r(t) - q(t)]Sa(t) - r(t)[a(t)S - b(t)K] = 0.$$

Choose $a(t), b(t)$ such that

$$a'(t) + [r(t) - q(t)]a(t) - r(t)a(t) = 0,$$
$$b'(t) - b(t)r(t) = 0,$$

and from the terminal condition,

$$a(T) = b(T) = 1.$$

The solution is

$$a(t) = e^{-\int_t^T q(\tau)d\tau}, \qquad b(t) = e^{-\int_t^T r(\tau)d\tau}.$$

Substitute it into (5.4.16), and we get the call—put parity (5.4.13). Thus the theorem is proved.

By the call—put parity (5.4.13), we have the **European put option pricing formula**

$$V(S,t) = Ke^{-\int_t^T r(\tau)d\tau} N(-\hat{d}_2) - Se^{-\int_t^T q(\tau)d\tau} N(-\hat{d}_1), \tag{5.4.17}$$

where $\hat{d}_1$, $\hat{d}_2$ are defined by (5.4.11), (5.4.12).

If in place of the continuous dividend paying assumption ($\hat{c}$), we assume

($\tilde{c}$) the underlying asset pays dividend Q on a predetermined date $t = t_1$ $(0 < t_1 < T)$ (if the asset is a stock, then Q is the dividend per share).

After the dividend payday $t = t_1$, there will be a change in stock price:

$$S(t_1 - 0) = S(t_1 + 0) + Q.$$

However, the option price must be continuous at $t = t_1$:

$$V(S(t_1 - 0), t_1 - 0) = V(S(t_1 + 0), t_1 + 0).$$

Therefore, S and V must satisfy the boundary condition at $t = t_1$:

$$V(S, t_1 - 0) = V(S - Q, t_1 + 0). \tag{5.4.18}$$

In order to set up the option pricing model (take call option as example), consider two periods $[0, t_1]$, $[t_1, T]$ separately.

In $\{0 \le S < \infty, \quad t_1 \le t \le T\}$, $V = V(S,t)$ satisfies the boundary-terminal value problem

$$\begin{cases} \dfrac{\partial V}{\partial t} + \dfrac{\sigma^2(t)}{2} S^2 \dfrac{\partial^2 V}{\partial S^2} + r(t) S \dfrac{\partial V}{\partial S} - r(t)V = 0, \\ V(S,T) = (S-K)^+. \end{cases}$$

By (5.4.18), in $\{0 \leq S < \infty, \quad 0 \leq t \leq t_1\}$, $V = V(S,t)$ satisfies

$$\begin{cases} \frac{\partial V}{\partial t} + \frac{\sigma^2(t)}{2} S^2 \frac{\partial^2 V}{\partial S^2} + r(t) S \frac{\partial V}{\partial S} - r(t) V = 0, \\ V(S, t_1) = V(S - Q, t_1 + 0). \end{cases}$$

By solving above problems, we can determine the premium $V(S_0, 0)$ to be paid at the initial date $t = 0$ (S_0 is the stock price at that time).

Remark Note that there is a subtle difference between the dividend-paying assumptions ($\hat{c}$) and ($\tilde{c}$) when we model the option price of dividend-paying assets.

In the case of assumption ($\hat{c}$), we used the dividend rate $q = q(t)$, which is related to the *return of the stock*. Thus in the time interval $[t_1, t_2]$, the dividend payment alone (if neglecting other factors affecting the stock price) will cause the stock price change from S_{t_1} to $S_{t_1} e^{-\int_{t_1}^{t_2} q(t)dt}$. By this model, if the dividend is paid at $t = t_1$ with the intensity d_Q,

$$\lim_{\Delta t \to 0} \int_{t_1}^{t_1 + \Delta t} q(t)dt = d_Q,$$

then at the payday $t = t_1$ the stock price will fall from S_{t_1} to $S_{t_1} e^{-d_Q}$. Thus we can derive from (5.4.17) the corresponding option pricing formula.

In the case of assumption ($\tilde{c}$), we used the dividend Q, which is related to the *stock price itself*. Therefore at the payday $t = t_1$, the stock price will fall from S_{t_1} to $S_{t_1} - Q$. Thus we have at $t = t_1$ the boundary condition (5.4.18) for the option price.

We should be aware of this difference when solving real problems.

Remark

For commodity options, the storage fee, which depends on the amount of the commodity, should also be taken into account.

Therefore, when applying the Δ-hedging technique, for the portfolio

$$\Pi = V - \Delta S,$$

there is

$$d\Pi = dV - \Delta dS + \Delta \hat{q} dt,$$

where $\Delta \hat{q} dt$ denotes the storage fee for Δ amount of commodity and period dt. Similar to the derivation we did before, choose

$$\Delta = \frac{\partial V}{\partial S},$$

such that Π is risk-free in $(t, t + dt)$. Then we get the terminal-boundary problem for the option price $V = V(S,t)$

$$\begin{cases} \frac{\partial V}{\partial t} + \frac{\sigma^2}{2}S^2\frac{\partial^2 V}{\partial S^2} + (rS + \hat{q})\frac{\partial V}{\partial S} - rV = 0, \\ V\mid_{t=T} = (S-K)^+. \end{cases} \tag{5.4.19}$$

This equation does not have a closed form solution in general. Numerical approach is required.

If the storage fee for Δ items of commodity and period dt is in the form of $\Delta\hat{q}Sdt$, proportional to the current price of the commodity, then (5.4.19) becomes

$$\frac{\partial V}{\partial t} + \frac{\sigma^2}{2}S^2\frac{\partial^2 V}{\partial S^2} + (r + \hat{q})S\frac{\partial V}{\partial S} - rV = 0.$$

And the option price is given by the Black-Scholes formula.

5.5 Generalized Black-Scholes Model (II) ——Binary Options and Compound Options

(A) There are two basic forms of **binary options** (take stock option as example):

1. *Cash-or-nothing call (CONC): If the stock price on the expiration date $(t = T)$ is below the strike price, the option is worthless; if the stock price is above the strike price, the holder gets \$1 in cash.*

2. *Asset-or nothing call (AONC): On the expiration date $(t = T)$, if the stock price is below the strike price, the option pays nothing; if the stock price is above the strike price, the option pays the stock price.*

If the basic assumptions in §5.4 hold, then the binary option can be modeled as

$$\begin{cases} \frac{\partial V}{\partial t} + \frac{\sigma^2}{2}S^2\frac{\partial^2 V}{\partial S^2} + (r - q)S\frac{\partial V}{\partial S} - rV = 0, & (5.5.1) \\ V\mid_{t=T} = \begin{cases} H(S-K), & \text{(CONC)} \\ SH(S-K), & \text{(AONC)} \end{cases} & (5.5.2) \end{cases}$$

where $H(x)$ is the Heviside function: $H(x) = 1$ for $x > 0$, $H(x) = 0$ for $x < 0$.

Consider a vanilla call option, a CONC and a AONC with the same strike price K and the same expiration date T. Their prices are denoted by V, V_C and V_A, respectively. On the expiration date $t = T$, these prices satisfy

$$V(S,T) = V_A(S,T) - KV_C(S,T).$$

In fact, by (5.5.2),

$$\begin{aligned} V(S,T) &= (S-K)^+ = (S-K)H(S-K) \\ &= SH(S-K) - KH(S-K) \\ &= V_A(S,T) - KV_C(S,T). \end{aligned}$$

And $V(S,t)$, $V_A(S,t)$ and $V_C(S,T)$ each satisfies the same Black-Scholes equation (5.5.1). In view of the linearity of the terminal-boundary problem, therefore in $\Sigma\{0 \leq S < \infty,\ 0 \leq t \leq T\}$,

$$V(S,t) = V_A(S,t) - KV_C(S,t). \tag{5.5.3}$$

i.e. *throughout the option's lifetime, a vanilla call is a combination of an AONC in long position and K times of CONC in short positions.*

What is the relation between V_A and V_C?

Theorem 5.2

$$V_A(S,t;r,q) = SV_C(S,t;q,\hat{r}). \tag{5.5.4}$$

where

$$\hat{r} = 2q - r - \sigma^2. \tag{5.5.5}$$

Proof Let $V_A(S,t) = Su(S,t)$.
It is straightforward to verify that $u(S,t)$ satisfies:

$$\frac{\partial u}{\partial t} + \frac{\sigma^2}{2}S^2\frac{\partial^2 u}{\partial S^2} + (r - q + \sigma^2)S\frac{\partial u}{\partial S} - qu = 0.$$

Define $\hat{r} = 2q - r - \sigma^2$, then the above equation can be written as

$$\frac{\partial u}{\partial t} + \frac{\sigma^2}{2}S^2\frac{\partial^2 u}{\partial S^2} + (q - \hat{r})S\frac{\partial u}{\partial S} - qu = 0. \tag{5.5.6}$$

At $t = T$,

$$u(S,T) = \frac{1}{S}V_A(S,T) = V_C(S,T). \tag{5.5.7}$$

In Σ, compare the terminal-boundary problem (5.5.6),(5.5.7) for $u(S,t)$, and the terminal-boundary problem (5.5.1),(5.5.2) for $V_C(S,t)$. If the constants r, q in (5.5.1) are replaced by q and $\hat{r}$, then $u(S,t)$ and $V_C(S,t)$ satisfy the same terminal-boundary value problem. By the uniqueness of the solution, we claim

$$u(x,t) = V_C(S,t;q,\hat{r}).$$

Thus (5.5.4) is proved.

Once the CONC price $V_C(S,t;r,q)$ is found, the AONC price $V_A(S,t;r,q)$ can be determined by (5.5.4).

In order to solve the CONC problem (5.5.1),(5.5.2), make transformation

$$\tau = T - t,$$
$$x = \ln\frac{S}{K}.$$

Then

$$H(S-K) = H(\frac{S}{K}-1) = H(e^x - 1) = H(x),$$

And (5.5.1),(5.5.2) is reduced to a Cauchy problem

$$\begin{cases} \frac{\partial V}{\partial \tau} = \frac{\sigma^2}{2}\frac{\partial^2 V}{\partial x^2} + (r - q - \frac{\sigma^2}{2})\frac{\partial V}{\partial x} - rV, \\ V(x,0) = H(x). \end{cases}$$

Analogous to the derivation in §5.3 of the Black-Scholes formula, we have

$$V(x,\tau) = e^{-r\tau}N(\frac{x + (r-q-\frac{\sigma^2}{2})\tau}{\sigma\sqrt{\tau}}),$$

where $N(x) = \frac{1}{\sqrt{2\pi}}\int_{-\infty}^{x} e^{-\frac{\omega^2}{2}}d\omega.$

Back to the original variables (S,t), we have

$$V_C(S,t;r,q) = e^{-r(T-t)}N(\frac{\ln\frac{S}{K} + (r-q-\frac{\sigma^2}{2})(T-t)}{\sigma\sqrt{T-t}}).$$

By (5.5.4) and the definition of $\hat{r}$ (5.5.5), we have

$$\begin{aligned} V_A(S,t;r,q) &= SV_C(S,t;q,\hat{r}) \\ &= Se^{-q(T-t)}N(\frac{\ln\frac{S}{K} + (q-\hat{r}-\frac{\sigma^2}{2})(T-t)}{\sigma\sqrt{T-t}}) \\ &= Se^{-q(T-t)}N(\frac{\ln\frac{S}{K} + (r-q+\frac{\sigma^2}{2})(T-t)}{\sigma\sqrt{T-t}}). \end{aligned}$$

(B) **Compound options**

A compound option is an option on another option. There are many varieties of compound options. Here we explain the simplest forms of compound options.

A compound option gives its owner the right to buy (sell) after a certain days (i.e. $t = T_1$) at a certain price $\hat{K}$ a call (put) option with the expiration date $t = T_2$ $(T_2 > T_1)$ and the strike price K. There are following forms of compound options:

1. At $t = T_1$ buy a call option on a call option;

2. At $t = T_1$ buy a call option on a put option;
3. At $t = T_1$ sell a put option on a call option;
4. At $t = T_1$ sell a put option on a put option.

Three risky assets are involved: the underlying asset (stock), the underlying option (stock option) and the compound option.

First, in domain $\Sigma_2\{0 \le S < \infty,\ 0 \le t \le T_2\}$ define the underlying option price, which can be given by the Black-Scholes formula, denoted as $V(S, t)$.

Then on $\Sigma_1\{0 \le S < \infty,\ 0 \le t \le T_1\}$ set up a PDE problem for the compound option $V_{co}(S, t)$. For this we again make use of the Δ-hedging technique to obtain the Black-Scholes equation for $V_{co}(S, t)$. At $t = T_1$, the corresponding terminal value is

$$V_{co}(S, T_1) = \begin{cases} (V(S, T_1) - \hat{K})^+, & (\text{"call" option}) \\ (\hat{K} - V(S, T_1))^+. & (\text{"put" option}) \end{cases}$$

For the case when r, q, σ are all constants, we can obtain a pricing formula for this form of the compound option. Take a call on a call at $t = T_1$ as example. At $t = 0$,

$$\begin{aligned} V_{co}(S, 0) = {} & Se^{-qT_2} M(a_1, b_1; \sqrt{\frac{T_1}{T_2}}) \\ & -Ke^{-rT_2} M(a_2, b_2; \sqrt{\frac{T_1}{T_2}}) - e^{rT_1} \hat{K} N(a_2), \end{aligned} \tag{5.5.8}$$

where

$$a_1 = \frac{\ln\frac{S}{S^*} + (r - q + \frac{\sigma^2}{2})T_1}{\sigma\sqrt{T_1}}, \quad a_2 = a_1 - \sigma\sqrt{T_1},$$

$$b_1 = \frac{\ln\frac{S}{K} + (r - q + \frac{\sigma^2}{2})T_2}{\sigma\sqrt{T_2}}, \quad b_2 = b_1 - \sigma\sqrt{T_2}$$

and S^* is the root of the following equation:

$$\begin{aligned} \hat{K} = {} & S^* e^{-q(T_2 - T_1)} N(\frac{\ln\frac{S^*}{K} + (r - q + \frac{\sigma^2}{2})(T_2 - T_1)}{\sigma\sqrt{T_2 - T_1}}) \\ & -Ke^{-r(T_2 - T_1)} N(\frac{\ln\frac{S^*}{K} + (r - q - \frac{\sigma^2}{2})(T_2 - T_1)}{\sigma\sqrt{T_2 - T_1}}), \end{aligned}$$

and $M(a, b; \rho)$ is the bivariate normal distribution function:

$$M(a, b; \rho) = \text{Prob}\{X \le a,\ Y \le b\},$$

where $X \sim N(0, 1)$, $Y \sim N(0, 1)$ are standard normal distribution, $Cov(X, Y) = \rho\ (-1 < \rho < 1)$.

Let $f_{(X,Y)}(x,y)$ denote its probability density function,

$$f_{(X,Y)}(x,y) = \frac{1}{2\pi\sqrt{1-\rho^2}}\exp\{-\frac{x^2 - 2\rho xy + y^2}{2(1-\rho^2)}\},$$

then

$$M(a,b;\rho) = \int_{-\infty}^{a} dx \int_{-\infty}^{b} f_{(X,Y)}(x,y)dy.$$

(C) **Chooser options (as you like it)**

Chooser option can be regarded as a special form of compound option. The option holder is given this right: at $t = T_1$ he can choose to let the option be a call option at strike price K_1, expiration date T_2 or let the option be a put option at strike price K_2, expiration date $\hat{T_2}$ $(T_2, \hat{T_2} > T_1 > 0)$.

Here four risky assets are involved: the underlying asset (stock), the underlying call option (stock option; strike price K_1, expiration date T_2), the underlying put option (stock option; strike price K_2, expiration date $\hat{T_2}$) and the chooser option. Denote

$V_C(S,t)$ as the underlying call option price,
$V_P(S,t)$ as the underlying put option price,

both are solutions given by the Black-Scholes formula.

In order to find the chooser option price $V_{ch}(S,t)$ on $\Sigma_1\{0 \le S < \infty,\ 0 \le t \le T_1\}$, we need to solve the following terminal-boundary value problem:

$$\begin{cases} \dfrac{\partial V}{\partial t} + \dfrac{1}{2}\sigma^2 S^2 \dfrac{\partial^2 V}{\partial S^2} + (r-q)S\dfrac{\partial V}{\partial S} - rV = 0, \\ V\mid_{t=T_1} = \max\{V_C(S,T_1), V_P(S,T_1)\}. \end{cases}$$

If the underlying call option V_C and put option V_P have the same strike price K and expiration date T_2, then by the call-put parity:

$$V_P(S,T_1) = V_C(S,T_1) + Ke^{-r(T_2-T_1)} - Se^{-q(T_2-T_1)},$$

thus

$$\begin{aligned} V\mid_{t=T_1} &= \max(V_C(S,T_1), V_P(S,T_1)) \\ &= V_C(S,T_1) + e^{-q(T_2-T_1)}(Ke^{-(r-q)(T_2-T_1)} - S)^+. \end{aligned}$$

Then by the superposition principle of the linear equations, we have

$$V_{ch}(S,t) = V_C(S,t) + e^{-q(T_2-T_1)}\hat{V}(S,t),$$

where $\hat{V}(S,t)$ is $e^{-q(T_2-T_1)}$ times of the price of a put option with expiration date T_1 and strike price $Ke^{-(r-q)(T_2-T_1)}$.

5.6 Numerical Methods (I) —— Finite Difference Method

With the computation power we enjoy nowadays, numerical methods are often preferred, although for European option pricing closed-form solutions do exist. Especially for complex option pricing problems, such as compound options and chooser options, numerical methods are particularly advantageous.

The binomial tree method (BTM) is the most commonly used numerical method in option pricing. In this section we will address the following questions:

a. How to solve the Black-Scholes equation by finite difference method (FDM)?

b. What is the relation between FDM and BTM?

c. How to prove the convergence of BTM, which is a stochastic algorithm, in the framework of the numerical solutions of partial differential equations?

(A) Introduction to finite difference method

Finite difference method is a discretization approach to the boundary value problems for partial differential equations by replacing the derivatives with differences.

If $y = f(x)$ is sufficiently smooth, then the differences corresponding to $f'(x)$ and $f''(x)$ are defined in the following forms:

$$f'(x) \sim \frac{f(x+\Delta x) - f(x)}{\Delta x} = (\frac{\Delta f}{\Delta x})_f, \qquad \text{(forward difference)}$$

$$f'(x) \sim \frac{f(x) - f(x-\Delta x)}{\Delta x} = (\frac{\Delta f}{\Delta x})_b, \qquad \text{(backward difference)}$$

$$f'(x) \sim \frac{f(x+\Delta x) - f(x-\Delta x)}{2\Delta x} = (\frac{\Delta f}{\Delta x})_c, \qquad \text{(central difference)}$$

$$f''(x) \sim \frac{f(x+\Delta x) - 2f(x) + f(x-\Delta x)}{\Delta x^2} = (\frac{\Delta^2 f}{\Delta x^2})_c. \qquad \text{(second central difference)}$$

By the Taylor expansion, we have the error estimates as follows

$$| f'(x) - (\frac{\Delta f}{\Delta x})_f |= O(\Delta x),$$

$$| f'(x) - (\frac{\Delta f}{\Delta x})_b |= O(\Delta x),$$

$$| f'(x) - (\frac{\Delta f}{\Delta x})_c |= O(\Delta x^2),$$

$$| f''(x) - (\frac{\Delta^2 f}{\Delta x^2})_c |= O(\Delta x^2).$$

There are several approaches to set up finite difference equations corresponding to the partial differential equations. Regarding the equation solving techniques, there are two basic types: *One type is the explicit finite difference scheme, whose solving process is explicit and solution can be obtained by direct computation; the other type is the implicit finite difference scheme, whose solution can only be obtained by solving a system of algebraic equations.*

To illustrate this, let us consider an initial-boundary value problem for the heat equation on $\{0 \le x < \infty,\ 0 \le t \le T\}$:

$$\begin{cases} \dfrac{\partial u}{\partial t} - a^2 \dfrac{\partial^2 u}{\partial x^2} = 0, & (0 \le x < \infty,\ t > 0) \quad (5.6.1) \\ u(0,t) = g(t), & (0 \le t \le T) \quad (5.6.2) \\ u(x,0) = \varphi(x). & (0 \le x < \infty) \quad (5.6.3) \end{cases}$$

In the domain $\{0 \le x < \infty,\ 0 \le t \le T\}$, we divide the x-axis into equally spaced nodes a distance Δx apart, and the t-axis into equally spaced nodes a distance Δt apart. Denote the mesh points by (x_m, t_n):

$$\begin{aligned} x_m &= m\Delta x, & (0 \le m < \infty) \\ t_n &= n\Delta t. & (0 \le n \le N, N = \tfrac{T}{\Delta t}) \end{aligned}$$

Denote the values of the function $u(x,t)$ at mesh points (x_m, t_n) by

$$u_m^n = u(x_m, t_n). \qquad (m = 0, 1, \ldots; n = 0, 1, \ldots, N)$$

Explicit finite difference scheme (Explicit FDS)

$$\begin{cases} (\frac{\Delta u}{\Delta t})_f - a^2(\frac{\Delta^2 u}{\Delta x^2})_c = 0, \\ u_0^n = g(t_n), \\ u_m^0 = \varphi(x_m). \end{cases}$$

i.e.

$$\begin{cases} (\dfrac{u_m^{n+1} - u_m^n}{\Delta t}) - a^2(\dfrac{u_{m+1}^n - 2u_m^n + u_{m-1}^n}{\Delta x^2}) = 0, & (5.6.4) \\ u_0^n = g(t_n), & (5.6.5) \\ u_m^0 = \varphi(x_m). & (5.6.6) \end{cases}$$

From (5.6.6), for the case $n = 0$, the value of u is given. Therefore if at $t = t_n$, the values of $u_m^n (m \ge 0)$ are known, then from the finite difference equation (5.6.4) we have the following recurrence equations

$$u_m^{n+1} = (1 - 2\alpha)u_m^n + \alpha u_{m+1}^n + \alpha u_{m-1}^n, \qquad (5.6.7)$$

and

$$u_0^{n+1} = g(t_{n+1}), \qquad (5.6.8)$$

where $\alpha = \dfrac{\Delta t}{\Delta x^2} a^2.$

We can compute the values of u at $t = t_{n+1}$ and obtain all u_m^{n+1} $(m \geq 0)$. Then by induction, we can evaluate all $u_m^n (m \geq 0,\ 0 \leq n \leq N)$. This is a typical explicit finite difference process.

Implicit finite difference scheme (Implicit FDS)

$$\begin{cases} (\frac{\Delta u}{\Delta t})_b - a^2(\frac{\Delta^2 u}{\Delta x^2})_c = 0, \\ u_0^{n+1} = g(t_{n+1}), \\ u_m^0 = \varphi(x_m) \end{cases}$$

i.e.

$$\begin{cases} (\frac{u_m^{n+1} - u_m^n}{\Delta t}) - a^2(\frac{u_{m+1}^{n+1} - 2u_m^{n+1} + u_{m-1}^{n+1}}{\Delta x^2}) = 0, & (5.6.9) \\ u_0^n = g(t_n), & (5.6.10) \\ u_m^0 = \varphi(x_m). & (5.6.11) \end{cases}$$

From (5.6.10), for the case $n = 0$, the value of u is given. Therefore if at $t = t_n$, values of $u_m^n (m \geq 0)$ are known, then by the finite difference equation (5.6.9) we have the recurrence equation

$$(1 + 2\alpha)u_m^{n+1} - \alpha u_{m+1}^{n+1} - \alpha u_{m-1}^{n+1} = u_m^n, \tag{5.6.12}$$

and

$$u_0^{n+1} = g(t_{n+1}). \tag{5.6.13}$$

where the unknowns are $u_m^{n+1} (m \geq 0)$.

Since (5.6.12) and (5.6.13) are a system of algebraic equations of an infinite number of unknowns, in order to solve them, usually we need to impose a boundary condition at $m = M$ (M is sufficiently large) to convert it to a system of linear equations of a finite number $(M - 1)$ of unknowns. There are many choices of boundary conditions, depending on the behavior of the solution at infinity. The simplest case is: the solution $u(x, t)$ and the initial value $\varphi(x)$ have the same behavior as $x \to \infty$. I.e. assuming

$$\lim_{x \to \infty} \frac{u(x,t)}{\varphi(x)} = 1, \qquad \forall t \in [0, T]$$

then at $x = M\Delta x = x_M$, we can impose a boundary condition as follows:

$$u_M^{n+1} = \varphi(x_M). \tag{5.6.14}$$

If $\lim_{x\to\infty} \varphi(x) = \varphi_\infty$ (constant), for simplicity, let

$$u_M^{n+1} = \varphi_\infty. \tag{5.6.15}$$

Under the boundary conditions (5.6.13) and (5.6.14) or (5.6.15), we get a linear system (5.6.12), which has $M-1$ unknowns u_m^{n+1} $(1 \le m \le M-1)$, i.e.

$$A\vec{u}^{n+1} = \vec{f}^{n+1},$$

where $\vec{u}^{n+1}$ and $\vec{f}^{n+1}$ are both $M-1$ dimensional vectors, A is $(M-1)\times(M-1)$ matrix:

$$\vec{u}^{n+1} = \begin{bmatrix} u_1^{n+1} \\ \vdots \\ u_{M-1}^{n+1} \end{bmatrix}, \qquad \vec{f}^{n+1} = \begin{bmatrix} f_1^{n+1} \\ \vdots \\ f_{M-1}^{n+1} \end{bmatrix},$$

$$A = \begin{bmatrix} 1+2\alpha & -\alpha & \dots & 0 \\ -\alpha & 1+2\alpha & \dots & 0 \\ \vdots & \ddots & \ddots & \vdots \\ 0 & 0 & -\alpha & 1+2\alpha \end{bmatrix},$$

and $\quad \alpha = a^2 \dfrac{\Delta t}{\Delta x^2}$,

$$\begin{aligned} f_1^{n+1} &= u_1^n + \alpha g(t_{n+1}), \\ f_i^{n+1} &= u_i^n, \qquad (2 \le i \le M-2) \\ f_{M-1}^{n+1} &= u_{M-1}^n + \alpha\varphi_\infty. \end{aligned}$$

There are two fundamental questions for any finite difference method: 1. As $\Delta t,\ \Delta x \to 0$, does the solution of the finite difference equation converge to the solution of the partial differential equation boundary problem? This is known as the **convergence problem** of the finite difference scheme. 2. When solving finite difference equations on computer, rounding errors are unavoidable. With decreasing mesh size, $\Delta t,\ \Delta x$ decrease, will the rounding errors be under control? Is it possible that these rounding errors do grow in magnitude at each iteration of the solution procedure, thus resulting in a totally wrong solution? This is called the **stability** of the scheme.

Definition 5.1 Suppose $L_\Delta u = 0$ is a finite difference equation obtained from discretization of the partial differential equation $Lu = 0$. If for any sufficiently smooth function $\omega(x,t)$ there is

$$\lim_{\Delta t, \Delta x \to 0} | L\omega - L_\Delta \omega | = 0,$$

then the finite difference scheme $L_\Delta u = 0$ is said to be **consistent** with $Lu = 0$.

Theorem 5.3(Lax's Equivalence Theorem)([35]) *Given a properly posed initial-boundary value problem and a finite difference scheme to it that satisfies the consistency condition, then stability is the necessary and sufficient condition for convergence.*

According to the numerical analysis theory of partial differential equation, for the initial-boundary value problem (5.6.1)—(5.6.3), the implicit finite difference scheme (5.6.9)—(5.6.11) is unconditionally stable, whereas the explicit finite difference scheme (5.6.4)—(5.6.6) is stable if $a^2\frac{\Delta t}{\Delta x^2} = \alpha \leq \frac{1}{2}$, and unstable if $\alpha > \frac{1}{2}$. This result indicates, although the explicit finite difference scheme is relatively simple in algorithm, but in order to obtain a reliable result, the time interval must satisfy the condition $\Delta t \leq \frac{1}{2a^2}\Delta x^2$. In contrast, although the implicit FDS requires solving a large system of linear equations in each step, the scheme is unconditionally stable, thus has no constraint on time interval Δt. That means if the computation accuracy is guaranteed, Δt can be large, and the result is still reliable.

Above results will be proved in the following when we introduce the FDS of the Black-Scholes equation.

(B) **Explicit FDS of the Black-Scholes equation**

In §5.2 we have shown the Black-Scholes equation can be reduced to a backward parabolic equation with constant coefficients under the transformation $x = \ln S$. In order to price the European call option, we need to solve the following terminal-boundary problem:

$$\begin{cases} \frac{\partial V}{\partial t} + \frac{\sigma^2}{2}\frac{\partial^2 V}{\partial x^2} + (r - q - \frac{\sigma^2}{2})\frac{\partial V}{\partial x} - rV = 0, & (5.6.16) \\ V\mid_{t=T} = (e^x - K)^+. & (5.6.17) \end{cases}$$

On the domain $\hat{\Sigma}\{-\infty < x < \infty,\ 0 \leq t \leq T\}$, construct a mesh:

$$x_m = m\Delta x, \qquad (-\infty < m < \infty)$$

$$t_n = n\Delta t. \qquad (0 \leq n \leq N, N = \frac{T}{\Delta t})$$

Define a function

$$V(x_m, t_n) = V_m^n.$$

Discretize the boundary problem(5.6.16),(5.6.17) as follows:

$$\begin{cases} \dfrac{V_m^{n+1}-V_m^n}{\Delta t}+\dfrac{\sigma^2}{2}\dfrac{V_{m+1}^{n+1}-2V_m^{n+1}+V_{m-1}^{n+1}}{\Delta x^2} \\ \qquad +(r-q-\dfrac{\sigma^2}{2})\dfrac{V_{m+1}^{n+1}-V_{m-1}^{n+1}}{2\Delta x}-rV_m^n=0, & (5.6.18) \\ V_m^N=(e^{m\Delta x}-K)^+. & (5.6.19) \end{cases}$$

By (5.6.19), for the case $n=N$, V_m^n is given; if V_m^{n+1} is known $(-\infty<m<\infty)$, then by (5.6.18), the value of V_m^n at $t=t_n=n\Delta t$ can be calculated from:

$$\begin{aligned} V_m^n=&\frac{1}{1+r\Delta t}[(1-\frac{\sigma^2\Delta t}{\Delta x^2})V_m^{n+1} \\ &+(\frac{\sigma^2\Delta t}{2\Delta x^2}+\frac{1}{2}(r-q-\frac{\sigma^2}{2})\frac{\Delta t}{\Delta x})V_{m+1}^{n+1} \\ &+(\frac{\sigma^2\Delta t}{2\Delta x^2}-\frac{1}{2}(r-q-\frac{\sigma^2}{2})\frac{\Delta t}{\Delta x})V_{m-1}^{n+1}]. \end{aligned} \tag{5.6.20}$$

Thus the scheme (5.6.18),(5.6.19) is a (backward) explicit FDS.

Theorem 5.4 *If* $\alpha=\dfrac{\sigma^2\Delta t}{\Delta x^2}\le 1$ *and*

$$1-\frac{1}{\sigma^2}|r-q-\frac{\sigma^2}{2}|\Delta x\ge 0, \tag{5.6.21}$$

then the scheme (5.6.18),(5.6.19) is stable.

Proof

In order to prove the stability of the scheme, without loss of generality, we only need to point out, if for the case $n=N$,

$$\max_{-\infty<m<\infty}|V_m^N|\le\epsilon, \tag{5.6.22}$$

then for any $0\le n<N$, there must be

$$\max_{-\infty<m<\infty}|V_m^n|\le C\epsilon, \tag{5.6.23}$$

where C is a constant independent of ϵ and n. To do it, we first show that (5.6.23) is true in the case $n=N-1$. By assumption (5.6.21), all coefficients of $V_m^{n+1}, V_{m+1}^{n+1}, V_{m-1}^{n+1}$ on the right side of (5.6.20) are nonnegative. By (5.6.22), we have

$$
\begin{aligned}
| V_m^{N-1} | &\leq \frac{1}{1+r\Delta t}[(1-\alpha) | V_m^N | + \frac{\alpha}{2}(1+\frac{1}{\sigma^2}(r-q-\frac{\sigma^2}{2})\Delta x) | V_{m+1}^N | \\
&\quad + \frac{\alpha}{2}(1-\frac{1}{\sigma^2}(r-q-\frac{\sigma^2}{2})\Delta x) | V_{m-1}^N |] \\
&\leq \frac{\epsilon}{1+r\Delta t}[1-\alpha+\frac{\alpha}{2}+\frac{\alpha}{2\sigma^2}(r-q-\frac{\sigma^2}{2})\Delta x \\
&\quad + \frac{\alpha}{2}-\frac{\alpha}{2\sigma^2}(r-q-\frac{\sigma^2}{2})\Delta x] \\
&= \frac{\epsilon}{1+r\Delta t}. \qquad (5.6.24)
\end{aligned}
$$

Thus by backward induction, we get (5.6.23), and thus have proved the theorem.

Remark By (5.6.24), we have

$$| V_m^n | \leq (\frac{1}{1+r\Delta t})^{N-n}\epsilon \leq e^{-\frac{r}{2}(T-t_n)}\epsilon.$$

i.e. the rounding error is decreasing.

Remark Corresponding to FDS (5.6.18),(5.6.19), what is the discrete form of the Black-Scholes equation in terms of the original variables (S, t)?

Let $u = e^{\Delta x}$,

$$S_m = u^m = e^{m\Delta x} = e^{x_m}.$$

For the domain $\{-\infty < x < \infty,\ 0 \leq t \leq T\}$ in (x, t) plane, the mesh is

$$
\begin{aligned}
x_m &= m\Delta x, \qquad (-\infty < m < \infty) \\
t_n &= n\Delta t. \qquad (0 \leq n \leq N)
\end{aligned}
$$

Correspondingly, in (S, t) plane, on the domain $\{0 \leq S < \infty,\ 0 \leq t \leq T\}$, the mesh is

$$S_m = u^m, \qquad (-\infty < m < \infty)$$

$$t_n = n\Delta t. \qquad (0 \leq n \leq N)$$

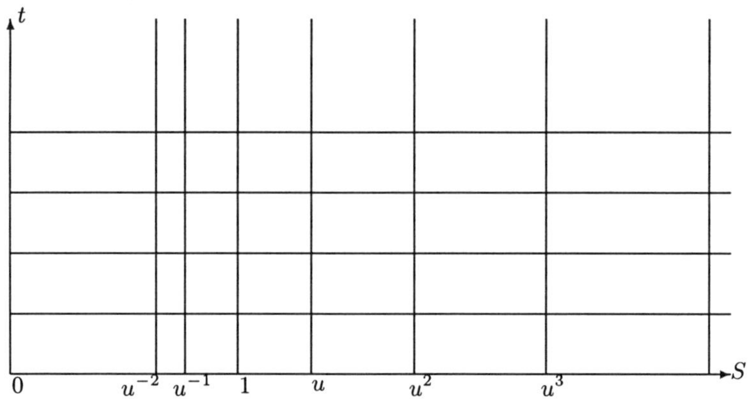

Thus (5.6.20) is of the form

$$V_m^n = \frac{1}{1+r\Delta t}[(1-\omega)V_m^{n+1} + (\frac{\omega}{2} + \frac{\sqrt{\omega}}{2\sigma}(r-q-\frac{\sigma^2}{2})\sqrt{\Delta t})V_{m+1}^{n+1}$$
$$+(\frac{\omega}{2} - \frac{\sqrt{\omega}}{2\sigma}(r-q-\frac{\sigma^2}{2})\sqrt{\Delta t})V_{m-1}^{n+1}],$$

where $\omega = \frac{\sigma^2 \Delta t}{(\ln u)^2}$. In particular for the case $\omega = 1$, there is

$$V_m^n = \frac{1}{1+r\Delta t}[\frac{1}{2}(1+\frac{\sqrt{\Delta t}}{\sigma}(r-q-\frac{\sigma^2}{2}))V_{m+1}^{n+1}$$
$$+\frac{1}{2}(1-\frac{\sqrt{\Delta t}}{\sigma}(r-q-\frac{\sigma^2}{2}))V_{m-1}^{n+1}]. \quad (5.6.25)$$

5.7 Numerical Methods (II) —— Binomial Tree Method and Finite Difference Method

BTM is essentially a stochastic algorithm. However, if S is regarded as a variable, and option price $V = V(S,t)$ is regarded as a function of S, t, then BTM is an explicit discrete algorithm for option pricing. If the higher orders of Δt can be neglected, we will be able to show that it is indeed a special form of the explicit FDS of the Black-Scholes equation.

In order to prove this, we need first to establish the relation between the parameters ρ, η, , u, d, q_u, q_d in BTM and the parameters r, q, σ in the Black-Scholes equation.

In fact, we discussed this in §4.2 when establishing continuous model of underlying asset price. But the derivation was heuristic, lack of rigor in mathematics. Here we will give a rigorous derivation of the relationship between the two sets of parameters, by comparing the continuous model (stochastic differential equation of the underlying asset price S_t)and the discrete model(BTM of the underlying asset price S_t).

Divide the time period $[0,T]$ into N equal intervals:

$$0 = t_0 < t_1 < \cdots < t_N = T,$$

where $t_n = n\Delta t, \Delta t = \frac{T}{N}$.

In §3.4 we established BTM for continuous dividend-paying asset. If S_n, the underlying asset price at $t = t_n$, is given, then at $t = t_{n+1}$, S_{n+1} has two possible values

$$S_{n+1} = \begin{cases} S_n u, & \text{up}, \\ S_n d, & \text{down}. \end{cases} \tag{5.7.1}$$

In a risk-neutral world, consider a continuous price model of the continuous dividend-paying asset:

$$\begin{cases} \frac{dS}{S} = (r-q)dt + \sigma dW_t \\ S(t_n) = S_n. \end{cases}$$

By the Itô formula, we have

$$d\ln S = (r - q - \frac{\sigma^2}{2})dt + \sigma dW_t.$$

Integrate both sides from t_n to t_{n+1}, and apply the initial condition at $t = t_n$, we get

$$\ln\frac{S_{n+1}}{S_n} = (r - q - \frac{\sigma^2}{2})\Delta t + \sigma\Delta W_n, \tag{5.7.2}$$

$(\Delta W_n = W_{t_{n+1}} - W_{t_n})$.

By (5.7.2)

$$E(\ln\frac{S_{n+1}}{S_n}) = (r - q - \frac{\sigma^2}{2})\Delta t \tag{5.7.3}$$

$$Var(\ln\frac{S_{n+1}}{S_n}) = \sigma^2\Delta t. \tag{5.7.4}$$

In a risk-neutral world, under the probability measure Q$\{q_u, q_d\}$:

$$q_u = \frac{\rho/\eta - d}{u - d}, \qquad q_d = \frac{u - \rho/\eta}{u - d}. \tag{5.7.5}$$

By (5.7.1) we get

$$E(\ln\frac{S_{n+1}}{S_n}) = q_u \ln u + q_d \ln d, \tag{5.7.6}$$

$$Var(\ln\frac{S_{n+1}}{S_n}) = q_u(\ln u)^2 + q_d(\ln d)^2 - (q_u\ln u + q_d\ln d)^2. \tag{5.7.7}$$

Under the assumption

$$ud = 1, \tag{5.7.8}$$

$$\eta = 1 + q\Delta t = e^{q\Delta t} + O(\Delta t^2), \tag{5.7.9}$$

$$\rho = 1 + r\Delta t = e^{r\Delta t} + O(\Delta t^2), \tag{5.7.10}$$

comparing (5.7.3),(5.7.4) and (5.7.6),(5.7.7), we get

$$(r - q - \frac{\sigma^2}{2})\Delta t = q_u \ln u + q_d \ln d,$$

$$\sigma^2 \Delta t = q_u (\ln u)^2 + q_d (\ln d)^2 - (q_u \ln u + q_d \ln d)^2.$$

By (5.7.8),(5.7.5), the above system of equations is reduced to

$$(2q_u - 1) \ln u = (r - q - \frac{\sigma^2}{2})\Delta t, \tag{5.7.11}$$

$$4q_u(1 - q_u)(\ln u)^2 = \sigma^2 \Delta t. \tag{5.7.12}$$

In order to solve u and q_u from (5.7.11),(5.7.12), by (5.7.12), let

$$u = e^{\alpha\sqrt{\Delta t}}, \tag{5.7.13}$$

α is to be determined. Substitute it into (5.7.11),(5.7.12) to get

$$\alpha(2q_u - 1) = (r - q - \frac{\sigma^2}{2})\sqrt{\Delta t}, \tag{5.7.14}$$

$$4q_u(1 - q_u)\alpha^2 \Delta t = \sigma^2 \Delta t. \tag{5.7.15}$$

By (5.7.14),

$$q_u = \frac{1}{2} + \frac{r - q - \frac{\sigma^2}{2}}{2\alpha}\sqrt{\Delta t}, \tag{5.7.16}$$

Substituting it into (5.7.15), we get

$$\alpha^2 - \sigma^2 = (r - q - \frac{\sigma^2}{2})^2 \Delta t,$$

i.e.

$$\alpha = \sigma + O(\Delta t). \tag{5.7.17}$$

Substituting into (5.7.16), ignoring higher orders of Δt, we have

$$q_u = \frac{1}{2} + \frac{r - q - \sigma^2/2}{2\sigma}\sqrt{\Delta t}, \tag{5.7.18}$$

$$q_d = \frac{1}{2} - \frac{r - q - \sigma^2/2}{2\sigma}\sqrt{\Delta t}. \tag{5.7.19}$$

Substituting (5.7.17) into (5.7.13), ignoring higher order terms of Δt, we get

$$u = e^{\sigma\sqrt{\Delta t}}, \qquad d = e^{-\sigma\sqrt{\Delta t}}. \tag{5.7.20}$$

(5.7.9),(5.7.10),(5.7.18)—(5.7.20) are the relationship between the parameters in BTM and the Black-Scholes equation.

Theorem 5.5 *If $ud = 1$, ignoring higher order terms of Δt, then for European option, pricing the BTM and the explicit FDS of the Black-Scholes equation $(\omega = \frac{\sigma^2 \Delta t}{(\ln u)^2} = 1)$ are equivalent.*

Proof As discussed in §3.5, if we construct a mesh in $\{0 \le S < \infty,\ 0 \le t \le T\}$

$$\begin{aligned} S_m &= S_0 u^m, \qquad & (m = 0, \pm 1, \pm 2, \dots) \\ t_n &= n\Delta t, \qquad & (n = 0, 1, 2, \dots, N) \end{aligned}$$

where $u > 1$, $\Delta t = \frac{T}{N}$. Then BTM for European option pricing can be written as

$$V_m^n = \frac{1}{\rho}[q_u V_{m+1}^{n+1} + q_d V_{m-1}^{n+1}], \tag{5.7.21}$$

and

$$V_m^N = (S_m - K)^+.$$

where

$$\rho = 1 + r\Delta t, \qquad \eta = 1 + q\Delta t,$$

$$q_u = \frac{\rho/\eta - d}{u - d}, \qquad q_d = 1 - q_u.$$

Let $S_0 = 1$, and by (5.7.10),(5.7.18),(5.7.19), then (5.7.21) can be written as

$$\begin{aligned} V_m^n = \frac{1}{1 + r\Delta t} & [(\tfrac{1}{2} + \frac{r - q - \sigma^2/2}{2\sigma}\sqrt{\Delta t})V_{m+1}^{n+1} \\ & + (\tfrac{1}{2} - \frac{r - q - \sigma^2/2}{2\sigma}\sqrt{\Delta t})V_{m-1}^{n+1}]. \end{aligned}$$

This is the explicit FDS formula (5.6.25) for the case $\omega = \frac{\sigma^2 \Delta t}{(\ln u)^2} = 1$. Thus the theorem is proved.

This equivalence theorem is very important. It transfers the BTM convergence study to the FDS framework. By Theorem 5.5 and the Lax's equivalence theorem (Theorem 5.3), we conclude: BTM as a discrete algorithm is stable, and its numerical solution, as $\Delta t \to 0$, must converge to that of the Black-Scholes (continuous) model. Thus we have proved the following.

Theorem 5.6 (Convergence of BTM for European option) *If*

$$1 - \left|\frac{r - q}{\sigma} - \frac{\sigma}{2}\right|\sqrt{\Delta t} > 0,$$

then as $\Delta t \to 0$*, there must be*

$$\lim_{\Delta t \to 0} V_\Delta(S,t) = V(S,t),$$

where $V_\Delta(S,t)$ *is the linear extrapolation of* V_m^n*.*

We can develop better discrete algorithms, more accurate than BTM, to solve the Black-Scholes equation, once we regard it as a problem of finding numerical solution of partial differential equations.

5.8 Properties of European Option Price

European option price depends on seven factors (take stock option as example): S (stock price), K (strike price), r (risk-free interest rate), q (dividend rate), T (expiration date) , t (time), σ (volatility).

In this section, we will find out, as one of the above seven factors changes, assuming all other factors remain fixed, what will happen to the option price?

Since European option price is given by the Black-Scholes formula, to answer the above question, we need to find out the sign of the partial derivatives of the option price with respect to each variable.

By the Black-Scholes formula, European call (put) option price $c(S,t)(p(S,t))$ can be written as

$$c(S,t) = e^{-q(T-t)}SN(\hat{d}_1) - e^{-r(T-t)}KN(\hat{d}_2),$$
$$p(S,t) = c(S,t) - Se^{-q(T-t)} + Ke^{-r(T-t)},$$

where

$$\hat{d}_1 = \frac{\ln\frac{S}{K} + (r - q + \frac{\sigma^2}{2})(T-t)}{\sigma\sqrt{T-t}},$$
$$\hat{d}_2 = \hat{d}_1 - \sigma\sqrt{T-t}.$$

(1) **Dependence on S and K**

By straightforward computation, we get

$$\frac{\partial \hat{d}_1}{\partial S} = \frac{\partial \hat{d}_2}{\partial S} = \frac{1}{S\sigma\sqrt{T-t}},$$

$$N'(\hat{d}_1) = \frac{K}{S}N'(\hat{d}_2)e^{-(r-q)(T-t)}.$$

Therefore we have

$$\frac{\partial c}{\partial S} = e^{-q(T-t)}N(\hat{d}_1) > 0,$$

$$\frac{\partial p}{\partial S} = -e^{-q(T-t)}[1 - N(\hat{d}_1)] < 0,$$

and

$$\frac{\partial c}{\partial K} = -e^{-r(T-t)}N(\hat{d_2}) < 0,$$

$$\frac{\partial p}{\partial K} = e^{-r(T-t)}[1 - N(\hat{d_2})] > 0.$$

That is, as S increases, call option price goes up, and put option price goes down; for options with different strike prices, call option price decreases with K, and put option price increases with K.

Financially, when the stock price goes up or the strike price goes down, the call option holders are more likely to gain more profits in the future, thus the call option price goes up; In contrast, the put option holders have smaller chance to gain profits in the future, thus the put option price goes down.

(2) **Dependence on r**

$$\frac{\partial c}{\partial r} = K(T-t)e^{-r(T-t)}N(\hat{d_2}) > 0,$$

$$\frac{\partial p}{\partial r} = -K(T-t)e^{-r(T-t)}[1 - N(\hat{d_2})] < 0.$$

That is, if the risk-free interest rate goes up, then the call option price goes up, but the put option price goes down.

Financially, the risk-free interest rate raise has two effects: for stock price, in a risk-neutral world, the expected return $E(\frac{dS}{S}) = (r-q)dt$ will go up; For cash flow, the cash K received at the future time $(t = T)$ would have a lower value $Ke^{-r(T-t)}$ at the present time t. Therefore, for put option holders, who will sell stocks for cash at the maturity $t = T$, thus the above two effects result in a decrease of the put option price. For call option holders, the effects are just the opposite, and the option price will go up.

(3) **Dependence on q**

$$\frac{\partial c}{\partial q} = -S(T-t)e^{-q(T-t)}N(\hat{d_1}) < 0,$$

$$\frac{\partial p}{\partial q} = S(T-t)e^{-q(T-t)}[1 - N(\hat{d_1})] > 0.$$

That is, if the dividend rate increases, then the call option price goes down, and the put option price goes up.

Financially, the dividend rate directly affects the stock price. In a risk-neutral world, as the dividend rate increases, the expected return of the stock $E(\frac{dS}{S}) = (r-q)dt$ decreases, thus the call option price decreases, but the put option price increases.

(4) **Dependence on σ**

$$\frac{\partial c}{\partial \sigma} = \frac{\partial p}{\partial \sigma} = e^{-q(T-t)}N'(\hat{d_1})\sqrt{T-t} > 0.$$

That is, when a stock has a high volatility σ, its option price (both call and put) goes up.

Financially, an increase of the volatility σ means an increase of the stock price fluctuation, i.e., increased investment risk. For the underlying asset itself (the stock), since $E(\sigma dW_t) = 0$, the risks (gain or loss) are symmetric. But this is not true for an individual option holder. Take a call option for example. The holder benefits from stock price increases, but has only limited downside risk in the event of stock price decreases, because the holder's loss is at most the option's premium. Therefore the stock price change has an asymmetric impact on the call option value. Therefore the call option price increases as the volatility increases. Same reasoning can be applied to the put option.

(5) **Dependence on T and t**

$$\frac{\partial c}{\partial t} = qSe^{-q(T-t)}N(\hat{d}_1) - rKe^{-r(T-t)}N'(\hat{d}_2) - \frac{\sigma e^{-q(T-t)}SN'(\hat{d}_1)}{2\sqrt{T-t}},$$

$$\frac{\partial p}{\partial t} = rKe^{-r(T-t)}[1 - N(\hat{d}_2)] - qSe^{-q(T-t)}[1 - N(\hat{d}_1)] - \frac{\sigma e^{-q(T-t)}SN'(\hat{d}_1)}{2\sqrt{T-t}},$$

$$\frac{\partial c}{\partial T} = -\frac{\partial c}{\partial t},$$

$$\frac{\partial p}{\partial T} = -\frac{\partial p}{\partial t}.$$

Since we do not know the sign of the right side of the above equations, we cannot predict in which direction the option price will change with t and T.

Financially, no matter how long is the option's lifetime T, a European option has only one exercise opportunity, hence a long expiration does not mean more gaining opportunity (this is unlike the case of American options). Therefore European options do not necessarily become more valuable as time to expiration increases. As for t, larger t, hence smaller $T - t$, means closer to the exercise day. Therefore, for European options we cannot predict whether the option price will go down or go up as the exercise day comes closer. However, there is an exception. In fact, in the case $q = 0$,

$$\frac{\partial c}{\partial t} = -rKe^{-r(T-t)}N(\hat{d}_2) - \frac{\sigma SN(\hat{d}_1)}{2\sqrt{T-t}} < 0.$$

i.e. with the expiration day coming closer, the call option on a non-dividend-paying stock will go down.

The above analysis of the European option price change is summarized in the following table:

variable	call option	put option
S (stock price)	+	−
K (strike price)	−	+
r (risk-free interest rate)	+	−
q (dividend rate)	−	+
σ (volatility)	+	+
T (expiration)	?	?
t (time)	?	?

Here, a "+" indicates that the option price is an increasing function, a "−" indicates that the option price is a decreasing function, and a "?" indicates it is uncertain whether increasing or decreasing.

5.9 Risk Management

When using option as a financial instrument to manage exposed risks, the following Greek letter parameters are of great importance:

$$\Delta = \frac{\partial V}{\partial S}.$$

Δ(Delta) is the partial derivative of the option or its portfolio price V with respect to the underlying asset price S. The seller of the option or its portfolio should buy Δ shares of the underlying asset to hedge the risk inherited in selling the option or portfolio.

$$\Gamma = \frac{\partial \Delta}{\partial S} = \frac{\partial^2 V}{\partial S^2}.$$

Γ(Gamma) is the partial derivative of Δ with respect to the underlying asset. Since Δ is a function of S and t, theoretically one must constantly adjust Δ to achieve the goal of the hedging (to eliminate the risk in selling the option or the portfolio). In practice, this is not feasible because of the transaction fee. Therefore in real operation one must choose the frequency of Δ wisely. This is reflected in the magnitude of Γ. A small Γ means Δ changes slowly, and there is no need to adjust in haste; Conversely, if Γ is large, then Δ is sensitive to change in S, there will be a risk if Δ is not adjusted in time.

$$\Theta = \frac{\partial V}{\partial t}.$$

Θ(Theta) is the rate of change in the option or portfolio price over time. The

Black-Scholes equation gives the relation between Δ, Γ and Θ.

$$\Theta = -\frac{\sigma^2}{2}S^2\Gamma - (r-q)S\Delta + rV.$$

$$\mathcal{V} = \frac{\partial V}{\partial \sigma}.$$

$\mathcal{V}$(Vega) is the partial derivative of the option or its portfolio price with respect to the volatility of the underlying asset.

The underlying asset volatility σ is the least known parameter in the Black-Scholes formula. It is practically impossible to give a precise value of σ. Instead, we consider the sensitivity of the corresponding option price over σ. This is the meaning of $\mathcal{V}$.

$$\rho = \frac{\partial V}{\partial r}.$$

ρ(Rho) is the partial derivative of the option or portfolio price with respect to the risk-free interest rate.

For European options, we have obtained the expressions of these Greeks in the previous section (§5.8). In this section we will explain how to use these parameters (especially Δ and Γ) in risk management.

Consider a specific example. Suppose a financial institution has sold a stock option OTC, and faces a risk due to the option price change. Therefore it wants to take a hedging strategy to manage the risk. *Ideally, a hedging strategy should guarantee an approximate balance of the expense and income, i.e., the money spent on hedging approximately equals the income from selling the option premiums.*

How does the hedging strategy work?

As we have explained in §5.2, construct a portfolio

$$\Pi = V - \Delta S,$$

and choose Δ such that the portfolio is risk-free in $(t, t+\Delta t)$, i.e.

$$dV_t - \Delta_t dS_t = r(V_t - \Delta_t S_t)dt.$$

It can be rewritten as

$$dV_t - rV_t dt = \Delta_t(dS_t - rS_t dt). \tag{5.9.1}$$

Let B_t be a risk-free bond, then

$$dB_t = rB_t dt. \tag{5.9.2}$$

Multiply both sides of (5.9.1) by $\frac{1}{B_t}$, and take (5.9.2) into account, we get

$$\frac{B_t dV_t - V_t dB_t}{B_t^2} = \Delta_t \frac{B_t dS_t - S_t dB_t}{B_t^2},$$

i.e.

$$d\left(\frac{V_t}{B_t}\right) = \Delta_t d\left(\frac{S_t}{B_t}\right). \tag{5.9.3}$$

This means that the change in the discounted price of the option equals the change in the discounted price of Δ_t shares of the stock, and the goal of hedging is thus achieved.

Integrate (5.9.3) over t in the option's lifetime, we get

$$\frac{V_T}{B_T} - \frac{V_0}{B_0} = \int_0^T \Delta_t d\left(\frac{S_t}{B_t}\right),$$

i.e.

$$V_T = V_0 e^{rT} + \int_0^T \Delta_t d(e^{r(T-t)} S_t).$$

Take the call option as example

$$V_0 e^{rT} = (S_T - K)^+ - \int_0^T \Delta_t d(e^{r(T-t)} S_t). \tag{5.9.4}$$

The right side of the above equation is the total cost to the option seller who takes the hedging strategy in order to hedge the risk in selling the option. The equation shows: if the hedging strategy (Δ_t) is adjusted constantly, then on the option expiration day, the total cost (not including the transaction fees) would exactly offset the interests if the option premium has been saved in a bank on the initial day.

In reality, the seller must pay a fee for each adjustment of the hedging strategy, and the hedging strategy can be adjusted only for a finite number of times. Nevertheless, (5.9.4) reminds us that an ideal hedging strategy should make the cost and gain equal.

In the following, we will consider an operation example to give a discrete form of the formula (5.9.4).

Suppose a hedging strategy is adjusted N times at $\{t_n\}_{n=0,1,\ldots,N-1}(0 = t_0 < t_1 < \cdots < t_{N-1} < T)$. For simplicity, let $t_{n+1} - t_n = \Delta t$ be a constant, i.e. $t_n = n\Delta t, \quad \Delta t = \frac{T}{N}$, then (5.9.4) in discrete form is

$$\begin{aligned} V_0 e^{rT} &= (S_T - K)^+ - \sum_{i=0}^{N-1} \Delta_i (e^{r(T-t_{i+1})} S_{i+1} - e^{r(T-t_i)} S_i) \\ &= (S_T - K)^+ - \Delta_N S_T + \sum_{i=1}^{N} e^{r(T-t_i)} S_i (\Delta_i - \Delta_{i-1}) + \Delta_0 e^{rT} S_0. \end{aligned}$$

where

$$\Delta_N = \left.\frac{\partial V}{\partial S}\right|_{t=t_N} = \begin{cases} H(S_T - K), & \text{(call option)} \\ -H(K - S_T), & \text{(put option)} \end{cases}$$

where $H(\alpha)$ is the Heaviside function. Take the call option as example, then

$$V_0 e^{rT} = -KH(S_T - K) + \Delta_0 S_0 e^{rT} + \sum_{i=1}^{N} e^{r(T-t_i)} S_i(\Delta_i - \Delta_{i-1}). \qquad (5.9.5)$$

Since in each time interval $[t, t + \Delta t]$, the interest for Z is $Zr\Delta t$, therefore, corresponding to the profit $Ze^{r\Delta t}$ in the continuous model, the profit should be $Z(1 + r\Delta t)$ in the discrete form. Thus (5.9.5) can be written as

$$\begin{aligned} V_0(1 + r\Delta t)^N &= -KH(S_T - K) + \Delta_0 S_0 (1 + r\Delta t)^N \\ &\quad + \sum_{i=1}^{N} (1 + r\Delta t)^{N-i} S_i(\Delta_i - \Delta_{i-1}). \end{aligned} \qquad (5.9.6)$$

The hedging operation is performed as follows: At $t = 0$ the seller buys $\Delta_0 = \left.\frac{\partial V}{\partial S}\right|_{(S_0,0)}$ shares of stock at S_0 per share, and borrows $\Delta_0 S_0$ from the bank. At $t = t_1$, to adjust the hedging share to $\Delta_1 = \left.\frac{\partial V}{\partial S}\right|_{(S_1,t_1)}$ (S_1 is the stock price at $t = t_1$), the seller needs to buy $\Delta_1 - \Delta_0$ shares at S_1 per share if $\Delta_1 > \Delta_0$, and sell $\Delta_0 - \Delta_1$ shares at S_1 per share if $\Delta_0 > \Delta_1$; and borrow (save) the money needed (gained) for (from) buying (selling) the stocks, and at $t = t_1$ pay the interest $\Delta_0 S_0 r\Delta t$ to the bank for the money borrowed at $t = t_0$. In general, at $t = t_n$, the seller owns Δ_n shares of stock, and has paid hedging cost D_n:

$$D_n = \Delta_0 S_0 (1 + r\Delta t)^n + \sum_{i=1}^{n} (1 + r\Delta t)^{n-i} S_i(\Delta_i - \Delta_{i-1}),$$

where $\Delta_i = \left.\frac{\partial V}{\partial S}\right|_{(S_i,t_i)}$, $(i = 0, 1, \ldots, n)$.

On the option expiration day $t = T$, the seller owns $\Delta_N = \left.\frac{\partial V}{\partial S}\right|_{(S_T,T)} = H(S_T - K)$ shares of stock, i.e. if $S_T > K$ (i.e. the option is **in the money**) the seller owns one share of stock, if $S_T < K$ (i.e. the option is **out of the money**) the seller owns no share of stock. If the option is in the money, the option holder will exercise the contract to buy one share of stock S from the seller with cash K; if the option is out of the money, the option holder will certainly choose not to exercise the contract. Therefore the seller's total hedging cost is

$$D_T = \Delta_0 S_0 (1 + r\Delta t)^N + \sum_{i=1}^{N} (1 + r\Delta t)^{N-i} S_i(\Delta_i - \Delta_{i-1}) - KH(S_T - K).$$

The above hedging strategy successfully hedges the risk in selling the option. In this deal the sellor's actual profit is

$$\text{profit} = V_0 e^{rT} - D_T,$$

where V_0 is the option premium. If there is a transaction fee for each hedging strategy adjustment, then the seller's profit is

$$\text{profit} = V_0 e^{rT} - D_T - \sum_{i=0}^{N-1} e_i,$$

where e_i is the fee for the i-th adjustment.

Remark In practical operation, hedging adjustment interval Δt is not a constant, and depends on $\Gamma = \frac{\partial \Delta}{\partial S}$. If Γ is large, adjustment is made more frequently; If Γ is small, adjustment can be made less frequently.

Summary:

1. In this chapter, we introduced a continuous model for the underlying asset price movement—the stochastic differential equation (5.2.1). Based on this model, using the Δ-hedging technique and the Itô *formula, we derived the Black-Scholes equation for the option price, by solving the terminal value problem of the Black-Scholes equation, we obtained a fair price for the European option, independent of each individual investor's risk preference—the Black-Scholes formula.*

2. As derivatives of an underlying asset, a variety of options can be set up in a various terminal-boundary problem for the Black-Scholes equation. To price these various options is to solve the Black-Scholes equation under various terminal-boundary conditions.

3. BTM is the most important discrete method of option pricing. When neglecting the higher orders of Δt, BTM is equivalent to an explicit finite difference scheme of the Black-Scholes equation. By the numerical solution theory of partial differential equation, we have proved the convergence of the BTM.

4. The option seller can manage the risk in selling the option by taking a hedging strategy. Since the amount of hedging shares $\Delta = \Delta(S,t)$ changes constantly, the seller needs to adjust Δ at appropriate frequency according to the magnitude of $\Gamma(S,t) = \frac{\partial \Delta}{\partial S}$, to achieve the goal of hedging.

Exercises

In the Black-Scholes framework, for the following forms of the call options, set up the mathematical model and find an expression of the option price (the premium).

1. Bermudan option. This type of option can be exercised on N predetermined dates $\{t_n\}, (0 < t_1 < \cdots < t_N < T)$. Write a mathematical model for the option,and find the premiums at $N = 1, t_1 = \frac{T}{2}$.

2. (Discrete) Barrier option. On N predetermined dates $\{t_n\}, (0 < t_1 < \cdots < t_N < T)$, if the asset price is below the barrier value $S = S_B (S_B < K)$, the option is knocked out. Write a mathematical model for the option, and find the premiums at $N = 1, t_1 = \frac{T}{2}$.

3. (Discrete) Callable option. On N predetermined dates $\{t_n\}, (0 < t_1 < \cdots < t_N < T)$, if the asset price exceeds $K_c (K_c > K)$, the seller of the option has the right to call back the option at price $K_c - K$. Write a mathematical model for the option,and find the premiums at $N = 1, t_1 = \frac{T}{2}$.

4. On N predetermined dates $\{t_n\}, (0 < t_1 < \cdots < t_N < T)$, the asset pays dividend at 1% rate. Write a mathematical model for the option, and find the premiums at $N = 1, t_1 = \frac{T}{2}$.

5. (Discrete) Asian option. The average of stock prices on N predetermined dates $\{t_n\}, (0 < t_1 < \cdots < t_N < T)$ is given by $J_T = \frac{1}{N}\sum_{i=1}^{N} S(t_i)$; A new call option is created by replacing S_T with the average price J_T. That is, at $t = T$,

$$\text{profit} = (J_T - K)^+.$$

Write a mathematical model for the option, and find the premiums at $N = 2, t_1 = \frac{T}{2}, t_2 = T$.

6. Prove the call on a call option pricing formula (5.5.8).

7. Find the call-put parity for call on a call option and put on a call option.

Chapter 6

American Option Pricing and Optimal Exercise Strategy

American option gives its holder the right to exercise the option at any time, thus more profiteering opportunity than European option offers. Consequently the price of American option cannot be less than that of an equivalent European option. Whether an American option holder can actually be benefited from this right at the cost of a higher premium depends on whether the holder can take advantage of the early exercise term and exercise the option at the best time to make profits. This should be considered by every American option holder. In mathematical theory, American option pricing is a free boundary problem. Here the **free boundary** is a boundary curve (to be determined) which divides the domain $\{0 \leq S < \infty, 0 \leq t \leq T\}$ into two parts: the **continuation region**, and the **stopping region**. In financial theory, this free boundary is called the **optimal exercise boundary**.

Obviously, every American option holder wants to know this boundary curve to make the best exercise strategy. Unfortunately, in contrast to European options, no closed-form solution has been found for American options. Therefore it is important to study its numerical solutions, approximate expressions, asymptotical expansions, and the solution itself (in particular the free boundary). We will discuss these topics in detail in this chapter.

Let us begin with the simplest model of American option, which has a closed-form solution.

6.1 Perpetual American Option

A **perpetual American option** has no expiry date, thus can be exercised at any time in its lifetime.

To be specific, let us consider a perpetual American put option. The put option holder can exercise the contract, i.e. to sell the underlying asset S at the strike price K, at any time.

Features of the Perpetual American option:

1. The option price does not dependent on time, i.e. $V = V(S)$. This is because the contract has no expiration date, thus its payoff does not depend on time but depends on the underlying asset's price only.

2. The option price is never lower than the payoff function, i.e.

$$V(S) \geq (S - K)^+, \qquad \text{(call option)}$$

$$V(S) \geq (K - S)^+, \qquad \text{(put option)}$$

since otherwise there would exist arbitrage opportunity(see Chapter 2).

3. Let $V_L(S,t)$ denote the value of an American option with the same strike price K, but with an expiration date $t = T$, then

$$V(S) \geq V_L(S,t). \tag{6.1.1}$$

That means, among all American options with the same strike price, the perpetual American option is the most expensive one. This is because with the same payoff, a perpetual American option has included all the profiteering opportunities of any American option with an expiration date.

4. According to the properties of American put option, the underlying asset's price range ($0 \leq S < \infty$) of a perpetual American put option can be divided into two regions: the continuation region Σ_1 and the stopping region Σ_2. When $S \in \Sigma_1$, the option price is greater than the exercise payoff,

$$V(S) > (K - S)^+, \tag{6.1.2}$$

therefore the holder should continue to keep the option to avoid loss. When $S \in \Sigma_2$, the option price equals the exercise payoff,

$$V(S) = (K - S)^+, \tag{6.1.3}$$

therefore the holder should exercise the option immediately to avoid loss.

In Chapter 2, we pointed out, when S is sufficiently small, the American put option should be exercised immediately, i.e. when $S \ll 1$, $S \in \Sigma_2$. On the other hand, when $S \geq K$, since the payoff is zero, the holder should continue to keep the option, i.e. when $S \geq K$, $S \in \Sigma_1$. Therefore we can conclude: there exists $S_0 \in (0, K)$, such that

$$\begin{aligned} \Sigma_1 &= \{S_0 \leq S < \infty\}, \\ \Sigma_2 &= \{0 \leq S < S_0\}, \end{aligned} \tag{6.1.4}$$

where S_0 is called **the optimal exercise boundary**. S_0 must be determined simultaneously with the option price $V(S)$.

In summary, for perpetual American put option, the pricing problem is to determine:

The option price $V(S)$ in Σ_1, and the optimal exercise boundary S_0.

Now we want to establish a pricing model in Σ_1.

Similar to what we did in the previous chapter, using the Δ-hedging principle, from the Itô formula, we can obtain a boundary value problem for $V(S)$:

$$\begin{cases} \frac{\sigma^2}{2} S^2 \frac{d^2V}{dS^2} + rS\frac{dV}{dS} - rV = 0, \qquad (S_0 < S < \infty) & (6.1.5) \\ V(S_0) = K - S_0, & (6.1.6) \\ V(\infty) = 0. & (6.1.7) \end{cases}$$

As we have reasoned in the feature (4) that $S_0 < K$, therefore when $S = S_0$ the option's payoff is $(K - S_0)^+ = K - S_0$.

(6.1.5)-(6.1.7) is a second order ordinary differential equation (ODE) boundary value problem given in $[S_0, \infty)$.

According to the ODE theory, we need to first find two linearly independent special solutions of (6.1.5).

To find special solutions, let $V = S^\alpha$, substituting it into (6.1.5) to get an algebraic equation of α:

$$\frac{\sigma^2}{2}\alpha^2 + (r - \frac{\sigma^2}{2})\alpha - r = 0. \tag{6.1.8}$$

It has two roots: $\alpha = 1$ and $\alpha = -\frac{2r}{\sigma^2}$. Thus the general solution of (6.1.5) is

$$V(S) = AS + BS^{-\frac{2r}{\sigma^2}}. \tag{6.1.9}$$

A, B can be determined from the boundary conditions (6.1.6), (6.1.7):

$$A = 0, \qquad B = S_0^{\frac{2r}{\sigma^2}}(K - S_0).$$

Thus we have found the solution of the ODE boundary value problem (6.1.5)—(6.1.7):

$$V(S, S_0) = \left(\frac{S_0}{S}\right)^{\frac{2r}{\sigma^2}}(K - S_0).$$

Note that the solution depends on S_0.

How can we determine S_0? Since S_0 *is the optimal exercise boundary, the value of the option must be maximized at* S_0, *i.e. the holder can get the maximum payoff by exercising the option at* $S = S_0$.

To distinguish with the boundary $S = S_0$ in the boundary value problem (6.1.5)—(6.1.7), here we denote the optimal exercise boundary as $S = S_0^*$. i.e.

$$V(S; S_0^*) = \max_{0 \le S_0 \le K} V(S; S_0) = \max_{0 \le S_0 \le K} \left(\frac{S_0}{S}\right)^{\frac{2r}{\sigma^2}}(K - S_0). \tag{6.1.10}$$

Let us denote $F(S_0) = \left(\frac{S_0}{S}\right)^{\frac{2r}{\sigma^2}} (K - S_0)$. Then

$$\frac{dF}{dS_0} = \left(\frac{S_0}{S}\right)^{\frac{2r}{\sigma^2}} \left[\frac{2rK}{\sigma^2 S_0} - \left(\frac{2r}{\sigma^2} + 1\right)\right].$$

Let $\frac{dF}{dS_0} = 0$ to determine S_0^*:

$$S_0^* = \frac{K}{1 + \frac{\sigma^2}{2r}}. \tag{6.1.11}$$

It is easy to check when $S_0 = S_0^*$, $V(S; S_0)$ reaches its maximum value

$$V(S) = V(S; S_0^*) = \frac{\sigma^2}{2r} \left(\frac{K}{1 + \frac{\sigma^2}{2r}}\right)^{\frac{2r+\sigma^2}{\sigma^2}} S^{-\frac{2r}{\sigma^2}}. \tag{6.1.12}$$

Now let us examine the geometrical meaning of (6.1.10).

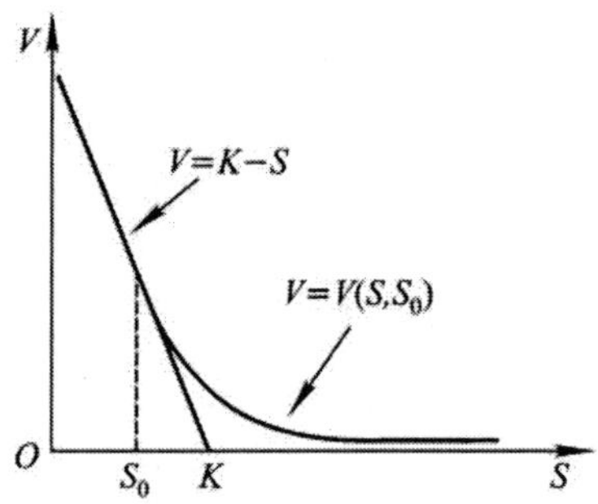

Let α be the slope of the option price curve $V = V(S; S_0)$ at $S = S_0$, i.e.

$$\alpha = \left.\frac{\partial V(S; S_0)}{\partial S}\right|_{S=S_0} = \frac{2r}{\sigma^2}(1 - \frac{K}{S_0}).$$

When $S_0 < S_0^*$, $\alpha < -1$, i.e. as $0 < S - S_0 \ll 1$,

$$\frac{V(S; S_0) - V(S_0; S_0)}{S - S_0} < -1,$$

i.e.

$$V(S; S_0) - (K - S_0) < -(S - S_0).$$

Thus when $S < S_0$, (S is sufficiently close to S_0,) there is

$$V(S; S_0) < K - S.$$

But this is impossible, since this contradicts to (6.1.2) and (6.1.3).

When $S_0 \geq S_0^*$, $\alpha \geq -1$. If and only if $S_0 = S_0^*$, $\alpha = -1$. Geometrically, this means if and only if $S_0 = S_0^*$, the option price curve $V = V(S; S_0)$ is tangent to the exercise payoff curve $V = K - S$ at $S = S_0$.

In the feature (4) of perpetual American option, (see (6.1.4)), we already pointed out: at the optimal exercise boundary $S = S_0$,

$$V(S) = \begin{cases} V(S; S_0), \ S \in \Sigma_1, \\ (K - S), \ \ S \in \Sigma_2, \end{cases}$$

where $\Sigma_1 = \{S_0 \leq S < \infty\}$, $\Sigma_2 = \{0 \leq S \leq S_0\}$.

Therefore *when the perpetual American option price passes the optimal exercise boundary $S = S_0$, i.e. when (6.1.11) is true, both the function V and its first derivative are continuous, i.e. both the price V and the hedge share Δ are continuous.*

In summary, *the principle of the perpetual American option pricing is to let the holder to exercise the optimal strategy, to maximize the option value, to gain the most profits. In mathematics, this principle is equivalent to selecting the exercise strategy ($S = S_0$), such that both the option price V itself and its first derivative $\Delta = \dfrac{dV}{dS}$ are continuous when passing the exercise boundary $S = S_0$.*

Thus we have the **perpetual American option pricing model:** find $\{V(S), S_0\}$, such that

$$\begin{cases} \mathcal{L}_\infty V = \dfrac{\sigma^2}{2} S^2 \dfrac{d^2V}{dS^2} + rS\dfrac{dV}{dS} - rV = 0 \quad (S_0 < S < \infty)\,, & (6.1.13) \\ V(S_0) = K - S_0, & (6.1.14) \\ V'(S_0) = -1, & (6.1.15) \\ V(\infty) = 0. & (6.1.16) \end{cases}$$

In mathematics, the ODE boundary value problem (6.1.13)—(6.1.16) is called **free boundary problem**, where S_0 is called **free boundary**.

Since superposition principle is not applicable to the free boundary (nonlinear) problem, $V(S)$ and S_0, which are correlated to each other, must be determined simultaneously.

Apart from being represented as an ODE free boundary problem (6.1.13)—(6.1.16), perpetual American option pricing can also be formulated as a **variational inequality** problem.

In this formulation, we restate (6.1.13)—(6.1.16) as follows: in $[0, \infty)$, find function $V = V(S)$, such that

(1) both $V(S)$ itself and $V'(S)$ are continuous in $[0, \infty)$, i.e. $V \in C^1_{[0,\infty)}$;

(2) in region Σ_1,

$$V(S) > (K-S)^+,$$
$$\mathcal{L}_\infty V(S) = 0;$$

(3) and in region Σ_2, (noticing $S_0 < K$)

$$V(S) = (K-S)^+ = K-S,$$
$$\mathcal{L}_\infty V(S) = -rK < 0;$$

Combining (1),(2),(3), the problem is to find $V(S) \in C^1_{[0,\infty)}$, with continuous second derivatives in each region in $[0,\infty)$, such that

$$V(S) \geq (K-S)^+,$$
$$\mathcal{L}_\infty V(S) \leq 0,$$
$$[V(S)-(K-S)^+]\mathcal{L}_\infty V(S) = 0,$$

or

$$\min\{-\mathcal{L}_\infty V, V-(K-S)^+\} = 0;$$

(4) $V(S)$ satisfies the boundary conditions

$$V(0) = K, V(\infty) = 0.$$

Combining(1)—(4), the problem is to find function $V = V(S) \in C^1_{[0,\infty)}$ with continuous second derivatives in each region, such that in $[0,\infty)$ it satisfies

$$\begin{cases} \min\left\{-\mathcal{L}_\infty V, V-(K-S)^+\right\} = 0, \qquad (0 < S < \infty) & (6.1.17) \\ V(0) = K, V(\infty) = 0. & (6.1.18) \end{cases}$$

This is called the **variational inequality** formulation.

Remark Historically, variational inequality was first encountered in classical mechanics problem.

Consider a string streched between A and B, with an obstacle Φ in the way. What is the shape of the string?

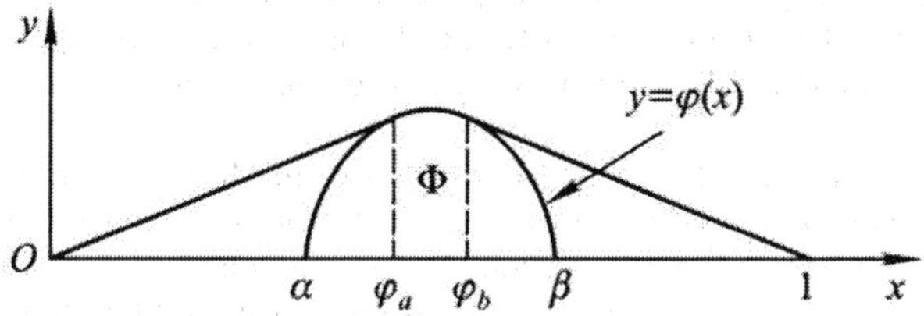

Let $y = Y(x)$ be the position function of the string, and $\Phi = \{(x,y)|y \leq \varphi(x), 0 \leq x \leq 1\}$, and $\varphi(0) < 0, \varphi(1) < 0$. Then $Y(x)$ must satisfy:

(1) $Y(x) \in C^1_{[0,1]}$, and $Y(0) = Y(1) = 0$,

(2) $Y(x) \geq \varphi(x)$,

(3) when $0 \leq x \leq \phi_a$ and $\phi_b \leq x \leq 1$, the string and the obstacle Φ are separated from each other, $Y(x) > \varphi(x)$, and no force is on the string, therefore

$$-Y^{''} = 0,$$

(4) when $\phi_a \leq x \leq \phi_b$, $Y(x) = \varphi(x)$, the string coincides with the obstacle, the obstacle exerts on the string a reaction force $f \geq 0$, thus

$$-Y'' = f \geq 0.$$

Combining (1)—(4), the problem is to find $y = Y(x) \in C^1_{[0,1]}$, such that

$$\begin{cases} \min\{-Y'', Y - \varphi(x)\} = 0, \qquad (0 \leq x \leq 1) & (6.1.19) \\ Y(0) = Y(1) = 0. & (6.1.20) \end{cases}$$

Using the principle of the minimal potential energy, the above equilibrium problem can also be formulated as the following **variation problem**: find $Y(x) \in \Omega$, such that

$$J(Y) = \min_{y(x) \in \Omega} J(y),$$

where $J(y)$ is the stress energy of the string:

$$J(y) = \frac{1}{2} \int_0^1 (\frac{dy}{dx})^2 dx,$$

and

$$\Omega = \{y(x)|y(x) \in C^1_{[0,1]}, y(0) = y(1) = 0, y(x) \geq \varphi(x)\}.$$

Here Ω is a convex set, $Y(x)$ is the solution of the variation problem given on the convex set. (6.1.19) is the Euler equation for this variation problem, and is therefore called **variational inequality.**

Remark In mathematics, the problem (6.1.17),(6.1.18) is often called the **obstacle problem**, and the payoff function $(K - S)^+$ called **obstacle**, the continuation region (the part not contacting the obstacle) called **separated set**, the stopping region called **coincident set**, and the optimal exercise boundary called **the boundary of the coincident set**, i.e. the free boundary.

(6.1.13)—(6.1.19) and (6.1.17),(6.1.18) are two mathematical formulations of the perpetual American put option pricing. In the former form the free boundary appears explicitly, and in the latter form, the free boundary is implicit. Each form has its own merit. One chooses a form according to the problem under study.

Remark Consider the dividend-paying case. If the dividend rate q is time-independent, then the mathematical model for the perpetual American put option is:

find $\{V(S), S_0\}$, such that

$$\begin{cases} \frac{\sigma^2}{2}S^2\frac{d^2V}{dS^2} + (r-q)S\frac{dV}{dS} - rV = 0, \qquad (S_0 < S < \infty) & (6.1.21) \\ V(S_0) = K - S_0, & (6.1.22) \\ V'(S_0) = -1, & (6.1.23) \\ V(\infty) = 0. & (6.1.24) \end{cases}$$

Let $V = S^\alpha$ and substitute it into (6.1.21) to obtain α's characteristic equation:

$$\frac{\sigma^2}{2}\alpha^2 + (r - q - \frac{\alpha^2}{2})\alpha - r = 0.$$

It has two roots

$$\alpha = \alpha_\pm = \omega \pm \sqrt{\omega^2 + \frac{2r}{\sigma^2}}, \tag{6.1.25}$$

where

$$\omega = \frac{-r + q + \frac{\sigma^2}{2}}{\sigma^2}.$$

It is easy to check

$$\alpha_- < 0 < \alpha_+.$$

Hence the general solution of the equation is

$$V(S) = AS^{\alpha_+} + BS^{\alpha_-}. \tag{6.1.26}$$

Applying the boundary condition (6.1.24) to determine

$$A = 0.$$

Applying the boundary conditions (6.1.22), (6.1.23), we get

$$BS_0^{\alpha_-} = K - S_0,$$

$$\alpha_- B S_0^{\alpha_- -1} = -1.$$

Solve it to determine

$$B = -\frac{1}{\alpha_-}\left(\frac{K}{1-1/\alpha_-}\right)^{1-\alpha_-},$$

$$S_0 = \frac{K}{1-1/\alpha_-}. \tag{6.1.27}$$

Substituting into (6.1.26) to get the solution

$$V = -\frac{1}{\alpha_-}\left(\frac{K}{1-1/\alpha_-}\right)^{1-\alpha_-} S^{\alpha_-}. \tag{6.1.28}$$

Remark How do we price perpetual American call options?

First, for dividend-paying perpetual American call option, the continuation region Σ_1 is $\{0 \le S \le S_0\}$, the stopping region Σ_2 is $\{S_0 \le S < \infty\}$, where S_0 is the optimal exercise boundary. Notice that $S_0 > K$, thus perpetual American call option price $V = V(S)$ satisfies the following free boundary problem:

$$\begin{cases} \frac{\sigma^2}{2} S^2 \frac{d^2V}{dS^2} + (r-q)S\frac{dV}{dS} - rV = 0 \quad (0 < S < S_0), & (6.1.29)\\ V(S_0) = S_0 - K, & (6.1.30)\\ V'(S_0) = 1, & (6.1.31)\\ V(0) = 0. & (6.1.32) \end{cases}$$

We can certainly take the same process as in the case of put option, to derive the pricing formula $V = V(S)$ and the optimal exercise boundary S_0. However, in order to obtain more knowledge, we introduce the following theorem, which states the call and put symmetry between the perpetual American options.

Theorem 6.1 *Let $V_c(S;r,q)$, $V_p(S;r,q)$, and $S_c(r,q)$, $S_p(r,q)$ be the price and the optimal exercise boundary of the dividend-paying perpetual American call and put options, respectively, then*

$$V_c(S;r,q) = \frac{S}{K} V_p\left(\frac{K^2}{S}; q, r\right), \tag{6.1.33}$$

$$\sqrt{S_c(r,q)S_p(q,r)} = K, \tag{6.1.34}$$

where K is the strike price.

Proof Let $V = V_p(y; q, r)$ and $S = S_p(q, r)$ be the solution of the following free boundary problem:

$$\begin{cases} \frac{\sigma^2}{2} y^2 \frac{d^2 V_p}{dy^2} + (q - r) y \frac{dV_p}{dy} - qV_p = 0, \quad (S_p < y < \infty) & (6.1.35) \\ V_p(S_p) = K - S_p, & (6.1.36) \\ V_p'(S_p) = -1, & (6.1.37) \\ V_p(\infty) = 0. & (6.1.38) \end{cases}$$

Define

$$W = \frac{K}{y} V_p(y), \tag{6.1.39}$$

$$S = \frac{K^2}{y}. \tag{6.1.40}$$

Under the transformation (6.1.40),

$$\text{domain}\{S_p \leq y < \infty\} \quad \Longrightarrow \quad \text{domain}\{0 < S \leq \frac{K^2}{S_p}\}.$$

Denote $\frac{K^2}{S_p} = S^*$, the free boundary conditions (6.1.36) and(6.1.37) then become

$$W(S^*) = \frac{K}{S_p}(K - S_p)\Big|_{S_p = \frac{K^2}{S^*}} = S^* - K, \tag{6.1.41}$$

and

$$\begin{aligned} \frac{dW}{dS}\Big|_{S=S^*} &= \left(\frac{dW}{dy}\frac{dy}{dS}\right)_{S=S^*} \\ &= \left(-\frac{K^2}{y^2}\right)\left(-\frac{K^2}{S^2}\right)\Big|_{S=S^*} = 1. \end{aligned} \tag{6.1.42}$$

And the boundary condition (6.1.38) becomes:

$$W(0) = \left[\frac{K}{y} V_p(y)\right]_{y=\infty} = 0. \tag{6.1.43}$$

Finally let us derive the ODE that $W(S)$ satisfies in $\{0 \leq S \leq S^*\}$. It is easy to find by straightforward computation:

$$y\frac{dV_p}{dy} = \frac{y}{K}\left[-S\frac{dW}{dS} + W\right],$$

$$y\frac{d}{dy}y\frac{dV_p}{dy} = \frac{y}{K}\left[S\frac{d}{dS}(S\frac{dW}{dS}) - 2S\frac{dW}{dS} + W\right].$$

Thus the differential equation (6.1.35) is transformed to

$$0 = \frac{\sigma^2}{2} y \frac{d}{dy} y \frac{dV_p}{dy} + (q - r - \frac{\sigma^2}{2}) y \frac{dV_p}{dy} - qV_p$$

$$= \frac{y}{K} \left\{ \frac{\sigma^2}{2} S \frac{d}{dS}(S \frac{dW}{dS}) + \left[-\sigma^2 - (q - r - \frac{\sigma^2}{2}) \right] S \frac{dW}{dS} \right.$$

$$\left. + \left[\frac{\sigma^2}{2} + (q - r - \frac{\sigma^2}{2}) - q \right] W \right\},$$

i.e.

$$\frac{\sigma^2}{2} S^2 \frac{d^2 W}{dS^2} + (r - q) S \frac{dW}{dS} - rW = 0. \qquad (6.1.44)$$

Combining (6.1.41)—(6.1.44), the pair $\{W(S), S^*\}$ in $[0, S^*]$ is the solution of the free boundary problem (6.1.29)—(6.1.32) for perpetual American call option pricing.

By the uniqueness of the solution of the free boundary problem (here we use without proof), we conclude

$$W(S) = V_c(S; r, q), \qquad S^* = S_c(r, q).$$

By transformation (6.1.39),(6.1.40), we can go back to the original variables $V_p(S; q, r)$ and $S_p(q, r)$, and arrive at the conclusion of the theorem.

Now let us derive the perpetual American call option price formula from the perpetual American put option price formula using Theorem 6.1.

We first point out

$$\alpha_-(q, r) = 1 - \alpha_+(r, q). \qquad (6.1.45)$$

This can be derived from (6.1.25):

$$\alpha_-(q, r) = \frac{-q + r + \frac{\sigma^2}{2}}{\sigma^2} - \frac{1}{\sigma^2} \sqrt{(q - r - \frac{\sigma^2}{2})^2 + 2\sigma^2 q}$$

$$= - \left[\frac{-r + q - \frac{\sigma^2}{2}}{\sigma^2} + \frac{1}{\sigma^2} \sqrt{(r - q - \frac{\sigma^2}{2})^2 + 2\sigma^2 r} \right]$$

$$= 1 - \alpha_+(r; q).$$

Thus by Theorem 6.1 and (6.1.45),

$$\begin{aligned}
V_c(S; r, q) &= \left[\frac{K}{y} V_p(y; q, r)\right]_{y=\frac{K^2}{S}} \\
&= \left\{ \frac{-K}{\alpha_-(q,r)} \left[\frac{K}{1 - 1/\alpha_-(q,r)}\right]^{1-\alpha_-(q,r)} y^{-1+\alpha_-(q,r)} \right\}_{y=\frac{K^2}{S}} \\
&= \frac{1}{\alpha_+(r,q) - 1} \left(1 - \frac{1}{\alpha_+(r,q)}\right)^{\alpha_+(r,q)} K^{1-\alpha_+(r,q)} S^{\alpha_+(r,q)},
\end{aligned}$$

and

$$\begin{aligned}
S_c(r,q) &= \frac{K^2}{S_p(q,r)} \\
&= K \frac{\alpha_-(q,r) - 1}{\alpha_-(q,r)} \\
&= K \frac{\alpha_+(r,q)}{\alpha_+(r,q) - 1}.
\end{aligned} \tag{6.1.46}$$

Corollary When $q = 0$,

$$\begin{aligned}
\alpha_+ &= \frac{-(r - \frac{\sigma^2}{2})}{\sigma^2} + \frac{1}{\sigma^2}\sqrt{(r - \frac{\sigma^2}{2})^2 + 2r\sigma^2} \\
&= -\frac{r}{\sigma^2} + \frac{1}{2} + (r + \frac{\sigma^2}{2})/\sigma^2 \\
&= 1.
\end{aligned}$$

Thus $S_c(r, 0) = \infty$. This says for perpetual American call option, if the underlying asset pays no dividend, then the holder should never consider early exercising the option. In this case, option price $V_c(S; r, 0) = S$.

6.2 Models of American Options

To be specific, let us still take non-dividend-paying American put option as example to establish the mathematical models.

For an American put option with expiration date $t = T$, there exist two regions: the continuation region Σ_1, where:

$$V(S,t) > (K - S)^+;$$

and the stopping region Σ_2, where:

$$V(S,t) = (K-S)^+.$$

Between these two regions lies the optimal exercise boundary $\Gamma : S = S(t)$.

Similar to the discussions in §6.1, we can conclude

$$\Sigma_1 = \{(S,t)|S(t) \le S < \infty, 0 \le t \le T\},$$

$$\Sigma_2 = \{(S,t)|0 \le S \le S(t), 0 \le t \le T\},$$

and

$$S(t) < K \qquad (0 \le t < T). \tag{6.2.1}$$

In Σ_1, using the Δ-hedging principle and the Itô formula, we can infer: when $(S,t) \in \Sigma_1$, the option price $V = V(S,t)$ satisfies the Black-Scholes equation:

$$\mathcal{L}V = \frac{\partial V}{\partial t} + \frac{\sigma^2}{2}S^2\frac{\partial^2 V}{\partial S^2} + rS\frac{\partial V}{\partial S} - rV = 0, \qquad (\Sigma_1) \tag{6.2.2}$$

On the optimal exercise boundary Γ,

$$V(S(t),t) = K - S(t), \tag{6.2.3}$$

$$\frac{\partial V}{\partial S}(S(t),t) = -1, \tag{6.2.4}$$

(notice that, because of (6.2.1), we can omit the "positive taking" symbol.) and when $S \to \infty$,

$$V \to 0, \tag{6.2.5}$$

at $t = T$,

$$V(S,T) = (K-S)^+. \tag{6.2.6}$$

This means in order to price American put option, we need to look for function pair $\{V(S,t), S(t)\}$ in Σ_1 , such that they satisfy the PDE problem (6.2.2)—(6.2.4). Since $S(t)$ is a free boundary, it is called a free boundary problem for a parabolic equation.

Remark The free boundary condition (6.2.4) indicates the option price's derivative (i.e. $\Delta = \frac{\partial V}{\partial S}$) is continuous at crossing the optimal exercise boundary. This fact, as we pointed out in §6.1, expresses the principle of American option pricing, i.e. the American option value is maximized by an exercise strategy that makes the option value and option derivative continuous.

Similar to §6.1, starting from the free boundary problem (6.2.2)—(6.2.4), we can get the variational inequality model for American put option pricing:

In domain $\Sigma : \{0 \le S < \infty, 0 \le t \le T\}$, look for function $V(S,t) \in C^1_\Sigma = V(S,t)|V, \frac{\partial V}{\partial S}$ continuous on Σ, where $\Sigma = \Sigma_1 \cup \Sigma_2 \cup \Gamma$, such that

(1) in the continuation region Σ_1,

$$\begin{aligned} V(S,t) &> (K-S)^+, \\ \mathcal{L}V &= 0, \end{aligned}$$

(2) in the stopping region Σ_2,

$$\begin{aligned} V(S,t) &= (K-S)^+, \\ \mathcal{L}V &= \mathcal{L}(K-S) = -rK < 0. \end{aligned}$$

(3) At the terminal time $t = T$,

$$V(S,t) = (K-S)^+.$$

(4) When $S \to \infty$,

$$V(S,t) \to 0.$$

Combining (1)—(4), we get the **variational inequality form of American put option pricing**:

find $\{V(S,t) \in C^1_\Sigma = V(S,t)|V, \frac{\partial V}{\partial S}$ continuous on $\Sigma\}$, such that

$$\begin{cases} \min\{-\mathcal{L}V, V-(K-S)^+\} = 0, & (\Sigma) & (6.2.7) \\ V(S,T) = (K-S)^+, & (0 \le S < \infty) & (6.2.8) \\ V \to 0. & (S \to \infty) & (6.2.9) \end{cases}$$

Remark For American option with a continuous dividend rate q, the model is

$$\begin{cases} \min\{-\mathcal{L}V, V-g(S)\} = 0, & (6.2.10) \\ V|_{t=T} = g(S). & (6.2.11) \end{cases}$$

where

$$\mathcal{L}V = \frac{\partial V}{\partial t} + \frac{\sigma^2}{2}S^2\frac{\partial^2 V}{\partial S^2} + (r-q)S\frac{\partial V}{\partial S} - rV, \quad (6.2.12)$$

$$g(S) = \begin{cases} (K-S)^+, & \text{(put option)} & (6.2.13) \\ (S-K)^+. & \text{(call option)} & (6.2.14) \end{cases}$$

It is natural to ask what relation exist between American call and put option prices.

In fact, we can use a similar procedure to extend the perpetual American call-put symmetry(Theorem 6.1) to American options in general.

Theorem 6.2 *Let $V_c(S,t;r,q)$, $V_p(S,t;r,q)$ and $S_c(t;r,q)$, $S_p(t;r,q)$ be the prices and the optimal exercise boundaries of the dividend-paying American call* *and put options with the same expiration date T and strike price K, respectively, then*

$$V_c(S,t;r,q) = \frac{S}{K} V_p(\frac{K^2}{S},t;q,r)$$

and

$$\sqrt{S_c(t,r,q)S_p(t;q,r)} = K,$$

where K is the option's strike price, r the risk-free interest rate, q the dividend rate.

The proof of this theorem is almost the same as the proof of Theorem 6.1. Therefore we leave it to the reader as an exercise.

6.3 Decomposition of American Options

Financially, a decomposition can be made to the American option price: a European option price plus another part due to the extra premium required by early exercising the contract. European option is priced by the Black-Scholes formula, and the extra premium obviously depends on the position of the optimal exercise boundary. In mathematics, we want to deduce the equation satisfied by the optimal exercise boundary $S = S(t)$ from this idea.

In order to deduce the integral equation of $S(t)$, we need to use the fundamental solution of the Black-Scholes equation.

Definition 6.1 $G(S,t;\xi,T)$ is called the **fundamental solution of the Black-Scholes equation** , if it satisfies the following terminal value problem to the Black-Scholes equation:

$$\begin{cases} \mathcal{L}V = \dfrac{\partial V}{\partial t} + \dfrac{\sigma^2}{2} S^2 \dfrac{\partial^2 V}{\partial S^2} + (r-q)S\dfrac{\partial V}{\partial S} - rV = 0, & (6.3.1) \\ V(S,T) = \delta(S-\xi), & (6.3.2) \end{cases}$$

where $0 < S < \infty, 0 < \xi < \infty, 0 < t < T, \delta(x)$ is the Dirac function. In order to obtain the expression of $G(S,t;\xi,T)$, define

$$x = \ln\frac{S}{\xi}, \qquad \tau = T - t. \tag{6.3.3}$$

Under the above transformation, (6.3.1),(6.3.2) becomes

$$\begin{cases} \dfrac{\partial V}{\partial \tau} - \dfrac{\sigma^2}{2}\dfrac{\partial^2 V}{\partial x^2} - (r - q - \dfrac{\sigma^2}{2})\dfrac{\partial V}{\partial x} + rV = 0, & (6.3.4) \\ V(x,0) = \frac{1}{\xi}\delta(x), & (6.3.5) \end{cases}$$

where $x \in R$, $0 < \tau \leq T$.

In deriving (6.3.5), we notice that under the transformation (6.3.3),

$$\delta(S-\xi)=\delta(\xi(e^x-1))=\frac{1}{\xi}\delta(e^x-1)=\frac{1}{\xi}\delta(x).$$

Similar to derivation in §5.3, make the transformation

$$V=e^{\alpha\tau+\beta x}u, \tag{6.3.6}$$

where

$$\beta=\frac{1}{2}-\frac{r-q}{\sigma^2}, \tag{6.3.7}$$

$$\alpha=-r-\frac{1}{2\sigma^2}\left(r-q-\frac{\sigma^2}{2}\right)^2. \tag{6.3.8}$$

Thus the initial value problem (6.3.4),(6.3.5) is reduced to

$$\begin{cases}\dfrac{\partial u}{\partial \tau}-\dfrac{\sigma^2}{2}\dfrac{\partial^2 u}{\partial x^2}=0 & (6.3.9)\\ u(x,0)=e^{-\beta x}\frac{1}{\xi}\delta(x)=\frac{1}{\xi}\delta(x). & (6.3.10)\end{cases}$$

Solution to the PDE initial value problem (6.3.9),(6.3.10) is

$$u(x,\tau)=\frac{1}{\xi\sigma\sqrt{2\pi\tau}}\exp\{-\frac{x^2}{2\sigma^2\tau}\}.$$

Substituting it into (6.3.6) and by (6.3.7),(6.3.8), we get

$$V(x,\tau)=\frac{1}{\xi\sigma\sqrt{2\pi\tau}}\exp\{-r\tau-\frac{1}{2\sigma^2\tau}[x+(r-q-\frac{\sigma^2}{2})\tau]^2\}.$$

Going back to the original variables (S,t) by (6.3.8), we get the **fundamental solution of the Black-Scholes equation**

$$\begin{aligned}G(S,t;\xi,T)=&\frac{e^{-r(T-t)}}{\xi\sigma\sqrt{2\pi(T-t)}}\\ &\cdot\exp\{-\tfrac{1}{2\sigma^2(T-t)}\left[\ln\tfrac{S}{\xi}+(r-q-\tfrac{\sigma^2}{2})(T-t)\right]^2\}.\end{aligned} \tag{6.3.11}$$

Theorem 6.3 *If the fundamental solution $G(S,t;\xi,\eta)$ is regarded as a function of ξ,η, then it is the fundamental solution of the adjoint equation of the Black-Scholes equation. That is, let*

$$v(\xi,\eta)=G(S,t;\xi,\eta),$$

then $v(\xi,\eta)$ *satisfies*

$$\begin{cases} \mathcal{L}^* v = -\dfrac{\partial v}{\partial \eta} + \dfrac{\sigma^2}{2}\dfrac{\partial^2}{\partial \xi^2}(\xi^2 v) - (r-q)\dfrac{\partial}{\partial \xi}(\xi v) - rv = 0, & (6.3.12) \\ v(\xi,t) = \delta(\xi - S), & (6.3.13) \end{cases}$$

where $0<\xi<\infty, 0<S<\infty, t<\eta$.[1]

Corollary Theorem 6.3 indicates, *if the fundamental solution of equation (6.3.12) is* $G^*(\xi,\eta;S,t)$, *then*

$$G(S,t;\xi,\eta) = G^*(\xi,\eta;S,t).$$

Proof of Theorem 6.3 Consider the integral

$$\begin{aligned} 0 = & \int_0^\infty dx \int_{t+\epsilon}^{\eta-\epsilon} [G^*(x,y;S,t)\mathcal{L}G(x,y;\xi,\eta) \\ & - G(x,y,\xi,\eta)\mathcal{L}^*G^*(x,y;S,t)]\,dxdy \\ = & \int_0^\infty dx \int_{t+\epsilon}^{\eta-\epsilon} \left\{ \frac{\partial}{\partial y}(G^*G) + \frac{\sigma^2}{2}\frac{\partial}{\partial x}(x^2 G^* \frac{\partial G}{\partial x}) \right. \\ & \left. - \frac{\sigma^2}{2}\frac{\partial}{\partial x}\left[G\frac{\partial}{\partial x}(x^2G^*)\right] + (r-q)\frac{\partial}{\partial x}(xGG^*)\right\} dy. \end{aligned}$$

Since when $x \to 0, \infty$,

$$\begin{aligned} & x^2 G^* \frac{\partial G}{\partial x} \to 0, \\ & G\frac{\partial}{\partial x}(x^2 G^*) \to 0, \\ & xGG^* \to 0. \end{aligned}$$

Thus

$$\int_0^\infty G^*(x,\eta-\epsilon;S,t)G(x,\eta-\epsilon;\xi,\eta)dx = \int_0^\infty G^*(x,t+\epsilon;S,t)G(x,t+\epsilon;\xi,\eta)dx.$$

---

[1] $\mathcal{L}^*v$, the adjoint operator of $\mathcal{L}u = \sum_{i,j=1}^n a_{ij}(x)\dfrac{\partial^2 u}{\partial x_i \partial x_j} + \sum_{i=1}^n b_i(x)\dfrac{\partial u}{\partial x_i} + c(x)u$, is defined by $\mathcal{L}^*v = \sum_{i,j=1}^n \dfrac{\partial^2}{\partial x_i \partial x_j}(a_{ij}(x)v) - \sum_{i=1}^n \dfrac{\partial}{\partial x_i}(b_i(x)v) + c(x)v$. $\mathcal{L}$ and $\mathcal{L}^*v$ satisfy

$$\int_\Omega (v\mathcal{L}u - u\mathcal{L}^*v)dx = 0, \qquad \forall u,v \in C_0^\infty(\Omega).$$

Let $\epsilon \to 0$, from the initial conditions (6.3.2) and (6.3.13)

$$\int_0^\infty G^*(x,\eta;S,t)\delta(x-\xi)dx$$

$$=\int_0^\infty \delta(x-S)G(x,t;\xi,\eta)dx,$$

i.e.

$$G^*(\xi,\eta;S,t)=G(S,t;\xi,\eta).$$

thus completes the proof of the theorem.

Now we can establish the decomposition formula of American option.

Theorem 6.4 *Let $V(S,t)$ be the American put option price, then*

$$V(S,t)=V_E(S,t)+e(S,t), \tag{6.3.14}$$

where $V_E(S,t)$ is the European put option price:

$$V_E(S,t)=Ke^{-r(T-t)}N(-\hat{d}_2)-Se^{-q(T-t)}N(-\hat{d}_1). \tag{6.3.15}$$

where $\hat{d}_1$ and $\hat{d}_2$ are defined by (5-4-11),(5-4-12). $e(S,t)$ is the early exercise premium,

$$e(S,t)=\int_t^T d\eta\int_0^{S(\eta)}(Kr-q\xi)G(S,t;\xi,\eta)d\xi. \tag{6.3.16}$$

where $G(S,t;\xi,\eta)$ is the fundamental solution of the Black-Scholes equation.

Proof For American put option, since in domain $\Sigma:\{0\le S<\infty, 0\le t<T\}$, the option price $V(S,t)$ has continuous first derivative , and in each region has continuous second derivative, thus $V(S,t)$ satisfies

$$-\mathcal{L}V(S,t)=\begin{cases}0, & (S,t)\in\Sigma_1,\\ Kr-qS, & (S,t)\in\Sigma_2,\end{cases} \tag{6.3.17}$$

where $\mathcal{L}$ is the Black-Scholes operator.

Multiply both sides of (6.3.17) by $G^*(\xi,\eta;S,t)$ and integrate on the domain $\{0\le\xi<\infty, t+\epsilon\le\eta\le T\}$. Since $\Sigma_2=\{0\le\xi\le S(\eta), 0\le\eta\le T\}$, and $S(\eta)$ is monotonic, therefore

$$\int_{t+\epsilon}^{T} d\eta \int_{0}^{S(\eta)} (Kr - q\xi) G^*(\xi, \eta; S, t) d\xi$$

$$= - \int_{t+\epsilon}^{T} d\eta \int_{0}^{\infty} G^*(\xi, \eta; S, t) \mathcal{L} V d\xi$$

$$= - \int_{t+\epsilon}^{T} d\eta \int_{0}^{\infty} [G^*(\xi, \eta; S, t) \mathcal{L} V(\xi, \eta)$$

$$- V(\xi, \eta) \mathcal{L}^* G^*(\xi, \eta; S, t)] \, d\xi$$

$$= - \int_{t+\epsilon}^{T} d\eta \int_{0}^{\infty} \left\{ \frac{\partial}{\partial \eta}(G^* V) + \frac{\sigma^2}{2} \frac{\partial}{\partial \xi}(\xi^2 G^* \frac{\partial V}{\partial \xi}) \right.$$

$$\left. - \frac{\sigma^2}{2} \frac{\partial}{\partial \xi}(V \frac{\partial}{\partial \xi}(\xi^2 G^*)) + (r - q) \frac{\partial}{\partial \xi}(\xi V G^*) \right\} d\xi.$$

Since when $\xi \to 0, \infty$

$$\xi^2 G^* \frac{\partial V}{\partial \xi} \longrightarrow 0,$$

$$V \frac{\partial}{\partial \xi}(\xi^2 G^*) \longrightarrow 0,$$

$$\xi V G^* \longrightarrow 0,$$

Thus we have

$$\int_{0}^{\infty} G^*(\xi, t + \epsilon; S, t) V(\xi, t + \epsilon) d\xi$$

$$= \int_{0}^{\infty} G^*(\xi, T; S, t) V(\xi, T) d\xi$$

$$+ \int_{t+\epsilon}^{T} d\eta \int_{0}^{S(\eta)} (Kr - q\xi) G^*(\xi, \eta; S, t) d\xi.$$

Let $\epsilon \to 0$, and consider (6.3.13) and the Corollary of Theorem 6.3, we get

$$V(S, t) = \int_{0}^{\infty} G(S, t; \xi, T)(K - \xi)^+ d\xi$$

$$+ \int_{t}^{T} d\eta \int_{0}^{S(\eta)} (Kr - q\xi) G(S, t; \xi, \eta) d\xi$$

$$= V_E(S, t) + e(S, t).$$

Q.E.D.

Expressions (6.3.14)—(6.3.16) indicate: if the optimal exercise boundary $S = S(t)$ is given, then American option price can be determined by (6.3.14)—(6.3.16).

How can we find the optimal exercise boundary $S = S(t)$? As a corollary of Theorem 6.4, we can obtain a nonlinear integral equation for the optimal exercise boundary $S = S(t)$.

Theorem 6.5 *The optimal exercise boundary of American put option $S = S(t)$ satisfies the following nonlinear Volterra integral equation of the second kind:*

$$\begin{aligned} S(t) = {} & K + S(t)e^{-q(T-t)}N\left(-\frac{-\ln\frac{S(t)}{K} + \beta_2(T-t)}{\sigma\sqrt{T-t}}\right) \\ & - Ke^{-r(T-t)}N\left(-\frac{-\ln\frac{S(t)}{K} + \beta_1(T-t)}{\sigma\sqrt{T-t}}\right) \\ & - Kr\int_t^T e^{-r(\eta-t)}\left[1 - N\left(\frac{\ln\frac{S(t)}{S(\eta)} + \beta_1(\eta-t)}{\sigma\sqrt{\eta-t}}\right)\right]d\eta \\ & + qS\int_t^T e^{-q(\eta-t)}\left[1 - N\left(\frac{\ln\frac{S(t)}{S(\eta)} + \beta_2(\eta-t)}{\sigma\sqrt{\eta-t}}\right)\right]d\eta, \end{aligned} \tag{6.3.18}$$

where

$$\beta_1 = r - q - \frac{\sigma^2}{2}, \tag{6.3.19}$$

$$\beta_2 = r - q + \frac{\sigma^2}{2}. \tag{6.3.20}$$

Proof By (6.3.16) and the fundamental solution expression (6.3.11), $e(S,t)$ can be expressed as

$$\begin{aligned} e(S,t) = {} & \int_t^T d\eta \int_0^{S(\eta)} (Kr - q\xi)\frac{e^{-r(\eta-t)}}{\sigma\xi\sqrt{2\pi(\eta-t)}} \\ & \cdot \exp\left\{-\frac{\left[\ln\frac{S}{\xi} + \beta_1(\eta-t)\right]^2}{2\sigma^2(\eta-t)}\right\}d\xi. \end{aligned} \tag{6.3.21}$$

Change the variable to

$$x = \frac{\ln \frac{S}{\xi} + \beta_1(\eta - t)}{\sigma\sqrt{\eta - t}},$$

$$dx = \frac{-\, d\xi}{\sigma\xi\sqrt{\eta - t}},$$

and (6.3.21) becomes

$$\begin{aligned}
e(S,t) &= \frac{Kr}{\sqrt{2\pi}} e^{-\, r(\eta-t)} \int_t^T d\eta \int_{\frac{\ln \frac{S}{S(\eta)} + \beta_1(\eta-t)}{\sigma\sqrt{\eta-t}}}^{\infty} e^{-x^2} dx \\
&\quad - \frac{qS}{\sqrt{2\pi}} \int_t^T e^{(\beta_1 - r)(\eta-t)} d\eta \int_{\frac{\ln \frac{S}{S(\eta)} + \beta_1(\eta-t)}{\sigma\sqrt{\eta-t}}}^{\infty} e^{-\, (\frac{x^2}{2} + \sigma\sqrt{\eta-t}x)} dx \\
&= Kr \int_t^T e^{-\, r(\eta-t)} \left[1 - N\left(\frac{\ln \frac{S}{S(\eta)} + \beta_1(\eta - t)}{\sigma\sqrt{\eta - t}}\right)\right] d\eta \\
&\quad - qS \int_t^T e^{-\, r(\eta-t)} d\eta \int_{\frac{\ln \frac{S}{S(\eta)} + \beta_1(\eta-t)}{\sigma\sqrt{\eta-t}}}^{\infty} e^{-\, \frac{1}{2}(x+\sigma\sqrt{\eta-t})^2 + (r-q)(\eta-t)} dx \\
&= Kr \int_t^T e^{-\, r(\eta-t)} \left[1 - N\left(\frac{\ln \frac{S}{S(\eta)} + \beta_1(\eta - t)}{\sigma\sqrt{\eta - t}}\right)\right] d\eta \\
&\quad - qS \int_t^T e^{-\, q(\eta-t)} \left[1 - N\left(\frac{\ln \frac{S}{S(\eta)} + \beta_2(\eta - t)}{\sigma\sqrt{\eta - t}}\right)\right] d\eta. \qquad (6.3.22)
\end{aligned}$$

Substituting (6.3.22) into (6.3.14), and taking into account

$$V(S(t), t) = K - S(t),$$

thus we have

$$K - S(t) = V_E(S(t), t) + e(S(t), t),$$

$$S(t) = K + S(t)e^{-q(T-t)}N\left(-\frac{\ln\frac{S(t)}{K} + \beta_1(T-t)}{\sigma\sqrt{T-t}}\right)$$

$$- Ke^{-r(T-t)}N\left(-\frac{\ln\frac{S(t)}{K} + \beta_2(T-t)}{\sigma\sqrt{T-t}}\right)$$

$$+ qS\int_t^T e^{-q(\eta-t)}\left[1 - N\left(\frac{\ln\frac{S(t)}{S(\eta)} + \beta_2(\eta-t)}{\sigma\sqrt{\eta-t}}\right)\right]d\eta$$

$$- Kr\int_t^T e^{-r(\eta-t)}\left[1 - N\left(\frac{\ln\frac{S(t)}{S(\eta)} + \beta_1(\eta-t)}{\sigma\sqrt{\eta-t}}\right)\right]d\eta.$$

Q.E.D.

While it is very difficult to solve the nonlinear integral equation (6.3.18), we can obtain an asymptotic expression of the optimal exercise boundary $S = S(t)$ near the terminal point $t = T$.

Remark We can use a similar derivation to obtain the expression of the early exercise premium for American call option:

$$e(S,t) = \int_t^T d\eta \int_{S(\eta)}^{\infty} (q\xi - Kr)G(S,t;\xi,\eta)d\xi,$$

and a nonlinear Volterra integral equation for the optimal exercise boundary $S = S(t)$.

6.4 Properties of American Option Price

A qualitative understanding of American option pricing is appropriate before we start the numerical studies. In contrast to European option, American option price, except for the perpetual option, does not have closed-form solutions in general. Therefore in studying the properties of American option we rely on the theoretical approach of partial differential equations. As discussed in the previous chapter §5.8, this requires a study on the properties of the derivatives of the solution with respect to the variables or parameters in the boundary-terminal value problem to parabolic equations. But since American option price satisfies a variational inequality, it is not differentiable. Therefore we introduce a **penalty function** $\beta_\epsilon(x)$, and set up a **penalty problem** corresponding to the variational inequality as its approximation. Then we will prove the assertion using the **maximum principle** for the parabolic equations. Moreover, since the payoff function

$(S-K)^+$ and $(K-S)^+$ are not differentiable at $S=K$, we will also need to smooth the payoff function to ensure the differentiability of the PDE problem.

Definition 6.2 Function $\beta_\epsilon(x)$ is called penalty function in $(-\infty,\infty)$, if

$$\beta_\epsilon(x) \in C^2_{(-\infty,\infty)},$$

$$\beta_\epsilon(x) \leq 0, \tag{6.4.1}$$

$$\beta_\epsilon(0) \leq -C_\epsilon, \qquad (C_\epsilon \geq 0) \tag{6.4.2}$$

$$\beta'_\epsilon(x) \geq 0, \tag{6.4.3}$$

$$\beta''_\epsilon(x) \leq 0, \tag{6.4.4}$$

and

$$\lim_{\epsilon\to 0}\beta_\epsilon(x) = \begin{cases} 0, & x \geq 0, \\ -\infty, & x < 0. \end{cases} \tag{6.4.5}$$

Under the transformation

$$x = \ln S, \qquad \tau = T - t$$

and

$$v(x,\tau) = V(S,t),$$

the variational inequality (6.2.10)—(6.2.11) becomes

$$\begin{cases} \min\left\{-\mathcal{L}_0 v, v-(K-e^x)^+\right\} = 0, & (6.4.6)\\ v(x,0) = (K-e^x)^+, & (6.4.7) \end{cases}$$

where

$$\mathcal{L}_0 v = \frac{\partial v}{\partial \tau} - \frac{\sigma^2}{2}\frac{\partial^2 v}{\partial x^2} - (r-q-\frac{\sigma^2}{2})\frac{\partial v}{\partial x} + rv.$$

Definition 6.3 In $\{x \in R, 0 \leq \tau \leq T\}$, the initial value problem to parabolic equations

$$\begin{cases} \mathcal{L}_\epsilon(v) = \frac{\partial v}{\partial \tau} - \frac{\sigma^2}{2}\frac{\partial^2 v}{\partial x^2} - (r-q-\frac{\sigma^2}{2})\frac{\partial v}{\partial x} \\ \qquad\qquad + rv + \beta_\epsilon(v - \Pi_\epsilon(K-e^x)) = 0, & (6.4.8)\\ v(x,0) = \Pi_\epsilon(K-e^x), & (6.4.9) \end{cases}$$

is called the **penalty problem** of the variational inequality (6.4.6), (6.4.7), where

$$\Pi_\epsilon(y) = \begin{cases} y & y \geq \epsilon, \\ \nearrow & |y| \leq \epsilon, \\ 0 & y \leq -\epsilon, \end{cases} \tag{6.4.10}$$

$$\Pi_\epsilon(y) \in C^\infty(R), 1 \geq \Pi'_\epsilon(y) \geq 0,$$
$$\Pi''_\epsilon(y) \geq 0, \lim_{\epsilon \to 0} \Pi_\epsilon(y) = y^+. \tag{6.4.11}$$

As a corollary of (6.4.10),(6.4.11), we have

$$\left|\Pi_\epsilon(y) - y\Pi'_\epsilon(y)\right| \leq \epsilon. \tag{6.4.12}$$

Let $D_T = \{(x,t)|a < x < b, 0 < t \leq T\}$, where $-\infty \leq a < b \leq \infty$; And $\partial_P D_T$ be the parabolic boundary of D_T. If a, b are finite,

$$\partial_P D = \{x = a, x = b, 0 \leq t \leq T\} \cup \{a \leq x \leq b, t = 0\};$$

If a, b are infinite,

$$\partial_P D = \{x \in R, t = 0\};$$

and

$$C^{2,1}(D_T) = \left\{u(x,t) \middle| u, \frac{\partial u}{\partial x}, \frac{\partial^2 u}{\partial x^2}, \frac{\partial u}{\partial t} \in C(D_T)\right\}.$$

Theorem 6.6(the maximum principle) *If $u(x,t) \in C^{2,1}(D_T) \cap C(\bar{D}_T)$, and*

$$|u(x,t)| \leq Me^{\alpha|x|^{2-\epsilon}}, \qquad (\alpha, \epsilon > 0)$$

and satisfies the linear parabolic equation in D:

$$\frac{\partial u}{\partial t} - a(x,t)\frac{\partial^2 u}{\partial x^2} + b(x,t)\frac{\partial u}{\partial x} + c(x,t)u = f(x,t),$$

where

$$a(x,t) \geq a_0 > 0,$$
$$c(x,t) \geq 0.$$

If $f(x,t) \leq 0$, $u(x,t)$ can only attain its nonnegative maximum at $\partial_P D_T$.

Remark The maximum principle also holds for higher dimensional parabolic equations. The proof can be found in textbooks.

For the penalty problem (6.4.8)—(6.4.9), we have the following conclusions ([15]).

Theorem 6.7(Convergence of the penalty problem) *If $v_\epsilon(x,t)$ is the solution of the penalty problem (6.4.8)—(6.4.9), then as $\epsilon \to 0$, in any finite and closed domain within $\overline{D}_T$, $v_\epsilon(x,t)$ converges uniformly to $v(x,t)$ which is the solution of the Cauchy problem (6.4.6)—(6.4.7).*

Now let us study the properties of the American option pricing using Theorem 6.7 and the maximum principle(Theorem 6.6).

To be specific, we will take American put option as example in performing rigid proof. Conclusions can be extended to American call option using the American call-put symmetry (Theorem 6.2).

Let $V = V(S,t) = v(x,\tau)$ be American put option price, and $v_\epsilon(x,\tau)$ be the solution of the corresponding penalty problem (6.4.8)—(6.4.9).

Theorem 6.8 *For American put option pricing,*

(1) if $S_1 \geq S_2$, *then*

$$V(S_1,t) \leq V(S_2,t); \tag{6.4.13}$$

(2) if $K_1 \geq K_2$, *then*

$$0 \leq V(S,t;K_1) - V(S,t;K_2) \leq K_1 - K_2. \tag{6.4.14}$$

Proof (6.4.13) and (6.4.14) can be proved in a similar way. We only prove the right side part of the inequality (6.4.14):

$$V(S,t;K_1) - V(S,t;K_2) \leq K_1 - K_2. \tag{6.4.15}$$

Define

$$W = K_1 - K_2 - v_1(x,\tau) + v_2(x,\tau),$$

where $v_i(x,\tau) = v_\epsilon(x,\tau;K_i), (i = 1,2)$.

Substitute it into equation (6.4.8),

$$\begin{aligned}
&\frac{\partial W}{\partial \tau} - \frac{\sigma^2}{2}\frac{\partial^2 W}{\partial x^2} - (r - q - \frac{\sigma^2}{2})\frac{\partial W}{\partial x} + rW \\
&\quad - \beta_\epsilon(v_1 - \Pi_\epsilon(K_1 - e^x)) + \beta_\epsilon(v_2 - \Pi_\epsilon(K_2 - e^x)) \\
&\quad = r(K_1 - K_2).
\end{aligned} \tag{6.4.16}$$

Since

$$\begin{aligned}
&- \beta_\epsilon(v_1 - \Pi_\epsilon(K_1 - e^x)) + \beta_\epsilon(v_2 - \Pi_\epsilon(K_2 - e^x)) \\
&\qquad = - \beta_\epsilon'(\xi)\left[v_1 - v_2 - (\Pi_\epsilon(K_1 - e^x) - \Pi_\epsilon(K_2 - e^x))\right] \\
&\qquad = \beta_\epsilon'(\xi)\left\{W - (1 - \Pi_\epsilon'(\eta))(K_1 - K_2)\right\},
\end{aligned}$$

where

$$\begin{aligned}
&\xi = \theta_1(v_1 - \Pi_\epsilon(K_1 - e^x)) + (1 - \theta_1)(v_2 - \Pi_\epsilon(K_2 - e^x)), \\
&\eta = \theta_2(K_1 - e^x) + (1 - \theta_2)(K_2 - e^x), \\
&\qquad (0 < \theta_1, \theta_2 < 1)
\end{aligned}$$

then (6.4.16) becomes

$$\frac{\partial W}{\partial \tau}-\frac{\sigma^2}{2}\frac{\partial^2 W}{\partial x^2}-(r-q-\frac{\sigma^2}{2})\frac{\partial W}{\partial x}+(r+\beta_\epsilon'(\xi))W$$

$$=\left[r+\beta_\epsilon'(\xi)(1-\Pi'(\eta))\right](K_1-K_2). \tag{6.4.17}$$

The initial value of W is:

$$W|_{\tau=0}=(K_1-K_2)-(\Pi_\epsilon(K_1-e^x)-\Pi_\epsilon(K_2-e^x))$$

$$=(1-\Pi_\epsilon'(\eta))(K_1-K_2). \tag{6.4.18}$$

By definitions of β_ϵ, Π_ϵ in (6.4.3),(6.4.11), we get

$$r+\beta_\epsilon'(\xi)>0,$$

$$r+\beta_\epsilon'(\xi)(1-\Pi_\epsilon'(\eta))>0,$$

$$1-\Pi_\epsilon'(\eta)\geq 0.$$

Since it is assumed $K_1 \geq K_2$, applying the maximum principle to the Cauchy problem (6.4.17),(6.4.18), we conclude $W \geq 0$, i.e.

$$v_\epsilon(x,\tau;K_1)-v_\epsilon(x,\tau;K_2)\leq K_1-K_2.$$

Let $\epsilon \to 0$, then by Theorem 6.7

$$V(S,t;K_1)-V(S,t;K_2)\leq K_1-K_2.$$

thus (6.4.15) is proved.

Lemma 6.1 *Suppose $v_\epsilon(x,\tau)$ is the solution of the penalty problem (6.4.8)—(6.4.9), then*

$$\frac{\partial v_\epsilon}{\partial x}-v_\epsilon\leq\frac{\sqrt{\epsilon}}{r}. \tag{6.4.19}$$

Proof In order to prove the lemma, we assume that β_ϵ is of the form

$$\beta_\epsilon(\alpha)=\frac{-1}{\sqrt{\epsilon}}\Pi_\epsilon(-\alpha), \tag{6.4.20}$$

where $\Pi_\epsilon(y)$ is defined in (6.4.10). It is easy to verify that $\beta_\epsilon(\alpha)$ defined above satisfies (6.4.1)—(6.4.4). Then by (6.4.12), $\beta_\epsilon(\alpha)$ satisfies the inequality:

$$\left|\beta_\epsilon(\alpha)-\alpha\beta_\epsilon'(\alpha)\right|\leq\sqrt{\epsilon}. \tag{6.4.21}$$

In fact, by the definition of $\beta_\epsilon(\alpha)$ in (6.4.20), and (6.4.12), we have

$$\begin{aligned}\left|\beta_\epsilon(\alpha)-\alpha\beta_\epsilon'(\alpha)\right| &= \left|-\frac{1}{\sqrt{\epsilon}}\Pi_\epsilon(-\alpha)-\frac{\alpha}{\sqrt{\epsilon}}\Pi_\epsilon'(-\alpha)\right| \\ &= \frac{1}{\sqrt{\epsilon}}\left|\Pi_\epsilon(-\alpha)-(-\alpha)\Pi_\epsilon'(-\alpha)\right| \\ &\leq \sqrt{\epsilon}.\end{aligned}$$

Now let us prove the inequality (6.4.19). Define

$$W=\frac{\partial v_\epsilon}{\partial x}-v_\epsilon-\frac{\sqrt{\epsilon}}{r},$$

It is easy to verify that W satisfies the equation:

$$\begin{aligned}&\frac{\partial W}{\partial \tau}-\frac{\sigma^2}{2}\frac{\partial^2 W}{\partial x^2}-(r-q-\frac{\sigma^2}{2})\frac{\partial W}{\partial x}+rW \\ &\quad+\beta_\epsilon'(\alpha)\left[\frac{\partial v_\epsilon}{\partial x}+\Pi_\epsilon'(K-e^x)e^x\right]-\beta_\epsilon(\alpha)=-\sqrt{\epsilon},\end{aligned}$$

i.e.

$$\begin{aligned}&\frac{\partial W}{\partial \tau}-\frac{\sigma^2}{2}\frac{\partial^2 W}{\partial x^2}-(r-q-\frac{\sigma^2}{2})\frac{\partial W}{\partial x}+(r+\beta_\epsilon'(\alpha))W \\ &\quad=-\sqrt{\epsilon}(1+\frac{1}{r}\beta_\epsilon'(\alpha))+\beta_\epsilon(\alpha)-\beta_\epsilon'(\alpha)[v_\epsilon+\Pi_\epsilon'(y)e^x],\end{aligned}$$

where $\alpha=v_\epsilon-\Pi_\epsilon(y)$, $y=K-e^x$.

Due to the inequality (6.4.21), and (6.4.3),(6.4.10), we have

$$\begin{aligned}&\frac{\partial W}{\partial \tau}-\frac{\sigma^2}{2}\frac{\partial^2 W}{\partial x^2}-(r-q-\frac{\sigma^2}{2})\frac{\partial W}{\partial x}+(r+\beta_\epsilon'(\alpha))W \\ &=-\sqrt{\epsilon}(1+\frac{1}{r}\beta_\epsilon'(\alpha))+\beta_\epsilon(\alpha)-\alpha\beta_\epsilon'(\alpha)-\beta_\epsilon'(\alpha)\left[\Pi_\epsilon(y)+\Pi_\epsilon'(y)e^x\right] \\ &\leq-\sqrt{\epsilon}(1+\frac{1}{r}\beta_\epsilon'(\alpha))+\sqrt{\epsilon}\leq 0;\end{aligned} \tag{6.4.22}$$

and at $\tau=0$,

$$W(x,0)=-\Pi_\epsilon'(K-e^x)e^x-\Pi_\epsilon(K-e^x)-\frac{\sqrt{\epsilon}}{r}<0. \tag{6.4.23}$$

Therefore, applying the maximum principle to the Cauchy problem (6.4.22),(6.4.23), we get

$$W(x,\tau) \le 0,$$

i.e.

$$\frac{\partial v_\epsilon}{\partial x} - v_\epsilon \le \frac{\sqrt{\epsilon}}{r}.$$

Thus completes the proof of the lemma.

Theorem 6.9 *For American put option pricing,*
(1) if $r_1 \ge r_2$, then

$$V(S,t;r_2) \ge V(S,t,r_1); \tag{6.4.24}$$

(2) if $q_1 \ge q_2$, then

$$V(S,t;q_1) \ge V(S,t,q_2). \tag{6.4.25}$$

Proof Since inequalities (6.4.24) and (6.4.25) can be proved similarly, let us take (6.4.24) as example.

Define

$$W = v_2(x,\tau) - v_1(x,\tau) + \frac{(r_1 - r_2)\sqrt{\epsilon}}{r_2 r_1},$$

where $v_i(x,\tau) = v_\epsilon(x,\tau;r_i)(i = 1,2)$. Substituting W into (6.4.8),

$$\begin{aligned} &\frac{\partial W}{\partial \tau} - \frac{\sigma^2}{2}\frac{\partial^2 W}{\partial x^2} - (r_2 - q - \frac{\sigma^2}{2})\frac{\partial W}{\partial x} + r_2 W \\ &\quad + \beta_\epsilon(v_2 - \Pi_\epsilon(K - e^x)) - \beta_\epsilon(v_1 - \Pi_\epsilon(K - e^x)) \\ &= \frac{(r_1 - r_2)\sqrt{\epsilon}}{r_1} + r_2(\frac{\partial v_1}{\partial x} - v_1) - r_1(\frac{\partial v_1}{\partial x} - v_1), \end{aligned}$$

Here $\beta_\epsilon(\alpha)$ is the penalty function as defined in (6.4.20). Thus by (6.4.19) (Lemma 6.1), we get

$$\begin{cases} \frac{\partial W}{\partial \tau} - \frac{\sigma^2}{2}\frac{\partial^2 W}{\partial x^2} - (r_2 - q - \frac{\sigma^2}{2})\frac{\partial W}{\partial x} + (r_2 + \beta'_\epsilon(\alpha))W \\ \qquad \ge (r_2 - r_1)\left[\frac{\partial v_1}{\partial x} - v_1 - \frac{\sqrt{\epsilon}}{r_1}\right] \ge 0, \\ W(x,0) = \frac{(r_1 - r_2)\sqrt{\epsilon}}{r_2 r_1}. \end{cases}$$

Thus by the maximum principle, $W(x,\tau)$ cannot take the negative minimum in $\{x \in R, 0 < \tau \leq T\}$. Then from $W(x, 0) > 0$, we infer

$$W(x, \tau) \geq 0,$$

i.e.

$$v_\epsilon(x, \tau; r_1) \leq v_\epsilon(x, \tau; r_2) + \frac{(r_1 - r_2)\sqrt{\epsilon}}{r_2 r_1}.$$

Let $\epsilon \to 0$, and by Theorem 6.7, we get (6.4.24).

Lemma 6.2 *If $v_\epsilon(x, \tau)$ is the solution of the penalty problem (6.4.8)—(6.4.9), then*

$$\frac{\partial v_\epsilon}{\partial \tau} \geq 0. \tag{6.4.26}$$

Proof Denote

$$W = \frac{\partial v_\epsilon}{\partial \tau}.$$

In domain $\overline{D}_T\{x \in R, 0 \leq \tau \leq T\}$, since $v_\epsilon(x, \tau)$, the solution of the penalty problem (6.4.8)—(6.4.9), is sufficiently smooth, W satisfies the Cauchy problem as follows:

$$\begin{cases} \dfrac{\partial W}{\partial \tau} - \dfrac{\sigma^2}{2}\dfrac{\partial^2 W}{\partial x^2} - (r - q - \dfrac{\sigma^2}{2})\dfrac{\partial W}{\partial x} + rW + \beta_\epsilon'(\alpha)W = 0, & (6.4.27) \\ W(x, 0) = \phi(x), & (6.4.28) \end{cases}$$

where

$$\begin{aligned} \phi(x) = \left.\frac{\partial v_\epsilon}{\partial \tau}\right|_{\tau=0} &= \left[\frac{\sigma^2}{2}\frac{\partial^2 v_\epsilon}{\partial x^2} + (r - q - \frac{\sigma^2}{2})\frac{\partial v_\epsilon}{\partial x} - r v_\epsilon - \beta_\epsilon(\alpha)\right]_{\tau=0} \\ &= \frac{\sigma^2}{2}\left(\Pi_\epsilon''(y)e^{2x} - \Pi_\epsilon'(y)e^x\right) - (r - q - \frac{\sigma^2}{2})\Pi_\epsilon'(y)e^x \\ &\quad - r\Pi_\epsilon(y) - \beta(0), \end{aligned}$$

where

$$y = K - e^x.$$

By (6.4.2) and (6.4.11),

$$\begin{aligned} \phi(x) &\geq -(r - q)\Pi_\epsilon'(y)e^x - r\Pi_\epsilon(y) + C_\epsilon \\ &\geq C_\epsilon - r\left[\Pi_\epsilon(y) - y\Pi_\epsilon'(y)\right] - rK\Pi_\epsilon'(y) \\ &\geq C_\epsilon - \frac{r\epsilon}{2} - rK. \end{aligned}$$

We can choose

$$-\beta_\epsilon(0) = C_\epsilon = rK + \frac{r}{2}\epsilon,$$

so that $\phi(x) \geq 0$. Then applying the maximum principle to the Cauchy problem (6.4.27),(6.4.28), we conclude in D_T

$$W(x,\tau) \geq 0,$$

i.e. (6.4.26) is true.

Theorem 6.10 *For American put option pricing,*

(1) if $t_1 \geq t_2$, then

$$V(S,t_2) \geq V(S,t_1); \tag{6.4.29}$$

(2) if $T_1 \geq T_2$, then when $0 \leq t \leq T_2$,

$$V(S,t;T_1) \geq V(S,t;T_2). \tag{6.4.30}$$

Proof Conclusion (6.4.29) is a direct corollary of (6.4.26). In order to prove (6.4.30), denote

$$W(x,\tau) = v_\epsilon(x,\tau;T_1) - v_\epsilon(x,\tau;T_2). \quad (\tau = T_2 - t)$$

It is easy to check that in domain $\{x \in R, 0 \leq \tau \leq T_2\}$, $W(x,\tau)$ satisfies the penalty problem

$$\begin{cases} \frac{\partial W}{\partial \tau} - \frac{\sigma^2}{2}\frac{\partial^2 W}{\partial x^2} - (r - q - \frac{\sigma^2}{2})\frac{\partial W}{\partial x} + (r + \beta_\epsilon'(\xi))W = 0, & (6.4.31) \\ W(x,\tau) = \phi(x), & (6.4.32) \end{cases}$$

where

$$\phi(x) = v_\epsilon(x,0;T_1) - v_\epsilon(x,0;T_2) = v_\epsilon(x,0;T_1) - \Pi_\epsilon(K - e^x).$$

Now back to the original time variable t

$$\begin{aligned} \phi(x) &= v_\epsilon(x,T_2;T_1) - \Pi_\epsilon(K - e^x) \\ &= v_\epsilon(x,T_2;T_1) - v_\epsilon(x,T_1;T_1) \\ &\geq 0. \end{aligned}$$

Applying the maximum principle to the Cauchy problem (6.4.31),(6.4.32), we conclude

$$W(x,\tau) \geq 0,$$

i.e.

$$v_\epsilon(x,\tau;T_1) \geq v_\epsilon(x,\tau;T_2).$$

Let $\epsilon \to 0$, and by Theorem 6.7, we get (6.4.30) .

Lemma 6.3 *If $v_\epsilon(x,\tau)$ is the solution of the penalty problem (6.4.8),(6.4.9), then*

$$\frac{\partial^2 v_\epsilon}{\partial x^2} - \frac{\partial v_\epsilon}{\partial x} \geq 0. \tag{6.4.33}$$

Proof Denote

$$W(x,\tau) = \frac{\partial^2 v_\epsilon}{\partial x^2} - \frac{\partial v_\epsilon}{\partial x},$$

Since the solution $v_\epsilon(x,\tau)$ of the penalty problem (6.4.8),(6.4.9) is sufficiently smooth in the problem domain, thus $W(x,\tau)$ satisfies the problem:

$$\begin{cases} \frac{\partial W}{\partial \tau} - \frac{\sigma^2}{2}\frac{\partial^2 W}{\partial x^2} - (r - q - \frac{\sigma^2}{2})\frac{\partial W}{\partial x} + (r + \beta_\epsilon'(\alpha))W = f(x,\tau), & (6.4.34) \\ W(x,0) = \phi(x), & (6.4.35) \end{cases}$$

where

$$\begin{aligned} f(x,\tau) &= -\,\beta_\epsilon''(\alpha)\left(\frac{\partial v_\epsilon}{\partial x} + \Pi_\epsilon'(y)e^x\right)^2 + \beta_\epsilon'(\alpha)\Pi_\epsilon''(y)e^{2x}, \\ \phi(x) &= \Pi''(y)e^{2x}, \\ \alpha &= v_\epsilon - \Pi_\epsilon(y), \\ y &= K - e^x. \end{aligned}$$

From (6.4.3),(6.4.4) and (6.4.11) we get

$$f(x,\tau) \geq 0,$$

$$\phi(x) \geq 0.$$

Applying the maximum principle to the Cauchy problem (6.4.34),(6.4.35), we get

$$W(x,\tau) \geq 0.$$

Thus the Lemma is proved.

Theorem 6.11 *If $\sigma_1 \geq \sigma_2$, then*

$$V(S,t;\sigma_1) \geq V(S,t;\sigma_2). \tag{6.4.36}$$

Proof Denote

$$W(x,\tau) = v_1(x,\tau) - v_2(x,\tau),$$

where $v_i(x,\tau) = v_\epsilon(x,\tau;\sigma_i), (i = 1,2)$. It is easy to check that in the domain $\overline{D}_T$, $W(x,\tau)$ satisfies the equation

$$\frac{\partial W}{\partial \tau} - \frac{\sigma_1^2}{2}\frac{\partial^2 W}{\partial x^2} - (r - q - \frac{\sigma_1^2}{2})\frac{\partial W}{\partial x} + (r + \beta_\epsilon'(\xi))W$$

$$= \frac{1}{2}(\sigma_1^2 - \sigma_2^2)\left(\frac{\partial^2 v_2}{\partial x^2} - \frac{\partial v_2}{\partial x}\right), \tag{6.4.37}$$

with the initial condition:

$$W(x,0) = 0. \tag{6.4.38}$$

From (6.4.33) and the theorem's assumption, the right side of equation (6.4.37) is nonnegative. Thus applying the maximum principle to the problem (6.4.37),(6.4.38), we get

$$W(x,\tau) \geq 0,$$

i.e.

$$v_\epsilon(x,\tau;\sigma_1) \geq v_\epsilon(x,\tau;\sigma_2).$$

Let $\epsilon \to 0$, and by Theorem 6.7, we get (6.4.36).

By American call-put symmetry

$$V_c(S,t;r,q) = \frac{S}{K}V_p(\frac{K^2}{S},t;q,r), \tag{6.4.39}$$

we can extend the properties of the American put option price (Theorems 6.8—6.11) to the American call option.

For simplicity of writing, we define points P, P_0 and Q:

$$P = (S,t;r,q,T,\sigma),$$

$$P_0 = (S_0,t_0;r_0,q_0,T_0,\sigma_0),$$

$$Q = (\frac{K^2}{S},t;q,r,T,\sigma).$$

Then (6.4.39) can be written as

$$V_c(P) = \frac{S}{K}V_p(P_0)\bigg|_{P_0=Q},$$

and assuming corresponding derivatives are meaningful, then:

$$\frac{\partial V_c}{\partial S} = \frac{1}{K}V_p(Q) - \frac{K}{S}\frac{\partial V_p}{\partial S_0}\bigg|_{P_0=Q} \geq 0,$$

$$\frac{\partial V_c}{\partial K} = -\frac{S}{K^2}V_p(Q) + 2\frac{\partial V_p}{\partial S_0}\bigg|_{P_0=Q} \leq 0,$$

$$\frac{\partial V_c}{\partial r} = \frac{S}{K}\frac{\partial V_p}{\partial q_0}\bigg|_{P_0=Q} \geq 0,$$

$$\frac{\partial V_c}{\partial q} = \frac{S}{K}\frac{\partial V_p}{\partial r_0}\bigg|_{P_0=Q} \leq 0,$$

$$\frac{\partial V_c}{\partial t} = \frac{S}{K}\frac{\partial V_p}{\partial t}(Q) \leq 0,$$

$$\frac{\partial V_c}{\partial T} = \frac{S}{K}\frac{\partial V_p}{\partial T}(Q) \geq 0,$$

$$\frac{\partial V_c}{\partial \sigma} = \frac{S}{K}\frac{\partial V_p}{\partial \sigma}(Q) \geq 0.$$

According to the above analysis of American option price, we get the following table: (here "+" indicates the option price is an increasing function of the variable, "–" indicates the option price is a decreasing function of the variable)

Variable	Call Option	Put Option
S(Stock Price)	+	–
K(Strike Price)	–	+
r(Risk-free Interest Rate)	+	–
q(Dividend Rate)	–	+
σ(Volatility)	+	+
T(Life)	+	+
t(time)	–	–

By comparing this table with the table in §5.8, we conclude:

(1) American option price has the same dependence as European option price on S, K, r, q, σ.

(2) In contrast to European option price, American option price has a definite dependence on the option lifetime T and time t. Financially, this is because for American options, whether put option or call option, an option with longer life has all the exercise opportunity that options with shorter life have, hence a long-life option must be worth at least as much as the short-life options. As for the time factor, since as t increases, $T - t$ decreases (the terminal time $t = T$ gets

closer), the profiteering opportunity from early exercising the option decreases, hence the option becomes less valuable.

6.5 Optimal Exercise Boundary

Since American option has early exercise term in the contract, the determination of the optimal exercise boundary is of special importance to the holder of American options. But as a free boundary, its determination is coupled with the determination of the option price. Therefore, a closed-form expression of the free boundary is not attainable in general.

In this section, we will use the PDE theory to make qualitative analysis on the optimal exercise boundary $S = S(t)$, including the position of $S(T)$, the monotonicity of $S(t)$, upper and lower bounds of $S(t)$ and convexity of $S(t)$ etc., and based on these, give an asymptotic expression of $S(t)$ near $t = T$. All these results will not only give us a good knowledge about the optimal exercise boundary, but will also help the numerical computation of the American option price.

First, let us determine the position of the optimal exercise boundary $S = S(t)$ at $t = T$.

Theorem 6.12 *Suppose* $\Gamma : \{S = S(t), (0 \leq t \leq T)\}$ *is the optimal exercise boundary for dividend-paying American option, then*

$$S(T) = \begin{cases} \min\left\{\frac{rK}{q}, K\right\}, & \textit{(put option)} \quad (6.5.1) \\ \max\left\{\frac{rK}{q}, K\right\}. & \textit{(call option)} \quad (6.5.2) \end{cases}$$

Proof First let us consider the American put option.

(A) If

$$q \leq r, \tag{6.5.3}$$

then we need to show $S(T) = K$.

Suppose otherwise, i.e., $S(T) \neq K$. As we already pointed out: since $V > 0$, therefore $S(T) < K$. Then in the continuation region Σ_1 there would exist a region $D_\delta : \{S(t) < S < K, T - \delta \leq t \leq T\}$, ($\delta$ sufficiently small), such that

$$\mathcal{L}V = 0,$$

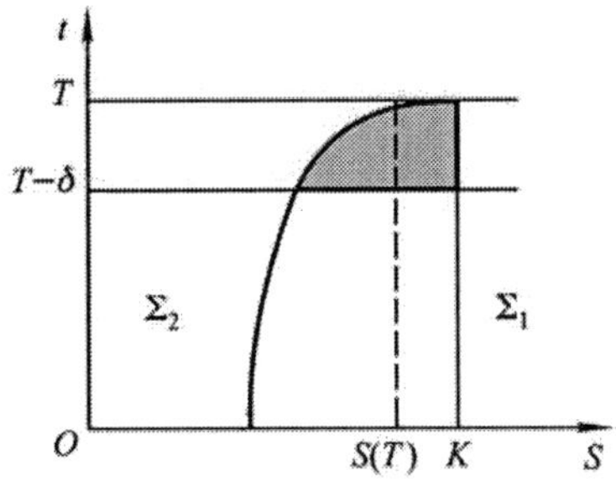

Then at $t = T$, $S(T) < S < K$,

$$\left.\frac{\partial V}{\partial t}\right|_{t=T} = -\left[\frac{\sigma^2}{2}S^2\frac{d^2V}{dS^2} + (r-q)S\frac{dV}{dS} - rV\right]_{t=T}$$

$$= -\left[\frac{\sigma^2}{2}S^2\frac{d^2(K-S)}{dS^2} + (r-q)S\frac{d(K-S)}{dS} - r(K-S)\right]$$

$$= rK - qS.$$

With (6.5.3) and $S < K$, there would be

$$\left.\frac{\partial V}{\partial t}\right|_{t=T} > 0.$$

But $V(S,T) = (K-S)$, therefore inside D_δ, there must be

$$V(S,t) < (K-S).$$

But this contradicts to the property $V \geq (K-S)^+$. Thus we conclude $S(T) = K$.

(B) If

$$r < q, \tag{6.5.4}$$

then we need to show $S(T) = \frac{rK}{q}$.

Suppose otherwise:

(a) If $S(T) < \frac{rK}{q}$. Since $\frac{r}{q}K < K$, then in Σ_1 there would exist a region $D_\delta^{(1)} : \left\{S(t) < S < \frac{rK}{q}, T-\delta \leq t \leq T\right\}$, such that

$$\mathcal{L}V = 0.$$

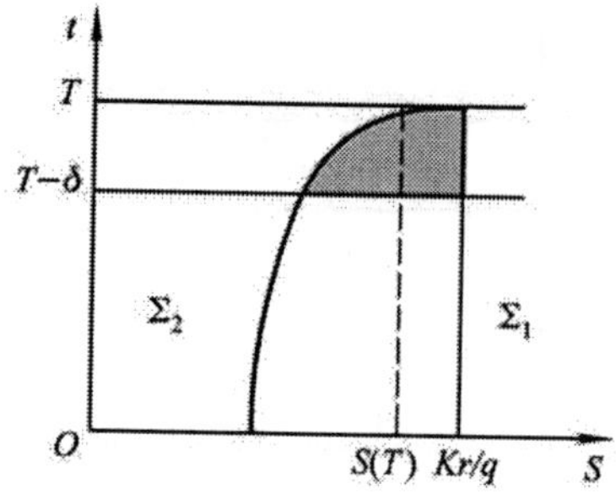

Then similar to (A), inside $D_\delta^{(1)}$, there would be

$$\left.\frac{\partial V}{\partial t}\right|_{t=T} = rK - qS > 0$$

and

$$V(S,t) < K - S.$$

This contradicts to the property $V(S,t) \geq (K-S)^+$.

(b) If $S(T) > \frac{r}{q}K$. Since $S(T) \geq K$, and (6.5.4), then in the stopping region of the option Σ_2 there would exist a region

$$D_\delta^{(2)} : \left\{\frac{r}{q}K < S < S(t), T - \delta \leq t \leq T\right\},$$

such that inside $D_\delta^{(2)}$,

$$V = K - S.$$

Then in $D_\delta^{(2)}$ there would be

$$-\mathcal{L}V = rK - qS < 0.$$

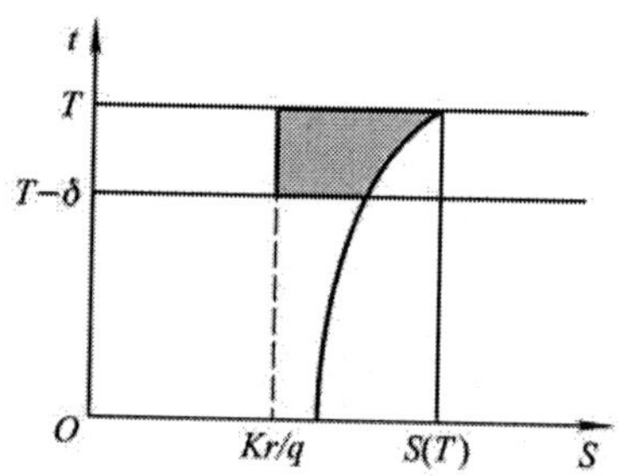

This contradicts to equation (6.2.10). Therefore there must be $S(T) = \frac{rK}{q}$.

Combining conclusions of (A) and (B), (6.5.1) is proved. Similarly one can prove (6.5.2).

Remark In the above proof, we made following two *a priori* assumptions:
(1) $S = S(t)$ is continuous;
(2) in addition, both $\frac{\partial V}{\partial t}, \frac{\partial^2 V}{\partial S^2}$ are continuous up to $t = T$ excluding $S = K$.
We omitted the proof of these two assumptions(see [15]).

Remark Based on the position $S(T)$ (6.5.1) for American put option, using American call-put symmetry (Theorem 6.2), we can derive directly the position of the optimal exercise boundary at the terminal time $S(T)$ (6.5.2) for American call option in Theorem 6.12.

In fact, from (6.1.34)

$$\begin{aligned} S_c(T; r, q) &= \frac{K^2}{S_p(T; q, r)} = \frac{K^2}{\min\left\{K, \frac{qK}{r}\right\}} \\ &= \begin{cases} K, & r < q, \\ \frac{r}{q}K, & r > q \end{cases} \\ &= \max(K, \frac{r}{q}K). \end{aligned}$$

Corollary *For American call option, if $q < r$, then*

$$S(T) = \frac{r}{q}K.$$

If $q \to 0$, then $S(T) \to \infty$.

Thus, using the PDE model of American option price, we have proved again : *non-dividend-paying American call option should never be exercised prior to the expiration date.*

Theorem 6.13 *Suppose $\Gamma : \{S = S(t), (0 \le t \le T)\}$ is the optimal exercise boundary of American option, then*

$$\begin{cases} S_p(t) \text{ is monotonic non-decreasing,} & \text{(put option)} \\ S_c(t) \text{ is monotonic non-increasing,} & \text{(call option)} \end{cases}$$

and for put option there are estimates as follows

$$S_{p,\infty} \le S_p(t) \le \min\left\{K, \frac{rK}{q}\right\}, \tag{6.5.5}$$

and for call option there are estiamtes as follows

$$\max\left\{K, \frac{rK}{q}\right\} \le S_c(t) \le S_{c,\infty}. \tag{6.5.6}$$

Here $S_{p,\infty}$ and $S_{c,\infty}$ are the optimal exercise boundary for the perpetual American put and call options, respectively. They have explicit expressions (6.1.27),(6.1.46) and (6.1.25).

Proof According to American call-put symmetry, we only need to prove for the case of American put option.

In fact, suppose $S(t)$ is not monotonic non-decreasing, (for simplicity of writing, we omit the subscript p, i.e. $S_p(t), S_{p,\infty}$ will be written as $S(t)$ and S_∞, respectively) i.e. there exists $0 \le t_1 \le t_2 \le T$, such that

$$S(t_1) > S(t_2).$$

Then at $t = t_2$,

$$\{0 \le S \le S(t_2), t = t_2\} \text{ belong to the stopping region } \Sigma_2,$$

$$\{S(t_2) \le S < \infty, t = t_2\} \text{ belong to the continuation region } \Sigma_1.$$

In particular $(S(t_1), t_2) \in \Sigma_1$, i.e.

$$V(S(t_1), t_2) > (K - S(t_1))^+.$$

But since $(S(t_1), t_1) \in \Gamma$, i.e.

$$V(S(t_1), t_1) = (K - S(t_1))^+,$$

thus we conclude: when $t_2 > t_1$

$$V(S(t_1), t_2) > V(S(t_1), t_1).$$

This contradicts to (6.4.29). Thus we have proved for American put option that the optimal exercise boundary $S = S(t)$ must be a monotonic non-decreasing function of t.

Due to the monotonicity of $S(t)$, when $0 \le t \le T$, there is

$$S(t) \le S(T) = \min\left\{K, \frac{rK}{q}\right\}. \tag{6.5.7}$$

Now let us prove the lower bound of $S(t)$.

Since American option price as a function of the expiration date T is monotone increasing (see (6.4.30)), financially, among all American options with the same strike price K, the perpetual American option is the most expensive, because it includes all the exercise opportunities that other American options have, i.e.

$$V(S,t;T) \leq V(S;\infty), \tag{6.5.8}$$

where $V(\cdot;T)$ denotes the price of American option with lifetime $T(0 < T \leq \infty)$.

Let S_∞ be the optimal exercise boundary of the perpetual American put option, so that when $0 \leq S \leq S_\infty$, there is

$$V(S,t;T) \leq V(S;\infty) = (K-S)^+.$$

By the arbitrage-free principle,

$$V(S,t;T) \geq (K-S)^+,$$

thus when $0 \leq S \leq S_\infty$

$$V(S,t;T) = (K-S)^+.$$

This indicates region $\{0 \leq S \leq S_\infty, 0 \leq t \leq T\} \subset \Sigma_2$(the stopping region), thus for all $t \in [0,T]$, there is

$$S(t) > S_\infty. \tag{6.5.9}$$

Q.E.D.

Remark *When $q = 0$, the optimal exercise boundary of American put option $\Gamma : S = S(t)$ is a convex curve, i.e. $S''(t) \geq 0$([8]).* The proof of this conclusion is not elementary and is thus omitted.

From Theorem 6.12, Theorem 6.13 and the above remark, although we do not have a quantitative expression of the optimal exercise boundary, we do have a basic understanding of its picture.

For American put option ($q \geq 0$)

(for $q = 0$, the convexity is proved)

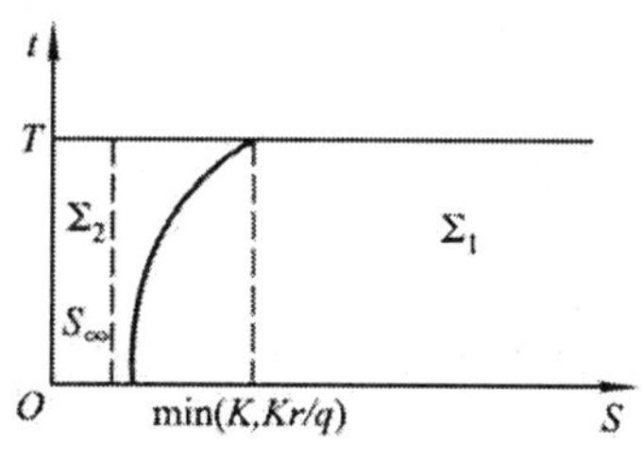

For American call option($q > 0$)

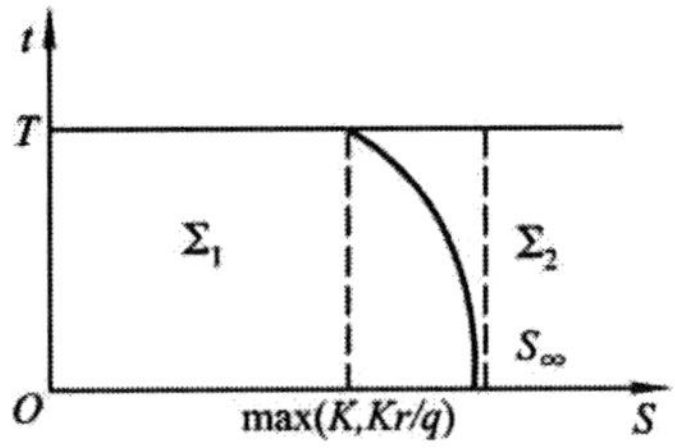

Now we need to find an approximate expression of the optimal exercise boundary, i.e. a quantitatively description of the optimal exercise boundary.

(A) Case $q < r$.

Theorem 6.14 *When $0 < T - t \ll 1$, for American put option's optimal exercise boundary $S = S(t)$, the following asymptotic expression holds*

$$\frac{K - S(t)}{K} \approx \sigma\sqrt{(T-t)|\ln(T-t)|}. \tag{6.5.10}$$

For simplicity we prove the theorem in the case of $q = 0$ only, since other cases can be treated similarly. Although the proof of the theorem is lengthy, the idea behind the proof is clear.

First, define a level curve $S = \hat{S}(t)$, which is the solution of the following functional equation:

$$V_E(\hat{S}(t), t) = K - \hat{S}(t), \tag{6.5.11}$$

i.e. $S = \hat{S}(t)$ is a curve on which the European put option price equals the exercise payoff. Since (see §5.8)

$$\frac{\partial V_E}{\partial S} = -\left[1 - N(\hat{d}_1)\right],$$

thus

$$\frac{\partial}{\partial S}[V_E - (K - S)] = N(\hat{d}_1) > 0$$

thus according to the implicit function theorem , the functional equation (6.5.11) has a unique solution $S = \hat{S}(t)$, which belongs to $C^{\infty}_{[0,T)}$, and $\hat{S}(T) = K$.

Lemma 6.4 *When* $0 \le t \le T$,

$$0 \le \hat{S}(t) - S(t) \le C(T-t)^{\frac{1}{2}}. \tag{6.5.12}$$

Before we prove the lemma, let us first look at its meaning. In fact, (6.5.12) leads to

$$\begin{aligned}\frac{K - S(t)}{K} &= \frac{K - \hat{S}(t)}{K} + \frac{\hat{S}(t) - S(t)}{K} \\ &\le \frac{K - \hat{S}(t)}{K} + \frac{C}{K}(T-t)^{\frac{1}{2}}.\end{aligned}$$

Therefore, the term at the right side of the asymptotic expression (6.5.10) comes mainly from $\dfrac{K - \hat{S}(t)}{K}$, where $\hat{S}(t)$ is a definite function to be determined by equation (6.5.11). Thus the proof of Theorem 6.14 is reduced to a rather elementary calculus problem.

Proof of Lemma 6.4 From (6.3.16) (where $q = 0$) we know: in domain $\Sigma : \{0 \le S < \infty, 0 \le t < T\}$

$$V(S,t) > V_E(S,t),$$

Thus on the curve $S = \hat{S}(t)$,

$$V(\hat{S}(t),t) > V_E(\hat{S}(t),t) = K - \hat{S}(t),$$

i.e. $S = \hat{S}(t)$ is in the continuation region Σ_1. Therefore,

$$S(t) < \hat{S}(t). \quad \forall t \in [0,T].$$

By the Taylor formula:

$$\begin{aligned}V(\hat{S}(t),t) &= V(S(t),t) + \frac{\partial V(S(t),t)}{\partial S}(\hat{S}(t) - S(t)) \\ &\quad + \frac{1}{2}\frac{\partial^2 V}{\partial S^2}\bigg|_{S=\xi}(\hat{S}(t) - S(t))^2,\end{aligned}$$

where $\xi \in (S(t), \hat{S}(t))$. By the free boundary conditions (6.2.3),(6.2.4), we get

$$\begin{aligned} V(\hat{S}(t),t) &= K - S(t) - (\hat{S}(t) - S(t)) \\ &\quad + \frac{1}{2}\frac{\partial^2 V}{\partial S^2}\bigg|_{S=\xi}(\hat{S}(t) - S(t))^2 \\ &= K - \hat{S}(t) + \frac{1}{2}\frac{\partial^2 V}{\partial S^2}\bigg|_{S=\xi}(\hat{S}(t) - S(t))^2. \end{aligned}$$

By (6.5.11) and (6.4.29),

$$\begin{aligned} V(\hat{S}(t),t) - V_E(\hat{S}(t),t) &= \frac{1}{2}\frac{\partial^2 V}{\partial S^2}\bigg|_{S=\xi}(\hat{S}(t) - S(t))^2 \\ &= \frac{[\hat{S}(t),t) - S(t)]^2}{\sigma^2\xi^2}\left[rV - \frac{\partial V}{\partial t} - rS\frac{\partial V}{\partial S}\right]_{S=\xi} \\ &\geq -[\hat{S}(t) - S(t)]^2]\,\frac{r}{\sigma^2\xi}\frac{\partial V}{\partial S}\bigg|_{S=\xi}. \end{aligned} \tag{6.5.13}$$

It is easy to check $u = \frac{\partial V}{\partial S}$ satisfies the following PDE problem in Σ_1:

$$\begin{cases} \frac{\partial u}{\partial t} + \frac{\sigma^2}{2}S^2\frac{\partial^2 u}{\partial S^2} + (r + \sigma^2)S\frac{\partial u}{\partial S} = 0, & (6.5.14) \\ u|_{t=T} = 0, & (6.5.15) \\ u|_{S=S(t)} = -1. & (6.5.16) \end{cases}$$

Let $u_E = \frac{\partial V_E}{\partial S}$, then in Σ_1, $u_E(S,t)$ also satisfies the same equation (6.5.14) and the terminal condition (6.5.15), but on $S = S(t)$ it satisfies the boundary condition

$$u_E|_{S=S(t)} = \frac{\partial V_E(S(t),t)}{\partial S}.$$

Since

$$\frac{\partial V_E(S(t),t)}{\partial S} \geq -1,$$

applying the maximum principle to the function $u_E - u$ in Σ_1, we get

$$u_E - u \geq 0,$$

i.e. in Σ_1,

$$\frac{\partial V}{\partial S} \leq \frac{\partial V_E}{\partial S}.$$

Substituting it into (6.5.13), we get

$$\begin{aligned} V(\hat{S}(t), t) - V_E(\hat{S}(t), t) &\geq -[\hat{S}(t) - S(t)]^2 \frac{r}{\sigma^2 \xi} \frac{\partial V_E}{\partial S}\bigg|_{S=\xi} \\ &= [\hat{S}(t) - S(t)]^2 \frac{r}{\sigma^2 \sqrt{2\pi}} \int_{d_1(\xi)}^{\infty} e^{-\frac{\alpha^2}{2}} d\alpha, \end{aligned} \tag{6.5.17}$$

where

$$d_1(\xi) = \frac{\ln \frac{\xi}{K} + (r + \frac{\sigma^2}{2})(T-t)}{\sigma\sqrt{T-t}}.$$

Since $\xi \in (S(t), \hat{S}(t))$, thus $\xi < K$, i.e.

$$d_1(\xi) \leq \frac{1}{\sigma}(r + \frac{\sigma^2}{2})\sqrt{T-t}.$$

Therefore, when $0 < T - t \ll 1$,

$$\frac{1}{\sqrt{2\pi}} \int_{d_1(\xi)}^{\infty} e^{-\frac{\alpha^2}{2}} d\alpha \geq \frac{1}{2\sqrt{2\pi}} \int_0^{\infty} e^{-\frac{\alpha^2}{2}} d\alpha = \frac{1}{4}.$$

Substituting it into (6.5.17), and by (6.3.16), we get

$$\begin{aligned} 0 &\leq \hat{S}(t) - S(t) \\ &\leq 2\sigma\sqrt{\frac{K}{r}}[V(\hat{S}(t), t) - V_E(\hat{S}(t), t)]^{\frac{1}{2}} \\ &\leq C(T-t)^{\frac{1}{2}}. \end{aligned}$$

Q.E.D.

In order to prove: when $0 < T - t \ll 1$,

$$\frac{K - \hat{S}(t)}{K} \approx \sigma\sqrt{(T-t)|\ln(T-t)|} \tag{6.5.18}$$

is true, let us review the functional equation (6.5.11) for $\hat{S}(t)$. With the expression of $V_E(S,t)$ (the Black-Scholes formula), (6.5.11) can be written as

$$K - \hat{S}(t) = Ke^{-r(T-t)}(1 - N(d_2)) - \hat{S}(t)(1 - N(d_1)),$$

i.e.

$$e^{-r(T-t)} - 1 = e^{\ln \frac{\hat{S}(t)}{K} + r(T-t)} N(d_1) - N(d_2), \tag{6.5.19}$$

where

$$d_1 = \frac{\ln \frac{\hat{S}(t)}{K} + (r + \frac{\sigma^2}{2})(T-t)}{\sigma\sqrt{T-t}},$$

$$d_2 = \frac{\ln \frac{\hat{S}(t)}{K} + (r - \frac{\sigma^2}{2})(T-t)}{\sigma\sqrt{T-t}}.$$

Let

$$\hat{y}(t) = \frac{1}{\sigma\sqrt{T-t}} \ln \frac{\hat{S}(t)}{K},$$

then (6.5.19) can be written as

$$\begin{aligned} 1 - e^{r(T-t)} &= N(\hat{y}(t) + (\frac{r}{\sigma} - \frac{\sigma}{2})\sqrt{T-t}) \\ &\quad - e^{\sigma\hat{y}(t)\sqrt{T-t} + r(T-t)} N(\hat{y}(t) + (\frac{r}{\sigma} + \frac{\sigma}{2})\sqrt{T-t}). \end{aligned} \tag{6.5.20}$$

Since $\hat{S}(t) < K$, therefore

$$\begin{aligned} 0 \geq \sigma\sqrt{T-t}\hat{y}(t) &= \ln \frac{\hat{S}(t)}{K} \\ &= \ln \left[1 - \frac{K - \hat{S}(t)}{K}\right] \\ &= -\frac{K - \hat{S}(t)}{K} + O(|K - \hat{S}(t)|^2). \end{aligned}$$

In order to prove (6.5.18), we only need to prove: as $0 < T - t \ll 1$, there exists the following asymptotic expansion for $\hat{y}(t)$,

$$\hat{y}(t) \approx -\sqrt{|\ln(T-t)|}. \tag{6.5.21}$$

For this, we need the following lemma.

Lemma 6.5 *Let $\tau = T - t$, then*

$$\lim_{\tau \to 0} \hat{y}(\tau) = -\infty. \tag{6.5.22}$$

Proof For simplicity of discussion, let us assume

$$\lim_{\tau \to 0} \hat{y}(\tau) = \beta$$

(In general, the limit can be replaced by its upper limit). Note that equation (6.5.20) can be rewritten as

$$\frac{1}{\sqrt{\tau}}(1 - e^{r\tau}) = \frac{1}{\sqrt{2\pi\tau}} \int_{\hat{y}+(\frac{r}{\sigma}+\frac{\sigma}{2})\sqrt{\tau}}^{\hat{y}+(\frac{r}{\sigma}-\frac{\sigma}{2})\sqrt{\tau}} e^{-\frac{\alpha^2}{2}} d\alpha$$

$$+ \frac{1}{\sqrt{2\pi\tau}}(1 - e^{r\tau+\sigma\sqrt{\tau}\hat{y}}) \int_{-\infty}^{\hat{y}+(\frac{r}{\sigma}+\frac{\sigma}{2})\sqrt{\tau}} e^{-\frac{\alpha^2}{2}} d\alpha.$$

Let $\tau \to 0$, we get

$$\frac{\sigma}{\sqrt{2\pi}} e^{-\frac{\beta^2}{2}} + \sigma\beta N(\beta) = 0.$$

It is easy to see, the above equation has a single root: $\beta = -\infty$. Q.E.D.

Lemma 6.6 *Let $\tau = T - t$, then*

$$\lim_{\tau \to 0} \sqrt{\tau}\hat{y}(\tau) = 0. \tag{6.5.23}$$

Proof (6.5.23) is verified by the definition of $\hat{y}(\tau)$ and $S(T) = K$ directly.

Now we can prove the asymptotic expression (6.5.21).

Lemma 6.7 *When $0 < T - t \ll 1$,*

$$\hat{y}(t) \approx -\sqrt{|\ln(T - t)|}. \tag{6.5.24}$$

Proof Since

$$N(\hat{y}(t) + (\frac{r}{\sigma} \pm \frac{\sigma}{2})\sqrt{T - t})$$

$$= N(\hat{y}) + N'(\hat{y})(\frac{r}{\sigma} \pm \frac{\sigma}{2})\sqrt{T - t} + R_{\pm}, \tag{6.5.25}$$

where

$$R_{\pm} = \frac{1}{2}N''(\hat{y} + \theta_{\pm}\sqrt{T-t})(\frac{r}{\sigma} \pm \frac{\sigma}{2})^2(T-t),$$

where

$$|\theta_{\pm}| \leq \frac{r}{\sigma} + \frac{\sigma}{2},$$

thus

$$\begin{aligned}|R_{\pm}| &\leq C(T-t) \max_{|\theta| \leq \frac{r}{\sigma} + \frac{\sigma}{2}} N''(\hat{y} + \theta\sqrt{T-t}) \\ &= C(T-t) \max_{|\theta| \leq \frac{r}{\sigma} + \frac{\sigma}{2}} |\hat{y} + \theta\sqrt{T-t}|e^{-\frac{|\hat{y}+\theta\sqrt{T-t}|^2}{2}}.\end{aligned}$$

Due to (6.5.22), thus

$$|R_{\pm}| = o(T-t). \tag{6.5.26}$$

Substituting (6.5.25),(6.5.26) into (6.5.20), we get

$$\begin{aligned}&(1 - e^{\sigma\sqrt{T-t}\hat{y}+r(T-t)})N(\hat{y}) - \frac{\sigma}{2}\sqrt{T-t}(1 + e^{\sigma\sqrt{T-t}\hat{y}+r(T-t)})N'(\hat{y}) \\ = \;& -r(T-t) + o(T-t). \end{aligned} \tag{6.5.27}$$

With the asymptotic expansion of $N(x)$ at $x = -\infty$

$$N(x) = \frac{1}{\sqrt{2\pi}}e^{-\frac{x^2}{2}}\left[-\frac{1}{x} + \frac{1}{x^3} + O(\frac{1}{x^5})\right], \tag{6.5.28}$$

and by Lemma 6.6, we get

$$\begin{aligned}1 - e^{\sigma\sqrt{T-t}\hat{y}+r(T-t)} =& -(\sigma\sqrt{T-t}\hat{y} + \frac{1}{2}\sigma(T-t)\hat{y}^2 \\ &+ O((T-t) + (\sqrt{T-t}|\hat{y}|)^3).\end{aligned} \tag{6.5.29}$$

Substituting (6.5.28),(6.5.29) into (6.5.27), and neglecting higher order terms of $T-t$, we get

$$-e^{-\frac{\hat{y}^2}{2}}\left[1 + O\left(\frac{1}{\hat{y}^2} + \frac{1}{2}\sqrt{T-t}\hat{y}\right)\right] = -\frac{\sqrt{2\pi}}{\sigma}r\sqrt{T-t} + o(\sqrt{T-t}),$$

i.e.

$$e^{-\frac{\hat{y}^2}{2}} = \frac{\sqrt{2\pi}}{\sigma} r\sqrt{T-t} + o(\sqrt{T-t}).$$

Thus we have

$$-\frac{\hat{y}^2}{2} \approx \frac{1}{2} \ln |T-t|,$$

i.e.

$$\hat{y} \approx -\sqrt{|\ln(T-t)|}.$$

Thus proves the Lemma 6.7.

By definition

$$\hat{y} = \frac{1}{\sigma\sqrt{T-t}} \ln \frac{\hat{S}(t)}{K},$$

thus

$$\frac{K - \hat{S}(t)}{K} \approx \sigma\sqrt{(T-t)|\ln(T-t)|}.$$

Then by (6.5.12), Theorem 6.14 is true.

Remark If $q = r$, then Theorem 6.14 is not true, and the asymptotic expression (6.5.10) will be replaced by

$$\frac{K - S(t)}{K} \approx \sqrt{2}\sigma\sqrt{(T-t)|\ln(T-t)|}.$$

The proof is similar. We refer the reader to [39].

(B) **Case** $q > r$.
As $q > r$,

$$S(T) = \frac{Kr}{q}. \tag{6.5.30}$$

We will prove the following asymptotic expansion for the optimal exercise boundary $S = S(t)$([13]).

Theorem 6.15 *Let $S = S(t)$ be the optimal exercise boundary of American put option, and $q > r$, then we have, as $0 < T - t \ll 1$,*

$$\frac{\frac{rK}{q} - S(t)}{\frac{rK}{q}} \approx \frac{\alpha}{\sqrt{2}}\sigma\sqrt{T-t}, \tag{6.5.31}$$

where α is the root of the following transcendental equation,

$$\alpha^3 e^{\frac{\alpha^2}{4}} \int_\alpha^\infty e^{-\frac{S^2}{4}} dS = 2(2-\alpha^2). \tag{6.5.32}$$

Proof In Σ_1 (the continuation region), American put option price satisfies the free boundary problem:

$$\begin{cases} \frac{\partial V}{\partial t} + \frac{\sigma^2}{2}S^2\frac{\partial^2 V}{\partial^2 S} + (r-q)S\frac{\partial V}{\partial S} - rV = 0, & (\Sigma_1) \\ V(S(t),t) = K - S(t), & (0 \le t \le T) \\ V_S(S(t),t) = -1, & (0 \le t \le T) \\ V(S,T) = (K-S)^+, & (\frac{rK}{q} \le S < \infty) \\ S(T) = \frac{rK}{q}, & \end{cases}$$

where $\Sigma_1 = \{(S,t)|S(t) \le S < \infty, 0 \le t \le T\}$.

Define

$$x = \ln\frac{S}{K}, \tag{6.5.34}$$

$$\tau = \frac{\sigma^2}{2}(T-t), \tag{6.5.35}$$

$$p = \frac{1}{K}(K - S - V), \tag{6.5.36}$$

$$x(\tau) = \ln\frac{S(t)}{K}, \tag{6.5.37}$$

$$x(0) = \ln\frac{r}{q}. \tag{6.5.38}$$

The new unknown function $\{p(x,\tau), x(\tau)\}$ satisfies a free boundary problem as follows:

$$\begin{cases} \dfrac{\partial p}{\partial \tau} = \dfrac{\partial^2 p}{\partial^2 x} + (k'-1)\dfrac{\partial p}{\partial x} - kp + f(x), & (\hat{\Sigma}_1) \\ p(x(\tau),\tau) = 0, & (0 \le \tau \le \hat{T}) \\ p_x(x(\tau),\tau) = 0, & (0 \le \tau \le \hat{T}) \\ p(x,0) = -(e^x - 1)^+, & (x^* \le x < \infty) \\ x(0) = x^*, \end{cases}$$

where $\hat{\Sigma}_1 = \{(x,\tau)|x(\tau) \le x < \infty, 0 \le \tau \le \hat{T}\}$,

$$\hat{T} = \frac{\sigma^2}{2}T, x^* = \ln\frac{r}{q}, \tag{6.5.39}$$

$$f(x) = (k'-k)e^x + k, \tag{6.5.40}$$

$$k = \frac{2r}{\sigma^2}, k' = \frac{2(r-q)}{\sigma^2}. \tag{6.5.41}$$

In order to obtain an asymptotic expansion of $x(\tau)$ at $\tau = 0$, let us observe the behavior of the solution $\{p(x,\tau), x(\tau)\}$ near $(x^*, 0)$.

By (6.5.40),(6.5.41), $f(x)$ has asymptotic expansion at $x = x^*$:

$$\begin{aligned} f(x) &= f(x^*) + f'(x^*)(x-x^*) + O(|x-x^*|^2) \\ &= \left[(k'-k)e^{x^*} + k\right] + (k'-k)e^{x^*}(x-x^*) + O(|x-x^*|^2) \\ &\approx -k(x-x^*). \end{aligned}$$

At $x = x^*$, since $q > r$, thus

$$p(x^*,0) = -\left(e^{x^*} - 1\right)^+ = -\left(\frac{r}{q} - 1\right)^+ = 0.$$

Therefore there exists a neighborhood of $x = x^*$, in which

$$p(x,0) = p_x(x,0) = 0.$$

Since $p(x,\tau)$ and $p_x(x,\tau)$ are continuous up to $\tau = 0$, thus near $x = x^*$, neglecting higher order terms of $|x - x^*|$, the free boundary problem can be reduced to

$$\begin{cases} \dfrac{\partial p}{\partial \tau} = \dfrac{\partial^2 p}{\partial x^2} - k(x - x^*), & (x(\tau) \le x < \infty, \tau > 0) \quad (6.5.42) \\ p(x(\tau), \tau) = 0, & (\tau \ge 0) \quad (6.5.43) \\ p_x(x(\tau), \tau) = 0, & (\tau \ge 0) \quad (6.5.44) \\ p(x, 0) = 0, & (x^* \le x < \infty) \quad (6.5.45) \\ x(0) = x^*. \end{cases}$$

By dimensional analysis, we know this problem has a self-similar solution:

$$p(x, \tau) = \tau^{\frac{3}{2}} W(\xi), \tag{6.5.46}$$

$$x(\tau) = x^* - \alpha\sqrt{\tau}, \tag{6.5.47}$$

where

$$\xi = \frac{x^* - x}{\sqrt{\tau}}. \tag{6.5.48}$$

By straightforward computation,

$$\frac{\partial p}{\partial \tau} = \frac{3}{2}\tau^{\frac{1}{2}} W(\xi) - \frac{1}{2}\frac{\partial W}{\partial \xi}(x^* - x),$$

$$\frac{\partial^2 p}{\partial x^2} = \tau^{\frac{1}{2}}\frac{\partial^2 W}{\partial \xi^2}.$$

Substituting into equation (6.5.42), we get

$$\frac{3}{2}\tau^{\frac{1}{2}} W - \frac{x^* - x}{2}\frac{\partial W}{\partial \xi} = \tau^{\frac{1}{2}}\frac{\partial^2 W}{\partial \xi^2} + k(x^* - x).$$

Multiplying both sides by $\tau^{-\frac{1}{2}}$, and noticing (6.5.48), we obtain a free boundary problem for an ordinary differential equation: find $\{W(\xi), \alpha\}$ such that:

$$\begin{cases} \dfrac{\partial^2 W}{\partial \xi^2} + \dfrac{\xi}{2}\dfrac{\partial W}{\partial \xi} - \dfrac{3}{2} W = -k\xi \quad (-\infty < \xi < \alpha), & (6.5.49) \\ W(\alpha) = 0, & (6.5.50) \\ W'(\alpha) = 0. & (6.5.51) \end{cases}$$

We need to add an asymptotic condition for W at $\xi \to -\infty$. Noticing that $\xi \to -\infty$ is equivalent to $\tau \to 0, x \neq x^*$, then by (6.5.45), (6.5.46), we get

$$\begin{aligned}\lim_{\xi \to -\infty} [W(\xi) - k\xi] &= \lim_{\tau \to 0, x \neq x^*} \left[\frac{p(x,\tau)}{\tau^{3/2}} - k\frac{x^* - x}{\sqrt{\tau}}\right] \\ &= \lim_{\tau \to 0, x \neq x^*} \left[\frac{p(x,\tau) - p(x,0)}{\tau^{3/2}} - k\frac{x^* - x}{\sqrt{\tau}}\right] \\ &= \lim_{\tau \to 0, x \neq x^*} \tau^{-1/2} \left[\int_0^1 p_\tau(x, \theta\tau) d\theta - k(x^* - x)\right] \\ &= \lim_{\tau \to 0, x \neq x^*} \tau^{-1/2} \int_0^1 p_{xx}(x, \theta\tau) d\theta.\end{aligned}$$

Since $p(x, \tau)$ is the solution of the free boundary problem (6.5.42)—(6.5.45) and $p(x, \tau) \equiv 0$ as $x > x^*$, we know from the regularity theory of parabolic equations: as $x > x^*$, $p_{xx}(x, 0) = p_{xxt}(x, 0) = 0$. Therefore the limit of the right side of the above equality is 0. Thus as $\xi \to -\infty$,

$$W \sim k\xi. \tag{6.5.52}$$

Thus under the transformation (6.5.46)—(6.5.48), the free boundary problem (6.5.42)—(6.5.45) is reduced to a free boundary problem to a second order ODE (6.5.49)—(6.5.52).

Now we need to find $\{W(\xi), \alpha\}$ that satisfies the free boundary problem (6.5.49)—(6.5.52).

The non-homogeneous ODE (6.5.49) has a special solution:

$$W = k\xi,$$

and its general solution is in the form

$$\begin{aligned}W(\xi) &= k\xi + A(\xi^3 + 6\xi) \\ &\quad + B\left[(\xi^2 + 4)e^{-\frac{\xi^2}{4}} + \frac{1}{2}(\xi^3 + 6\xi)\int_{-\infty}^{\xi} e^{-\frac{S^2}{4}} dS\right].\end{aligned} \tag{6.5.53}$$

And by the boundary condition (6.5.52),

$$A = 0. \tag{6.5.54}$$

By boundary conditions (6.5.50),(6.5.51),

$$0 = k\alpha + BR(\alpha),$$

$$0 = k + BR'(\alpha),$$

i.e.

$$B[R(\alpha) - \alpha R'(\alpha)] = 0,$$

where

$$R(\xi) = (\xi^2 + 4)e^{-\frac{\xi^2}{4}} + \frac{1}{2}(\xi^3 + 6\xi)\int_{-\infty}^{\xi} e^{-\frac{S^2}{4}}dS.$$

Let α be the root of the equation $R(\alpha) - \alpha R'(\alpha) = 0$, i.e. α satisfies equation (6.5.32), then

$$B = \frac{-k\alpha}{R(\alpha)}, \tag{6.5.55}$$

Substituting (6.5.54),(6.5.55) into (6.5.53), we find

$$W(\xi) = k\xi - k\alpha\frac{R(\xi)}{R(\alpha)}.$$

Substituting this into (6.5.46),(6.5.47), we get the asymptotic expansion of $p(x, \tau)$ at $(x^*, 0)$:

$$p(x,\tau) = k\tau^{\frac{3}{2}}\left[\xi - \alpha\frac{1}{R(\alpha)}R(\frac{x^* - x}{\sqrt{\tau}})\right]$$

and

$$x(\tau) = x^* - \alpha\sqrt{\tau}.$$

Then by transformation (6.5.34)—(6.5.38), we get the asymptotic expansion of $V(S,t)$ and $S(t)$ at $(\frac{rK}{q}, T)$. This completes the proof of Theorem 6.15.

Remark By American call-put symmetry, we can obtain the expression of the optimal exercise boundary for American call option near the expiration date $t = T$, as $q < r$,

$$\frac{S(t) - \frac{rK}{q}}{\frac{rK}{q}} = \frac{\sigma}{\sqrt{2}}\alpha\sqrt{T - t},$$

where α is the root of the transcendental equation (6.5.32).

Remark By numerical computation, an approximate value of the root α of equation (6.5.32) is determined to be

$$\alpha \approx 0.9034\ldots$$

6.6 Numerical Method (I)——Finite Difference Method

American option pricing is a free boundary problem to the Black-Scholes equation. Except for the perpetual American option, in general there is no closed-form expression of the option price. Therefore numerical methods are particularly important for American option pricing. In the next two sections, we focus on the difference method and the line method. The former is based on the discretization of the variational inequality (6.2.7)—(6.2.9), and the latter is based on the discretization of the free boundary problem (6.2.2)—(6.2.6). To be specific, in the following we consider non-dividend-paying American put option only. Other cases can be treated similarly.

(A) Explicit Difference Scheme

For variational inequality (6.2.7)—(6.2.9) given in $\Sigma : \{0 \leq S < \infty, 0 \leq t \leq T\}$, make the transformation

$$x = \ln \frac{S}{K} \tag{6.6.1}$$

and

$$v(x,t) = \frac{1}{K} V(S,t). \tag{6.6.2}$$

Thus it is reduced to

$$\begin{cases} \min\{-\mathcal{L}_0 v, v - (1-e^x)^+\} = 0, \quad (x \in \mathbf{R}, 0 \leq t \leq T) & (6.6.3) \\ v(x,T) = (1-e^x)^+, \quad (x \in \mathbf{R}) & (6.6.4) \end{cases}$$

where

$$\mathcal{L}_0 v = \frac{\partial v}{\partial t} + \frac{\sigma^2}{2}\frac{\partial^2 v}{\partial x^2} + (r - \frac{\sigma^2}{2})\frac{\partial v}{\partial x} - rv. \tag{6.6.5}$$

In the region $\{x \in \mathbf{R}, 0 \leq t \leq T\}$, make a mesh

$$Q = \{(n\Delta t, j\Delta x) | 0 \leq n \leq N, j \in \mathbf{Z}\},$$

where $\mathbf{Z}$ is the set of natural numbers, $\Delta t = \frac{T}{N}, \Delta x > 0$. At each mesh point, define a function

$$v_j^n = v(j\Delta x, n\Delta t), \tag{6.6.6}$$

$$\varphi_j = \varphi(j\Delta x) = (1 - e^{j\Delta x})^+. \tag{6.6.7}$$

Let

$$\left(\frac{\partial v}{\partial t}\right)_{n+1,j} = \frac{v_j^{n+1} - v_j^n}{\Delta t},$$

$$\left(\frac{\partial v}{\partial x}\right)_{n+1,j} = \frac{v_{j+1}^{n+1} - v_{j-1}^{n+1}}{2\Delta x},$$

$$\left(\frac{\partial^2 v}{\partial x^2}\right)_{n+1,j} = \frac{v_{j+1}^{n+1} - 2v_j^{n+1} + v_{j-1}^{n+1}}{\Delta x^2}.$$

Substituting them into (6.6.3)—(6.6.4), we get the equation for the mesh point $(j\Delta x, (n+1)\Delta t)$:

$$\begin{cases} \min\left\{-\frac{v_j^{n+1} - v_j^n}{\Delta t} - \frac{\sigma^2}{2}\frac{v_{j+1}^{n+1} - 2v_j^{n+1} + v_{j-1}^{n+1}}{\Delta x^2} - (r - \frac{\sigma^2}{2})\frac{v_{j+1}^{n+1} - v_{j-1}^{n+1}}{2\Delta x} \right. \\ \left. \qquad + rv_j^n, v_j^n - \varphi_j\right\} = 0, \quad (0 \le n \le N-1, j \in \mathbf{Z}) & (6.6.8) \\ v_j^N = \varphi_j. & (6.6.9) \end{cases}$$

Due to the fact

$$\min(A, B) = 0 \Longleftrightarrow \min(\alpha A, B) = 0, \quad (\alpha > 0)$$

and

$$\min(C - A, C - B) = 0 \Longleftrightarrow C = \max(A, B),$$

thus in equation (6.6.8), let $\alpha = \Delta t$, and we get

$$\min\{(1 + r\Delta t)v_j^n - (1 - \omega)v_j^{n+1} - av_{j+1}^{n+1} - cv_{j-1}^{n+1}, v_j^n - \varphi_j\} = 0, \tag{6.6.10}$$

here

$$\omega = \frac{\sigma^2 \Delta t}{\Delta x^2},$$

$$a = \frac{\omega}{2} + \frac{\Delta t}{2\Delta x}(r - \frac{\sigma^2}{2}),$$

$$c = \omega - a.$$

Then in (6.6.8), let $\alpha = \frac{1}{1+r\Delta t}$, we get

$$\min\left\{v_j^n - \frac{1}{1+r\Delta t}\left[(1-\omega)v_j^{n+1} + av_{j+1}^{n+1} + cv_{j-1}^{n+1}\right], v_j^n - \varphi_j\right\} = 0.$$

i.e.

$$v_j^n = \max\left\{\frac{1}{1+r\Delta t}\left[(1-\omega)v_j^{n+1} + av_{j+1}^{n+1} + cv_{j-1}^{n+1}\right], \varphi_j\right\}, \quad (0 \le n \le N-1, j \in \mathbf{Z}) \tag{6.6.11}$$

Thus v_j^n can be computed in the following steps:

(1) Define φ_j by $\varphi(x) = (1 - e^x)^+$. Find the value of v_j^n at $n = N$ by (6.6.9);

(2) By (6.6.11) and backward induction, find $v_j^n (0 \le n \le N-1)$ step by step; In particular as $n = 0$, we get the American option premium.

Since this algorithm does not involve solving a set of algebraic equations, it is an **explicit difference scheme** (backward). Obviously, this algorithm is nonlinear.

Theorem 6.16(Convergence of the explicit difference scheme for American option) *If*

$$\omega = \frac{\sigma^2 \Delta t}{\Delta x^2} \le 1$$

and

$$\frac{1}{\sigma^2}\left|r - \frac{\sigma^2}{2}\right| \Delta x \le 1,$$

then the explicit difference scheme(6.6.9),(6.6.11) is convergent, i.e.

$$\lim_{\Delta t, \Delta x \to 0} v_\Delta(x,t) = v(x,t),$$

where $v_\Delta(x,t)$ is the linear interpolation of the lattice function $v(j\Delta x, n\Delta t) = v_j^n$, and $v(x,t)$ is a viscosity solution of the variational inequality (6.6.3),(6.6.4).

The definition of the viscosity solution and the proof of this result involve a lot of PDE theoretical knowledge, and will not be discussed in this book. We refer the reader to [21].

Theorem 6.17 *For American put option, the BTM and the explicit difference scheme (6.6.9),(6.6.11) of the variational inequality (6.6.3),(6.6.4) at $\omega = 1$ are equivalent.*

Proof Similar to the proof of Theorem 5.5, in the domain $\Sigma : \{0 \le S < \infty, 0 \le t \le T\}$, make a mesh

$$S_j = Ku^j, \qquad (j = 0, \pm 1, \pm 2, \dots)$$

$$t_n = n\Delta t, \qquad (n = 0, 1, \dots, N)$$

where $u > 0, \Delta t = \frac{T}{N}$. Then American option valuation formula can be written as

$$V_j^n = \max\left\{\frac{1}{\rho}[qV_{j+1}^{n+1} + (1-q)V_{j-1}^{n+1}], \Phi_j\right\}, \tag{6.6.12}$$

where

$$ud = 1,$$

$$q = \frac{\rho - d}{u - d},$$

$$\rho = 1 + r\Delta t,$$

$$\Phi_j = (K - S_j)^+.$$

Let

$$\Delta x = \ln u,$$

$$x_j = j\Delta x = j \ln u = \ln \frac{S_j}{K},$$

$$v_j^n = \frac{1}{K}V_j^n, \varphi_j = \frac{1}{K}\Phi_j.$$

Then by (5.7.18),

$$q = \frac{1}{2} + \frac{1}{2\sigma}(r - \frac{\sigma^2}{2})\sqrt{\Delta t} + O(\Delta t).$$

Neglecting higher order terms, (6.6.12) can be written as

$$v_j^n = \max\left\{\frac{1}{1+r\Delta t}\left[(\frac{1}{2}+\frac{r-\frac{\sigma^2}{2}}{2\sigma}\sqrt{\Delta t})v_{j+1}^{n+1} + (\frac{1}{2}-\frac{r-\frac{\sigma^2}{2}}{2\sigma}\sqrt{\Delta t})v_{j-1}^{n+1}\right], \varphi_j\right\}. \tag{6.6.13}$$

Comparing (6.6.11) with (6.6.13), in (6.6.11), let $\omega = 1$, i.e.

$$\frac{\sigma^2 \Delta t}{\Delta x^2} = 1,$$

then in (6.6.11), the coefficient a can be represented as

$$a = \frac{1}{2} + \frac{\Delta t}{2\Delta x}(r - \frac{\sigma^2}{2}) = \frac{1}{2} + \frac{1}{2\sigma}(r - \frac{\sigma^2}{2})\sqrt{\Delta t}.$$

Thus (6.6.13) and (6.6.11) (as $\omega = 1$) are equivalent.

From Theorem 6.17 and the convergence theorem of the explicit difference scheme of American option, we get:

Theorem 6.18(Convergence theorem of the BTM of American put option) *If* $\frac{1}{\sigma^2}\left|r - \frac{\sigma^2}{2}\right|\Delta x \le 1$, *then when* $\Delta t \to 0$, *the BTM of American put option converges to the cohesive solution of the variational inequality (6.6.3),(6.6.4).*

(B) Implicit Difference Scheme

To solve American put option pricing problem (6.6.3),(6.6.4) by implicit difference scheme, first we need to truncate the infinite mesh at $-N_1$ and N_2, $(N_1, N_2 > 0)$, and add boundary conditions on the two boundaries $\{x = -N_1, 0 \le t \le T\}$ and $\{x = N_2, 0 \le t \le T\}$.

From the properties of American option, if N_1 is sufficiently large, the boundary $\{x = -N_1, 0 \le t \le T\}$ must be in the stopping region Σ_2, hence

$$v(-N_1, t) = \varphi(-N_1), \tag{6.6.14}$$

where $\varphi(x) = (1 - e^x)^+$.

And since $v \to 0$ as $x \to \infty$, therefore if N_2 is sufficiently large, on the boundary $\{x = N_2, 0 \le t \le T\}$, there is

$$v(N_2, t) = 0. \tag{6.6.15}$$

Thus on $\{-N_1 \le x \le N_2, 0 \le t \le T\}$, $v(x,t)$ satisfies the variational inequality

$$\begin{cases} -\frac{\partial v}{\partial t} - \frac{\sigma^2}{2}\frac{\partial^2 v}{\partial x^2} - (r - \frac{\sigma^2}{2})\frac{\partial v}{\partial x} + rv \ge 0, & (6.6.16) \\ v \ge \varphi(x), & (6.6.17) \\ (-\frac{\partial v}{\partial t} - \frac{\sigma^2}{2}\frac{\partial^2 v}{\partial x^2} - (r - \frac{\sigma^2}{2})\frac{\partial v}{\partial x} + rv)(v - \varphi(x)) = 0. & (6.6.18) \end{cases}$$

In the region $\{-N_1 \le x \le N_2, 0 \le t \le T\}$ make a mesh

$$(j\Delta x, n\Delta t), \qquad (-n_1 \le j \le n_2, 0 \le n \le N)$$

where $\Delta t = \frac{T}{N}, \Delta x = \frac{N_1}{n_1} = \frac{N_2}{n_2}$. Define lattice function

$$v_j^n = v(j\Delta x, n\Delta t),$$

And discretize the variational inequality (6.6.14)—(6.6.18): let

$$\left(\frac{\partial v}{\partial t}\right)_{n,j} = \frac{v_j^{n+1} - v_j^n}{\Delta t},$$

$$\left(\frac{\partial v}{\partial x}\right)_{n,j} = \frac{v_{j+1}^n - v_{j-1}^n}{2\Delta x},$$

$$\left(\frac{\partial^2 v}{\partial x^2}\right)_{n,j} = \frac{v_{j+1}^n - 2v_j^n + v_{j-1}^n}{\Delta x^2}.$$

Thus we have

$$\begin{cases} -av_{j+1}^n + bv_j^n - cv_{j-1}^n \ge v_j^{n+1}, & (6.6.19) \\ v_j^n \ge \varphi_j, & (6.6.20) \\ \left[-av_{j+1}^n + bv_j^n - cv_{j-1}^n - v_j^{n+1}\right]\left[v_j^n - \varphi_j\right] = 0, & (6.6.21) \\ v_{-n_1}^n = \varphi_{-n_1}, & (6.6.22) \\ v_{n_2}^n = 0, & (6.6.23) \\ v_j^N = \varphi_j, & (6.6.24) \end{cases}$$

$$(-n_1+1 \le j \le n_2-1, 0 \le n \le N-1)$$

where

$$a = \frac{\omega}{2} + \frac{\omega}{2\sigma^2}(r - \frac{\sigma^2}{2})\Delta x,$$

$$c = \omega - a,$$

$$b = 1 + \omega + r\Delta t,$$

$$\omega = \frac{\sigma^2 \Delta t}{\Delta x^2},$$

$$\varphi_j = (1 - e^{j\Delta x})^+.$$

Remark It is not difficult to prove that the results of Theorem 3.5 remain valid for the scheme (6.6.19)–(6.6.24).

(6.6.19)—(6.6.21) can be rewritten in the matrix form

$$\begin{cases} \mathbf{A}\mathbf{V}^n \ge \theta^n, & (6.6.25) \\ \mathbf{V}^n \ge \mathbf{\Phi}, & (6.6.26) \\ (\mathbf{A}\mathbf{V}^n - \theta^n)_j(\mathbf{V}^n - \mathbf{\Phi})_j = 0, \quad (-n_1+1 \le j \le n_2-1) & (6.6.27) \end{cases}$$

where

$$\mathbf{A} = \begin{bmatrix} b & -c & & & 0 \\ -a & b & -c & & \\ & \ddots & \ddots & \ddots & \\ & & -a & b & -c \\ 0 & & & -a & b \end{bmatrix},$$

$$\mathbf{V}^n = \begin{bmatrix} v_{n_2-1}^n \\ \vdots \\ v_{-n_1+1}^n \end{bmatrix},$$

$$\theta^n = \begin{bmatrix} \theta_{n_2-1}^n \\ \vdots \\ \theta_{-n_1+1}^n \end{bmatrix},$$

$$\mathbf{\Phi} = \begin{bmatrix} \varphi_{n_2-1} \\ \vdots \\ \varphi_{-n_1+1}. \end{bmatrix},$$

where it follows from the boundary conditions (6.6.22), (6.6.23),

$$\theta^n_{n_2-1} = v^{n+1}_{n_2-1} + av^n_{n_2} = v^{n+1}_{n_2-1},$$

$$\theta^n_{-n_1+1} = v^{n+1}_{-n_1+1} + cv^n_{-n_1} = v^{n+1}_{-n_1+1} + c\varphi_{-n_1},$$

$$\theta^n_j = v^{n+1}_j. \quad (-n_1 + 2 \le j \le n_2 - 2)$$

The algorithm is as follows:
(1) Define φ_j according to $\varphi(x) = (1 - e^x)^+$. By (6.6.24)

$$v^N_j = \varphi_j. \quad (-n_1 \le j \le n_2)$$

(2) By backward induction, we solve the discrete scheme of the variational inequality (6.6.25)—(6.6.27) to find $v^n_j (0 \le n \le N-1)$ step by step.

If v^{n+1}_j is known, how can we solve the discrete scheme of the variational inequality (6.6.25)—(6.6.27) to get $v^n_j, (-n_1 + 1 \le j \le n_2 - 1)$?

We will follow the idea of the Gauss elimination method. To solve the equations, we first reduce matrix **A** to a lower triangular matrix, then solve the equations step by step. *Since it involves inequality, after each elementary operation, we must check the sign of the proportional divisors.* The solution-finding procedure goes as follows.

Let us start from the last two equations in (6.6.25):

$$-av^n_{-n_1+3} + bv^n_{-n_1+2} - cv^n_{-n_1+1} \ge \theta^n_{-n_1+2}, \tag{6.6.28}$$

$$-av^n_{-n_1+2} + bv^n_{-n_1+1} \ge \theta^n_{-n_1+1}. \tag{6.6.29}$$

Let Δx be sufficiently small, such that

$$1 - \frac{1}{\sigma^2}\left|r - \frac{\sigma^2}{2}\right|\Delta x > 0,$$

thus

$$a > 0, c > 0.$$

(6.6.29) $\times \frac{c}{b}$ + (6.6.28), then (6.6.28) becomes

$$-av^n_{-n_1+3} + (b - \frac{ac}{b})v^n_{-n_1+2} \geq \theta^n_{-n_1+2} + \frac{c}{b}\theta^n_{-n_1+1}. \quad (6.6.30)$$

Since $\frac{c}{b} > 0$, therefore under above elementary operations, the sign of the inequality is preserved. Denote

$$b_{-n_1+2} = b - \frac{ac}{b}.$$

Thus (6.6.30) can be written as

$$-av^n_{-n_1+3} + b_{-n_1+2}v^n_{-n_1+2} \geq \hat{\theta}^n_{-n_1+2}, \quad (6.6.31)$$

where $\hat{\theta}_{-n_1+2}$ represents the right side of the inequality (6.6.30).

In order to repeat the above procedures, we need to make sure that b_{-n_1+2} is positive. In fact

$$b_{-n_1+2} = \frac{1}{b}(b^2 - ac) > \frac{1}{b}\left[(1+\omega)^2 - \frac{\omega^2}{4}\right] > 0.$$

Then combine the 3rd-to-the-last equation in (6.6.25) with (6.6.31). And repeat the procedure in a similar way. In general, use above elementary operation to obtain the inequality :

$$-av^n_{k+1} + b_k v^n_k \geq \hat{\theta}^n_k \quad (6.6.32)$$

and as will be verified soon,

$$b_k > 0.$$

Then combine it with the $n_1 + k + 1$-to-the-last equation in (6.6.25), i.e. consider the inequality (6.6.32) and

$$-av^n_{k+2} + bv^n_{k+1} - cv^n_k \geq \theta^n_{k+1}. \quad (6.6.33)$$

(6.6.32) $\times \frac{c}{b_k}$ + (6.6.33), we get

$$-av^n_{k+2} + (b - \frac{ac}{b_k})v^n_{k+1} \geq \hat{\theta}_{k+1}$$

(here we make use of $\frac{c}{b_k} > 0$), where

$$\hat{\theta}^n_{k+1} = \theta^n_{k+1} + \frac{c}{b_k}\hat{\theta}^n_k.$$

Denote

$$b_{k+1} = b - \frac{ac}{b_k},$$

If we can prove all B_m defined by

$$B_{m+1} = b - \frac{ac}{B_m} \qquad (1 \le m \le M) \tag{6.6.34}$$

and

$$B_1 = b \tag{6.6.35}$$

are positive, in view of the the same results as mentioned in Theorem 3.5, then we can conclude: the discrete scheme of the variational inequality (6.6.25)—(6.6.27) is equivalent to the variational inequality

$$\begin{cases} \tilde{\mathbf{A}}\mathbf{V}^n \ge \hat{\theta}^n, & (6.6.36) \\ \mathbf{V}^n \ge \mathbf{\Phi}, & (6.6.37) \\ (\tilde{\mathbf{A}}\mathbf{V}^n - \hat{\theta}^n)_j(\mathbf{V}^n - \mathbf{\Phi})_j = 0, \quad (-n_1 + 1 \le j \le n_2 - 1) & (6.6.38) \end{cases}$$

where $\tilde{\mathbf{A}}$ is the lower triangular matrix

$$\tilde{\mathbf{A}} = \begin{bmatrix} b_{n_2-1} & & & 0 \\ -a & \ddots & & \\ & \ddots & \ddots & \\ 0 & & -a & b_{-n_1+1} \end{bmatrix}, \tag{6.6.39}$$

$$\hat{\theta}^n = \begin{bmatrix} \hat{\theta}^n_{n_2-1} \\ \vdots \\ \hat{\theta}^n_{-n_1+1} \end{bmatrix}$$

Lemma 6.8 *If $b^2 - 4ac > 0$, then equations (6.6.34),(6.6.35) have the following solution:*

$$B_m = \frac{J_m}{J_{m-1}}, \qquad (2 \le m \le M) \tag{6.6.40}$$

where

$$J_1 = b, \tag{6.6.41}$$

$$J_m = \sum_{i=0}^{m} (\alpha_+)^{m-i}(\alpha_-)^i, \qquad (m \geq 2) \tag{6.6.42}$$

and

$$\alpha_\pm = \frac{b \pm \sqrt{b^2 - 4ac}}{2}. \tag{6.6.43}$$

Proof Multiplying the difference equation (6.6.34) by B_m, we get

$$B_{m+1}B_m = bB_m - ac. \qquad (m \geq 1)$$

Then multiplying both sides by $B_{m-1} \dots B_1$, and from (6.6.40),(6.6.41) and (6.6.35), we obtain the difference equation for $J_m = \prod_{i=1}^{m} B_i$:

$$J_{m+1} - bJ_m + acJ_{m-1} = 0, \qquad (m \geq 2) \tag{6.6.44}$$

with the initial conditions

$$J_1 = b, \tag{6.6.45}$$

$$J_2 = J_1 B_2 = b(b - \frac{ac}{b}) = b^2 - ac. \tag{6.6.46}$$

In order to solve the difference equation (6.6.44) under the initial conditions (6.6.45),(6.6.46), let

$$J_m = \xi^m.$$

Substituting it into (6.6.44), we get

$$\xi^2 - b\xi + ac = 0.$$

This quadratic equation is called the characteristic equation of the difference equation (6.6.44). The two roots are

$$\xi = \alpha_\pm = \frac{b \pm \sqrt{b^2 - 4ac}}{2}.$$

Thus the general solution of (6.6.44) has the form

$$J_m = A(\alpha_+)^m + B(\alpha_-)^m. \tag{6.6.47}$$

Applying initial conditions (6.6.45),(6.6.46), we get

$$\alpha_+ A + \alpha_- B = b,$$

$$\alpha_+^2 A + \alpha_-^2 B = b^2 - ac.$$

And solve them to determine

$$A = \frac{\alpha_+}{\sqrt{b^2 - 4ac}},$$

$$B = \frac{-\alpha_-}{\sqrt{b^2 - 4ac}}.$$

Substituting them into (6.6.47), we get

$$\begin{aligned} J_m &= \frac{1}{\sqrt{b^2 - 4ac}} \left[(\alpha_+)^{m+1} - (\alpha_-)^{m+1}\right] \\ &= \frac{\alpha_+ - \alpha_-}{\sqrt{b^2 - 4ac}} \sum_{i=0}^{m} (\alpha_+)^{m-i} \alpha_-^i \\ &= \sum_{i=0}^{m} (\alpha_+)^{m-i} \alpha_-^i . \end{aligned}$$

Thus (6.6.42) is proved. And by definition of J_m,

$$B_m = \frac{J_m}{J_{m-1}}. \qquad (m \geq 2)$$

Thus proves the lemma.

Now let us check the condition of Lemma 6.8

$$b^2 - 4ac > 0.$$

By definition,

$$\begin{aligned} b &= 1 + \omega + r\Delta t, \\ a &= \frac{\omega}{2} + \beta\sqrt{\Delta t}, \\ c &= \frac{\omega}{2} - \beta\sqrt{\Delta t}. \end{aligned}$$

Thus the condition is

$$b^2 - 4ac = (1 + \omega + r\Delta t)^2 - 4\left(\frac{\omega^2}{4} - \beta^2 \Delta t\right) > 0,$$

where

$$\beta = \frac{\sqrt{\omega}}{2\sigma}(r - \frac{\sigma^2}{2}),$$

$$\omega = \frac{\sigma^2 \Delta t}{\Delta x^2}.$$

Since

$$\alpha_- = \frac{ac}{\alpha_+} = \frac{\omega^2}{4\alpha_+}\left[1 - \frac{\Delta x^2}{\sigma^4}(r - \frac{\sigma^2}{2})^2\right],$$

Thus if

$$1 - \frac{\Delta x}{\sigma^2}\left|r - \frac{\sigma^2}{2}\right| \geq 0,$$

then

$$\alpha_+ > \alpha_- \geq 0,$$

and by (6.6.41),(6.6.42), we have

$$J_m > 0, \qquad (1 \leq m \leq M)$$

and

$$B_m = \frac{J_m}{J_{m-1}}. \qquad (2 \leq m \leq M)$$

Thus we have proved: all elements b_k $(-n_1 + 1 \leq k \leq n_2 - 1)$ on the main diagonal of the lower triangular matrix $\tilde{\mathbf{A}}$ are positive.

Theorem 6.19 *The discrete scheme of the variational inequality (6.6.36)—(6.6.38) has solution*

$$v^n_{n_2-1} = \max\left\{\frac{1}{b_{n_2-1}}\hat{\theta}^n_{n_2-1}, \varphi_{n_2-1}\right\}, \qquad (6.6.48)$$

$$v^n_j = \max\left\{\frac{1}{b_j}[\hat{\theta}^n_j + av^n_{j+1}], \varphi_j\right\}, \quad (-n_1 + 1 \leq j \leq n_2 - 2). \qquad (6.6.49)$$

Proof Let us first examine the first row of (6.6.36)—(6.6.38), i.e. for $j = n_2 - 1$ case:

$$\begin{cases} b_{n_2-1}v_{n_2-1}^n \geq \hat{\theta}_{n_2-1}^n, \\ v_{n_2-1}^n \geq \varphi_{n_2-1}, \\ (b_{n_2-1}v_{n_2-1}^n - \hat{\theta}_{n_2-1}^n)(v_{n_2-1}^n - \varphi_{n_2-1}) = 0. \end{cases}$$

Rewrite them in the following form

$$\min\{v_{n_2-1}^n - \frac{1}{b_{n_2-1}}\hat{\theta}_{n_2-1}^n, v_{n_2-1}^n - \varphi_{n_2-1}\} = 0,$$

then the solution can be expressed as follows:

$$v_{n_2-1}^n = \max\left\{\frac{1}{b_{n_2-1}}\hat{\theta}_{n_2-1}^n, \varphi_{n_2-1}\right\}.$$

Substituting this result into the 2nd row of (6.6.36)—(6.6.38), i.e. for the case $j = n_2 - 2$, similarly, we get:

$$\min\{-av_{n_2-1}^n + b_{n_2-2}v_{n_2-2}^n - \hat{\theta}_{n_2-2}^n, v_{n_2-2}^n - \varphi_{n_2-2}\} = 0.$$

Since $v_{n_2-1}^n$ has been found, thus we have

$$v_{n_2-2}^n = \max\left\{\frac{1}{b_{n_2-2}}[\hat{\theta}_{n_2-2}^n + av_{n_2-1}^n], \varphi_{n_2-2}\right\}.$$

Repeating the procedure, and using backward induction, we can obtain (6.6.48),(6.6.49). Thus proves the theorem.

If $1 - \frac{1}{\sigma}(r - \frac{\sigma^2}{2})\sqrt{\Delta t} > 0$, we can similarly prove the convergence of the approximate solution obtained by the implicit difference scheme, when $\Delta t, \Delta x \to 0$. In contrast to the explicit difference scheme, we do not need to assume $\omega = \dfrac{\sigma^2 \Delta x^2}{\Delta t} \leq 1$.

6.7 Numerical Methods(II)——Line Method

Consider non-dividend-paying American put option modeled as a free boundary problem, i.e. to find $\{V(S,t), S(t)\}$, such that in region Σ_1 : $\{S(t) \leq S < \infty, 0 \leq t \leq T\}$ they satisfy the following free boundary problem:

$$\begin{cases} \frac{\partial V}{\partial t} + \frac{\sigma^2}{2} S^2 \frac{\partial^2 V}{\partial S^2} + rS\frac{\partial V}{\partial S} - rV = 0, \qquad (\Sigma) & (6.7.1) \\ V(S(t),t) = K - S(t), & (6.7.2) \\ V_S(S(t),t) = -1, & (6.7.3) \\ V(S,T) = (K-S)^+, & (6.7.4) \\ V(S,t) \to 0, \qquad (S \to \infty) & (6.7.5) \\ S(T) = K. & (6.7.6) \end{cases}$$

Since obviously we can normalize the strike price K by transformation $\hat{S} = \frac{S}{K}, \hat{V} = \frac{V}{K}, \hat{S}(t) = \frac{S(t)}{K}$, without loss of generality, we can assume $K = 1$.

Divide $[0,T]$ into N equal intervals:

$$0 = t_0 < t_1 < \cdots < t_N = T,$$

$$t_n = n\Delta t, \Delta t = \frac{T}{N}.$$

At each line $t = t_n$, define

$$V_n(S) = V(S, t_n) \text{ and } S_n = S(t_n),$$

so that they satisfy a system of free boundary problems obtained by discretizing (6.7.1)—(6.7.6) in time t, i.e. to find $\{V_n(S), S_n\}, (n = 0, 1, \ldots, N)$, so that

$$\begin{cases} \frac{V_{n+1}(S) - V_n(S)}{\Delta t} + \frac{\sigma^2}{2} S^2 \frac{d^2 V_n}{dS^2} + rS\frac{dV_n}{dS} - rV_n = 0, & (6.7.7) \\ \qquad (S_n \le S < \infty) & \\ V_n(S_n) = 1 - S_n, & (6.7.8) \\ \frac{dV_n}{dS}(S_n) = -1, & (6.7.9) \\ V_n(S) \to 0, \qquad (S \to \infty) & (6.7.10) \\ V_N(S) = (1-S)^+, & (6.7.11) \\ S_N = 1, & (6.7.12) \end{cases}$$

where $0 \le n \le N-1$.

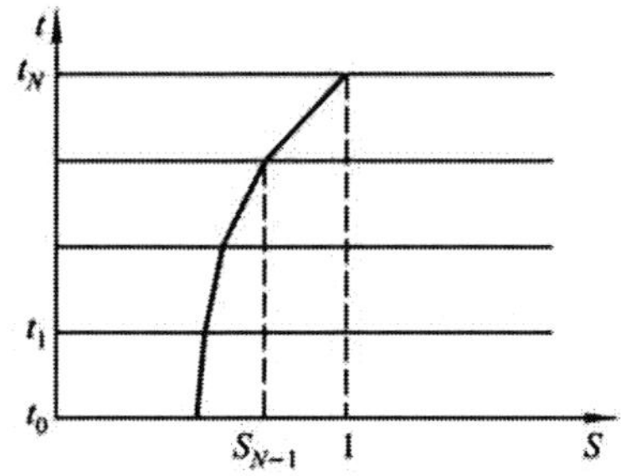

The algorithm for solving the above system of free boundary problems is as follows:

(1) Since $V_N(S) = (1-S)^+, \quad (0 \le S < \infty)$

$$S_N = 1.$$

Thus we have found the value of $\{V_n(S), S_n\}$ when $n = N$.

(2) By induction, if $\{V_{n+1}(S), S_{n+1}\}$ is given, and $S_{n+1} \le 1$, define

$$\hat{V}_{n+1}(S) = \begin{cases} V_{n+1}(S), & S_{n+1} \le S < \infty, \\ 1 - S, & 0 \le S \le S_{n+1}. \end{cases}$$

Obviously $\hat{V}_{n+1}(S) \in C^1_{[0,\infty)}$.

(3) In region $\{S_n \le S < \infty\}$, solve the following free boundary problem to second order ODE:

$$\begin{cases} \mathcal{L}_\Delta V_n = \frac{\sigma^2}{2} S^2 \frac{d^2 V_n}{dS^2} + rS\frac{dV_n}{dS} - (r + \frac{1}{\Delta t})V_n = \frac{-1}{\Delta t}\hat{V}_{n+1}(S), \quad (S_n \le S < \infty) & (6.7.13) \\ V_n(S_n) = 1 - S_n, & (6.7.14) \\ \frac{dV_n}{dS}(S_n) = -1, & (6.7.15) \\ V_n(S) \to 0, \quad (S \to \infty) & (6.7.16) \end{cases}$$

to get$\{V_n, S_n\}$. And repeat the procedure.

(4) There are many methods to solve the free boundary problem (6.7.13)—(6.7.16). For this special case, we can obtain a closed-form solution of equation (6.7.13). In the following, we will explain how to find V_n and S_n([6]) by solving the equation directly.

How can we find $V_{N-1}(S)$ and S_{N-1}? (6.7.13) is a nonhomogeneous second order ODE. First we need to find the general solution of the corresponding homogeneous equation: let

$$V_n(S) = S^\alpha.$$

Substituting it into (6.7.13), we get

$$K(\alpha) = \frac{\sigma^2}{2}\alpha(\alpha - 1) + r\alpha - (r + \frac{1}{\Delta t}) = 0. \tag{6.7.17}$$

Equation (6.7.17) is called the characteristic equation of the ODE (6.7.13). It has two roots:

$$\alpha_\pm = \gamma \pm \frac{\rho}{2},$$

where

$$\gamma = \frac{1}{2} - \frac{r}{\sigma^2},$$

$$\rho = \frac{2}{\sigma^2}\sqrt{(r + \frac{\sigma^2}{2})^2 + \frac{2\sigma^2}{\Delta t}}.$$

Thus

$$\alpha_+ > 0 > \alpha_-.$$

Thus homogeneous equation corresponding to (6.7.13) has a general solution of the form:

$$V(S) = d_1 S^{\alpha_+} + d_2 S^{\alpha_-}.$$

From properties of the optimal exercise boundary, we can assume $S_{N-1} < 1$. Then the right side of equation (6.7.13) is a piecewise polynomial, i.e. equation (6.7.13) can be written as

$$\begin{cases} \mathcal{L}_\Delta V_{N-1} = 0, & (1 \le S < \infty) \quad (6.7.18) \\ \mathcal{L}_\Delta V_{N-1} = -\frac{1}{\Delta t}(1 - S), & (S_{N-1} \le S < 1) \quad (6.7.19) \\ V_{N-1}, V'_{N-1} \text{ are continuous at } S = 1. & \quad (6.7.20) \end{cases}$$

Since the inhomogeneous equation (6.7.19) has a special solution

$$v = \frac{1}{1 + r\Delta t} - S,$$

hence the general solution of the equations (6.7.18)—(6.7.19) is

$$V_{N-1}(S) = \begin{cases} d_1^{(1)} S^{\alpha_+} + d_2^{(1)} S^{\alpha_-} + \frac{1}{1+r\Delta t} - S, & (S_{N-1} \le S \le 1) \quad (6.7.21) \\ d_1^{(2)} S^{\alpha_+} + d_2^{(2)} S^{\alpha_-}, & (1 \le S < \infty) \quad (6.7.22) \end{cases}$$

where the constants $d_i^{(m)} (i, m = 1, 2)$ and S_{N-1} are to be determined by the boundary conditions (6.7.14)—(6.7.16) and the consistency conditions (6.7.20).

By (6.7.16), we find

$$d_1^{(2)} = 0; \tag{6.7.23}$$

By (6.7.20), we find

$$d_2^{(2)} = d_1^{(1)} + d_2^{(1)} - \frac{r\Delta t}{1+r\Delta t}, \tag{6.7.24}$$

$$\alpha_- d_2^{(2)} = \alpha_+ d_1^{(1)} + \alpha_- d_2^{(1)} - 1; \tag{6.7.25}$$

By the free boundary conditions (6.7.14), (6.7.15), we get

$$d_1^{(1)} S_{N-1}^{\alpha_+} + d_2^{(1)} S_{N-1}^{\alpha_-} - \frac{r\Delta t}{1+r\Delta t} = 0, \tag{6.7.26}$$

$$\alpha_+ d_1^{(1)} S_{N-1}^{\alpha_+ - 1} + \alpha_- d_2^{(1)} S_{N-1}^{\alpha_- - 1} = 0; \tag{6.7.27}$$

By (6.7.24),(6.7.25), we find

$$d_1^{(1)} = d_2^{(2)} - d_2^{(1)} + \frac{r\Delta t}{1+r\Delta t},$$

$$\frac{\alpha_+}{\alpha_-} d_1^{(1)} = d_2^{(2)} - d_2^{(1)} + 1/\alpha_-.$$

Thus

$$d_1^{(1)} (\alpha_+ - \alpha_-)/\alpha_- = \frac{1}{\alpha_-} - \frac{r\Delta t}{1+r\Delta t},$$

i.e.

$$d_1^{(1)} = \frac{1}{\rho}(1 - \frac{r\Delta t \alpha_-}{1+r\Delta t}). \tag{6.7.28}$$

By (6.7.26) $\times \alpha_-$ − (6.7.27) $\times S_{N-1}$, we obtain the equation for the free boundary point S_{N-1}:

$$\rho S_{N-1}^{\alpha_+} d_1^{(1)} + \frac{r\Delta t \alpha_-}{1 + r\Delta t} = 0,$$

i.e.

$$(1 - \frac{r\Delta t \alpha_-}{1 + r\Delta t}) S_{N-1}^{\alpha_+} = -\frac{r\Delta t \alpha_-}{1 + r\Delta t}. \tag{6.7.29}$$

It is easy to see: $0 < S_{N-1} < 1$. Substituting $d_1^{(1)}, S_{N-1}$ into (6.7.27), we find

$$d_2^{(1)} = -\frac{\alpha_+}{\alpha_-} d_1^{(1)} S_{N-1}^{\alpha_+ - \alpha_-}. \tag{6.7.30}$$

Then substituting $d_1^{(1)}$ and $d_2^{(1)}$ into (6.7.24), we get $d_2^{(2)}$. Thus we have found $\{V_{N-1}(S), S_{N-1}\}$:

$$V_{N-1}(S) = \begin{cases} 1 - S, & (0 \le S \le S_{N-1}) \\ d_1^{(1)} S^{\alpha_+} + d_2^{(1)} S^{\alpha_-} + \frac{1}{1 + r\Delta t} - S, & (S_{N-1} \le S \le 1) \\ d_2^{(2)} S^{\alpha_-}, & (1 \le S < \infty) \end{cases}$$

where $d_1^{(1)}, d_2^{(1)}, d_2^{(2)}$ and S_{N-1} are defined in (6.7.28),(6.7.30),(6.7.23) and (6.7.29), and they can be determined by the following procedure:

$$d_1^{(2)} \to d_1^{(1)} \to S_{N-1} \to d_2^{(1)} \to d_2^{(2)}$$

Since in $[0, \infty)$, $V_{N-1}(S)$ consists of a piecewise function, therefore in order to find a special solution of the equation with this function as a nonhomogeneous term on the right side, we need the following lemma.

Lemma 6.9 *Consider the nonhomogeneous ODE:*

$$\mathcal{L}_\Delta(W) = \frac{\sigma^2}{2} S^2 \frac{d^2 W}{dS^2} + rS\frac{dW}{dS} - (r + \frac{1}{\Delta t})W = S^\omega \frac{1}{\Delta t} \tag{6.7.31}$$

where ω is the single root of the characteristic equation (6.7.17), i.e.

$$K(\omega) = \frac{\sigma^2}{2}\omega(\omega - 1) + r\omega - (r + \frac{1}{\Delta t}) = 0, \tag{6.7.32}$$

$$K'(\omega) \neq 0;$$

Then the equation (6.7.31) has a special solution

$$W(S) = \frac{1}{\Delta t K'(\omega)} S^{\omega} \ln S.$$

Proof Substituting the expression of W into equation (6.7.31), we get

$$\begin{aligned}
\mathcal{L}_{\Delta} W &= \frac{1}{\Delta t K'(\omega)} \left[\left(\frac{\sigma^2}{2}\omega(\omega-1) + r\omega - (r + \frac{1}{\Delta t})\right) S^{\omega} \ln S \right. \\
&\quad \left. + \left(\frac{\sigma^2}{2}(2\omega - 1) + r\right) S^{\omega} \right] \\
&= \frac{1}{\Delta t K'(\omega)} \left(\frac{\sigma^2}{2}(2\omega - 1) + r\right) S^{\omega} \\
&= \frac{1}{\Delta t} S^{\omega}.
\end{aligned}$$

Now we look for $\{V_{N-2}(S), S_{N-2}\}$, which satisfies

$$\begin{cases}
\mathcal{L}_{\Delta} V_{N-2} = -\frac{1}{\Delta t} d_2^{(2)} S^{\alpha_-}, \quad (1 \le S \le \infty) & (6.7.33) \\
\mathcal{L}_{\Delta} V_{N-2} = -\frac{1}{\Delta t}\left(d_1^{(1)} S^{\alpha_+} + d_2^{(1)} S^{\alpha_-}\right) - \left(\frac{1}{1 + r\Delta t} - S\right)\frac{1}{\Delta t}, & (6.7.34) \\
\qquad (S_{N-1} \le S \le 1) & \\
\mathcal{L}_{\Delta} V_{N-2} = -\frac{1}{\Delta t}(1 - S), \quad (S_{N-2} \le S \le S_{N-1}) & (6.7.35) \\
V_{N-2}, V'_{N-2} \text{ are continuous at } S = 1, & (6.7.36) \\
V_{N-2}, V'_{N-2} \text{ are continuous at } S = S_{N-1}, & (6.7.37) \\
V_{N-2}(S_{N-2}) = 1 - S_{N-2}, & (6.7.38) \\
V'_{N-2}(S_{N-2}) = -1, & (6.7.39) \\
V_{N-2}(S) \to 0. \quad (S \to \infty) & (6.7.40)
\end{cases}$$

Equation (6.7.35) has a special solution

$$W_1(S) = \frac{1}{1 + r\Delta t} - S. \tag{6.7.41}$$

And by Lemma 6.9, equations (6.7.33), (6.7.34) have special solutions

$$W_2(S) = -\frac{1}{\Delta t}\left[d_1^{(1)}\frac{1}{K'(\alpha_+)}S^{\alpha_+}\ln S + d_2^{(1)}\frac{1}{K'(\alpha_-)}S^{\alpha_-}\ln S\right]$$

$$+\frac{1}{(1+r\Delta t)^2} - S, \tag{6.7.42}$$

$$W_3(S) = -\frac{1}{\Delta t}d_2^{(2)}\frac{1}{K'(\alpha_-)}S^{\alpha_-}\ln S, \tag{6.7.43}$$

Therefore in region $\{S_{N-2} < S < \infty\}$, the general solution of equations (6.7.33)—(6.7.35) is

$$V_{N-2}(S) = \begin{cases} W_1(S) + \hat{d}_1^{(1)}S^{\alpha_+} + \hat{d}_2^{(1)}S^{\alpha_-} \ (S_{N-2} \le S \le S_{N-1}) & (6.7.44) \\ W_2(S) + \hat{d}_1^{(2)}S^{\alpha_+} + \hat{d}_2^{(2)}S^{\alpha_-} \ (S_{N-1} \le S \le 1) & (6.7.45) \\ W_3(S) + \hat{d}_1^{(3)}S^{\alpha_+} + \hat{d}_2^{(3)}S^{\alpha_-} \ (1 \le S < \infty) & (6.7.46) \end{cases}$$

The six coefficients $d_i^{(m)}(m = 1,2,3, i = 1,2)$ and the free boundary point S_{N-2} will be determined from the four consistency conditions (6.7.36), (6.7.37), two free boundary conditions (6.7.38), (6.7.39) and a condition at infinity (6.7.40).

By (6.7.40), we find

$$\hat{d}_1^{(3)} = 0. \tag{6.7.47}$$

By (6.7.36), we get

$$W_2(1) + \hat{d}_1^{(2)} + \hat{d}_2^{(2)} = W_3(1) + \hat{d}_2^{(3)}, \tag{6.7.48}$$

$$W_2'(1) + \alpha_+\hat{d}_1^{(2)} + \alpha_-\hat{d}_2^{(2)} = W_3'(1) + \alpha_-\hat{d}_2^{(3)}. \tag{6.7.49}$$

Since $W_2(1) = \dfrac{1}{(1+r\Delta t)^2} - 1, W_3(1) = 0$, thus from (6.7.48), (6.7.49), we find

$$\hat{d}_1^{(2)} = \frac{1}{\rho}\left\{\alpha_-\left[\frac{1}{(1+r\Delta t)^2} - 1\right] - [W_2'(1) - W_3'(1)]\right\}. \tag{6.7.50}$$

From (6.7.37), we get

$$W_1(S_{N-1}) + \hat{d}_1^{(1)}S_{N-1}^{\alpha_+} + \hat{d}_2^{(1)}S_{N-1}^{\alpha_-}$$
$$= W_2(S_{N-1}) + \hat{d}_1^{(2)}S_{N-1}^{\alpha_+} + \hat{d}_2^{(2)}S_{N-1}^{\alpha_-}, \tag{6.7.51}$$

$$W_1'(S_{N-1}) + \alpha_+ \hat{d}_1^{(1)} S_{N-1}^{\alpha_+ - 1} + \alpha_- \hat{d}_2^{(1)} S_{N-1}^{\alpha_- - 1}$$
$$= W_2'(S_{N-1}) + \alpha_+ \hat{d}_1^{(2)} S_{N-1}^{\alpha_+ - 1} + \alpha_- \hat{d}_2^{(2)} S_{N-1}^{\alpha_- - 1},$$

Eliminating $\hat{d}_2^{(1)}$ and $\hat{d}_2^{(2)}$, we find

$$\hat{d}_1^{(1)} = \hat{d}_1^{(2)} + \frac{\alpha_-[W_1(S_{N-1}) - W_2(S_{N-1})] - S_{N-1}[W_1'(S_{N-1}) - W_2'(S_{N-1})]}{\rho S_{N-1}^{\alpha_+}}. \tag{6.7.52}$$

By free boundary conditions (6.7.38), (6.7.39), we get

$$W_1(S_{N-2}) + \hat{d}_1^{(1)} S_{N-2}^{\alpha_+} + \hat{d}_2^{(1)} S_{N-2}^{\alpha_-} = 1 - S_{N-2},$$

$$W_1'(S_{N-2}) + \alpha_+ \hat{d}_1^{(1)} S_{N-2}^{\alpha_+ - 1} + \alpha_- \hat{d}_2^{(1)} S_{N-2}^{\alpha_- - 1} = -1. \tag{6.7.53}$$

Eliminating $\hat{d}_2^{(1)}$, and noticing $W_1(S) = \frac{1}{1 + r\Delta t} - S, W_1'(S) = -1$, we obtain the equation for S_{N-2}:

$$\hat{d}_1^{(1)} S_{N-2}^{\alpha_+} = \frac{-\alpha_-}{\rho}\left[1 - \frac{1}{1 + r\Delta t}\right]. \tag{6.7.54}$$

Substituting (6.7.50), (6.7.52) into (6.7.54), we get a transcendental equation for S_{N-2}. It is easy to see, $S_{N-2} < S_{N-1}$.

Back to (6.7.53), we can determine $\hat{d}_2^{(1)}$. Since $\hat{d}_1^{(2)}, \hat{d}_1^{(1)}, \hat{d}_2^{(1)}$ have been determined, we can find $\hat{d}_2^{(2)}$ from (6.7.51), then substituting it into (6.7.48) to determine $\hat{d}_2^{(3)}$. By now we have determined all coefficients $\hat{d}_i^{(m)} (m = 1, 2, 3, i = 1, 2)$ and S_{N-2}. The procedure goes as follows:

$$\hat{d}_1^{(3)} \to \hat{d}_1^{(2)} \to \hat{d}_1^{(1)} \to S_{N-2} \to \hat{d}_2^{(1)} \to \hat{d}_2^{(2)} \to \hat{d}_2^{(3)}.$$

Let us use the backward induction. Suppose when $t = t_{n+1}$, $V_{n+1}(S) \in C^1_{[0,\infty)}$ and $S_{n+1} (n \geq 0)$ are given. The function $V_{n+1}(S)$ can be defined in the following way. Divide $[0, \infty)$ into $N - n$ subintervals:

$$[0, S_{n+1}], \ldots, [S_{N-1}, 1], [1, \infty).$$

In $0 \leq S \leq S_{n+1}$,

$$V_{n+1}(S) = 1 - S = M_1(S);$$

In $[S_{n+1}, \infty)$, function $V_{n+1}(S)$ is defined as follows. In interval $[S_{n+j-1}, S_{n+j}]$,

$$V_{n+1}(S) = M_j(S), \quad j = 2, \ldots, N - n + 1,$$

where

$$S_N = 1,$$

$$S_{N+1} = \infty,$$

$$M_j(S) = \sum_{i=1}^{n-2} c_i^{(j)} S^{\alpha_+}(lnS)^i + \sum_{i=1}^{n-2} d_i^{(j)} S^{\alpha_-}(lnS)^i + e^{(j)}S + f^{(j)}.$$

Here $c_i^{(j)}, d_i^{(j)}, e^{(j)}, f^{(j)}$ are constants, and α_+, α_- are the roots of the characteristic equation (6.7.17). Thus in order to find the values of $V_n(S)$ and S_n at $t = t_n$, we first rewrite the free boundary problem (6.7.13)—(6.7.16) as

$$\begin{cases} \mathcal{L}_\Delta V_n = -\frac{1}{\Delta t} M_1(S), & (S_n \le S \le S_{n+1}) \quad (6.7.55) \\ \mathcal{L}_\Delta V_n = -\frac{1}{\Delta t} M_2(S), & (S_{n+1} \le S \le S_{n+2}) \quad (6.7.56) \\ \cdots\cdots & \\ \mathcal{L}_\Delta V_n = -\frac{1}{\Delta t} M_{N-n}(S), & (S_{N-1} \le S \le 1) \quad (6.7.57) \\ \mathcal{L}_\Delta V_n = -\frac{1}{\Delta t} M_{N-n+1}(S), & (1 \le S < \infty) \quad (6.7.58) \end{cases}$$

and

$$V_n(S), V_n'(S) \text{ are continuous at } S = S_{n+1}, \quad (6.7.59)$$

$$\cdots\cdots$$

$$V_n(S), V_n'(S) \text{ are continuous at } S = 1, \quad (6.7.60)$$

and

$$V_n(S_n) = 1 - S_n, \quad (6.7.61)$$

$$V_n'(S_n) = -1, \quad (6.7.62)$$

$$V_n(\infty) = 0. \quad (6.7.63)$$

$V_n(S)$ as a solution of the free boundary problem (6.7.55)—(6.7.63) can be expressed in the following form:

$$V_n(S) = \begin{cases} W_1(S) + \tilde{d}_1^{(1)} S^{\alpha_+} + \tilde{d}_2^{(1)} S^{\alpha_-}, & (S_n \le S \le S_{n+1}) \\ \ldots\ldots & \\ W_{N-n+1}(S) + \tilde{d}_1^{(N-n+1)} S^{\alpha_+} + \tilde{d}_2^{(N-n+1)} S^{\alpha_-}, & (1 \le S < \infty) \end{cases}$$

where $W_i(S)(i = 1, \ldots, N - n + 1)$ is the special solution (see Lemma 6.10) to the nonhomogeneous ODE (6.7.55)—(6.7.58) with $-\frac{1}{\Delta t} M_i(S)$ at the right side, respectively. The $2(N - n + 1)$ unknown constants $\tilde{d}_j^{(m)}(m = 1, \ldots, N - n + 1; j = 1, 2)$ and the free boundary point $S = S_n$ can be determined by the consistency conditions (6.6.59),(6.7.60) at $S = 1, S_{N-1}, \ldots, S_{n+1}$, the free boundary conditions (6.7.61)(6.7.62), and the condition at infinity (6.7.63), altogether $2(N - n + 1) + 1$ equations. They can be determined by the following process:

$$\tilde{d}_1^{(n+1)} \to \tilde{d}_1^{(n)} \to \cdots \to \tilde{d}_1^{(1)} \to S_n \to \tilde{d}_2^{(1)} \to \tilde{d}_2^{(2)} \to \cdots \to \tilde{d}_2^{(n+1)}$$

The actual procedure is rather tedious, but all operations are explicit, and there is no need to solve a large system of equations. This is an advantage of this method.

Next we show how to obtain the special solution to the nonhomogeneous ODE with $S^{\alpha_\pm}(\ln S)^j$ at the right side.

Lemma 6.10 *Consider nonhomogeneous ODE*

$$\mathcal{L}_\Delta(W) = \frac{\sigma^2}{2} S^2 \frac{d^2 W}{dS^2} + rS \frac{dW}{dS} - (r + \frac{1}{\Delta t})W = S^\omega (\ln S)^j,$$

where ω is a root of the characteristic equation (6.7.17), i.e.

$$K(\omega) = \frac{\sigma^2}{2}\omega(\omega - 1) + r\omega - (r + \frac{1}{\Delta t}) = 0,$$

$$K'(\omega) \neq 0.$$

It has a special solution

$$W(S) = \sum_{i=1}^{j+1} C_i S^\omega (\ln S)^i,$$

where $C_i(1 \leq i \leq j+1)$ *are given by the following recurrence formula:*

$$C_i = \frac{-\sigma^2(i+1)}{2K'(\omega)} C_{i+1}, \qquad (i = 1, 2, \ldots, j)$$

$$C_{j+1} = \frac{1}{(j+1)K'(\omega)}.$$

Proof By straightforward calculation,

$$\mathcal{L}_\Delta(S^\omega(\ln S)^i) = iK'(\omega)S^\omega(\ln S)^{i-1} + \frac{\sigma^2}{2} i(i-1)(\ln S)^{i-2}S^\omega, \qquad (i \geq 1)$$

thus

$$\begin{aligned}
\mathcal{L}_\Delta(W) &= \mathcal{L}_\Delta\left(\sum_{i=1}^{j+1} C_i S^\omega (\ln S)^i\right) \\
&= \sum_{i=1}^{j+1} iC_i K'(\omega)(\ln S)^{i-1} S^\omega + \sum_{i=1}^{j} \frac{\sigma^2}{2} i(i+1)C_{i+1}(\ln S)^{i-1} S^\omega \\
&= (j+1)C_{j+1}K'(\omega)(\ln S)^j S^\omega \\
&\quad + \sum_{i=1}^{j} i\left[K'(\omega)C_i + \frac{\sigma^2}{2}(i+1)C_{i+1}\right](\ln S)^{i-1}S^\omega.
\end{aligned}$$

To satisfy the equation

$$\mathcal{L}_\Delta(\omega) = S^\omega(\ln S)^j,$$

there must be

$$(j+1)C_{j+1}K'(\omega) = 1,$$

$$K'(\omega)C_i + \frac{\sigma^2}{2}(i+1)C_{i+1} = 0. \quad (1 \leq i \leq j)$$

Q.E.D.

6.8 Other Types of American Options

(A) American Binary Option

American binary option: during the contract's lifetime, whenever the underlying asset price S_t exceeds the strike price K, the contract can be exercised to receive \$1 in cash.

The math model for this type of American option is not a free boundary problem, since the underlying asset price at the exercise time is fixed: $S_t = K$.

Let $V(S,t)$ be the option price, then it satisfies:

$$\begin{cases} \frac{\partial V}{\partial t} + \frac{\sigma^2}{2} S^2 \frac{\partial^2 V}{\partial S^2} + (r-q) S \frac{\partial V}{\partial S} - rV = 0, \quad (0 < S < K) & (6.8.1) \\ V(K,t) = 1, & (6.8.2) \\ V(S,T) = H(S-K) = 0. \quad (0 < S < K) & (6.8.3) \end{cases}$$

Let

$$V(S,t) = V_0(S) - u(S,t), \tag{6.8.4}$$

where $V_0(S)$ is the price of the perpetual American binary option, i.e. $V_0(S)$ satisfies

$$\begin{cases} \frac{\sigma^2}{2} S^2 \frac{d^2 V_0}{dS^2} + (r-q) S \frac{dV_0}{dS} - rV_0 = 0, \quad (0 < S < K) & (6.8.5) \\ V_0(K) = 1. & (6.8.6) \end{cases}$$

Similar to discussion in §6.1, let

$$V_0(S) = A\left(\frac{S}{K}\right)^{\alpha_+} + B\left(\frac{S}{K}\right)^{\alpha_-}, \tag{6.8.7}$$

where $\alpha_\pm$ is the root of the characteristic equation:

$$\frac{\sigma^2}{2}\alpha(\alpha-1) + (r-q)\alpha - r = 0, \tag{6.8.8}$$

i.e.

$$\alpha_\pm = \frac{-(r-q-\frac{\sigma^2}{2}) \pm \sqrt{(r-q-\frac{\sigma^2}{2})^2 + 2\sigma^2 r}}{\sigma^2}. \tag{6.8.9}$$

Thus

$$\alpha_+ > 0 > \alpha_-.$$

Since $V_0(0)$ is finite,

$$B = 0.$$

And by boundary condition (6.8.8),

$$A = 1.$$

Thus, denoting $\alpha_+ = \alpha$, the solution of (6.8.5)—(6.8.6) is of the form

$$V_0 = \left(\frac{S}{K}\right)^{\alpha}. \tag{6.8.10}$$

Substituting it into (6.8.4), we obtain the initial-boundary value problem for function $u(S,t) = V_0(S) - V(S,t)$:

$$\begin{cases} \frac{\partial u}{\partial t} + \frac{\sigma^2}{2} S^2 \frac{\partial^2 u}{\partial S^2} + (r-q) S \frac{\partial u}{\partial S} - ru = 0, \quad (0 < S < K) & (6.8.11) \\ u(K,t) = 0, & (6.8.12) \\ u(S,T) = \left(\frac{S}{K}\right)^{\alpha}. \quad (0 < S < K) & (6.8.13) \end{cases}$$

Change the variable to

$$x = \ln \frac{K}{S}. \tag{6.8.14}$$

Then $u(x,t)$ satisfies the one side bounded problem:

$$\begin{cases} \frac{\partial u}{\partial t} + \frac{\sigma^2}{2} \frac{\partial^2 u}{\partial x^2} - (r - q - \frac{\sigma^2}{2}) \frac{\partial u}{\partial x} - ru = 0, & (0 < x < \infty) \\ u(0,t) = 0, & (0 \le t \le T) \\ u(x,T) = e^{-\alpha x}. & (0 < x < \infty) \end{cases}$$

Suppose $u(x,t)$ can be written as

$$u = e^{ax + b(T-t)} W, \tag{6.8.15}$$

where

$$a = \frac{1}{\sigma^2}(r - q - \frac{1}{2}\sigma^2),$$

$$b = -r - \frac{1}{2\sigma^2}(r - q - \frac{1}{2}\sigma^2)^2.$$

Then $W(x,t)$ satisfies

$$\begin{cases} \dfrac{\partial W}{\partial t}+\dfrac{\sigma^2}{2}\dfrac{\partial^2 W}{\partial x^2}=0, & (0<x<\infty) \\ W(0,t)=0, & (0\le t\le T) \\ W(x,T)=e^{-(\alpha+a)x}. & (0<x<\infty) \end{cases}$$

Using the image method, we perform an odd extension by defining an odd function $\varphi(x)$:

$$\varphi(x)=\begin{cases} e^{-(\alpha+a)x}, & x>0, \\ -e^{(\alpha+a)x}, & x<0. \end{cases}$$

Consider the Cauchy problem given in the domain $\{x\in R, 0\le t\le T\}$:

$$\begin{cases} \dfrac{\partial W}{\partial t}+\dfrac{\sigma^2}{2}\dfrac{\partial^2 W}{\partial x^2}=0, & (x\in R, 0\le t\le T) & (6.8.16) \\ W(x,T)=\varphi(x). & (x\in R) & (6.8.17) \end{cases}$$

Since $\varphi(x)$ is an odd function, $W(x,t)$ must also be an odd function of x, and hence necessarily satisfies the boundary condition at $x=0$:

$$W(0,t)=0.$$

By the Poisson formula, the solution to the Cauchy problem (6.8.16),(6.8.17) is

$$\begin{aligned} W(x,t)&=\int_{-\infty}^{\infty}\frac{1}{\sigma\sqrt{2\pi(T-t)}}e^{-\frac{(x-\xi)^2}{2\sigma^2(T-t)}}\varphi(\xi)d\xi \\ &=\frac{1}{\sigma\sqrt{2\pi(T-t)}}\int_0^{\infty}\left[e^{-\frac{(x-\xi)^2}{2\sigma^2(T-t)}}-e^{-\frac{(x+\xi)^2}{2\sigma^2(T-t)}}\right]e^{-(\alpha+a)\xi}d\xi. \end{aligned}$$

Substitute it into (6.8.15) to get $u(x,t)$. Then go back to the original variable to get $u(S,t)$. Then substituting into (6.8.4), we get the valuation of American binary option.

In particular if $q=0$, then $\alpha=1$, and

$$V(S,t)=\left(\frac{K}{S}\right)^{\frac{2r}{\sigma^2}}N(d_3)+\left(\frac{S}{K}\right)N(d_1),$$

where

$$d_1=\frac{\ln\frac{S}{K}+(r-\frac{\sigma^2}{2})(T-t)}{\sigma\sqrt{T-t}}, \qquad (6.8.18)$$

$$d_3 = \frac{\ln \frac{S}{K} - (r - \frac{\sigma^2}{2})(T-t)}{\sigma\sqrt{T-t}}. \tag{6.8.19}$$

The derivation is left to the reader.

(B) Bermudan Option

Bermudan option: early exercise is allowed at certain predetermined times during the lifetime of the contract, and no early exercise allowed, just like European option, at other times.

Let $0 \le t_1 < \cdots < t_N = T$ be the allowed early exercise times for a put option. Then

$$V(S,t) = \begin{cases} V_N(S,t), \; t_{N-1} \le t \le t_N, \\ \vdots \qquad\qquad \vdots \\ V_1(S,t), \;\; 0 \le t \le t_1. \end{cases}$$

and in each region $\{0 \le S < \infty, t_{i-1} \le t \le t_i\}$,

$$\begin{cases} \frac{\partial V_i}{\partial t} + \frac{\sigma^2}{2} S^2 \frac{\partial^2 V_i}{\partial S^2} + (r-q)S\frac{\partial V_i}{\partial S} - rV_i = 0, \\ V_i(S,t_i) = \max\{V_{i+1}(S,t_i), (K-S)^+\}, \qquad (i = 1, \ldots, N) \end{cases}$$

where $V_{N+1}(S,t_N) = (K-S)^+$.

(C) American Capped Call Options

Add the following term to an ordinary American call option contract: when the underlying asset price exceeds the upper limit $L(L > K)$ as specified in the contract, the option writer has the right to purchase back the option at the price $L - K$. The motivation behind this term is obvious: the option writer wants to manage the risk inherent in selling American call options.

For American call options with above terms, its payoff function is

$$\text{payoff} = (\min(S_t, L) - K)^+,$$

Hence its mathematical model is a variational inequality given in region

$\Sigma^L\{0 \le S \le L; 0 \le t \le T\}$:

$$\begin{cases} \min\{-\mathcal{L}V, V-(S-K)^+\}=0, & (\Sigma^L) \\ V(L,t)=L-K, & (0\le t\le T) \\ V(S,T)=(S-K)^+. & (0\le S\le L) \end{cases}$$

(D) American Options with Warning Time (Make Your Mind Up)

The contract requires a warning period before the option is exercised. Once the decision is made, the option holder cannot change mind, i.e. the holder must exercise the option upon expiration of the warning period in any circumstance.

Suppose the holder makes a decision at t_0 and the warning time is τ_0. Then at $t_0+\tau_0$, the payoff for the holder of the American call option is

$$\text{payoff} = S-K.$$

Note that there is no "positive taking" operation in the above function. This indicates that the holder must exercise the contract even if the asset is out of the money.

Let $V(S,t_0+\tau)(0\le\tau\le\tau_0)$ be the price of the American call option with warning time, then during the warning time, V satisfies the initial value problem to the Black-Scholes equations:

$$\begin{cases} \frac{\partial V}{\partial \tau}+\frac{\sigma^2}{2}\frac{\partial^2 V}{\partial S^2}+(r-q)S\frac{\partial V}{\partial S}-rV=0, & (0\le S<\infty, 0\le\tau\le\tau_0) \\ V|_{\tau=\tau_0}=S-K. & (0\le S<\infty) \end{cases}$$

It has a solution

$$V(S,t_0+\tau)=Se^{-q(\tau_0-\tau)}-Ke^{-r(\tau_0-\tau)}.$$

Hence at $\tau=0$ when the holder makes the decision, the intrinsic value of the option is

$$V(S,t_0)=Se^{-q\tau_0}-Ke^{-r\tau_0}.$$

Then, the price of the American call option with warning time τ_0 must satisfy

$$V(S,t)\ge Se^{-q\tau_0}-Ke^{-r\tau_0}.$$

Based on the above analysis, we can formulate the problem as a variational inequality in domain $\Sigma\{0 \le S < \infty, 0 \le t \le T\}$:

$$\begin{cases} \min\{-\mathcal{L}V, V-(Se^{-q\tau_0}-Ke^{-r\tau_0})\}=0, & (\Sigma) \\ V(S,T)=(S-K)^+. & (0\le S<\infty) \end{cases}$$

Summery

1. The main feature of American option is its early exercise right. During the lifetime of the option, the holder needs to watch closely the asset price to decide whether to hold or exercise the option.

According to whether the option's intrinsic price exceeds or equals the early exercise payoff, the domain of $V(S,t)$ is divided into two regions: the continuation region in which

$$V(S,t) > (S-K)^+, \qquad \textit{(call option)}$$

$$V(S,t) > (K-S)^+; \qquad \textit{(put option)}$$

and the stopping region in which

$$V(S,t) = (S-K)^+, \qquad \textit{(call)}$$

$$V(S,t) = (K-S)^+. \qquad \textit{(put)}$$

The interface is called the optimal exercise boundary. Holders of American options need to know "picture" to have an optimal exercise strategy.

2. The math model of American option pricing is a free boundary problem——the obstacle problem, in which the obstacle is the payoff function of the option, the coincidence set of the solution and the obstacle is the stopping region of the option, and the boundary of the coincidence set is a free boundary, which is the optimal exercise boundary of American option.

This mathematical model has two equivalent formulations:

a. Variational inequality. In this form, the solution domain is the whole region $\Sigma = \{0 \le S < \infty, 0 \le t \le T\}$, and the free boundary is implicit in the problem statement.

b. Free boundary problem. In this form, the solution domain is restricted to the continuation region Σ_1*:*

$$\Sigma_1 = \{0 \leq S \leq S(t), 0 \leq t \leq T\}, \qquad \textit{(call)}$$

$$\Sigma_1 = \{S(t) \leq S \leq \infty, 0 \leq t \leq T\}. \qquad \textit{(put)}$$

The free boundary $S = S(t)$ *as the boundary of the problem appears explicitly in the problem statement.*

3. As a nonlinear PDE problem, American option price in general cannot be given in a closed form, except for the perpetual American option. Therefore, the study of the properties of the optimal exercise boundary is of great importance for American option pricing.

Let $S_c(t), S_p(t)$ *and* $S_{c,\infty}, S_{p,\infty}$ *be the optimal exercise boundaries for ordinary American call, put option and perpetual American call, put options with the same strike price, respectively. Then for the American call option, we have:*

$$S_c(t) \text{ monotonic decreasing, convex;}$$

$$\max(\frac{rK}{q}, K) = S_c(T) \leq S_c(t) < S_{c,\infty},$$

and its asymptotic expansion at $t = T$*:*

$$S_c(t) \approx \begin{cases} K(1 + \sigma\sqrt{(T-t)|\ln(T-t)|}), & q > r, \\ K(1 + \sqrt{2}\sigma\sqrt{(T-t)|\ln(T-t)|}), & q = r, \\ \frac{rK}{q}(1 + \frac{\sigma\alpha}{\sqrt{2}}\sqrt{T-t}), & q < r. \end{cases}$$

For the American put option, we have

$$S_p(t) \text{ monotonic increasing, convex;}$$

$$S_{p,\infty} < S_p(t) \leq S_p(T) = \min(\frac{rK}{q}, K),$$

and its asymptotic expansion at $t = T$:

$$S_p(t) \approx \begin{cases} K(1 - \sigma\sqrt{(T-t)|\ln(T-t)|}), & q < r, \\ K(1 - \sqrt{2}\sigma\sqrt{(T-t)|\ln(T-t)|}), & q = r, \\ \frac{rK}{q}(1 - \frac{\sigma\alpha}{\sqrt{2}}\sqrt{T-t}), & q > r, \end{cases}$$

where α *is the root of the transcendental equation*

$$\alpha^3 e^{\alpha^2/4} \int_\alpha^\infty e^{-\omega^2/4} d\omega = 2(2 - \alpha^2).$$

If the optimal exercise boundary $S = S(t)$ *is known, or approximately determined, then American option price* $V(S,t)$ *can be determined or approximately given by (6.3.14)—(6.3.16).*

4. American option price in general can only be obtained by numerical methods. Two methods are introduced in this chapter:

a. The difference method (explicit and implicit schemes);

b. The line method.

As a natural extension of §5.7, we have shown that when neglecting the higher order terms, the BTM of American option pricing (described in §3.5) is equivalent to a special case of the explicit difference scheme, thus provides a foundation for proving the convergence of the BTM of American option pricing in the framework of PDE.

5. While the call-put parity does not hold for American options, there exists the American call-put symmetry

$$V_c(S,t;r,q) = \frac{S}{K} V_p(\frac{K^2}{S}, t; q, r)$$

and

$$\sqrt{S_c(t;r,q)S_p(t;q,r)} = K,$$

where V_c, V_p *and* S_c, S_p *are the prices and the optimal exercise boundary of American call option and put option, respectively.*

Exercises

1. Consider the dividend-paying (dividend rate $q \geq 0$) perpetual American call option. Write out its mathematical model and solve it directly, to find its premium and the exercise boundary.

2. Study how the perpetual American option price is affected by the volatility σ, and explain the financial meaning.

3. American straddle option is a contract with early exercise term, and its payoff function is

$$\begin{aligned}\text{payoff} &= |S-K| \\ &= (S-K)^+ + (K-S)^+.\end{aligned}$$

Set up a mathematical model for the dividend-paying perpetual American straddle option, and find the premium and the optimal exercise boundary. Moreover, can its premium be represented as the sum of a perpetual American call option and a perpetual American put option? Why? Compare their premiums.

4. Write out the mathematical model for the perpetual American call option with warning time, and find the premium and the optimal exercise boundary.

5. Prove(Theorem 6.2)American call-put symmetry:

$$V_c(S,t;r,q) = \frac{S}{K} V_p(\frac{K^2}{S}, t; q, r)$$

and

$$\sqrt{S_c(t;r,q)S_p(t;q,r)} = K,$$

where $V_c(S,t;r,q), V_p(S,t;r,q)$ and $S_c(t;r,q), S_p(t;q,r)$ are the price and the optimal exercise boundary of dividend-paying American (call, put) options with the same expiration date T and strike price K, respectively.

6. Show that inequality (6.4.25) is true. I.e. if $q_1 \geq q_2$, the American put option price V satisfies

$$V(S,t;q_1) \geq V(S,t;q_2),$$

If $V(S,t;q)$ is the American call option price, how will the above relation be modified?

7. Show that for the American capped call option, the optimal exercise boundary $\hat{S}(t)$ is

$$\hat{S}(t) = \min(L, S(t)),$$

where L is the upper limit specified in the contract, $S(t)$ is the optimal exercise boundary for the American call option without cap.

8. Find the premium and optimal exercise boundary for the perpetual American capped call option.

9. Show that among all American call options with the same strike price, the perpetual American call option is the most expensive one. I.e. if $V_T(S,t)$ is the price of American call option with expiration date $t=T$, $V_\infty(S)$ is the perpetual American call option price with the same strike price, then for all $T>0$, there must be

$$V_T(S,t) \leq V_\infty(S), \qquad (0 \leq t \leq T)$$

and

$$S_T(t) \leq S_\infty,$$

here $S_T(t)$ and S_∞ are the optimal exercise boundary for American call option and the perpetual American call option with the same expiration date T, respectively.

Chapter 7

Multi-Asset Option Pricing

The price movement of two or more risky assets can be described by a system of stochastic differential equations. Options derived from two or more underlying risky assets are called **multi-asset options**. Multi-asset option price satisfies a multidimensional parabolic partial differential equation. Different types of multi-asset options are distinguished by their payoff functions. Hence a given multi-asset option pricing problem can be modeled as a terminal-boundary value problem to a multidimensional parabolic PDE with appropriate terminal condition. Since the dimension of the PDE is determined by the number of the underlying risky assets, which can be very large, even if an explicit solution can be obtained, it will still be very difficult to evaluate the expression. Thus, an important question in multi-asset option pricing is whether a given multi-asset option pricing problem can be reduced to a 1-D problem by introducing suitable composed variables?

7.1 Stochastic Models of Multi-Assets Pricing

In order to price multi-asset options, we need first to establish the price movement model for the underlying multi-assets. Let S_i be the price of the i-th risky asset ($i = 1, \ldots, n$). Suppose S_i satisfies a stochastic differential equation (SDE) of the following form:

$$\frac{dS_i}{S_i} = \mu_i dt + \sigma_i dW_i, \qquad (i = 1, \ldots, n) \tag{7.1.1}$$

where $dW_i (i = 1, \ldots, n)$ are standard Brownian motion which satisfy

$$E(dW_i) = 0, \tag{7.1.2}$$

$$Var(dW_i) = dt, \tag{7.1.3}$$

$$Cov(dW_i, dW_j) = \rho_{ij} dt. \quad (i \neq j) \tag{7.1.4}$$

Here $Cov(\cdot, \cdot)$ denotes the covariance. By the definition of covariance and (7.1.2),

$$\begin{aligned} Cov(dW_i, dW_j) &= E([dW_i - E(dW_i)][dW_j - E(dW_j)]) \\ &= E(dW_i dW_j), \quad (i \neq j) \end{aligned}$$

The prices of multi-assets can also be modeled as:

$$\frac{dS_i}{S_i} = \mu_i dt + \sum_{j=1}^{m} \sigma_{ij} dW_j, \quad (i = 1, \ldots, n) \tag{7.1.5}$$

where $dW_i (i = 1, \ldots, n)$ are one-dimensional Brownian motions, i.e.

$$E(dW_i) = 0, \tag{7.1.6}$$

$$Var(dW_i) = dt, \tag{7.1.7}$$

$$Cov(dW_i, dW_j) = 0, \quad (i \neq j) \tag{7.1.8}$$

SDE (7.1.5) can be written in vector form:

$$d\vec{S} = \vec{a} dt + [\sigma] d\vec{W}_t,$$

where

$$\vec{S} = \begin{bmatrix} S_1 \\ \vdots \\ S_n \end{bmatrix}, \vec{a} = \begin{bmatrix} \mu_1 S_1 \\ \vdots \\ \mu_n S_n \end{bmatrix}, \vec{W}_t = \begin{bmatrix} W_{1t} \\ \vdots \\ W_{mt} \end{bmatrix},$$

$$[\sigma] = \begin{bmatrix} \sigma_{11} S_1 & \ldots & \sigma_{1m} S_1 \\ \vdots & & \vdots \\ \sigma_{n1} S_n & \ldots & \sigma_{nm} S_n \end{bmatrix} = [S][\sigma_0],$$

here

$$[S] = \begin{bmatrix} S_1 & & 0 \\ & \ddots & \\ 0 & & S_n \end{bmatrix},$$

$$[\sigma_0] = \begin{bmatrix} \sigma_{11} & \dots & \sigma_{1m} \\ \vdots & & \vdots \\ \sigma_{n1} & \dots & \sigma_{nm} \end{bmatrix}.$$

7.2 Black-Scholes Equation

Let $S_1, \dots, S_n$ be n risky assets (e.g., stock, foreign exchange rate,...), satisfying geometric Brownian motion (7.1.5).

Let V be an option derived from the underlying assets $S_1, \dots, S_n$, as a function of $n+1$ variables $S_1, \dots, S_n$ and t:

$$V = V(S_1, \dots, S_n, t). \tag{7.2.1}$$

Δ-hedging principle

Choose Δ_i shares of asset $S_i (i = 1, \dots, n)$ to hedge against the option $V(S_1, \dots, S_n, t)$, i.e. to construct a portfolio Π:

$$\Pi = V(S_1, \dots, S_n, t) - \sum_{i=1}^{n} \Delta_i S_i, \tag{7.2.2}$$

such that it is risk-free in $(t, t+dt)$.

From the Itô formula for the multivariate stochastic process, we have

$$\begin{aligned} d\Pi &= dV - \sum_{i=1}^{n} \Delta_i dS_i - \sum_{i=1}^{n} \Delta_i S_i q_i dt \\ &= \left(\frac{\partial V}{\partial t} + \frac{1}{2} \sum_{i,j=1}^{n} a_{ij} S_i S_j \frac{\partial^2 V}{\partial S_i \partial S_j} \right) dt \\ &\quad + \sum_{i=1}^{n} \frac{\partial V}{\partial S_i} dS_i - \sum_{i=1}^{n} \Delta_i dS_i - \sum_{i=1}^{n} \Delta_i S_i q_i dt, \end{aligned} \tag{7.2.3}$$

where q_i is the dividend rate of asset S_i, and

$$a_{ij} = \sum_{k=1}^{m} \sigma_{ik}\sigma_{jk}, \qquad (i, j = 1, \ldots, n)$$

i.e.

$$A = [a_{ij}] = \sigma_0 \sigma_0^T,$$

where σ_0^T is the transpose of matrix σ_0.

In order that Π is risk-free in $(t, t+dt)$, i.e.

$$d\Pi = r\Pi dt = r(V - \sum_{i=1}^{n} \Delta_i S_i)dt, \tag{7.2.4}$$

we choose

$$\Delta_i = \frac{\partial V}{\partial S_i}. \tag{7.2.5}$$

Substituting (7.2.5) into (7.2.3),(7.2.4), and eliminating dt, we get

$$\frac{\partial V}{\partial t} + \frac{1}{2} \sum_{i,j=1}^{n} a_{ij} S_i S_j \frac{\partial^2 V}{\partial S_i \partial S_j} + \sum_{i=1}^{n} (r - q_i) S_i \frac{\partial V}{\partial S_i} - rV = 0. \tag{7.2.6}$$

This equation is called the **Black-Scholes equation for multi-asset options**.

Since the quadratic form

$$\eta^T A \eta = \eta^T \sigma_0 \sigma_0^T \eta = |\sigma_0^T \eta|^2 \geq 0, \qquad \forall \eta \in \mathbf{R}^n$$

thus $A = [a_{ij}]$ is a symmetrical nonnegative matrix. Therefore equation (7.2.6) is a multidimensional parabolic equation.

Denoting the option payoff function at maturity $(t = T)$ by $P(S_1, \ldots, S_n)$, then the **mathematical model of the European multi-asset option** is: solve PDE (7.2.6) in domain $\Sigma : \{0 \leq S_i < \infty (i = 1, \ldots, n); 0 \leq t \leq T\}$ with the terminal condition

$$V(S_1, \ldots, S_n, T) = P(S_1, \ldots, S_n). \tag{7.2.7}$$

7.3 Black-Scholes Formula

The terminal value problem to multidimensional Black-Scholes equation (7.2.6),(7.2.7) has a solution.

By transformation

$$x_i = \ln S_i, \tag{7.3.1}$$

(7.2.6) becomes

$$\frac{\partial V}{\partial t} + \frac{1}{2}\sum_{i,j=1}^{n} a_{ij}\frac{\partial^2 V}{\partial x_i \partial x_j} + \sum_{i=1}^{n}(r - q_i - \frac{a_{ii}}{2})\frac{\partial V}{\partial x_i} - rV = 0. \tag{7.3.2}$$

In vector form,

$$\frac{\partial V}{\partial t} + \frac{1}{2}\nabla_x^T A \nabla_x V + \vec{b}^T \nabla_x V - rV = 0, \tag{7.3.3}$$

where

$$A = [a_{ij}],$$

$$\vec{b} = \begin{bmatrix} r - q_1 - \frac{a_{11}}{2} \\ \vdots \\ r - q_n - \frac{a_{nn}}{2} \end{bmatrix}, \tag{7.3.4}$$

$$\nabla_x = \begin{bmatrix} \frac{\partial}{\partial x_1} \\ \vdots \\ \frac{\partial}{\partial x_n} \end{bmatrix},$$

and $\vec{b}^T$ is the transpose of matrix (vector) $\vec{b}$.

By transformation $\vec{z} = B\vec{x}$,

$$\begin{bmatrix} z_1 \\ \vdots \\ z_n \end{bmatrix} = \begin{bmatrix} b_{11} & \dots & b_{1n} \\ \vdots & & \vdots \\ b_{n1} & \dots & b_{nn} \end{bmatrix} \begin{bmatrix} x_1 \\ \vdots \\ x_n \end{bmatrix}, \tag{7.3.5}$$

where B is chosen such that under the new coordinates $(z_1, \dots, z_n)$, the coefficients of the second order derivative term in equation (7.3.3) are diagonalized, and due to

$$\nabla_x = B^T \nabla_z,$$

equation (7.3.3) becomes

$$\frac{\partial V}{\partial t} + \frac{1}{2}\nabla_z^T (BAB^T)\nabla_z V + (B\vec{b})^T \nabla_z V - rV = 0. \tag{7.3.6}$$

Since A is a symmetric matrix, there must exist an orthogonal transformation B such that BAB^T is a diagonal matrix, i.e. there exists transformation (7.3.5) satisfying

$$B^T B = BB^T = I, \tag{7.3.7}$$

such that

$$BAB^T = \Lambda = \begin{bmatrix} \lambda_1 & & 0 \\ & \ddots & \\ 0 & & \lambda_n \end{bmatrix}, \tag{7.3.8}$$

where $\lambda_1, \ldots, \lambda_n$ are the eigenvalues of the symmetric matrix A, which are the real roots of the characteristic equation of A:

$$\det |A - \lambda I| = 0. \tag{7.3.9}$$

Suppose $\vec{\xi_i}$ is the eigenvector corresponding to the eigenvalue λ_i, i.e.

$$(A - \lambda_i I)\vec{\xi_i} = 0, \tag{7.3.10}$$

and

$$\vec{\xi_i}^T \vec{\xi_i} = |\vec{\xi_i}|^2 = 1.$$

Then by transformation (7.3.5), with

$$B = \begin{bmatrix} \vec{\xi_1}^T \\ \vdots \\ \vec{\xi_n}^T \end{bmatrix} = \begin{bmatrix} \xi_{11} & \xi_{12} & \cdots & \xi_{1n} \\ \vdots & & & \vdots \\ \xi_{n1} & \xi_{n2} & \cdots & \xi_{nn} \end{bmatrix}, \tag{7.3.11}$$

equation (7.3.6) will be reduced to

$$\frac{\partial V}{\partial t} + \frac{1}{2} \sum_{i=1}^{n} \lambda_i \frac{\partial^2 V}{\partial z_i^2} + \sum_{i=1}^{n} (\vec{\xi_i}^T \vec{b}) \frac{\partial V}{\partial z_i} - rV = 0. \tag{7.3.12}$$

Therefore under transformation (7.3.5), the terminal value problem of the Black-Scholes equation (7.2.6),(7.2.7) becomes a Cauchy problem:

$$\begin{cases} \text{Equation (7.3.12)}, \\ V(z_1, \ldots, z_n, T) = \hat{P}(z_1, \ldots, z_n), \end{cases} \tag{7.3.13}$$

where $\hat{P}(z_1, \ldots, z_n) = P(e^{x_1}, \ldots, e^{x_n})$. To solve it, we need first to find the fundamental solution of equation (7.3.12), i.e. a solution of (7.3.12) with the terminal condition:

$$V(z_1, \dots, z_n, T) = \delta(z_1 - z_1^0, \dots, z_n - z_n^0), \tag{7.3.14}$$

where $\delta(z_1, \dots, z_n)$ is the multidimensional Dirac function

$$\delta(z_1, \dots, z_n) = \delta(z_1) \dots \delta(z_n).$$

Let

$$V = e^{\vec{\omega}^T \vec{z} + \beta(T-t)} W, \tag{7.3.15}$$

where β is a constant, $\vec{\omega}$ is a n-dimensional vector:

$$\vec{\omega} = \begin{bmatrix} \omega_1 \\ \vdots \\ \omega_n \end{bmatrix}.$$

Substituting (7.3.15) into equation (7.3.12), we get

$$\frac{\partial W}{\partial t} + \frac{1}{2} \sum_{i=1}^{n} [\lambda_i \omega_i + (\vec{\xi}_i^T \vec{b})] \frac{\partial W}{\partial z} + \frac{1}{2} \sum_{i=1}^{n} \lambda_i \frac{\partial^2 W}{\partial z_i^2}$$

$$- [r + \beta - \frac{1}{2}(\vec{\omega}^T \Lambda \vec{\omega}) - \vec{b}^T B^T \vec{\omega}] W = 0.$$

Choose

$$\omega_i = -\frac{1}{\lambda_i} (\vec{\xi}_i^T \vec{b}) \tag{7.3.16}$$

i.e.

$$\vec{\omega} = -\Lambda^{-1} B \vec{b}, \tag{7.3.17}$$

and

$$\begin{aligned} \beta &= -r + \frac{1}{2} \vec{\omega}^T \Lambda \vec{\omega} + \vec{b}^T B^T \vec{\omega} \\ &= -r + \frac{1}{2} (B\vec{b})^T \Lambda^{-1} \Lambda \Lambda^{-1} (B\vec{b}) - \vec{b}^T B^T \Lambda^{-1} B \vec{b} \\ &= -r + \frac{1}{2} (B\vec{b})^T \Lambda^{-1} (B\vec{b}) - (B\vec{b})^T \Lambda^{-1} (B\vec{b}) \\ &= -r - \frac{1}{2} (B\vec{b})^T \Lambda^{-1} (B\vec{b}). \end{aligned} \tag{7.3.18}$$

Then under the transformation (7.3.15), equation (7.3.12) is reduced to

$$\frac{\partial W}{\partial t} + \frac{1}{2}\sum_{i=1}^{n} \lambda_i \frac{\partial^2 W}{\partial z_i^2} = 0. \tag{7.3.19}$$

And the terminal condition (7.3.14) becomes

$$W(z_1, \ldots, z_n, T) = e^{-\vec{\omega}^T \vec{z_0}} \delta(z_1 - z_1^0, \ldots, z_n - z_n^0), \tag{7.3.20}$$

where

$$\vec{z_0} = \begin{bmatrix} z_1^0 \\ \vdots \\ z_n^0 \end{bmatrix}.$$

According to the theory of the heat equation, the solution to the problem (7.3.19), (7.3.20) is of the form:

$$\begin{aligned} W(z, t, ; z_0) &= e^{-\vec{\omega}^T \vec{z_0}} \prod_{i=1}^{n} \frac{1}{\sqrt{2\pi\lambda_i(T-t)}} e^{-\frac{(z_i - z_i^0)^2}{2\lambda_i(T-t)}} \\ &= e^{-\vec{\omega}^T \vec{z_0}} \left[\frac{1}{2\pi(T-t)}\right]^{\frac{n}{2}} (\det \Lambda^{-1})^{\frac{1}{2}} \\ &\quad \cdot \exp\left(-\frac{(\vec{z} - \vec{z_0})^T \Lambda^{-1} (\vec{z} - \vec{z_0})}{2(T-t)}\right). \end{aligned}$$

Back to the original function V and variable $\vec{x}$, we obtain the fundamental solution $\Gamma(x, t; x_0)$ to the Cauchy problem (7.3.2), (7.3.13) as follows:

$$\begin{aligned} \Gamma(x, t; x_0) = &\left[\frac{1}{2\pi(T-t)}\right]^{\frac{n}{2}} \frac{e^{-r(T-t)}}{|\det A|^{\frac{1}{2}}} \\ &\cdot \exp\left\{-\frac{(B(\vec{x} - \vec{x}_0))^T \Lambda^{-1} (B(\vec{x} - \vec{x}_0))}{2(T-t)}\right. \\ &\left. - \frac{1}{2}(B\vec{b})^T \Lambda^{-1} (B\vec{b})(T-t) - (\Lambda^{-1} B\vec{b})^T B(\vec{x} - \vec{x}_0)\right\}. \end{aligned}$$

Since

$$B^T \Lambda^{-1} B = B^{-1} \Lambda^{-1} (B^{-1})^T = (B^T \Lambda B)^{-1} = A^{-1},$$

thus

$$\Gamma(x,t;x_0) = \left[\frac{1}{2\pi(T-t)}\right]^{\frac{n}{2}} \frac{e^{-r(T-t)}}{|\det A|^{\frac{1}{2}}} \cdot$$

$$\exp\left\{-\frac{1}{2(T-t)}\left[(\vec{x}-\vec{x}_0+\vec{b}(T-t))^T A^{-1}(\vec{x}-\vec{x}_0+\vec{b}(T-t))\right]\right\} \tag{7.3.21}$$

Then the solution of the Cauchy problem (7.3.12),(7.3.13) has the form

$$V(x,t) = \int_{-\infty}^{\infty}\cdots\int_{-\infty}^{\infty}\Gamma(x,t;\xi)\hat{P}(\xi_1,\ldots,\xi_n)d\xi_1\ldots d\xi_n.$$

Back to the original variables $S_1,\ldots,S_n$ by (7.3.1), we obtain the European multi-asset option pricing formula:

$$V(S,t) = \left[\frac{1}{2\pi(T-t)}\right]^{\frac{n}{2}} \frac{e^{-r(T-t)}}{|\det A|^{\frac{1}{2}}}$$

$$\cdot\int_0^{\infty}\cdots\int_0^{\infty}\frac{P(\eta_1,\ldots,\eta_n)}{\eta_1,\ldots,\eta_n}\exp\left[-\frac{\vec{\alpha}^T A^{-1}\vec{\alpha}}{2(T-t)}\right]d\eta_1\ldots d\eta_n, \tag{7.3.22}$$

where

$$\vec{\alpha} = \begin{bmatrix}\alpha_1\\ \vdots\\ \alpha_n\end{bmatrix},$$

and

$$\alpha_i = \ln\frac{S_i}{\eta_i} + (r - q_i - \frac{a_{ii}}{2})(T-t). \quad (i=1,\ldots,n) \tag{7.3.23}$$

(7.3.22) is called the **Black-Scholes formula for European multi-asset options.**

Remark (7.3.22) indicates that there exists a closed-form expression for any European multi-asset option. However, this is a multiple integral with singularities in the integrand. When a large number of assets are involved, the integral has high multiplicity and is very difficult to evaluate. Thus, finding a closed-form expression is only the first step in solving the pricing problem of the European multi-asset option. We still need to find a simple way to get special solution to the problem for each concrete form of the payoff function.

7.4 Rainbow Options

There are three general categories of European multi-asset options:

(I) **rainbow options,**

(II) **basket options,**

(III) **quanto options.**

For each category of multi-asset options, we will explain its financial meaning, specify its payoff function upon maturity, and derive the option pricing formula. In particular, we will find out whether it can be reduced to a one-dimensional problem.

As a rainbow is a combination of various colors, a rainbow option is a combination of various underlying assets. The value of a rainbow option depends on the performance of the underlying assets. According to the payoff structure, rainbow options have the following forms:

(A) Better-of options

The holder of better-of option receives exercise payoff associated with the better performer of the underlying assets.

Example An investor considers to invest in stock index A or stock index B, but is not sure which index will bring a higher return. By buying a better-of option, the investor is guaranteed to receive a higher return according to the better of the two indexes at maturity.

There are two types of better-of options:

(1) According to the price,

$$\text{payoff } = \max(\alpha_1 S_1(T), \ldots, \alpha_n S_n(T)),$$

where $S_i(T)$ is the price of the i-th risky asset at $t = T$, and α_i is a coefficient so that all risky asset prices are at the same level.

(2) According to the growth rate,

$$\text{payoff (rate) } = \max(\hat{S}_1(T), \ldots, \hat{S}_n(T)),$$

where $\hat{S}_i(T)$ is the price growth rate of the i-th risky asset at $t = T$. Since

$$\hat{S}_i(T) = \frac{S_i(T) - S_i(0)}{S_i(0)} = \frac{S_i(T)}{S_i(0)} - 1,$$

thus

$$\max(\hat{S}_1(T),\ldots,\hat{S}_n(T)) = \max(\alpha_1 S_1(T),\ldots,\alpha_n S_n(T)) - 1,$$

where

$$\alpha_i = \frac{1}{S_i(0)}, \qquad (i = 1,\ldots,n)$$

In general, the payoff function of a European better-of option can be written as

$$\text{payoff } = \max(S_1(T),\ldots,S_n(T)),$$

where $S_i(t)$ can be either the same-level price, or the growth rate, of the i-th risky asset.

Mathematical model for better-of options: to solve the multivariate Black-Scholes equation (7.2.6) with the terminal condition:

$$V(S_1,\ldots,S_n,T) = \max\{S_1,\ldots,S_n\}. \tag{7.4.1}$$

Its solution is given by the multi-asset Black-Scholes formula (7.3.22), i.e.

$$V(S_1,\ldots,S_n,t) = \left[\frac{1}{2\pi(T-t)}\right]^{\frac{n}{2}} e^{-r(T-t)} \det|A|^{-\frac{1}{2}}$$

$$\cdot \int_0^\infty \cdots \int_0^\infty \frac{\max(\eta_1,\ldots,\eta_n)}{\eta_1,\ldots,\eta_n} \exp\left\{-\frac{\vec{\alpha}^T A^{-1}\vec{\alpha}}{2(T-t)}\right\} d\eta_1\ldots d\eta_n,$$

where $\vec{\alpha}$ is defined by (7.3.23).

Remark Closely related to the better-of option, another form of rainbow option is the worse-of option. Its exercise payoff is

$$\text{payoff } = \min(S_1(T),\ldots,S_n(T)).$$

(B) Out-performance options

The exercise payoff of out-performance option is based on the difference in the performance of two assets.

Example An investor holding a position in a risky asset A, not sure whether A will outperform B, can purchase an out-performance option so that payoff will be based on the difference if risky asset B outperforms A. Thus the exercise payoff of the option is $\max(S_B(T) - S_A(T), 0)$, where $S_A(T), S_B(T)$ can be either the same-level price, or the price growth rate, of the risky assets A, B.

Mathematical model of out-performance options: to solve equation (7.2.6) with the terminal condition:

$$V(S_1, S_2, T) = \max\{S_2 - S_1, 0\}. \tag{7.4.2}$$

Remark A similar form of option is the spread option. Its exercise payoff function is

$$V(S_1, S_2, T) = \max(S_2 - S_1 - K, 0), \tag{7.4.3}$$

where K is the strike price.

Remark Another form related to the out-performance option is the **options to exchange one asset to another**. By purchasing an option to exchange one asset for another, an investor holding a position in a risky asset A can exchange A for another risky asset B, or trade A for B by adding cash K, when B outperforms A.

Mathematical model of options to exchange one asset for another: to solve equation (7.2.6) with the terminal condition (7.4.2) or equation (7.2.6) with the terminal condition (7.4.3).

Remark A European better-of (worse-of) two assets option can be decomposed into a risky asset and an option to exchange one asset for another. In fact, since European option pricing is a linear problem, the payoff function of a better-of (worse-of) option can be written as

$$\max(S_1(T), S_2(T)) = S_1(T) + \max(S_2(T) - S_1(T), 0)$$

and

$$\min(S_1(T), S_2(T)) = S_2(T) - \max(S_2(T) - S_1(T), 0).$$

(C) Maximum call options and **minimum call options**

A maximum call option offers its holder n choices: to buy risky asset S_i at strike price K_i, $(i = 1, \ldots, n)$. The option holder can choose the best performer at the expiration date to get the maximum payoff. The payoff at the expiration date is

$$\text{payoff } = \max\{(S_1(T) - K_1)^+, \ldots, (S_n(T) - K_n)^+\}.$$

Mathematical model of the maximum call options: solve equation (7.2.6) with the terminal condition

$$V(S_1, \dots, S_n, T) = \max\{(S_1 - K_1)^+, \dots, (S_n - K_n)^+\}. \tag{7.4.4}$$

Its solution is given by the Black-Scholes formula (7.3.22).

Remark For maximum call options, if

$$K_1 = \cdots = K_n = K,$$

then the payoff function is reduced to

$$\begin{aligned} V(S_1, \dots, S_n, T) &= \max\{(S_1 - K), \dots, (S_n - K), 0\} \\ &= (\max\{S_1, \dots, S_n\} - K)^+ . \end{aligned} \tag{7.4.5}$$

This kind of the maximum call options is often regarded as a generalization of the single asset vanilla call option.

Remark Corresponding to the maximum (minimum) call options, we may also consider the **maximum (minimum) put options**. In particular, if $K_1 = \cdots = K_n = K$, its payoff function is

$$\text{payoff } = (K - \max(S_1, \dots, S_n))^+ \tag{7.4.6}$$

or

$$\text{payoff } = (K - \min(S_1, \dots, S_n))^+. \tag{7.4.7}$$

This is often regarded as a generalization of the vanilla put option on a single asset.

In the following, we will discuss which of the rainbow option pricing problems can be reduced to a one-dimensional problem. For some problems, by introducing a new variable as combination of the original ones, the equation, the terminal and boundary conditions, and the domain will depend on this new variable only.

The out-performance and better-of (worse-of) options of two risky assets can each be reduced to a one-dimensional problem.

Let us begin with the out-performance option.

The mathematical model of the out-performance option pricing is the terminal-boundary value problem (7.2.6), (7.4.2): i.e. in domain Σ :

$\{(S_1, S_2, t)|0 \leq S_1 < \infty, 0 \leq S_2 < \infty, 0 \leq t \leq T\}$, solve the problem

$$\begin{cases} \frac{\partial V}{\partial t} + \frac{1}{2}\left[a_{11}S_1^2\frac{\partial^2 V}{\partial S_1^2} + 2a_{12}S_1S_2\frac{\partial^2 V}{\partial S_1 \partial S_2} + a_{22}S_2^2\frac{\partial^2 V}{\partial S_2^2}\right] \\ \qquad + (r - q_1)S_1\frac{\partial V}{\partial S_1} + (r - q_2)S_2\frac{\partial V}{\partial S_2} - rV = 0, & (7.4.8) \\ V(S_1, S_2, T) = \max(S_2 - S_1, 0). & (7.4.9) \end{cases}$$

Let

$$\xi = \frac{S_1}{S_2}, \tag{7.4.10}$$

and

$$u(\xi, t) = V(S_1, S_2, t)/S_2. \tag{7.4.11}$$

Then we have

$$\frac{\partial V}{\partial S_1} = S_2\frac{\partial u}{\partial \xi}\frac{\partial \xi}{\partial S_1} = \frac{\partial u}{\partial \xi},$$

$$\frac{\partial V}{\partial S_2} = u + S_2\frac{\partial u}{\partial \xi}\frac{\partial \xi}{\partial S_2} = u - \xi\frac{\partial u}{\partial \xi},$$

$$\frac{\partial^2 V}{\partial S_1^2} = \frac{1}{S_2}\frac{\partial^2 u}{\partial \xi^2},$$

$$\frac{\partial^2 V}{\partial S_1 \partial S_2} = \frac{\partial^2 u}{\partial \xi^2}\frac{\partial \xi}{\partial S_2} = -\frac{\xi}{S_2}\frac{\partial^2 u}{\partial \xi^2},$$

$$\frac{\partial^2 V}{\partial S_2^2} = \frac{\partial u}{\partial \xi}\frac{\partial \xi}{\partial S_2} - \frac{\partial u}{\partial \xi}\frac{\partial \xi}{\partial S_2} - \xi\frac{\partial^2 u}{\partial \xi^2}\frac{\partial \xi}{\partial S_2} = \frac{\xi^2}{S_2}\frac{\partial^2 u}{\partial \xi^2}.$$

Substituting these into equation (7.4.8), we get

$$\frac{\partial u}{\partial t} + \frac{1}{2}\left[a_{11} - 2a_{12} + a_{22}\right]\xi^2\frac{\partial^2 u}{\partial \xi^2} + (q_2 - q_1)\xi\frac{\partial u}{\partial \xi} - q_2 u = 0. \tag{7.4.12}$$

By transformation (7.4.10),(7.4.11), the terminal condition (7.4.9) becomes

$$u(\xi, T) = \frac{1}{S_2}V(S_1, S_2, T) = \frac{1}{S_2}\max(S_2 - S_1, 0) = (1 - \xi)^+. \tag{7.4.13}$$

And the problem domain Σ is transformed to:

$$\{0 \leq \xi < \infty, 0 \leq t \leq T\}.$$

Thus under the transformation (7.4.10),(7.4.11), the problem (7.4.8),(7.4.9) in domain Σ is reduced to a European-like put option pricing problem with (ξ, t) as the variables. By the Black-Scholes formula, the solution is

$$u(\xi, t) = -e^{-q_1(T-t)}\xi N(-\hat{d}_1) + e^{-q_2(T-t)}N(-\hat{d}_2), \tag{7.4.14}$$

where

$$\hat{d}_1 = \frac{\ln \xi + \left[q_2 - q_1 + \frac{1}{2}(a_{11} - 2a_{12} + a_{22})\right](T-t)}{\sqrt{(a_{11} - 2a_{12} + a_{22})(T-t)}}, \tag{7.4.15}$$

$$\hat{d}_2 = \hat{d}_1 - \sqrt{(a_{11} - 2a_{12} + a_{22})(T-t)}. \tag{7.4.16}$$

Back to the original variable (S_1, S_2, t) by reversing the transformation (7.4.10),(7.4.11), we get

$$V(S_1, S_2, t) = S_2 e^{-q_2(T-t)}N(-\tilde{d}_2) - S_1 e^{-q_1(T-t)}N(-\tilde{d}_1), \tag{7.4.17}$$

$$\tilde{d}_1 = \frac{\ln \frac{S_1}{S_2} + \left[q_2 - q_1 + \frac{1}{2}(a_{11} - 2a_{12} + a_{22})\right](T-t)}{\sqrt{(a_{11} - 2a_{12} + a_{22})(T-t)}}, \tag{7.4.18}$$

$$\tilde{d}_2 = \tilde{d}_1 - \sqrt{(a_{11} - 2a_{12} + a_{22})(T-t)}. \tag{7.4.19}$$

The better-of two risky assets option pricing model: in domain Σ solve equation (7.4.8) with the terminal condition:

$$V(S_1, S_2, T) = \max(S_1, S_2). \tag{7.4.20}$$

By the same transformation (7.4.10),(7.4.11), $u(\xi, t)$ satisfies equation (7.4.12) in domain $\{0 \leq \xi < \infty, 0 \leq t \leq T\}$ and the terminal condition:

$$u(\xi, T) = \frac{1}{S_2}V(S_1, S_2, T) = \max(\xi, 1) = (1-\xi)^+ + \xi. \tag{7.4.21}$$

Then, $u(\xi, t)$ can be expressed as the sum of a vanilla put option (7.4.14) and a function $\xi e^{-q_1(T-t)}$. Back to the original variable (S_1, S_2, t), we get

$$V(S_1, S_2, t) = S_2\left[\frac{S_1}{S_2}(1 - N(-\tilde{d}_1))e^{-q_1(T-t)} + e^{-q_2(T-t)}N(-\hat{d}_2)\right]$$

$$= S_1 e^{-q_1(T-t)}N(d_{1,2}) + S_2 e^{-q_2(T-t)}N(d_{2,1}), \tag{7.4.22}$$

where

$$d_{1,2} = \frac{\ln\frac{S_1}{S_2} + \left[q_2 - q_1 + \frac{1}{2}(a_{11} - 2a_{12} + a_{22})\right](T-t)}{\sqrt{(a_{11} - 2a_{12} + a_{22})(T-t)}}, \tag{7.4.23}$$

$$d_{2,1} = \frac{\ln\frac{S_2}{S_1} + \left[q_1 - q_2 + \frac{1}{2}(a_{11} - 2a_{12} + a_{22})\right](T-t)}{\sqrt{(a_{11} - 2a_{12} + a_{22})(T-t)}}. \tag{7.4.24}$$

7.5 Basket Options

The payoff of basket options is

$$\text{payoff} = (\sum_{i=1}^{n} \alpha_i S_i - K)^+, \tag{7.5.1}$$

where α_i is the portion of the i-th asset S_i in the basket.

Basket options are usually used in trading two or more foreign currencies. Let S_i be the exchange rate of the i-th foreign currency, and K be the weighted average exchange rate based on the exchange rates of all underlying currencies.

According to the portfolio theory, the volatility of the basket is in general smaller than that of each individual currency. Therefore the basket option premium is less than the sum of the premiums of all individual options on each underlying currency.

From the multivariate Black-Scholes formula we can get the pricing formula for the basket options.

Is it possible to reduce the basket option pricing problem to a 1-D problem? The answer is negative! The reason is that the basket option price is based on the **arithmetic mean** of n asset prices, whereas the price of each asset makes **geometric Brownian motion**. However, *if the payoff of a basket option is the geometric mean of n underlying assets, i.e. if the payoff function is*

$$\textit{payoff} = (\prod_{i=1}^{n} S_i^{\alpha_i} - K)^+, \tag{7.5.2}$$

where $\sum \alpha_i = 1, \alpha_i \geq 0$, *then the pricing problem can be reduced to a 1-D problem.*

By transformation

$$x_i = \ln S_i, \tag{7.5.3}$$

equation (7.2.6) becomes (7.3.2), and the payoff function becomes

$$(\prod_{i=1}^{n} S_i^{\alpha_i} - K)^+ = \left(\exp\{\sum_{i=1}^{n} \alpha_i x_i\} - K\right)^+. \tag{7.5.4}$$

Change the variables to

$$\xi = \sum_{i=1}^{n} \alpha_i x_i, \tag{7.5.5}$$

thus,

$$\frac{\partial V}{\partial x_i} = \frac{\partial V}{\partial \xi}\alpha_i,$$

$$\frac{\partial^2 V}{\partial x_i \partial x_j} = \alpha_i \alpha_j \frac{\partial^2 V}{\partial \xi^2}.$$

and equation (7.3.2) is reduced to

$$\frac{\partial V}{\partial t} + \frac{1}{2}\hat{\sigma}^2 \frac{\partial^2 V}{\partial \xi^2} + (r - \hat{q} - \frac{1}{2}\hat{\sigma}^2)\frac{\partial V}{\partial \xi} - rV = 0, \tag{7.5.6}$$

where

$$\hat{\sigma}^2 = \sum_{i,j=1}^{n} a_{ij}\alpha_i\alpha_j,$$

$$\hat{q} = \sum_{i=1}^{n} \alpha_i \left(q_i + \frac{a_{ii}}{2}\right) - \frac{\hat{\sigma}^2}{2}.$$

and the terminal condition (7.5.4) is reduced to

$$V(\xi, T) = (e^{\xi} - K)^+. \tag{7.5.7}$$

Then by the Black-Scholes formula of the vanilla European call options, we can get the expression of $V(\xi, t)$, and back to the original variable $(S_1, \ldots, S_n, t)$, we get

$$V = e^{-\hat{q}(T-t)} S_1^{\alpha_1} \ldots S_n^{\alpha_n} N(\hat{d}_1) - e^{-r(T-t)} K N(\hat{d}_2), \tag{7.5.8}$$

where

$$\hat{d}_1 = \frac{\ln \frac{S_1^{\alpha_1} \ldots S_n^{\alpha_n}}{K} + \left[r - \hat{q} + \frac{\hat{\sigma}^2}{2}\right](T-t)}{\hat{\sigma}\sqrt{(T-t)}}, \tag{7.5.9}$$

$$\hat{d}_2 = \hat{d}_1 - \hat{\sigma}\sqrt{T-t}. \tag{7.5.10}$$

7.6 Quanto Options

Quanto options are cross-currency contracts. In addition to the risk due to the fluctuations of the foreign asset price, there is also a risk due to the fluctuations of the exchange rate for that foreign currency.

Example Suppose a US investor wants to buy a European call option on a certain European company stock at strike price K (Euro). What should be the premium of the option in USD?

Here are two risky assets: one is the European stock price S_1 (in Euro), and the other is the USD/Euro exchange rate S_2. At option maturity, the exchange rate can either be

(1) the spot exchange rate $S_2(t)$, or

(2) a spot exchange rate $S_2(t)$ which will be no less than a guaranteed rate S_2^0.

Correspondingly, the payoff function at maturity is either

$$\text{payoff function} = S_2(T)(S_1(T) - K)^+ \tag{7.6.1}$$

or

$$\begin{aligned} \text{payoff function} &= \max(S_2(T), S_2^0)(S_1(T) - K)^+ \\ &= (S_2(T) - S_2^0)^+(S_1^{(T)} - K)^+ + S_2^0(S_1^{(T)} - K)^+. \end{aligned} \tag{7.6.2}$$

Now let us establish the PDE for quanto option price (in USD).

Suppose

$$\frac{dS_1}{S_1} = \mu_1 dt + \sigma_1 dW_1, \tag{7.6.3}$$

$$\frac{dS_2}{S_2} = \mu_2 dt + \sigma_2 dW_2, \tag{7.6.4}$$

where S_1 is the European stock price (in Euro), S_2 is the USD/Euro rate. Also assume the Brownian motion with correlations,

$$E(dW_i) = 0, Var(dW_i) = dt, \qquad (i = 1, 2)$$

$$Cov(dW_1, dW_2) = \rho dt. \quad (|\rho| < 1)$$

Let the option price be V (in USD):

$$V = V(S_1, S_2, t).$$

By Δ-hedging, construct a portfolio Π (in USD):

$$\Pi = V - \Delta_1 S_2 S_1 - \Delta_2 S_2. \tag{7.6.5}$$

Choose Δ_1, Δ_2 such that Π is risk-free in $(t, t + dt)$, i.e.

$$d\Pi = r_1 \Pi dt, \tag{7.6.6}$$

$$d\Pi = dV - \Delta_1 d(S_1 S_2) - \Delta_2 dS_2 - \Delta_1 S_2 S_1 q dt - \Delta_2 S_2 r_2 dt,$$

where r_1 is the risk-free interest rate in home country, and r_2 is the risk-free interest rate in the foreign country, and q is the dividend rate of the risky asset S_1. By the Itô formula, we have

$$\begin{aligned} dV = & \left\{ \frac{\partial V}{\partial t} + \frac{1}{2}[\sigma_1^2 S_1^2 \frac{\partial^2 V}{\partial S_1^2} + 2\rho\sigma_1\sigma_2 S_1 S_2 \frac{\partial^2 V}{\partial S_1 \partial S_2} \right. \\ & \left. + \ \sigma_2^2 S_2^2 \frac{\partial^2 V}{\partial S_2^2}] \right\} dt + \frac{\partial V}{\partial S_1} dS_1 + \frac{\partial V}{\partial S_2} dS_2, \end{aligned} \tag{7.6.7}$$

$$d(S_1 S_2) = S_1 dS_2 + S_2 dS_1 + \sigma_1 \sigma_2 S_1 S_2 \rho dt. \tag{7.6.8}$$

Thus from (7.6.6)—(7.6.8),

$$
\begin{aligned}
&r_1(V - \Delta_1 S_1 S_2 - \Delta_2 S_2)dt \\
&= \left\{ \frac{\partial V}{\partial t} + \frac{1}{2}[\sigma_1^2 S_1^2 \frac{\partial^2 V}{\partial S_1^2} + 2\rho\sigma_1\sigma_2 S_1 S_2 \frac{\partial^2 V}{\partial S_1 \partial S_2} \right. \\
&+ \left. \sigma_2^2 S_2^2 \frac{\partial^2 V}{\partial S_2^2}] - \Delta_1 \sigma_1 \sigma_2 S_1 S_2 \rho \right\} dt - \Delta_1 S_1 S_2 q dt \\
&- \Delta_2 S_2 r_2 dt + (\frac{\partial V}{\partial S_1} - \Delta_1 S_2) dS_1 \\
&+ (\frac{\partial V}{\partial S_2} - \Delta_1 S_1 - \Delta_2) dS_2.
\end{aligned} \tag{7.6.9}
$$

Choose

$$\Delta_1 S_2 = \frac{\partial V}{\partial S_1},$$

$$\Delta_1 S_1 + \Delta_2 = \frac{\partial V}{\partial S_2}.$$

i.e.

$$\Delta_1 = \frac{1}{S_2}\frac{\partial V}{\partial S_1}, \tag{7.6.10}$$

$$\Delta_2 = \frac{\partial V}{\partial S_2} - \frac{S_1}{S_2}\frac{\partial V}{\partial S_1}. \tag{7.6.11}$$

Substituting (7.6.10),(7.6.11) into (7.6.9), we have

$$
\begin{aligned}
&\frac{\partial V}{\partial t} + \frac{1}{2}[\sigma_1^2 S_1^2 \frac{\partial^2 V}{\partial S_1^2} + 2\rho\sigma_1\sigma_2 S_1 S_2 \frac{\partial^2 V}{\partial S_1 \partial S_2} + \sigma_2^2 S_2^2 \frac{\partial^2 V}{\partial S_2^2}] \\
&\quad + (r_1 - q - \sigma_1\sigma_2\rho) S_1 \frac{\partial V}{\partial S_1} + (r_1 - r_2) S_2 \frac{\partial V}{\partial S_2} \\
&\quad + (r_2 - r_1) S_1 \frac{\partial V}{\partial S_1} - r_1 V = 0.
\end{aligned}
$$

i.e.

$$\frac{\partial V}{\partial t} + \frac{1}{2}\left[\sigma_1^2 S_1^2 \frac{\partial^2 V}{\partial S_1^2} + 2\rho\sigma_1\sigma_2 S_1 S_2 \frac{\partial^2 V}{\partial S_1 \partial S_2} + \sigma_2^2 S_2^2 \frac{\partial^2 V}{\partial S_2^2}\right]$$

$$+ (r_1 - \hat{q}_1) S_1 \frac{\partial V}{\partial S_1} + (r_1 - \hat{q}_2) S_2 \frac{\partial V}{\partial S_2} - r_1 V = 0, \qquad (7.6.12)$$

where

$$\hat{q}_1 = r_1 - r_2 + q + \sigma_1\sigma_2\rho, \qquad (7.6.13)$$

$$\hat{q}_2 = r_2. \qquad (7.6.14)$$

The payoff function at $t = T$ (see (7.6.1), (7.6.2)) is either

$$V(S_1, S_2, T) = S_2(S_1 - K)^+ \qquad (7.6.15)$$

or

$$V(S_1, S_2, T) = \max(S_2, S_2^0)(S_1 - K)^+. \qquad (7.6.16)$$

Therefore the mathematical model of quanto options is a two dimensional PDE terminal value problem (7.6.12), (7.6.15) or (7.6.12), (7.6.16). By the multivariate Black-Scholes formula (7.3.22), we can give an explicit expression of the option price. Take the terminal value problem (7.6.12), (7.6.15) as example,

$$\begin{aligned} V(S_1, S_2, t) &= \frac{1}{2\pi(T-t)} e^{-r_1(T-t)} \frac{1}{\sigma_1\sigma_2\sqrt{1-\rho^2}} \\ &\cdot \int_0^\infty \int_0^\infty \frac{(\eta_1 - K)^+}{\eta_1} \exp\left[-\frac{\sigma_2^2\alpha_1^2 - 2\rho\sigma_1\sigma_2\alpha_1\alpha_2 + \sigma_1^2\alpha_2^2}{2\sigma_1^2\sigma_2^2(1-\rho^2)(T-t)}\right] d\eta_1 d\eta_2, \end{aligned} \qquad (7.6.17)$$

where

$$\alpha_1 = \ln\frac{S_1}{\eta_1} + (r_2 - q - \sigma_1\sigma_2\rho - \frac{\sigma_1^2}{2})(T-t),$$

$$\alpha_2 = \ln\frac{S_2}{\eta_2} + (r_1 - r_2 - \frac{\sigma_2^2}{2})(T-t).$$

Note: in deriving (7.6.17) from (7.3.22), we used

$$A = \begin{bmatrix} \sigma_1^2 & \rho\sigma_1\sigma_2 \\ \rho\sigma_1\sigma_2 & \sigma_2^2 \end{bmatrix},$$

$$\det A = \sigma_1^2\sigma_2^2(1-\rho^2),$$

$$A^{-1} = \frac{1}{\det A}\begin{bmatrix} \sigma_2^2 & -\rho\sigma_1\sigma_2 \\ -\rho\sigma_1\sigma_2 & \sigma_1^2 \end{bmatrix}.$$

7.7 American Multi-Asset Options

As in the case of American single-asset options, the mathematical model of **American multi-asset options** pricing is a parabolic variational inequality.

Define

$$\Sigma = \left\{ (S_1, \ldots, S_n, t) | \, (S_1, \ldots, S_n) \in \mathbf{R}_+^n, 0 \le t < T \right\},$$

$$(\mathbf{R}_+^n = \{(S_1, \ldots, S_n) | 0 \le S_i < \infty, i = 1, \ldots, n\}.)$$

And let $V = V(S_1, \ldots, S_n, t)$ be the American option price. Then V is the solution to the following problem in Σ:

$$\begin{cases} \min\left\{-\frac{\partial V}{\partial t} - \mathcal{L}V, V - P(S_1, \ldots, S_n)\right\} = 0, \quad (\Sigma) & (7.7.1) \\ V(S_1, \ldots, S_n) = P(S_1, \ldots, S_n), \quad (\mathbf{R}_+^n) & (7.7.2) \end{cases}$$

where $\mathcal{L}$ is the multivariate Black-Scholes differential operator given by (7.2.6):

$$\mathcal{L}V = \frac{1}{2}\sum_{i,j=1}^{n} a_{ij}S_iS_j\frac{\partial^2 V}{\partial S_i \partial S_j} + \sum_{i=1}^{n}(r - q_i)S_i\frac{\partial V}{\partial S_i} - rV,$$

and $P(S_1, \ldots, S_n)$ is the payoff function. Equation (7.7.1) indicates: in the continuation region Σ_1:

$$\frac{\partial V}{\partial t} + \mathcal{L}V = 0,$$

$$V > P(S_1, \ldots, S_n);$$

and in the stopping region Σ_2:

$$\frac{\partial V}{\partial t} + \mathcal{L}V \le 0,$$

$$V = P(S_1, \ldots, S_n).$$

The interface Γ between Σ_1 and Σ_2 is the optimal exercise boundary of the American multi-asset option. *V as a function of $n+1$ variables $(S_1, \ldots, S_n, t)$, and its derivatives with respect to $S_1, \ldots, S_n$, i.e. V and $\nabla_x V$, are continuous in the entire region $\Sigma = \Sigma_1 \bigcup \Gamma \bigcup \Sigma_2$,.* As in the case of American single-asset options, we can also formulate (7.7.1),(7.7.2) as a free boundary problem. However, for American multi-asset options, the structure of the optimal exercise boundary (i.e. the free boundary) can be extremely complicated, therefore we need to combine various payoff functions $P(S_1, \ldots, S_n)$ to study the behavior of the boundary Γ.

To study the behavior of the optimal exercise boundary Γ, we need to first study the properties of the option price $V = V(S_1, \ldots, S_n, t)$. Similar to what we did in §6.4, we study the signs of $\frac{\partial V}{\partial S_i}, \frac{\partial V}{\partial t}$ by introducing a penalty function. Since the procedures are analogous, we only give the conclusions, and leave the proof to the reader.

Theorem 7.1 *Suppose the payoff function $P(S_1, \ldots, S_n)$ satisfies:*

(1) $P(S_1, \ldots, S_n)$ is a Lipschitz continuous function;

(2) There exists $P_\varepsilon(S_1, \ldots, S_n) \in C^\infty(\mathbf{R}_+^n)$, such that

$$\lim_{\varepsilon \to 0} P_\varepsilon(S_1, \ldots, S_n) = P(S_1, \ldots, S_n),$$

and is uniformly convergent in any finite bounded domain within $\mathbf{R}_+^n$;

(3) $$\frac{\partial P_\varepsilon}{\partial S_i} > 0 \ \left(or\ \frac{\partial P_\varepsilon}{\partial S_i} < 0\right), \tag{7.7.3}$$

and in any finite bounded domain D within $\mathbf{R}_+^n$, there exists a constant C_D which depends on D only and is independent of ϵ, such that

$$\mathcal{L}P_\varepsilon \geq C_D, \tag{7.7.4}$$

then the solution of the American multi-asset option pricing problem (7.7.1),(7.7.2) has the following properties:

(1) $V(S_1, \ldots, S_n, t)$ is a nondecreasing (monotone increasing) function of $S_i (i = 1, \ldots n)$,

(2) $V(S_1, \ldots, S_n, t)$ is a nonincreasing function of t.

Now let us study the properties of the optimal exercise boundary for American multi-asset options with a specific payoff function.

(A) **American better-of option on two assets**

The mathematical model is: ([20])

$$\begin{cases} \min\left\{-\frac{\partial V}{\partial t} - \mathcal{L}V, V - P(S_1, S_2)\right\} = 0, \quad (\Sigma) & (7.7.5)\\ V|_{t=T} = P(S_1, S_2), \quad (S_1, S_2 \in \mathbf{R}_+^2) & (7.7.6)\end{cases}$$

where

$$\begin{aligned}\mathcal{L}V = {} & \frac{1}{2}\left[\sigma_1^2 S_1^2 \frac{\partial^2 V}{\partial S_1^2} + 2\rho\sigma_1\sigma_2 S_1 S_2 \frac{\partial^2 V}{\partial S_1 \partial S_2} + \sigma_2^2 S_2^2 \frac{\partial^2 V}{\partial S_2^2}\right] \\ & + (r - q_1) S_1 \frac{\partial V}{\partial S_1} + (r - q_2) S_2 \frac{\partial V}{\partial S_2} - rV = 0, \end{aligned} \tag{7.7.7}$$

$$P(S_1, S_2) = \max(S_1, S_2). \tag{7.7.8}$$

Similar to §7.4, we introduce the transformation (see (7.4.10),(7.4.11))

$$\xi = \frac{S_1}{S_2}, \qquad u(\xi, t) = \frac{V(S_1, S_2, t)}{S_2}. \tag{7.7.9}$$

Under the above transformation, the problem (7.7.5),(7.7.6) is reduced to the following one dimensional problem: in

$$\hat{\Sigma} = \{(\xi, t)\,|0 \le \xi \le \infty, 0 \le t \le T\},$$

solve:

$$\begin{cases} \min\left\{-\frac{\partial u}{\partial t} - \frac{1}{2}\hat{\sigma}^2\xi^2\frac{\partial^2 u}{\partial \xi^2} - (q_2 - q_1)\xi\frac{\partial u}{\partial \xi}\right. \\ \qquad\qquad \left. + q_2 u, u - \max(\xi, 1)\right\} = 0, & (7.7.10) \\ u\,|_{t=T} = \max(\xi, 1), & (7.7.11)\end{cases}$$

where

$$\hat{\sigma}^2 = \sigma_1^2 + 2\rho\sigma_1\sigma_2 + \sigma_2^2. \tag{7.7.12}$$

If

$$q_1, q_2 > 0, \tag{7.7.13}$$

then we can write $\hat{\Sigma}$ as $\hat{\Sigma}_1 \cup \hat{\Gamma} \cup \hat{\Sigma}_2$, where $\hat{\Sigma}_1$ is the "continuation region" of the option:

$$u > \max(\xi, 1),$$

$$\frac{\partial u}{\partial t} + \frac{1}{2}\hat{\sigma}^2\xi^2\frac{\partial^2 u}{\partial \xi^2} + (q_2 - q_1)\xi\frac{\partial u}{\partial \xi} - q_2 u = 0;$$

$\hat{\Sigma}_2$ is the "stopping region" of the option:

$$u = \max(\xi, 1),$$

$$\frac{\partial u}{\partial t} + \frac{1}{2}\hat{\sigma}^2\xi^2\frac{\partial^2 u}{\partial \xi^2} + (q_2 - q_1)\xi\frac{\partial u}{\partial \xi} - q_2 u \leq 0;$$

$\hat{\Gamma}$ is the interface of $\hat{\Sigma}_1$ and $\hat{\Sigma}_2$.

Theorem 7.2 *If (7.7.13) is true, then for the problem (7.7.10), (7.7.11), the continuation region is:*

$$\hat{\Sigma}_1 = \{(\xi, t)\,|\xi_1(t) \leq \xi \leq \xi_2(t), 0 \leq t \leq T\},$$

where

$$\xi_1(T) = \xi_2(T) = 1,$$

$$\begin{aligned}&\xi_1(t) \textit{ nondecreasing,}\\&\xi_2(t) \textit{ nonincreasing.}\end{aligned}$$

In $\hat{\Sigma}_1$, u satisfies the free boundary problem:

$$\begin{cases} \frac{\partial u}{\partial t} + \frac{1}{2}\hat{\sigma}^2\xi^2\frac{\partial^2 u}{\partial \xi^2} + (q_2 - q_1)\xi\frac{\partial u}{\partial \xi} - q_2 u = 0, \quad (\hat{\Sigma}_1) & (7.7.14)\\ u(\xi_1(t), t) = 1, \quad (0 \leq t \leq T) & (7.7.15)\\ \frac{\partial u}{\partial \xi}(\xi_1(t), t) = 0, \quad (0 \leq t \leq T) & (7.7.16)\\ u(\xi_2(t), t) = \xi, \quad (0 \leq t \leq T) & (7.7.17)\\ \frac{\partial u}{\partial \xi}(\xi_2(t), t) = 1. \quad (0 \leq t \leq T) & (7.7.18)\end{cases}$$

Proof We first prove $\partial\hat{\Sigma}_1 \bigcap \{t = T\}$, the intersection of the boundary $\partial\hat{\Sigma}_1$ of $\hat{\Sigma}_1$ and the line $t = T$, cannot be an open set. Suppose otherwise, i.e. there exists $(a, b) \in \partial\hat{\Sigma}_1 \bigcap \{t = T\}$. Since u satisfies the parabolic equation (7.7.14) in $\hat{\Sigma}_1$, thus due to the regularity of the solution of parabolic equation, at $t = T$, excluding $\xi = 1$, in (a, b) there is

$$\begin{aligned}\frac{\partial u}{\partial t}|_{t=T} &= \left[-\frac{1}{2}\hat{\sigma}^2\xi^2\frac{\partial^2}{\partial \xi^2} - (q_2 - q_1)\xi\frac{\partial}{\partial \xi} + q_2\right]\max(\xi, 1)\\ &= \begin{cases} q_1\xi, \ \xi > 1,\\ q_2, \ \ \xi < 1.\end{cases}\end{aligned}$$

By assumption (7.7.13), $\frac{\partial u}{\partial t}|_{t=T} > 0$ within (a, b) (excluding $\xi = 1$). Thus in the neighborhood of $t = T$, u is strictly increasing, i.e.

$$u(\xi, t) < u(\xi, T) = \max(1, \xi).$$

This contradicts to $u \geq \max(1, \xi)$.

Let $\partial\hat{\Sigma}_1$ be the boundary of $\hat{\Sigma}_1$, then by Theorem 7.1, $u(\xi, t)$ is nondecreasing with respect to ξ. Thus by similar argument as above, we claim

$$\partial\hat{\Sigma}_1 \cap \{t = T\} = \text{point}(1, T),$$

and the following two continuous rays originating from $(1, T)$ are the free boundaries: $\xi = \xi_1(t)$ and $\xi = \xi_2(t)$, where $\xi_1(t) < 1 < \xi_2(t)$. In $\partial\hat{\Sigma}_1$, u satisfies the free boundary conditions (7.7.15),(7.7.16) and (7.7.17),(7.7.18).

Now let us examine the intersection of each line $\xi = \xi_0$ and $\partial\hat{\Sigma}_1$.

It follows from the previous arguments, there exists $0 \leq \tau(\xi_0) \leq T$, such that the line segment $\{(\xi, \tau) \,|\xi = \xi_0 \,, \tau(\xi_0) \ \leq \tau \leq T\}$ belongs to the "stopping" region $\hat{\Sigma}_2$. Here

$$\begin{aligned} \tau(1) &= T, \\ \tau(\xi_0) &< T, \qquad (\xi_0 \neq 1) \end{aligned}$$

By Theorem 7.1, $V(\xi, t)$ is nondecreasing with respect to t, thus the line $\xi = \xi_0$ and $\partial\hat{\Sigma}_1$ may either

(1) intersect once (at a point or a segment)

or

(2) not intersect at all.

Thus we have proved

$$\xi_1(t) < 1 < \xi_2(t)$$

and

$$\xi_1(t) \text{ nondecreasing,}$$

$$\xi_2(t) \text{ nonincreasing.}$$

Thus competes the proof of Theorem 7.2.

Remark In fact, by the regularity of the solution of parabolic equation and the strong maximum principle, we can further show that the line $\xi = \xi_0$ and $\partial\hat{\Sigma}_1$ cannot intersect at a segment, i.e. $\xi_1(t)$ and $\xi_2(t)$ must be strictly increasing and decreasing, respectively.

Back to the original variables (S_1, S_2, t), we get the price of the American better-of option:

$$V(S_1, S_2, t) = S_2 u(\frac{S_1}{S_2}, t) = \begin{cases} S_2, & 0 \le \frac{S_1}{S_2} \le \xi_1(t), \\ S_2 u(\frac{S_1}{S_2}, t), & \xi_1(t) \le \frac{S_1}{S_2} \le \xi_2(t), \\ S_1, & \xi_2(t) \le \frac{S_1}{S_2} < \infty, \end{cases} \tag{7.7.19}$$

where the optimal exercise boundary consists of surfaces Γ_1 and Γ_2:

$$\Gamma_1 : S_1 = \xi_1(t) S_2, \tag{7.7.20}$$

and

$$\Gamma_2 : S_1 = \xi_2(t) S_2, \tag{7.7.21}$$

where $\xi_1(T) = \xi_2(T) = 1$, $\xi_1(t) \uparrow, \xi_2(t) \downarrow$.

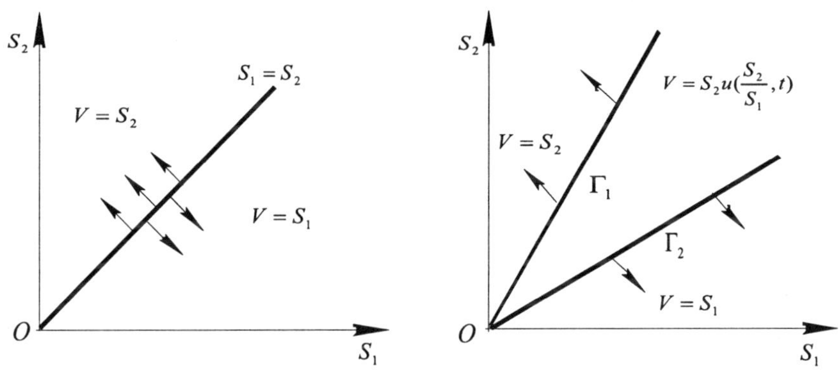

Left figure: At $t = T, \Gamma_1$ and Γ_2 degenerate to a ray: $S_1 = S_2$.
Right figure: At $t < T$, positions of Γ_1, Γ_2

This shows how the optimal exercise boundary Γ for American better-of options evolves with time t according to the following picture: At $t = T$, Γ_1 and Γ_2 coincide to the ray $S_1 = S_2$. When $t < T$, the optimal exercise boundary lines separate. At any given time t, the optimal exercise boundary consists of two rays originating from $(0, 0)$: $S_1 = \xi_1(t) S_2$ and $S_1 = \xi_2(t) S_2$. Between them lies the continuation region, and beyond them lies the stopping region. At $t = 0$, the optimal exercise boundary rays are $S_1 = \xi_1(0) S_2$ and $S_1 = \xi_2(0) S_2$. Now we ask: is it possible to estimate the lower bound of $\xi_1(0)$ and the upper bound of $\xi_2(0)$?

To answer this question, we consider the model of the perpetual American better-of option pricing. Similar to §6.1, this is an elliptic obstacle problem:

$$\begin{cases} \min\{-\mathcal{L}V_\infty, V_\infty - \max(S_1, S_2)\} = 0, \quad (\mathbf{R}_+^2) & (7.7.22) \\ V_\infty(0, S_2) = S_2, \quad (S_1 \in \mathbf{R}_+) & (7.7.23) \\ V_\infty(S_1, 0) = S_1. \quad (S_2 \in \mathbf{R}_+) & (7.7.24) \end{cases}$$

Under the transformation

$$V_\infty = S_2 W, \tag{7.7.25}$$

$$\xi = \frac{S_1}{S_2}. \tag{7.7.26}$$

the free boundary problem (7.7.22)—(7.7.24) is reduced an ODE obstacle problem in domain $\mathbf{R}_+$:

$$\begin{cases} \min\{-\frac{1}{2}\hat{\sigma}^2\xi^2\frac{d^2W}{d\xi^2} - (q_2 - q_1)\xi\frac{dW}{d\xi} + q_2 W, \\ \qquad W - \max(1, \xi)\} = 0, \quad (\xi \in \mathbf{R}_+) & (7.7.27) \\ W(0) = 1, & (7.7.28) \\ W(\xi) \sim \xi, \quad (\xi \to \infty) & (7.7.29) \end{cases}$$

where $\hat{\sigma}$ is defined in (7.7.12).

Similar to §6.1, the obstacle problem (7.7.27)—(7.7.29) is equivalent to the following free boundary problem: find $\{W(\xi); \xi_1^0, \xi_2^0\}$ such that

$$\begin{cases} \frac{1}{2}\hat{\sigma}^2\xi^2\frac{d^2W}{d\xi^2} + (q_2 - q_1)\xi\frac{dW}{d\xi} - q_2 W = 0, \quad (\xi_1^0 < \xi < \xi_2^0) & (7.7.30) \\ W(\xi_1^0) = 1, & (7.7.31) \\ W'(\xi_1^0) = 0, & (7.7.32) \\ W(\xi_2^0) = \xi_2^0, & (7.7.33) \\ W'(\xi_2^0) = 1. & (7.7.34) \end{cases}$$

The general solution to equation (7.7.30) is

$$W = A\left(\frac{\xi}{\xi_1^0}\right)^{\alpha_1} + B\left(\frac{\xi}{\xi_2^0}\right)^{\alpha_2}, \tag{7.7.35}$$

where $\alpha_i (i = 1, 2)$ are the two roots of the characteristic equation:

$$\frac{1}{2}\hat{\sigma}^2\alpha(\alpha - 1) + (q_2 - q_1)\alpha - q_2 = 0,$$

i.e.

$$\alpha_i = \omega + (-1)^i\theta, \quad (i = 1, 2) \tag{7.7.36}$$

where

$$\omega = \frac{1}{2} + \frac{1}{\hat{\sigma}^2}(q_1 - q_2), \tag{7.7.37}$$

$$\theta = \sqrt{\frac{1}{4} + \frac{q_1}{\hat{\sigma}^2} + \frac{(q_1 - q_2)^2}{\hat{\sigma}^4}}. \tag{7.7.38}$$

It follows from the assumption (7.7.13) that

$$\alpha_1 < 0, \quad \alpha_2 > 0.$$

A, B, ξ_1^0, ξ_2^0 can be determined from the free boundary conditions (7.7.31)—(7.7.34):

$$A\left(\frac{\xi_2^0}{\xi_1^0}\right)^{\alpha_1} + B = \xi_2^0,$$

$$A\frac{\alpha_1}{\xi_1^0}\left(\frac{\xi_2^0}{\xi_1^0}\right)^{\alpha_1 - 1} + B\frac{\alpha_2}{\xi_2^0} = 1,$$

$$A + B\left(\frac{\xi_1^0}{\xi_2^0}\right)^{\alpha_2} = 1,$$

$$A\frac{\alpha_1}{\xi_1^0} + B\frac{\alpha_2}{\xi_2^0}\left(\frac{\xi_1^0}{\xi_2^0}\right)^{\alpha_2 - 1} = 0.$$

Solving the above system of equations, we get A, B, ξ_1^0, ξ_2^0. Then substituting them into (7.7.35), we get

$$\xi_1^0 = \beta_1^{\frac{\alpha_1 - 1}{\alpha_2 - \alpha_1}} \beta_2^{\frac{1 - \alpha_2}{\alpha_2 - \alpha_1}},$$

$$\xi_2^0 = \beta_1^{\frac{\alpha_1}{\alpha_2 - \alpha_1}} \beta_2^{\frac{-\alpha_2}{\alpha_2 - \alpha_1}},$$

$$W(\xi) = \frac{\alpha_1}{\alpha_1 - \alpha_2}\beta_1^{\frac{\alpha_2(1-\alpha_1)}{\alpha_2 - \alpha_1}} \beta_2^{-\frac{\alpha_2(1+\alpha_2)}{\alpha_2 - \alpha_1}} \xi^{\alpha_2}$$

$$+ \frac{\alpha_2}{\alpha_2 - \alpha_1}\beta_2^{\frac{\alpha_1(\alpha_2 - 1)}{\alpha_2 - \alpha_1}} \beta_1^{\frac{\alpha_1(1-\alpha_1)}{\alpha_2 - \alpha_1}} \xi^{\alpha_1}, \qquad (\xi_1^0 < \xi < \xi_2^0)$$

where

$$\beta_i = \frac{\alpha_i - 1}{\alpha_i}. \qquad (i = 1, 2) \tag{7.7.39}$$

Back to the original variables S_1, S_2 and V_∞ (see (7.7.25), (7.7.26)), we get the pricing formula of the perpetual American better-of option:

$$V_\infty(S_1,S_2)=\begin{cases} S_2, & 0\le \frac{S_1}{S_2}=\xi_1^0,\\ \frac{\alpha_1}{\alpha_1-\alpha_2}\beta_1^{\frac{\alpha_2(1-\alpha_1)}{\alpha_2-\alpha_1}}\beta_2^{-\frac{\alpha_2(1+\alpha_2)}{\alpha_2-\alpha_1}}S_1^{\alpha_2}S_2^{1-\alpha_2} & \\ \quad +\frac{\alpha_2}{\alpha_2-\alpha_1}\beta_1^{\frac{\alpha_1(1-\alpha_1)}{\alpha_2-\alpha_1}}\beta_2^{\frac{\alpha_1(\alpha_2-1)}{\alpha_2-\alpha_1}}S_1^{\alpha_1}S_2^{1-\alpha_1}, & \xi_1^0\le\frac{S_1}{S_2}\le\xi_2^0,\\ S_1, & \xi_2^0\le\frac{S_1}{S_2}<\infty. \end{cases}$$

$$\Gamma_1: \quad S_1=\xi_1^0 S_2,$$

$$\Gamma_2: \quad S_1=\xi_2^0 S_2.$$

Positions of the optimal exercise boundary Γ_1 and Γ_2 for the perpetual American better-of option

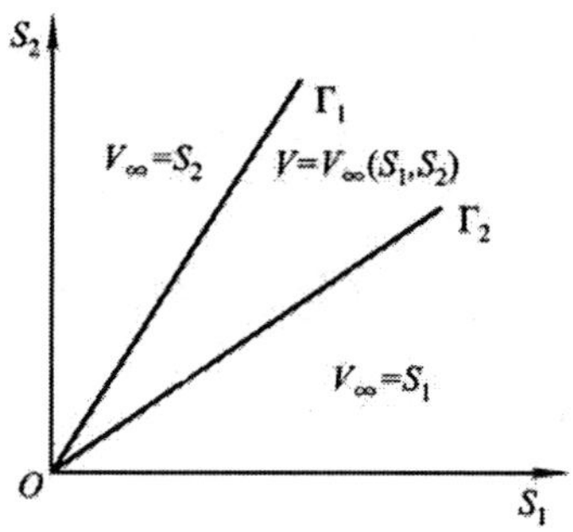

Since the perpetual American better-of option is the most expensive one comparing to other American better-of options with the same strike price, thus

$$\max\{S_1,S_2\}\le V(S_1,S_2,t)\le V_\infty(S_1,S_2).$$

Thus we have

$$\xi_1^0<\xi_1(t)<\xi_1(T)=1=\xi_2(T)<\xi_2(t)<\xi_2^0.$$

Thus for American better-of option's optimal exercise boundary Γ_1 and Γ_2, we have the following two valuation relations for their slopes:

$$\xi_1(t)>\xi_1^0=\beta_1^{\frac{\alpha_1-1}{\alpha_2-\alpha_1}}\beta_2^{\frac{1-\alpha_2}{\alpha_2-\alpha_1}},$$

$$\xi_2(t)<\xi_2^0=\beta_1^{\frac{\alpha_1}{\alpha_2-\alpha_1}}\beta_2^{\frac{-\alpha_2}{\alpha_2-\alpha_1}},$$

where $\alpha_1, \alpha_2, \beta_1, \beta_2$ are defined in (7.7.36)—(7.3.39).

Remark The above analysis of the optimal exercise boundary for American better-of options is made under the assumption (7.7.13). If one of the dividend rates $q_i (i = 1, 2)$ is 0, then the behavior of the optimal exercise boundary should be modified.

Without losing generality, let us assume

$$q_1 > 0, q_2 = 0. \tag{7.7.40}$$

Then under transformation (7.7.9), the problem (7.7.5),(7.7.6) is reduced to

$$\begin{cases} \min\left\{-\frac{\partial u}{\partial t} - \frac{1}{2}\hat{\sigma}^2\xi^2\frac{\partial^2 u}{\partial \xi^2} + q_1\xi\frac{\partial u}{\partial \xi}, u - \max(\xi, 1)\right\} = 0, & (7.7.41) \\ u(\xi, T) = \max(\xi, 1). & (7.7.42) \end{cases}$$

Thus corresponding to Theorem 7.2, we have

Theorem 7.3 *If assumption (7.7.40) is true, then for the problem (7.7.41),(7.7.42), the continuation region is*

$$\tilde{\Sigma}_1 = \{(\xi, t) \mid 0 \leq \xi \leq \xi_2(t), 0 \leq t \leq T\},$$

where

$$\xi_2(T) = 1,$$

$$\xi_2(t) \text{ nonincreasing,}$$

and in $\tilde{\Sigma}_1$, u satisfies the following free boundary problem:

$$\begin{cases} \frac{\partial u}{\partial t} + \frac{1}{2}\hat{\sigma}^2\xi^2\frac{\partial^2 u}{\partial \xi^2} - q_1\xi\frac{\partial u}{\partial \xi} = 0, \ (\tilde{\Sigma}_1) \\ u(\xi_2(t), t) = \xi, & (0 \leq t \leq T) \\ \frac{\partial u}{\partial \xi}(\xi_2(t), t) = 1, & (0 \leq t < T) \\ u(0, t) = 1. & (0 \leq t \leq T) \end{cases}$$

i.e. for problem (7.7.41),(7.7.42) there is only one free boundary $\xi = \xi_2(t)$, in $\hat{\Sigma} = \{0 \leq \xi < \infty, 0 \leq t \leq T\}$, u is of the form

$$u(\xi, t) = \begin{cases} u(\xi, t), \ 0 \leq \xi \leq \xi_2(t), \\ \xi, \qquad \xi_2(t) \leq \xi < \infty. \end{cases}$$

Back to the original variables, the option price is

$$V(S_1, S_2, t) = \begin{cases} S_2 u(\frac{S_2}{S_1}, t), \ 0 \leq \frac{S_1}{S_2} \leq \xi_2(t), \\ S_1, \qquad \xi_2(t) \leq \frac{S_1}{S_2} < \infty. \end{cases}$$

and the optimal exercise boundary is

$$\Gamma : S_1 = \xi_2(t) S_2. \tag{7.7.43}$$

The proof of Theorem 7.3 is left to the reader.

Consider the perpetual American better-of option, under assumption (7.7.40), by transformation (7.7.25),(7.7.26), $\{W(\xi), \xi_2^0\}$ satisfies the free boundary problem as follows:

$$\begin{cases} -\frac{1}{2}\hat{\sigma}^2 \xi^2 \frac{d^2 W}{d\xi^2} + q_1 \xi \frac{dW}{d\xi} = 0, \qquad 0 < \xi < \xi_2^0, & (7.7.44) \\ W(\xi_2^0) = \xi_2^0, & (7.7.45) \\ W'(\xi_2^0) = 1, & (7.7.46) \\ W(0) = 1. & (7.7.47) \end{cases}$$

Its characteristic equation is

$$\frac{1}{2}\hat{\sigma}^2 \alpha(\alpha - 1) - q_1 \alpha = 0,$$

which has two roots α_1, α_2:

$$\alpha_i = \omega + (-1)^i \theta, \qquad (i = 1, 2)$$

where

$$\theta = \omega = \frac{1}{2} + \frac{1}{\hat{\sigma}^2} q_1,$$

thus

$$\alpha_1 = 0 < \alpha_2.$$

The solution of the free boundary problem (7.7.44)—(7.7.47) is of the form:

$$\omega = A + B \left(\frac{\xi}{\xi_2^0} \right)^{\alpha_2}. \tag{7.7.48}$$

Applying the free boundary conditions (7.7.45),(7.7.46) and (7.7.47), we get

$$A = 1,$$

$$A + B = \xi_2^0,$$

$$\frac{\alpha_2 B}{\xi_2^0} = 1.$$

Solving the system, we get A, B and ξ_2^0. Substituting them into (7.7.47), we get

$$W = 1 + \frac{1}{\alpha_2 - 1}(\frac{\xi}{\xi_2^0})^{\alpha_2},$$

$$\xi_2^0 = \frac{\alpha_2}{\alpha_2 - 1}.$$

Back to the original variables (S_1, S_2), we get

$$V_\infty(S_1, S_2) = \begin{cases} S_2 + \frac{(\xi_2^0)^{-\alpha_2}}{\alpha_2 - 1} S_1^{\alpha_2} S_2^{\alpha_2 - 1}, & 0 \leq \frac{S_1}{S_2} \leq \xi_2^0, \\ S_1, & \xi_2^0 \leq \frac{S_1}{S_2} \leq \infty. \end{cases}$$

Since

$$\max(S_1, S_2) \leq V(S_1, S_2, t) \leq V_\infty(S_1, S_2),$$

thus we have an estimate for the slope the of the optimal exercise boundary (7.7.43) under assumption (7.7.40):

$$\xi_2(t) < \xi_2^0 = \frac{\alpha_2}{\alpha_2 - 1} = \frac{\hat{\sigma}^2}{2q_1} + 1.$$

Remark If both underlying assets are non-dividend-paying, i.e., $q_i(i = 1, 2) = 0$, then as in the case of single-asset option, it is unwise to early exercise the American better-of option. Then American better-of option has the same price as European better-of option, and there is no optimal exercise boundary.

(B) American call-max options on two risky assets

For American call-max options on two risky assets, the exercise payoff is:

$$P(S_1, S_2) = (\max(S_1, S_2) - K)^+. \tag{7.7.49}$$

It can be regarded as a generalization of the American better-of option discussed in (A), since American better-of option is the $K = 0$ case of American call-max options on two risky assets.

American call-max options on two risky assets ($K > 0$) is a typical 2-D problem. We will make an in-depth qualitative study of its optimal exercise boundary by mathematical analysis. In particular we will make use of the results of the optimal exercise boundary for American better-of options and of the relation between the optimal exercise boundaries of these two American options to gain a deep understanding of the behavior of the optimal exercise boundary for American call-max options on two risky assets. ([20])

The mathematical model for American call-max options on two risky assets: in domain

$$\Sigma : \{(S_1, S_2) \in \mathbf{R}_+^2, 0 \leq t \leq T\}$$

solve the variational inequality

$$\begin{cases} \min\left\{-\frac{\partial V}{\partial t} - \mathcal{L}V, V - P(S_1, S_2)\right\} = 0, \quad (\Sigma) & (7.7.50) \\ V\mid_{t=T} = P(S_1, S_2), \quad (S_1, S_2) \in \mathbf{R}_+^2 & (7.7.51) \end{cases}$$

where $P(S_1, S_2)$ is defined in (7.7.49), and

$$\mathcal{L}V = \frac{1}{2}\left[\sigma_1^2 S_1^2 \frac{\partial^2 V}{\partial S_1^2} + 2\rho\sigma_1\sigma_2 S_1 S_2 \frac{\partial^2 V}{\partial S_1 \partial S_2} + \sigma_2^2 S_2^2 \frac{\partial^2 V}{\partial S_2^2}\right]$$
$$+ (r - q_1)S_1 \frac{\partial V}{\partial S_1} + (r - q_2)S_2 \frac{\partial V}{\partial S_2} - rV. \tag{7.7.52}$$

By transformation

$$x_i = \ln S_i, \qquad (i = 1, 2)$$

the problem (7.7.50),(7.7.51) becomes

$$\begin{cases} \min\left\{-\frac{\partial V}{\partial t} - \mathcal{L}_0 V, V - p(x_1, x_2)\right\} = 0, \quad (x_1, x_2) \in \mathbf{R}^2, 0 \le t \le T, & (7.7.53) \\ V\mid_{t=T} = p(x_1, x_2), \quad (x_1, x_2) \in \mathbf{R}^2, & (7.7.54) \end{cases}$$

where

$$\mathcal{L}_0 V = \frac{1}{2}\left[\sigma_1^2 \frac{\partial^2 V}{\partial x_1^2} + 2\rho\sigma_1\sigma_2 \frac{\partial^2 V}{\partial x_1 \partial x_2} + \sigma_2^2 \frac{\partial^2 V}{\partial x_2^2}\right]$$
$$+ (r - q_1 - \frac{\sigma_1^2}{2})\frac{\partial V}{\partial x_1} + (r - q_2 - \frac{\sigma_2^2}{2})\frac{\partial V}{\partial x_2} - rV, \tag{7.7.55}$$

$$p(x_1, x_2) = P(e^{x_1}, e^{x_2}) = (\max(e^{x_1}, e^{x_2}) - K)^+. \tag{7.7.56}$$

To show that the option price is monotonic with respect to S_1, S_2, t, K (i.e. x_1, x_2, t, K), we need to introduce $p_\epsilon(x_1, x_2) \in C^\infty(\mathbf{R}^2)$ according to the conditions of Theorem 7.1. Therefore we define a function $p_\epsilon(x_1, x_2)$:

$$p_\epsilon(x_1, x_2) = \Pi_\epsilon(F_\epsilon(x_1, x_2) - K), \qquad (\epsilon > 0) \tag{7.7.57}$$

where

$$\Pi_\epsilon(s) = \begin{cases} s, & s \ge \epsilon, \\ \nearrow, & -\epsilon \le s \le \epsilon \\ 0, & s \le -\epsilon. \end{cases} \tag{7.7.58}$$

and

$$\left.\begin{aligned}&\Pi_\epsilon(s)\in C^\infty(\mathbf{R}),\\&0\le \Pi_\epsilon'(s)\le 1,\\&\Pi_\epsilon''(s)\ge 0,\end{aligned}\right\} \tag{7.7.59}$$

$$\lim_{\epsilon\to 0}\Pi_\epsilon(s)=s^+.$$

And define

$$F_\epsilon(x_1,x_2)=\frac{e^{x_1}+e^{x_2}}{2}+\frac{e^{x_1}-e^{x_2}}{2}h(\frac{e^{x_1}-e^{x_2}}{2\epsilon}), \tag{7.7.60}$$

where

$$h(S)=\frac{2}{\pi}\arctan S. \tag{7.7.61}$$

It is easy to check:

$$\begin{aligned}&h'(S)\ge 0,\\&0\le 2h'(S)+Sh''(S)\le \tfrac{4}{\pi},\\&0\le 1\pm[h(S)+Sh'(S)]\le 2.\end{aligned} \tag{7.7.62}$$

Then we have

$$\lim_{\epsilon\to 0}F_\epsilon(x_1,x_2)=\max(e^{x_1},e^{x_2}).$$

And therefore

$$\lim_{\epsilon\to 0}p_\epsilon(x_1,x_2)=(\max(e^{x_1},e^{x_2})-K)^+=p(x_1,x_2).$$

Obviously, $p_\epsilon(x_1,x_2)$ is monotonic with respect to x_1, x_2, K.

To check condition (7.7.4) of Theorem 7.1, we only need to examine the lower bound of $\mathcal{L}_0 p_\epsilon(x_1,x_2)$.

Since

$$(F_\epsilon)_{x_1x_1}=\frac{e^{2x_1}}{4\epsilon}\left[2h'(S)+Sh''(S)\right]+\frac{e^{x_1}}{2}\left[1+h(S)+Sh'(S)\right],$$

$$(F_\epsilon)_{x_1x_2}=\frac{e^{x_1+x_2}}{4\epsilon}\left[-2h'(S)-Sh''(S)\right],$$

$$(F_\epsilon)_{x_2x_2}=\frac{e^{2x_2}}{4\epsilon}\left[2h'(S)+Sh''(S)\right]+\frac{e^{x_2}}{2}\left[1-h(S)-Sh'(S)\right],$$

where

$$S=\frac{e^{x_1}-e^{x_2}}{2\epsilon},$$

thus by straightforward computation, from (7.7.59),(7.7.62), we get

$$
\begin{aligned}
\mathcal{L}p_\epsilon = & \frac{1}{2}\Pi_\epsilon^{''}(F_\epsilon - K)\left[\sigma_1^2(F_{\epsilon x_1})^2 + 2\rho\sigma_1\sigma_2 F_{\epsilon x_1} F_{\epsilon x_2}\right. \\
& + \left.\sigma_2^2(F_{\epsilon x_2})^2\right] + \frac{1}{8\epsilon}\Pi_\epsilon^{'}(F_\epsilon - K)\left[2h'(S) + Sh''(S)\right] \\
& \cdot \left[\sigma_1^2 e^{2x_1} - 2\rho\sigma_1\sigma_2 e^{x_1+x_2} + \sigma_2^2 e^{2x_2}\right] \\
& + \frac{e^{x_1}}{2}(r - q_1)\Pi_\epsilon^{'}(F_\epsilon - K)(1 + h(S) + Sh'(S)) \\
& + \frac{e^{x_2}}{2}(r - q_2)\Pi_\epsilon^{'}(F_\epsilon - K)(1 - h(S) - Sh'(S)) \\
& - r\Pi_\epsilon(F_\epsilon - K) \\
\geq & \, r\left[-\Pi_\epsilon(F_\epsilon - K) + \Pi_\epsilon^{'}(F_\epsilon - K)(F_\epsilon - K)\right] \\
& + \Pi_\epsilon^{'}(F_\epsilon - K)\left[rK - \max(q_1, q_2)F_\epsilon\right] \\
& + \frac{4\epsilon}{\pi}\Pi_\epsilon^{'}(F_\epsilon - K)(r - \max(q_1, q_2))\frac{S^2}{1 + S^2}.
\end{aligned}
$$

Define $D = \{0 \leq S_i \leq M(i = 1, 2)\}$, then since

$$\max_D F_\epsilon \leq e^M,$$

thus from

$$\Pi_\epsilon(S) - S\Pi_\epsilon^{'}(S) \leq \Pi_\epsilon(0) \leq \frac{\epsilon}{2},$$

we get

$$\mathcal{L}p_\epsilon \geq -\frac{\epsilon}{2}r - \max(q_1, q_2)\left[e^M + \frac{4\epsilon}{\pi}\right].$$

If

$$\frac{\epsilon}{2}r < 1, M > 1,$$

then

$$\mathcal{L}P_\epsilon \geq -1 - 2\max(q_1, q_2)e^M.$$

thus we have verified that there exists a ϵ-independent lower bound C_D for $\mathcal{L}p_\epsilon$ (see (7.7.4)). By Theorem 7.1, we infer the following properties of American call-max option price $V(S_1, S_2, t)$:

(1) If $\hat{S}_i \geq S_i \quad (i = 1, 2)$, then

$$V(\hat{S}_1, \hat{S}_2, t) \geq V(S_1, S_2, t); \tag{7.7.63}$$

(2) If $\hat{K} \geq K$, then

$$0 \leq V(S_1, S_2, t, K) - V(S_1, S_2, t; \hat{K}) \leq \hat{K} - K; \tag{7.7.64}$$

(3) If $\hat{t} \geq t$, then

$$V(S_1, S_2, \hat{t}) - V(S_1, S_2, t) \leq 0. \tag{7.7.65}$$

Now we study the behavior of American call-max options according to (7.7.63)—(7.7.65). Suppose $\Gamma(t, K)$ is the optimal exercise boundary for $V(S_1, S_2, t; K)$,

$$\Gamma(t, K) = \Gamma_1(t, K) \cup \Gamma_2(t, K),$$

where

$$\Gamma_1(t, K) = \partial\Sigma_2(t, K) \cap \{S_1 \geq S_2 > 0\}, \tag{7.7.66}$$

$$\Gamma_2(t, K) = \partial\Sigma_2(t, K) \cap \{S_2 > S_1 > 0\}, \tag{7.7.67}$$

where $\Sigma_2(t, K)$ is the stopping region of the American call-max option at time t, i.e.

$$\Sigma_2(t, K) = \{(S_1, S_2) \mid V(S_1, S_2, t; K) = P(S_1, S_2; K), (S_1, S_2) \in R_+^2\}. \tag{7.7.68}$$

Theorem 7.4 *If $q_i > 0, (i = 1, 2)$, then*

$$\Sigma_2(T, K) = \left\{(S_1, S_2) \mid S_1 \geq S_2, S_1 \geq \max(K, \frac{Kr}{q_1}); \right.$$
$$\left. S_2 > S_1, S_2 \geq \max(K, \frac{Kr}{q_2})\right\}. \tag{7.7.69}$$

Proof If (S_1^0, S_2^0, T) belongs to the continuation region $\Sigma_1(T, K)$, and the payoff function $P(S_2, S_2)$ is differentiable in the neighborhood of (S_1^0, S_2^0), then due to the regularity of the solution to parabolic equations, in the neighborhood of (S_1^0, S_2^0, T), $V(S_1, S_2, t)$ satisfies equation

$$\frac{\partial V}{\partial t} + \mathcal{L}V = 0.$$

Thus

$$\frac{\partial V}{\partial t}\Big|_{(S_1^0, S_2^0, T)} = -\mathcal{L}(V|_{t=T})\Big|_{(S_1^0, S_2^0)} = -\mathcal{L}(P(S_1, S_2))\Big|_{(S_1^0, S_2^0)}.$$

By straightforward computation, we get

$$\mathcal{L}(P(S_1, S_2)) = Kr - S_1 q_1 \qquad \text{as } S_1 \geq S_2,\ S_1 > K,$$

$$= Kr - S_2 q_2, \qquad \text{as } S_2 > S_1,\ S_2 > K.$$

Thus in the regions

$$S_1 \geq S_2 \text{ and } S_1 > \max(K, \frac{Kr}{q_1}) \tag{7.7.70}$$

and

$$S_2 > S_1 \text{ and } S_2 > \max(K, \frac{Kr}{q_2}), \tag{7.7.71}$$

we have

$$\mathcal{L}(P(S_1, S_2)) < 0,$$

i.e. when (S_1^0, S_2^0, T) satisfies conditions (7.7.70), (7.7.71),

$$\frac{\partial V}{\partial t}\bigg|_{(S_1^0, S_2^0, T)} > 0.$$

But this contradicts to property (3) of V (see (7.7.65)). Thus

$$\Sigma_2(T, K) \supset \left\{(S_1, S_2) \mid S_1 \geq S_2, S_1 > \max\left(K, \frac{Kr}{q_1}\right);\right.$$
$$\left. S_2 > S_1, S_2 > \max\left(K, \frac{Kr}{q_2}\right)\right\}.$$

Therefore, in order to prove Theorem 7.4, we only need to point out that all points not belonging to the set on the righthand side of the above expression must belong to the continuation region $\Sigma_1(T, K)$.

In fact, since for points in region $\{(S_1, S_2) | K > \max(S_1, S_2)\}$, $P(S_1, S_2) \equiv 0$, thus the set must belong to $\Sigma_1(T, K)$. Moreover, if $\frac{Kr}{q_1} > K$, then at $t = T$, the set $\left\{(S_1, S_2) \mid S_1 \geq S_2, K \leq S_1 < \frac{Kr}{q_1}\right\}$ must also belong to $\Sigma_1(T, K)$. Suppose otherwise, i.e. it belongs to $\Sigma_2(T, K)$, then since in $\Sigma_2(t, K)$

$$V(S_1, S_2, t) \equiv P(S_1, S_2),$$

then there must be

$$\frac{\partial V}{\partial t} + \mathcal{L}V \leq 0.$$

But from the payoff function at $t = T$ (7.7.49), for those points $S_1 \geq S_2$ and $K \leq S_1 < \frac{Kr}{q_1}$,

$$\mathcal{L}P(S_1, S_2) > 0.$$

This results in contradiction. Therefore the region $\left\{(S_1, S_2) \middle| S_1 \geq S_2,\ K \leq S_1 < \frac{Kr}{q_1}\right\}$ must belong to region $\Sigma_1(T, K)$.

By the same argument, region $\left\{(S_1, S_2) \mid S_2 > S_1, K \leq S_2 < \frac{Kr}{q_2}\right\}$ must belong to the continuation region $\Sigma_1(T, K)$. Thus completes the proof of the Theorem.

Theorem 7.5 *If $t_2 > t_1$, then*

$$\Sigma_2(t_2, K) \supset \Sigma_2(t_1, K); \tag{7.7.72}$$

If $K_2 > K_1$, then

$$\Sigma_2(t, K_2) \subset \Sigma_2(t, K_1). \tag{7.7.73}$$

Proof The relation (7.7.72) is a corollary of the option price property (3) (see(7.7.65)). In fact, suppose otherwise, i.e. there exist (S_1^0, S_2^0) and $t = t_1^0, t_2^0$ with $t_2^0 > t_1^0$, such that:

$$(S_1^0, S_2^0, t_1^0) \in \Sigma_2(t_1^0, K),$$

but

$$(S_1^0, S_2^0, t_2^0) \in \Sigma_1(t_2^0, K).$$

Then we have

$$V(S_1^0, S_2^0, t_2^0) > P(S_1^0, S_2^0) = V(S_1^0, S_2^0, t_1^0).$$

But this contradicts to (7.7.65).

The relation (7.7.73) is a corollary of the option price property (2) (see (7.7.64)). In fact, suppose otherwise, then there exist (S_1^0, S_2^0) and $t = t_0$, such that when $K_2 > K_1$,

$$(S_1^0, S_2^0, t_0) \in \Sigma_2(t, K_2),$$

but

$$(S_1^0, S_2^0, t_0) \in \Sigma_1(t, K_1).$$

Due to (7.7.64), we have

$$\begin{aligned} P(S_1^0, S_2^0; K_2) &= V(S_1^0, S_2^0, t_0; K_2) \\ &\geq V(S_1^0, S_2^0, t_0; K_1) - K_2 + K_1 \\ &> P(S_1^0, S_2^0; K_1) - K_2 + K_1, \end{aligned}$$

i.e.

$$(\max(S_1^0, S_2^0) - K_2)^+ + K_2 > (\max(S_1^0, S_2^0) - K_1)^+ + K_1. \tag{7.7.74}$$

Thus there must be

$$\max(S_1^0, S_2^0) < K_2, \tag{7.7.75}$$

otherwise, if

$$\max(S_1^0, S_2^0) \geq K_2 > K_1,$$

then

$$(\max(S_1^0, S_2^0) - K_2)^+ + K_2 = \max(S_1^0, S_2^0) = (\max(S_1^0, S_2^0) - K_1)^+ + K_1.$$

This contradicts to (7.7.74).

But (7.7.75) and $(S_1^0, S_2^0, t_0) \in \Sigma_2(t, K_2)$ (see (7.7.73)) are contradictory, therefore (S_1^0, S_2^0, t_0) must belong to $\Sigma_2(t, K_1)$. Thus we have proved (7.7.73).

Corollary *By (7.7.73), at any given time t,*

$$\Sigma_2(t, K) \subset \Sigma_2(t, 0), \qquad \forall K > 0. \tag{7.7.76}$$

Corollary *By (7.7.72), for a given strike price K, the stopping region of the American call-max option starts from $t = T$, and $\Sigma_2(t, K)$ (see (7.7.69)) narrows down with decreasing t, i.e. when further away from the expiration date.*

Now we can give a qualitative description of the evolving picture of the optimal exercise boundary of the American call-max options.

At $t = T$, Γ_1 and Γ_2 partly coincide along $S_1 = S_2$, and $\Sigma_2(T, K)$ is determined by (7.7.69).

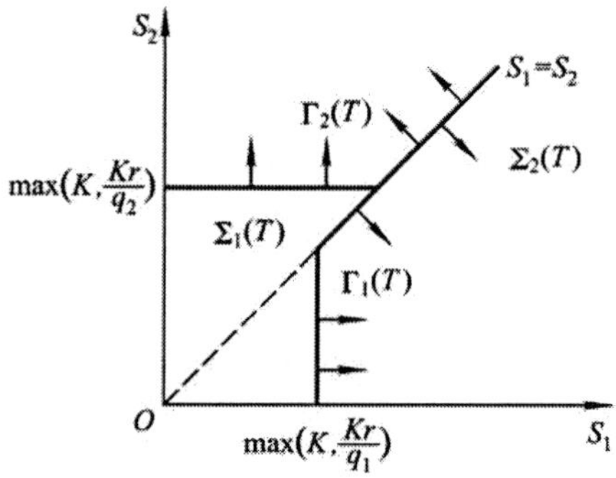

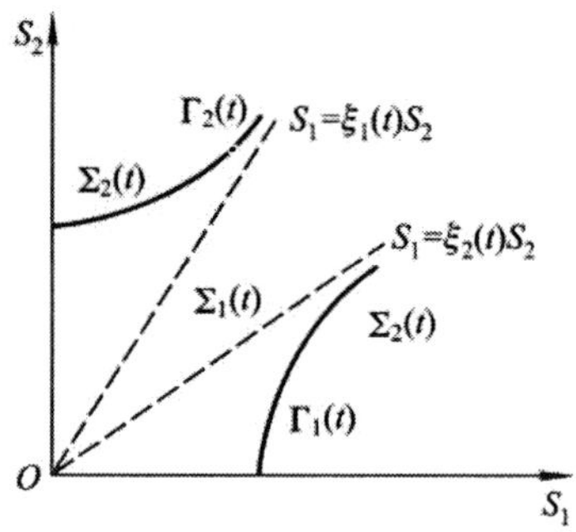

When $t < T, \Sigma_2(t, 0)$ is separated and depart from $S_1 = S_2$, and by (7.7.76), $\Sigma_2(t, K)$ is also separated in the same way, and expands, one branch moving in $S_1 > S_2$ region, denoted by $\Sigma_2^{(1)}(t, K)$, the other branch moving in $S_1 < S_2$ region, and denoted by $\Sigma_2^{(2)}(t, K)$. Their boundaries in $\{S_1 > S_2\}$ and $\{S_2 > S_1\}$

are denoted by $\Gamma_1(t,K)$ and $\Gamma_2(t,K)$, respectively.

Theorem 7.6 *American call-max option price $V(S_1,S_2,t)$ is a convex function of S_1, S_2, i.e. for arbitrary $0 \le \lambda \le 1$,*

$$(1-\lambda)V(S_1,S_2,t) + \lambda V(S_1+\Delta S_1, S_2+\Delta S_2, t) \ge V(S_1+\lambda\Delta S_1, S_2+\lambda\Delta S_2, t),$$

where $(S_1,S_2),(S_1+\Delta S_1, S_2+\Delta S_2) \in \mathbf{R}_+^2$.

For the proof of this theorem, we refer the reader to [20]. As a corollary of the theorem, we have:

Theorem 7.7 *For American call-max options, the stopping regions $\Sigma_2^{(1)}(t)$ and $\Sigma_2^{(2)}(t)(0 \le t < T)$ are convex sets.*

Proof Without losing generality, let $Q(S_1,S_2,t), Q_0(S_1^0,S_2^0,t) \in \Sigma_2^{(1)}(t)$. Let $\overline{QQ_0}$ be the line segment connecting Q and Q_0. For any point $Q_\lambda \in \overline{QQ_0}$, $(0 \le \lambda \le 1)$, its coordinates can be written as

$$Q_\lambda = (S_1^0 + \lambda(S_1 - S_1^0), S_2^0 + \lambda(S_2 - S_2^0), t)$$

Since $V(S_1,S_2,t)$ is convex with respect to S_1, S_2, thus

$$\begin{aligned} 0 &\le (1-\lambda)V(S_1^0,S_2^0,t) + \lambda V(S_1,S_2,t) \\ &\quad - V(S_1^0 + \lambda(S_1 - S_1^0), S_2^0 + \lambda(S_2 - S_2^0), t) \\ &= (1-\lambda)P(S_1^0,S_2^0) + \lambda P(S_1,S_2) \\ &\quad - V(S_1^0 + \lambda(S_1 - S_1^0), S_2^0 + \lambda(S_2 - S_2^0), t). \end{aligned} \tag{7.7.77}$$

Since $Q, Q_0 \in \Sigma_2^{(1)}(t)$, thus

$$S_1 > S_2, S_1^0 > S_2^0,$$

and

$$S_1 > \max(K, \frac{Kq_1}{r}), S_1^0 > \max(K, \frac{Kq_1}{r}),$$

thus

$$P(S_1,S_2) = S_1 - K,$$

$$P(S_1^0,S_2^0) = S_1^0 - K.$$

Therefore (7.7.77) can be rewritten as

$$\begin{aligned} V(S_1^0 + \lambda(S_1 - S_1^0), S_2^0 + \lambda(S_2 - S_2^0), t) \\ &\leq (1-\lambda)(S_1^0 - K) + \lambda(S_1 - K) \\ &= S_1^0 + \lambda(S_1 - S_1^0) - K \\ &= P(S_1^0 + \lambda(S_1 - S_1^0), S_2^0 + \lambda(S_2 - S_2^0)). \end{aligned}$$

Since $V(Q_\lambda) \geq P(S_1^0 + \lambda(S_1 - S_1^0), S_2^0 + \lambda(S_2 - S_2^0))$, thus

$$V(S_1^0 + \lambda(S_1 - S_1^0), S_2^0 + \lambda(S_2 - S_2^0), t) = P(S_1^0 + \lambda(S_1 - S_1^0), S_2^0 + \lambda(S_2 - S_2^0)),$$

i.e.

$$Q_\lambda \in \Sigma_2^{(1)}, \qquad (0 \leq \lambda \leq 1)$$

Thus the theorem is proved.

Finally, we give the following results for the optimal exercise boundary of American call-max options.

Theorem 7.8 *For the American call-max option, the optimal exercise boundaries $\Gamma_1(t)$ and $\Gamma_2(t)$ have the following properties:*

(1) There exist $\varphi_1(S_1, t)$ and $\varphi_2(S_2, t)$, such that

$$\Gamma_1(t): \qquad S_2 = \varphi_1(S_1, t),$$

$$\Gamma_2(t): \qquad S_1 = \varphi_2(S_2, t);$$

(2) $\varphi_1(S_1, t)$ and $\varphi_2(S_2, t)$ are nondecreasing convex function of S_i, $(i = 1, 2)$, respectively;

(3)

$$\lim_{S_1 \to \infty} \frac{\varphi_1(S_1, t)}{S_1} = \frac{1}{\xi_2(t)},$$

$$\lim_{S_2 \to \infty} \frac{\varphi_2(S_2, t)}{S_2} = \xi_1(t),$$

where $S_1 = \xi_1(t) S_2$ and $S_1 = \xi_2(t) S_2$ are the optimal exercise boundaries of American better-of option.

We refer the reader to [20] for the proof of this theorem.

Conclusion (3) of Theorem 7.8 indicates: for the American call-max option with an arbitrary strike price K, its optimal exercise boundaries $\Gamma_1(t, K)$ and $\Gamma_2(t, K)$, have $\Gamma_1(t, 0)$ and $\Gamma_2(t, 0)$ (i.e. the optimal exercise boundaries of American better-of option) as their asymptotic lines.

Summary

1. Multi-asset option pricing is modeled as a backward multivariate parabolic PDE terminal value problem. The terminal condition is given by the payoff function of the option. Explicit solutions exist for European multi-asset options.

2. Pricing problem of out-performance options and options to exchange one set for another, whether European or American style, can be reduced to a 1-D problem.

3. Although there is no explicit expression in general for multi-asset American option price, an evolving picture of the optimal exercise boundary can be obtained by PDE analysis. This is very useful for understanding the option pricing and numerical computation.

Exercises

Suppose $S_1, \dots, S_n$ are prices of n risky assets, and in $[0, T]$ their movements satisfy the SDE system (7.1.5)—(7.1.8). Show that:

1. If $V = V(S_1 \dots, S_n, t)$ is the European option price with a payoff at $t = T$ being

$$V(S_1, \dots, S_n, T) = \sum_{i=1}^{n} \Phi_i(S_i),$$

then

$$V(S_1, \dots, S_n, t) = \sum_{i=1}^{n} V_i(S_i, t),$$

where $V_i(S_i, t)$, $(i = 1, ..., n)$ is the solution to the following problem:

$$\begin{cases} \dfrac{\partial V_i}{\partial t} + \dfrac{\hat{\sigma}_i{}^2}{2} S_i^2 \dfrac{\partial^2 V_i}{\partial S_i^2} + (r - q_i) S_i \dfrac{\partial V_i}{\partial S_i} - r V_i = 0, \\ \qquad\qquad (0 < S_i < \infty, 0 \le t < T) \\ V_i(S_i, T) = \Phi_i(S_i), \end{cases}$$

where

$$\hat{\sigma}_i^2 = \sum_{j=1}^{m} \sigma_{ij}^2.$$

2. Let $C = C(S_1, \dots, S_n, t)$ and $P = P(S_1, \dots, S_n, t)$ be the prices of the arithmetic-mean basket call and put options, respectively. And their payoffs at maturity $(t = T)$ are given by

$$C(S_1, \dots, S_n, T) = \left(\sum_{i=1}^{n} \alpha_i S_i - K \right)^+,$$

$$P(S_1, \dots, S_n, T) = \left(K - \sum_{i=1}^{n} \alpha_i S_i \right)^+,$$

where $\alpha_i \geq 0, \quad (i = 1, \ldots, n)$

$$\sum_{i=1}^{n} \alpha_i = 1.$$

Find the call-put parity formula for the arithmetic-mean basket options.

3. Let $C = C(S_1, ..., S_n, t)$ and $P = P(S_1, ..., S_n, t)$ be the prices of geometric-mean basket call and put option, respectively. And their payoffs at maturity $(t = T)$ are

$$C(S_1, \ldots, S_n, T) = \left(\prod_{i=1}^{n} S_i^{\alpha_i} - K\right)^+,$$

$$P(S_1, \ldots, S_n, T) = \left(K - \prod_{i=1}^{n} S_i^{\alpha_i}\right)^+,$$

where $\alpha_i \geq 0, \quad (i = 1, ..., n,)$

$$\sum_{i=1}^{n} \alpha_i = 1.$$

Find the call-put parity formula for the geometric-mean basket options.

4. Let $C = C(S_1, S_2, t)$ and $P = P(S_1, S_2, t)$ be the prices of call-max and put-max options, respectively. And at maturity $(t = T)$, their payoff functions are

$$C(S_1, S_2, T) = (\max(S_1, S_2) - K)^+,$$
$$P(S_1, S_2, T) = (K - \max(S_1, S_2))^+.$$

Find the call-put parity formula.

5. Let $C = C(S_1, S_2, t)$ and $P = P(S_1, S_2, t)$ be the prices of the quanto call, put options, respectively. And at maturity $(t = T)$, their payoff functions are

$$C(S_1, S_2, T) = S_2(S_1 - K)^+,$$

$$P(S_1, S_2, T) = S_2(K - S_1)^+.$$

Find the call-put parity formula for quantos options. (Consider two cases: a. the foreign security S_1 pays no dividend. b. The foreign security S_1 pays dividend at rate $q > 0$.)

6. Let $V(S_1, S_2, t)$ and $U(S_1, S_2, t)$ be the prices of the better-of and worse-of options of two assets S_1, S_2, respectively, and their payoffs at maturity $(t = T)$ be

$$V(T) = \max(S_1(T), S_2(T)),$$

and

$$U(T) = \min(S_1(T), S_2(T)).$$

Find the pricing formula for these two options.

7. Let $V(S_1, S_2, t)$ and $U(S_1, S_2, t)$ be the prices of call-max and call-min options, and their payoffs at maturity ($t = T$) be

$$V(S_1, S_2, T) = \max\{(S_1 - K_1)^+, (S_2 - K_2)^+\}$$

and

$$U(S_1, S_2, T) = \min\{(S_1 - K_1)^+, (S_2 - K_2)^+\}.$$

Find the call-max-call-min parity.

8. Let S_1, S_2 be two risky assets, with dividend rates $q_1 > 0, q_2 > 0$. And let $V(S_1, S_2)$ be the perpetual American out-performance option with a payoff

$$V(S_1, S_2) = (S_1 - S_2)^+.$$

Find the option price formula and the position of the optimal exercise boundary.

9. Let $V(S_1, S_2, t)$ be a quanto call option. Its payoff at maturity ($t = T$) is:

$$\text{payoff } = S_2(T)(S_1(T) - K)^+.$$

Find a hedging strategy for the writer of the option to manage the risk.

10. Let S_1, S_2 be two risky assets with dividend rates $q_1 \geq 0, q_2 \geq 0$; and let $V(S_1, S_2, t)$ be an American out-performance option with the expiration date T. Make a qualitative analysis of the optimal exercise boundary of the option.

Chapter 8

Path-Dependent Options (I) —— Weakly Path-Dependent Options

The European options we have seen in the previous chapters have a common feature: the option's payoff depends on the underlying asset's price on the expiration day only regardless the historical path of the underlying asset's price. In the next two chapters, we will study **path-dependent options**, *whose payoff is determined not only by the asset price on the expiration day, but is also affected by how the asset price changes during the option's lifetime.*

According to how strongly an option's payoff is tied to the underlying asset's price history, path-dependent options are divided into two classes. In the first class, known as weakly path-dependent options, the payoff depends on whether the asset price has reached certain predetermined price level or levels. In the second class, known as strongly path-dependent options, the payoff depends on the price history in part or all of the option's lifetime.

Barrier option is the most important type of the weakly path-dependent options. It has many variations. Indeed, American options also belong to the weakly path-dependent options.

8.1 Barrier Options

Barrier option is a type of European options whose payoff depends not only on the underlying asset's price on the expiration day, but also on whether the underlying asset's price has reached a predetermined price (known as the barrier) during the option's lifetime.

Barrier options can be divided into two kinds according to the status of the option when the underlying asset price reaches the barrier. **Knock-out option**: once the asset price hits the barrier level, the option is **extinguished**. If the barrier is hit from above, it is called **down-and-out option**; If the barrier is hit from below, it is called **up-and-out option**. The other kind is **knock-in options**: once the asset price hits the barrier, the option is **activated**. The barrier level is also called the **trigger**. Similarly, regarding the relation between the spot price and the trigger, there are **down-and-in options** and **up-and-in options**.

Each kind of the above options can be a call or a put. In summary, there are 8 cases of payoff functions for the barrier options as shown below:

barrier option(S_B—trigger)

Knock-out

$$\textbf{down-and-out}\begin{cases}(S_T-K)^+I_{\{S_t>S_B,\quad t\in[0,T]\}} & \text{(call)}\\ (K-S_T)^+I_{\{S_t>S_B,\quad t\in[0,T]\}} & \text{(put)}\end{cases}$$

$$\textbf{up-and-out}\begin{cases}(S_T-K)^+I_{\{S_t<S_B,\quad t\in[0,T]\}} & \text{(call)}\\ (K-S_T)^+I_{\{S_t<S_B,\quad t\in[0,T]\}} & \text{(put)}\end{cases}$$

Knock-in

$$\textbf{down-and-in}\begin{cases}(S_T-K)^+[1-I_{\{S_t>S_B,\quad t\in[0,T]\}}] & \text{(call)}\\ (K-S_T)^+[1-I_{\{S_t>S_B,\quad t\in[0,T]\}}] & \text{(put)}\end{cases}$$

$$\textbf{up-and-in}\begin{cases}(S_T-K)^+[1-I_{\{S_t<S_B,\quad t\in[0,T]\}}] & \text{(call)}\\ (K-S_T)^+[1-I_{\{S_t<S_B,\quad t\in[0,T]\}}] & \text{(put)}\end{cases}$$

where $I_\omega(S)$ (I_ω in short) is the characteristic function of the set ω,

$$I_\omega(S)=\begin{cases}1, & S\in\omega,\\ 0, & S\notin\omega\end{cases}$$

If we regard $(S_T-K)^+$ or $(K-S_T)^+$ as payoff of the vanilla option, then it is obvious:

payoff of knock-out +payoff of knock-in=payoff of vanilla option

Since European option pricing problem is a linear one, the following relation between the price of a barrier option and the price of the corresponding European option holds:

$$\begin{aligned}V_{\text{vanilla}}(S,t)&=V_{\text{up-and-out}}(S,t)+V_{\text{up-and-in}}(S,t)\\&=V_{\text{down-and-out}}(S,t)+V_{\text{down-and-in}}(S,t).\end{aligned}\tag{8.1.1}$$

The financial meaning of the above equality is clear: when the barrier $S=S_B$ is reached, both the knock-in and knock-out (having the same strike price K and expiration time T) are triggered, and the net effect is the same as a vanilla European option.

Barrier options are very popular in financial markets. Investors are attracted to barrier options because barrier options are cheaper than European options. This depends on the investor's view of the future price of the underlying asset. Take a down-and-out call as example. If an investor believes once the asset price falls to the barrier ($S=S_B$), the chance for the price to return to $S>K$ is so small that the investor would rather give up the possible chance of making profit when the asset price reaches and exceeds the barrier S_B at maturity $t = T$, and renounce the option. Thus the investor can save the option premium, but is at risk of getting no profit if the asset price falls to S_B temporarily and keeps rising hereafter so that on the expiration day $S_T > K$.

In the following example we can see how premiums for various barrier options compare with the premium of the vanilla option.

Example Consider a stock call option with 6 month expiration. We assume the spot price is \$145, risk-free interest rate $r = 6\%$, dividend rate $q = 3\%$, volatility $\sigma = 0.295$.

option type	strike price K	barrier S_B	premium
vanilla	\$145		\$12.87
up-and-out	\$145	\$160	\$0.17
up-and-out	\$145	\$190	\$4.46
up-and-in	\$145	\$160	\$12.70
up-and-in	\$145	\$190	\$8.41
down-and-out	\$145	\$130	\$10.48
down-and-out	\$145	\$110	\$12.83
down-and-in	\$145	\$130	\$2.39
down-and-in	\$145	\$110	\$0.04

Partial differential equation model for barrier options:

For barrier options, **domain, boundary condition** at barrier $S = S_B$, and **terminal condition** at $t = T$ are different for different cases: **"knock-out"** and **"knock-in"**, **"up"** and **"down"**, **"call"** and **"put"**.

(1) **Domain** Let D be the domain,

going "up", the asset price must be below the barrier:

$$D = \{(S,t)|0 \le S \le S_B, \quad 0 \le t \le T\},$$

going "down", the asset price must be above the barrier:

$$D = \{(S,t)|S_B \le S < \infty, \quad 0 \le t \le T\};$$

(2) **Boundary condition at $S = S_B$**

when "out", the option price must be 0:

$$V(S_B, t) = 0,$$

when "in", the option price must be the same as vanilla option price:

$$V(S_B, t) = V_{\text{vanilla}}(S_B, t);$$

(3) **Terminal condition at $t = T$**

"knock-out call"

$$V(S,T) = (S-K)^+, \qquad \begin{pmatrix} 0 \le S \le S_B & \text{up} \\ S_B \le S < \infty & \text{down} \end{pmatrix}$$

"knock-in call"

$$V(S,T) = 0, \qquad \begin{pmatrix} 0 \le S \le S_B & \text{up} \\ S_B \le S < \infty & \text{down} \end{pmatrix}$$

"knock-out put"

$$V(S,T) = (K-S)^+, \qquad \begin{pmatrix} 0 \le S \le S_B & \text{up} \\ S_B \le S < \infty & \text{down} \end{pmatrix}$$

"knock-in put"

$$V(S,T) = 0; \qquad \begin{pmatrix} 0 \le S \le S_B & \text{up} \\ S_B \le S < \infty & \text{down} \end{pmatrix}$$

(4) **The partial differential equation**
All kinds of barrier options satisfy the same Black-Scholes equation,

$$\frac{\partial V}{\partial t} + \frac{1}{2}\sigma^2 S^2 \frac{\partial^2 V}{\partial S^2} + (r-q)S\frac{\partial V}{\partial S} - rV = 0.$$

In summary, barrier option pricing is a terminal-boundary problem of the Black-Scholes equation. Comparing to vanilla option pricing, it has one more boundary $S = S_B$ and a corresponding boundary condition. Its domain, boundary condition and terminal condition will be defined according to the type of the barrier option.

Solution

Take the down-and-out call option as example. We will find its closed form solution. Pricing problem of other types of barrier options can be solved similarly.

Mathematical model of the European down-and-out call option is:

$$\begin{cases} \dfrac{\partial V}{\partial t} + \dfrac{1}{2}\sigma^2 S^2 \dfrac{\partial^2 V}{\partial S^2} + (r-q)S\dfrac{\partial V}{\partial S} - rV = 0, & (D) \quad (8.1.2) \\ V(S,T) = (S-K)^+, & (S_B \le S < \infty) \quad (8.1.3) \\ V(S_B,t) = 0, & (0 \le t \le T) \quad (8.1.4) \end{cases}$$

where $D = \{S_B < S < \infty,\ 0 \le t \le T\}$.

Under the transformation

$$x = \ln\frac{S}{S_B}, \tag{8.1.5}$$

$$V = S_B u, \tag{8.1.6}$$

the above problem becomes

$$\begin{cases} \frac{\partial u}{\partial t} + \frac{1}{2}\sigma^2\frac{\partial^2 u}{\partial x^2} + (r - q - \frac{\sigma^2}{2})\frac{\partial u}{\partial x} - ru = 0, & (8.1.7) \\ \qquad (x \in \mathbf{R}_+, 0 \le t \le T) & \\ u(x,T) = (e^x - K_B)^+, \qquad (0 < x < \infty) & (8.1.8) \\ u(0,t) = 0, \qquad (0 \le t \le T) & (8.1.9) \end{cases}$$

where $\quad K_B = \frac{K}{S_B}$.

Introduce a new function W as follows:

$$u = e^{\alpha x + \beta(T-t)}W, \tag{8.1.10}$$

where

$$\alpha = -\frac{1}{\sigma^2}(r - q - \frac{\sigma^2}{2}),$$
$$\beta = -r - \frac{1}{2\sigma^2}(r - q - \frac{\sigma^2}{2})^2.$$

By the transformation (8.1.10), we get a terminal-boundary value problem for W in $\{x \in \mathbf{R}_+,\ 0 \le t \le T\}$:

$$\begin{cases} \frac{\partial W}{\partial t} + \frac{1}{2}\sigma^2\frac{\partial^2 W}{\partial x^2} = 0, & (8.1.11) \\ W(x,T) = e^{-\alpha x}(e^x - K_B)^+, & (8.1.12) \\ W(0,t) = 0. & (8.1.13) \end{cases}$$

Applying the image method, define

$$\varphi(x) = \begin{cases} e^{-\alpha x}(e^x - K_B)^+, & x > 0, \\ -e^{\alpha x}(e^{-x} - K_B)^+, & x < 0. \end{cases} \tag{8.1.14}$$

Obviously $\varphi(x)$ is an odd function, $\varphi(x) = -\varphi(-x)$. Now consider the Cauchy problem in $\{x \in \mathbf{R}, 0 \le t \le T\}$:

$$\begin{cases} \frac{\partial W}{\partial t} + \frac{1}{2}\sigma^2\frac{\partial^2 W}{\partial x^2} = 0 \ (x \in \mathbf{R}, \quad 0 \le t \le T) & (8.1.15) \\ W(x,T) = \varphi(x). \qquad (x \in \mathbf{R}) & (8.1.16) \end{cases}$$

Since its solution must be an odd function, thus in D $W(x,t)$ satisfies the boundary-terminal value problem (8.1.11)—(8.1.13).

The solution of the Cauchy problem (8.1.15),(8.1.16) can be written in the form of the Poisson formula:

$$\begin{aligned}
W(x,t) &= \frac{1}{\sigma\sqrt{2\pi(T-t)}}\int_{-\infty}^{\infty} e^{-\frac{(x-\xi)^2}{2\sigma^2(T-t)}}\varphi(\xi)d\xi \\
&= \frac{1}{\sigma\sqrt{2\pi(T-t)}}[\int_0^{\infty} e^{-\frac{(x+\xi)^2}{2\sigma^2(T-t)}}\varphi(-\xi)d\xi \\
&\quad + \int_0^{\infty} e^{-\frac{(x-\xi)^2}{2\sigma^2(T-t)}}\varphi(\xi)d\xi] \\
&= \frac{1}{\sigma\sqrt{2\pi(T-t)}}\int_0^{\infty}[e^{-\frac{(x-\xi)^2}{2\sigma^2(T-t)}} - e^{-\frac{(x+\xi)^2}{2\sigma^2(T-t)}}]e^{-\alpha\xi}(e^{\xi}-K_B)^+d\xi.
\end{aligned}$$

Back to the original function $u(x,t)$ by (8.1.10), we get

$$\begin{aligned}
u(x,t) &= \frac{e^{-r(T-t)}}{\sigma\sqrt{2\pi(T-t)}}\int_{\ln K_B}^{\infty} e^{-\frac{[(x-\xi)+(r-q-\frac{\sigma^2}{2})(T-t)]^2}{2\sigma^2(T-t)}}(e^{\xi}-K_B)d\xi \\
&\quad - \frac{e^{-r(T-t)-\frac{2}{\sigma^2}(r-q-\frac{\sigma^2}{2})x}}{\sigma\sqrt{2\pi(T-t)}}\int_{lnK_B}^{\infty} e^{-\frac{[(x+\xi)-(r-q-\frac{\sigma^2}{2})(T-t)]^2}{2\sigma^2(T-t)}}(e^{\xi}-K_B)d\xi \\
&= \frac{e^{x-q(T-t)}}{\sqrt{2\pi}}\int_{-\infty}^{\frac{x-\ln K_B+(r-q+\frac{\sigma^2}{2})(T-t)}{\sigma\sqrt{(T-t)}}} e^{-\frac{\omega^2}{2}}d\omega \\
&\quad - \frac{1}{\sqrt{2\pi}}K_B e^{-r(T-t)}\int_{-\infty}^{\frac{x-\ln K_B+(r-q-\frac{\sigma^2}{2})(T-t)}{\sigma\sqrt{(T-t)}}} e^{-\frac{\omega^2}{2}}d\omega \\
&\quad - \frac{e^{-\frac{2}{\sigma^2}(r-q)x-r(T-t)}}{\sqrt{2\pi}}\int_{-\infty}^{\frac{-x-\ln K_B+(r-q+\frac{\sigma^2}{2})(T-t)}{\sigma\sqrt{(T-t)}}} e^{-\frac{\omega^2}{2}}d\omega \\
&\quad + \frac{K_B}{\sqrt{2\pi}}e^{-r(T-t)-\frac{2}{\sigma^2}(r-q-\frac{\sigma^2}{2})x}\int_{-\infty}^{\frac{-x-\ln K_B+(r-q-\frac{\sigma^2}{2})(T-t)}{\sigma\sqrt{(T-t)}}} e^{-\frac{\omega^2}{2}}d\omega.
\end{aligned}$$

By (8.1.5),(8.1.6), back to the original variable (S,t) and function $V(S,t)$, we get

$$\begin{aligned}
V(S,t) &= Se^{-q(T-t)}N(d_1) - Ke^{-r(T-t)}N(d_2) - S_B\left(\frac{S}{S_B}\right)^{-\frac{2}{\sigma^2}(r-q)}e^{-q(T-t)}N(d_3) \\
&\quad -Ke^{-r(T-t)}\left(\frac{S}{S_B}\right)^{1-\frac{2}{\sigma^2}(r-q)}N(d_4) \\
&= V_{\text{vanilla}}(S,t) - \left(\frac{S}{S_B}\right)^{-\frac{2}{\sigma^2}(r-q)+1}[\frac{S_B^2}{S}e^{-q(T-t)}N(d_3) - Ke^{-r(T-t)}N(d_4)],
\end{aligned} \tag{8.1.17}$$

where

$$d_1 = \frac{\ln \frac{S}{K} + (r - q + \frac{\sigma^2}{2})(T-t)}{\sigma\sqrt{T-t}},$$

$$d_2 = d_1 - \sigma\sqrt{T-t},$$

$$d_3 = \frac{\ln \frac{S_B^2}{SK} + (r - q + \frac{\sigma^2}{2})(T-t)}{\sigma\sqrt{T-t}},$$

$$d_4 = d_3 - \sigma\sqrt{T-t}.$$

The solution (8.1.17) can be written as

$$V_{\text{down-and-out}}(S,t) = V_{\text{vanilla}}(S,t) - \left(\frac{S}{S_B}\right)^{-\frac{2}{\sigma^2}(r-q)+1} V_{\text{vanilla}}\left(\frac{S_B^2}{S}, t\right). \quad (8.1.18)$$

By (8.1.1) we get

$$V_{\text{down-and-in}}(S,t) = \left(\frac{S}{S_B}\right)^{-\frac{2}{\sigma^2}(r-q)+1} V_{\text{vanilla}}\left(\frac{S_B^2}{S}, t\right). \quad (8.1.19)$$

Similarly we can obtain the valuation formulas for $V_{\text{up-and-out}}(S,t)$ and $V_{\text{up-and-in}}(S,t)$.

In order to obtain the pricing formulas for put barrier options, we introduce the following call-put parity for the barrier options.

Theorem 8.1 *For down-and-out options, the following call-put parity holds*

$$p_{\text{down-and-out}}(S,t) + SN(\hat{d}_1) = c_{\text{down-and-out}}(S,t) + Ke^{-r(T-t)}N(\hat{d}_2) + \left(\frac{S}{S_B}\right)^{-\frac{2}{\sigma^2}(r-q)+1} \left[\frac{S_B^2}{S}N(\hat{d}_3) - Ke^{-r(T-t)}N(\hat{d}_4)\right], \quad (8.1.20)$$

where

$$\hat{d}_1 = \frac{\ln \frac{S}{S_B} + (r - q + \frac{\sigma^2}{2})(T-t)}{\sigma\sqrt{T-t}},$$

$$\hat{d}_2 = \hat{d}_1 - \sigma\sqrt{T-t},$$

$$\hat{d}_3 = \frac{\ln \frac{S_B}{S} + (r - q + \frac{\sigma^2}{2})(T-t)}{\sigma\sqrt{T-t}},$$

$$\hat{d}_4 = \hat{d}_3 - \sigma\sqrt{T-t}.$$

Proof Let W be the difference between a down-and-out call and a down-and-out put:

$$W = c_{\text{down-and-out}}(S,t) - p_{\text{down-and-out}}(S,t).$$

It is easy to show that W(S,t) satisfies the terminal-boundary value problem in $D = \{S_B < S < \infty, \quad 0 \le t \le T\}$:

$$\begin{cases} \frac{\partial W}{\partial t} + \frac{1}{2}\sigma^2 S^2 \frac{\partial^2 W}{\partial S^2} + (r-q)S\frac{\partial W}{\partial S} - rW = 0, & (D) \\ W(S,T) = S - K, & (S_B < S < \infty) \\ W(S_B, t) = 0. & (0 \le t < T) \end{cases}$$

Under the transformation (8.1.5) and

$$W = S_B u,$$

the problem is reduced to

$$\begin{cases} \frac{\partial u}{\partial t} + \frac{1}{2}\sigma^2 \frac{\partial^2 u}{\partial x^2} + (r - q - \frac{\sigma^2}{2})\frac{\partial u}{\partial x} - ru = 0, \ (x \in \mathbf{R}_+, \ 0 \le t < T) \\ u(x,T) = e^x - K_B, & (0 \le x < \infty) \\ u(0,t) = 0. & (0 \le t \le T) \end{cases}$$

The solution can be found to be

$$\begin{aligned} u(x,t) = & \frac{e^{x-q(T-t)}}{\sqrt{2\pi}} \int_{-\infty}^{\frac{x+(r-q+\frac{\sigma^2}{2})(T-t)}{\sigma\sqrt{T-t}}} e^{-\frac{\omega^2}{2}} d\omega \\ & - \frac{1}{\sqrt{2\pi}} \frac{K}{S_B} e^{-r(T-t)} \int_{-\infty}^{\frac{x+(r-q-\frac{\sigma^2}{2})(T-t)}{\sigma\sqrt{T-t}}} e^{-\frac{\omega^2}{2}} d\omega \\ & - \frac{e^{-\frac{2}{\sigma^2}(r-q)x - q(T-t)}}{\sqrt{2\pi}} \int_{-\infty}^{\frac{-x+(r-q+\frac{\sigma^2}{2})(T-t)}{\sigma\sqrt{T-t}}} e^{-\frac{\omega^2}{2}} d\omega \\ & + \frac{K}{S_B} \frac{e^{-r(T-t)-[\frac{2}{\sigma^2}(r-q)-1]x}}{\sqrt{2\pi}} \int_{-\infty}^{\frac{-x+(r-q-\frac{\sigma^2}{2})(T-t)}{\sigma\sqrt{T-t}}} e^{-\frac{\omega^2}{2}} d\omega. \end{aligned}$$

Back to the original variable (S,t) and W, we arrive at the conclusion of the theorem.

Similarly we can prove call-put parity for other types of barrier options. By these parity formulas, we can readily write out the valuation formula for a put barrier option from that of the call barrier option.

8.2 Time-Dependent Barrier Options

If the barrier changes with time, the option is called **time-dependent barrier option**. There are two types of time-dependent barrier options:

(A) Moving barrier options

Let barrier S_B be a known function of time t, $S = S_B(t)$. In general, the price of this kind of options does not have a closed form expression, unless S_B is an exponential function of t.

Take a down-and-out call as example. In the domain $D = \{(S,t)\,|S_B(t) \le S < \infty,\ \ 0 \le t \le T\}$, we solve the following terminal-boundary value problem of the Black-Scholes equation:

$$\begin{cases} \dfrac{\partial V}{\partial t} + \frac{1}{2}\sigma^2 S^2 \dfrac{\partial^2 V}{\partial S^2} + (r-q)S\dfrac{\partial V}{\partial S} - rV = 0, & (D) \quad (8.2.1) \\ V(S_B(t),t) = 0, & (0 \le t \le T) \quad (8.2.2) \\ V(S,T) = (S-K)^+. & (S_B(T) < S < \infty) \quad (8.2.3) \end{cases}$$

By the transformation

$$x = \ln \frac{S}{S_B(t)}, \tag{8.1.5}$$

$$V = S_B(T)u, \tag{8.1.6}$$

the problem (8.2.1)—(8.2.3) is reduced to the following problem for $u(x,t)$ in domain $\{x \in \mathbf{R}_+,\ 0 \le t \le T\}$:

$$\begin{cases} \dfrac{\partial u}{\partial t} + \frac{1}{2}\sigma^2 \dfrac{\partial^2 u}{\partial x^2} + [r - q - \frac{\sigma^2}{2} - \alpha(t)]\dfrac{\partial u}{\partial x} - ru = 0, & (8.2.4) \\ u(0,t) = 0, & (8.2.5) \\ u(x,0) = (e^x - K_B)^+, & (8.2.6) \end{cases}$$

where

$$K_B = \frac{K}{S_B(T)}, \tag{8.2.7}$$

$$\alpha(t) = \frac{1}{S_B}\frac{dS_B}{dt}. \tag{8.2.8}$$

If

$$\alpha(t) = \alpha(\text{a constant}), \tag{8.2.9}$$

then the solution of

$$\frac{dS_B}{dt} = \alpha S_B(t)$$

is

$$S_B(t) = S_B(T)e^{-\alpha(T-t)}. \tag{8.2.10}$$

Then (8.2.4) becomes:

$$\frac{\partial u}{\partial t} + \frac{1}{2}\sigma^2 \frac{\partial^2 u}{\partial x^2} + [r - \hat{q} - \frac{\sigma^2}{2}]\frac{\partial u}{\partial x} - ru = 0, \tag{8.2.11}$$

where

$$\hat{q} = \alpha + q.$$

Then by (8.1.17), we get

$$\begin{aligned} V(S,t) &= Se^{-(q+\alpha)(T-t)}N(d_1^*) - Ke^{-r(T-t)}N(d_2^*) \\ &\quad - \left(\frac{S}{S_B(t)}\right)^{-\frac{1}{\sigma^2}(r-q-\alpha)+1} [\frac{S_B(t)}{S}e^{-(q+\alpha)(T-t)}N(d_3^*) - Ke^{-r(T-t)}N(d_4^*)], \end{aligned} \tag{8.2.12}$$

where

$$d_1^* = \frac{\ln\frac{S}{K} + (r - q - \alpha + \frac{\sigma^2}{2})(T-t)}{\sigma\sqrt{T-t}},$$

$$d_2^* = d_1^* - \sigma\sqrt{T-t},$$

$$d_3^* = \frac{\ln\frac{S_B^2(T)}{SK} + (r - q - \alpha + \frac{\sigma^2}{2})(T-t)}{\sigma\sqrt{T-t}},$$

$$d_4^* = d_3^* - \sigma\sqrt{T-t}.$$

(B) Partial barrier options

The barrier is set up only during predetermined time windows in the option's lifetime. For an up-and-out partial barrier option, in days when the barrier is set up, the asset price S_t with respect to the barrier S_B can be one of the following three cases:

(a) $S_t < S_B$: the underlying asset price stays below the barrier.

(b) During the period, there exists $t = t_0$ such that $S_{t_0} = S_B$ (the asset price hits the barrier).

(c) $S_t > S_B$: the asset price crossed S_B before the period and then stays above the barrier S_B during the period.

For up-and-out partial barrier options, if case (c) happens, there are two types of barrier options:

Type (I): *The barrier is active.*

For this type of options, the payoff function on the expiration date (take a call option as example) is

$$\text{payoff function} = (S_T - K)^+ I_{\{S_t < S_B, \quad t\in\Pi\}},$$

where Π denotes barrier active period, I_ω is the characteristic function of ω.

Type (II): *The barrier is inactive. It mean that according to the contract, the barrier is triggered only if the barrier is crossed, either from above or below, during the period.*

For this type of options, the payoff function on the expiration date is

$$\text{payoff function} = (S_T - K)^+[I_{\{S_t<S_B,\quad t\in\Pi\}} + I_{\{S_t>S_B,\quad t\in\Pi\}}].$$

Now we set up the partial differential equation models for these two types of barrier options.

Consider an up-and-out partial barrier option. Its lifetime is $[0, T]$. Suppose the barrier is set up in the period Π which consists of two intervals: $[t_1, t_2]$ and $[t_3, T]$, where

$$0 < t_1 < t_2 < t_3 < T,$$

and corresponding trigger values are S_B and $\hat{S}_B$. Suppose the asset price change as follows:

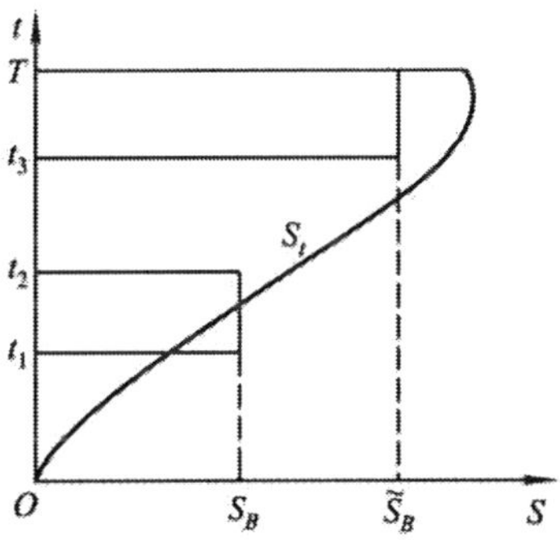

Then in $[t_1, t_2]$, for both Type(I) and Type (II) options, the barrier is considered triggered; But in $[t_3, T]$, the barrier is considered triggered for type (I) but not for type (II) options. In fact, the difference between type I and type II can be regarded as in the barrier levels.

As shown in the figure, for type (II) partial barrier options, barriers are represented by the two vertical line segments at $\{S = S_B, t_1 \le t \le t_2\}$ and $\{S = \hat{S_B}, t_3 \le t \le T\}$, where the option price satisfies the knock-out boundary

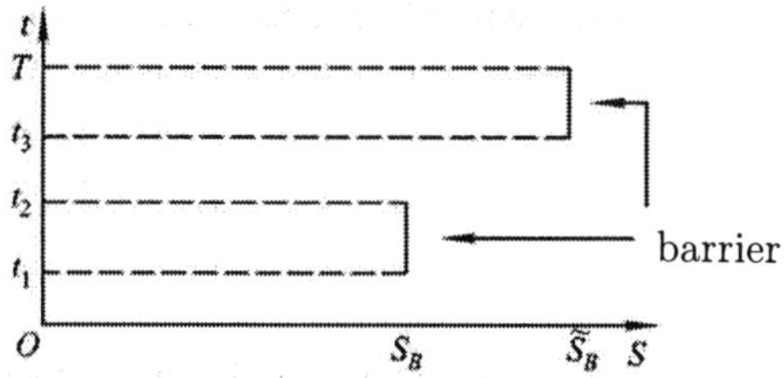

Type (II) partial barrier options

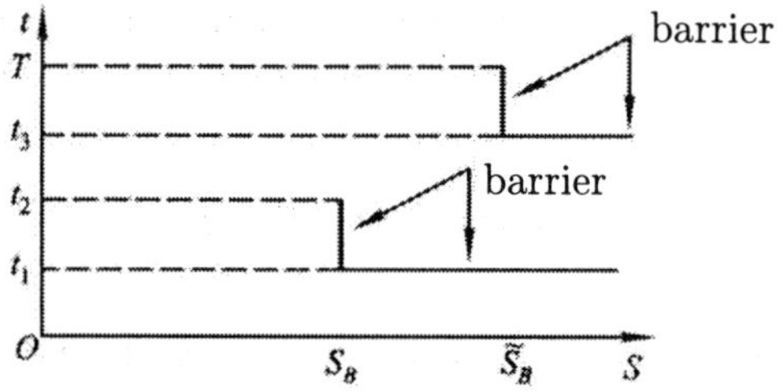

Type (I) partial barrier options

conditions:

$$V(S_B, t) = 0, \qquad (t_1 \le t \le t_2) \tag{8.2.13}$$

$$V(\hat{S_B}, t) = 0. \qquad (t_3 \le t \le T) \tag{8.2.14}$$

For type (I) partial barrier options, in addition to the two vertical line segments $\{S = S_B, t_1 \le t \le t_2\}$ and $\{S = \hat{S_B}, t_3 \le t \le T\}$, where option price satisfies the knock-out boundary conditions (8.2.13), (8.2.14), barriers are set also on the two horizontal line segments $\{S_B \le S < \infty,\ t = t_1\}$ and $\{\hat{S}_B \le S < \infty,\ t = t_3\}$, where the option price satisfies the knock-out "boundary" conditions:

$$V(S, t_1) = 0, \qquad (S_B \le S < \infty) \tag{8.2.15}$$

and

$$V(S, t_3) = 0. \qquad (\hat{S}_B \le S < \infty) \tag{8.2.16}$$

Therefore the pricing model for these two types of partial barrier options is:

In $[t_3, T]$**:**

Type (I) $\quad D_{\mathrm{I}} = \{0 \le S \le \hat{S}_B, \quad t_3 \le t \le T\}$:

$$\begin{cases} \mathcal{L}V = 0, & (D_{\mathrm{I}}) \\ V(\hat{S}_B, t) = 0, & (t_3 \le t \le T) \\ V(S, T) = (S - K)^+; & (0 \le S \le \hat{S}_B) \end{cases}$$

Type (II) $D_{\rm II}^1 = \{0 \le S \le \hat{S}_B, \quad t_3 \le t \le T\}$ and $D_{\rm II}^2 = \{\hat{S}_B \le S < \infty, \quad t_3 \le t \le T\}$:

$$\begin{cases} \mathcal{L}\tilde{V}_1 = 0, & (D_{\rm II}^1) \\ \tilde{V}_1(\hat{S}_B, t) = 0, & (t_3 \le t \le T) \\ \tilde{V}_1(S,T) = (S-K)^+, & (0 \le S \le \hat{S}_B) \end{cases}$$

and

$$\begin{cases} \mathcal{L}\tilde{V}_2 = 0, & (D_{\rm II}^2) \\ \tilde{V}_2(\hat{S}_B, t) = 0, & (t_3 \le t \le T) \\ \tilde{V}_2(S,T) = (S-K)^+; & (\hat{S}_B \le S < \infty) \end{cases}$$

In $[t_2, t_3]$**:**
Type (I) $\tilde{D} = \{0 \le S < \infty, \quad t_2 \le t \le t_3\}$:

$$\begin{cases} \mathcal{L}V = 0, & (\tilde{D}) \\ V(S,t_3) = \begin{cases} V(S, t_3+0), & (0 \le S \le \hat{S}_B) \\ 0; & (\hat{S}_B \le S < \infty) \end{cases} \end{cases}$$

Type (II) $\tilde{D}$:

$$\begin{cases} \mathcal{L}\tilde{V} = 0, & (\tilde{D}) \\ \tilde{V}(S,t_3) = \begin{cases} \tilde{V}_1(S, t_3+0), & (0 \le S \le \hat{S}_B) \\ \tilde{V}_2(S, t_3+0); & (\hat{S}_B \le S < \infty) \end{cases} \end{cases}$$

In $[t_1, t_2]$**:**
Type (I) $\hat{D}_{\rm I} = \{0 \le S < S_B, \quad t_1 \le t \le t_2\}$:

$$\begin{cases} \mathcal{L}V = 0, & (\hat{D}_{\rm I}) \\ V(S_B, t) = 0, & t_1 \le t \le t_2 \\ V(S,t_2) = V(S, t_2+0); & (0 \le S \le S_B) \end{cases}$$

Type (II) $\hat{D}_{\rm II}^1 = \{0 \le S \le S_B, \quad t_1 \le t \le t_2\}$ and $\hat{D}_{\rm II}^2 = \{S_B \le S < \infty, \quad t_1 \le t \le t_2\}$:

$$\begin{cases} \mathcal{L}\tilde{V}_1 = 0, & (\hat{D}_{\rm II}^1) \\ \tilde{V}_1(S_B, t) = 0, & (t_1 \le t \le t_2) \\ \tilde{V}_1(S,t_2) = \tilde{V}(S, t_2+0) & (0 \le S \le S_B) \end{cases}$$

and

$$\begin{cases} \mathcal{L}\tilde{V}_2 = 0, & (\hat{D}^2_{\text{II}}) \\ \tilde{V}_2(S_B, t) = 0, & (t_1 \le t \le t_2) \\ \tilde{V}_2(S, t_2) = \tilde{V}(S, t_2 + 0); & (S_B \le S < \infty) \end{cases}$$

In $[0, t_1]$:

Type (I) $\hat{D} = \{0 \le S < \infty, \quad 0 \le t \le t_1\}$:

$$\begin{cases} \mathcal{L}V = 0, & (\hat{D}) \\ V(S, t_1) = \begin{cases} V(S, t_1 + 0), & (0 \le S \le S_B) \\ 0; & (S_B \le S < \infty) \end{cases} \end{cases}$$

Type (II) $\hat{D} = \{0 \le S < \infty, \quad 0 \le t \le t_1\}$:

$$\begin{cases} \mathcal{L}\tilde{V} = 0, & (\hat{D}) \\ \tilde{V}(S, t_1) = \begin{cases} \tilde{V}_1(S, t_1 + 0), & 0 \le S \le S_B \\ \tilde{V}_2(S, t_1 + 0); & S_B \le S < \infty \end{cases} \end{cases}$$

In the above,

$$\mathcal{L}V = \frac{\partial V}{\partial t} + \frac{1}{2}\sigma^2 S^2 \frac{\partial^2 V}{\partial S^2} + (r - q)S\frac{\partial V}{\partial S} - rV.$$

8.3 Reset Options

Reset option is such a contract, when the underlying asset price reaches a predetermined level, the strike price will be reset, to give the option holder more profit opportunity.

Such reset can occur once or multiple times. Reset options can be divided into two types:

(I) Reset options with predetermined dates: *The strike price can be reset on predetermined dates.*

Take a call option as example. Let $0 < t_1 < \cdots < t_n < T$. On the initial day ($t = 0$), the strike price is set to K. At $t = t_1$, if the asset price $S(t_1)$ is below K, then the strike price is reset to $S(t_1)$ (otherwise the original price K), and so on. In general, at $t = t_m$ $(1 \le m \le n)$, the reset strike price K_m is given by

$$\begin{aligned} K_m &= \min(K_{m-1}, S(t_m)), \\ K_0 &= K. \end{aligned}$$

(II) Reset options with predetermined levels: *The strike price can be reset to predetermined price levels.*

Take a call option as example. Let $K > K_1 > K_2 > \cdots > K_n$. On the initial day ($t = 0$), the strike price is K. If the asset price falls to a predetermined level K_1, then the strike price is reset to K_1, and so on. In general, if the asset price falls from K_{m-1} to K_m, then the strike price is reset to K_m, $\quad (1 \le m \le n)$.

Why do we discuss reset options with barrier options? In fact, a reset process is equivalent to a combination of two barrier options: knock out a barrier option at the "old" strike price, and simultaneously knock in a barrier option at the "new" strike price.

Since the interpretation of the barrier is different for the two types of reset options, their mathematical models are different. For simplicity, we consider reset call options only, and allow only single reset.

Type I—— reset options with predetermined dates.

At $t_1 \in (0, T)$, if the asset price $S(t_1) < K$ (K is the strike price at initial date $t = 0$), then the strike price is reset to

$$\hat{K} = \min(K, S(t_1)).$$

The barrier setting is illustrated in the figure below

$$\{0 \le S \le K,\ t = t_1\}.$$

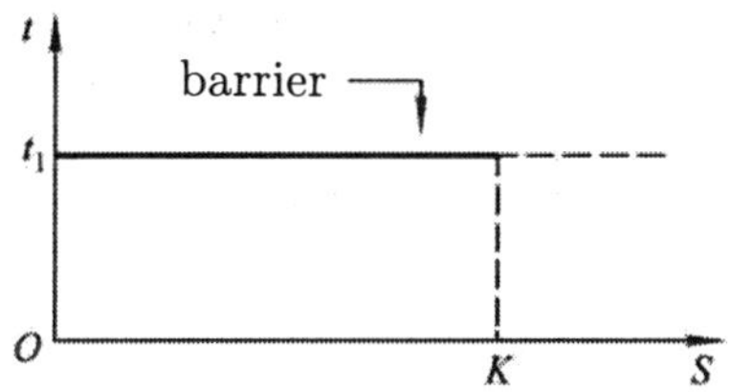

In $[t_1, T]$, solve

$$\begin{cases} \mathcal{L}V = 0, & (0 \le S < \infty,\ t_1 \le t \le T) \\ V(S,T) = (S - \hat{K})^+, & (S \in \mathbf{R}_+) \end{cases}$$

where $\mathcal{L}V = \dfrac{\partial V}{\partial t} + \frac{1}{2}\sigma^2 S^2 \dfrac{\partial^2 V}{\partial S^2} + (r-q)S\dfrac{\partial V}{\partial S} - rV.$

The solution is of the form

$$V = V(S, t; \hat{K}).$$

The asset price at $t = t_1$ is a known constant $S(t_1)$.

If $S(t_1) \ge K$, then $\hat{K} = K$ in $[t_1, T]$, and the option price is

$$V = V(S, t; K),$$

If $S(t_1) < K$, then $\hat{K} = S(t_1)$ in $[t_1, T]$, and the option price is

$$V = V(S, t; S(t_1)).$$

Thus at $t = t_1$, we have

$$V(S(t_1), t_1) = \begin{cases} V(S(t_1), t_1; K), & S(t_1) \geq K, \\ V(S(t_1), t_1; S(t_1)), & S(t_1) < K. \end{cases}$$

Define a function $\hat{V}(S)$:

$$\hat{V}(S) = \begin{cases} V(S, t_1; K), & S \geq K, \\ V(S, t_1; S), & S < K. \end{cases}$$

In $[t, t_1]$, solve

$$\begin{cases} \mathcal{L}V = 0, & (0 \leq S < \infty,\ 0 \leq t \leq t_1) \\ V(S, t_1) = \hat{V}(S). & (S \in \mathbf{R}_+) \end{cases}$$

In particular, we can evaluate $V(S, 0)$, since at each step the solution has a closed form expression constructed from the fundamental solutions of the Black-Scholes operator.

Type II—— reset options with predetermined levels.

If the asset price falls to $K_1 < K$, then reset the strike price to K_1. The barrier setting is

$$\{S = K_1, \quad 0 \leq t \leq T\}.$$

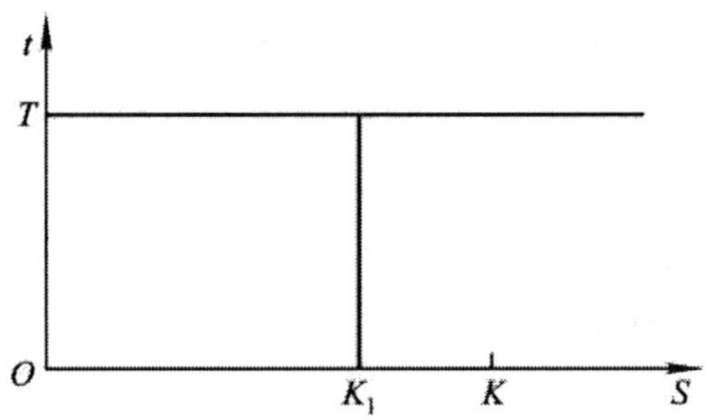

First, in $D\{0 \leq S < \infty,\ 0 \leq t \leq T\}$, solve

$$\begin{cases} \mathcal{L}\tilde{V} = 0, & (D) \\ \tilde{V}(S, T) = (S - K_1)^+, & (\mathbf{R}_+) \end{cases}$$

to find

$$\tilde{V} = \tilde{V}(S, t; K_1).$$

Then the price for reset options with predetermined levels satisfies a terminal boundary problem in $D\{K_1 \leq S < \infty,\ 0 \leq t \leq T\}$ as follows:

$$\begin{cases} \mathcal{L}V = 0, & (K_1 \leq S < \infty,\ 0 \leq t \leq T) \\ V(K_1, t) = V(K_1, t; K_1), & (0 \leq t \leq T) \\ V(S,T) = (S-K)^+. & (K_1 \leq S < \infty) \end{cases}$$

It is easy to see that the reset option price $V(S,t)$ can be decomposed into

$$\begin{aligned} V(S,t) = {} & V_{\text{down-and-out}}(S, t; K; K_1) \\ & + V_{\text{down-and-in}}(S, t; K_1; K_1), \end{aligned} \tag{8.3.1}$$

where $V_{\text{down-and-out(in)}}(S, t; K; S_B)$ denotes the price of a down-and-out (in) barrier option with strike price K and barrier level S_B. The financial meaning is that the price of this type of reset options can be decomposed into a knock-out barrier option at strike price K and a knock-in barrier option at strike price K_1. Therefore, it has closed form solution.

Remark The mathematical model and the solution procedure for the above two types of the reset options can be extended to the multiple reset options, although the expression will be rather complicated. Interested readers can refer [9] and [25].

8.4 Modified Barrier Options

A barrier option's premium is lower than its corresponding vanilla option, and is therefore more attractive to the investors. But barrier options create a number of problems for both option buyers and sellers :

1. The holder of a knock-out barrier option loses the investment if an asset price spike hits the barrier.
2. When the asset price approaches the barrier level, conflicting interests of the option holders and sellers tend to trigger short-term market manipulations.
3. Δ, the hedging share, is discontinuous at the barrier. When the asset price approaches the barrier, the seller must re-balance the hedging strategy.

Various modifications to barrier options have been introduced to overcome these problems. We call them **modified barrier options**. In this section we will explain three types of modified barrier options.

Take a down-and-out call option as example. The basic idea is: *when the asset price falls across the barrier S_B, the contract does not end abruptly. Instead, it goes through a phaseout process.* There are several ways to describe this process.

(1) When the asset price falls to the region $S \le S_B$, the option payoff decreases at a killing rate ρ. The payoff function on the expiration date is given by

$$V(S,T) = (S_T - K)^+ e^{-\rho\tau_T}, \tag{8.4.1}$$

where τ_t is the occupation time, which is the total amount of time in $[0,t]$ when the asset price S is below S_B (including S_B itself),

$$\tau_t = \text{mes}\{t' | S(t') \le S_B,\ 0 \le t' \le t\},$$

or

$$\tau_t = \int_0^t H(S_B - S_\tau) d\tau, \tag{8.4.2}$$

where

$$H(S) = \begin{cases} 1, & S \ge 0, \\ 0, & S < 0. \end{cases} \tag{8.4.3}$$

This phaseout process indicates: although the option does not extinguish, its payoff decreases continuously during the occupation time. This type of barrier options is called **step option.**

(2) Once the asset price falls to below S_B, a clock starts to measure the time outside the barrier S_B, so that when the **accumulated** occupation time below S_B (including S_B) reaches a predetermined number of days D, the option extinguishes. The payoff of the option remains the same before the accumulated time reaches D. The payoff function on the expiration day is

$$V(S_T, T, \tau_T) = (S_T - K)^+ I_{\{\tau_T < D\}}. \tag{8.4.4}$$

This type of option is called **Parasian options.**

(3) When the asset price falls to S_B, again a clock starts to measure the time outside the barrier S_B. But the count method differs from (2). If the **continuous** occupation time below S_B (excluding S_B) reaches a predetermined time D, the option extinguishes. That means, if the asset price returns to S_B before the continuous occupation time reaches D, then the clock will be reset to zero.

$\hat{\tau}_t$, the continuous occupation time below S_B(excluding S_B), is given by

$$\hat{\tau}_t = t - g_t = t - \sup\{t' | S(t') \ge S_B \quad 0 \le t' \le t\}. \tag{8.4.5}$$

The payoff function on the expiration day is

$$V(S_T, T, \hat{\tau}_T) = (S_T - K)^+ I_{\{\hat{\tau}_T < D\}}. \tag{8.4.6}$$

This type of option is called **Parisian options**.

Let us examine the difference between the accumulated occupation time τ_t and the continuous occupation time $\hat{\tau}_t$.

In the following figure, τ_t and $\hat{\tau}_t$ are drawn for an imagined asset price curve S_t and a given barrier level S_B.

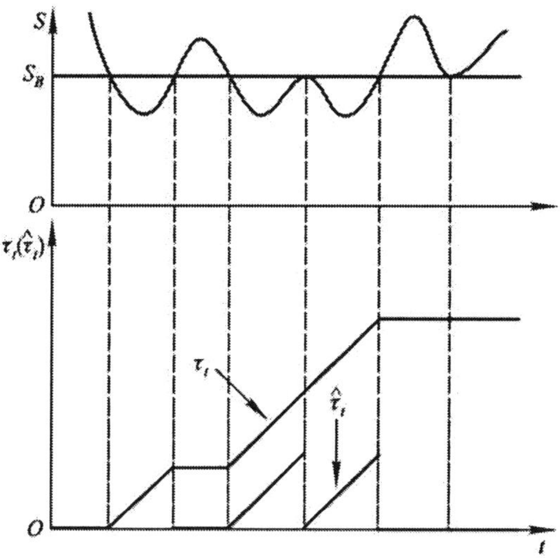

Remark Step option, Parasian option, Parisian option and barrier option are related to each other as follows:

(1) As $\rho \to \infty$, step option becomes barrier option,
(2) As $\rho \to 0$, step option becomes vanilla option,
(3) As $D \to T$, Parasian option and Parisian option become vanilla option,
(4) As $D \to 0$, Parasian option and Parisian option become barrier option.

Take the down-and-out option as example. From (8.4.2) and (8.4.5), the definition of τ_t and $\hat{\tau}_t$, it is easy to see

$$\frac{d\tau_t}{dt} = \frac{d\hat{\tau}_t}{dt} = \begin{cases} 0, & S_t > S_B, \\ 1, & S_t < S_B. \end{cases} \tag{8.4.7}$$

Notice that at $S_t = S_B$, $\frac{d\tau_t}{dt}$ and $\frac{d\hat{\tau}_t}{dt}$ differ greatly (see above figure). Suppose the option price is

$$V = V(S, \tau, t),$$

(here τ denotes either τ_t or $\hat{\tau}_t$.)
We will apply the Δ-hedging technique by constructing a portfolio Π:

$$\Pi = V - \Delta S,$$

and choose Δ, such that Π is risk-free in $(t, t+dt)$. Since

$$d\Pi = dV - \Delta dS,$$

and by the Itô formula:

$$\begin{aligned} dV &= \frac{\partial V}{\partial t}dt + \frac{\partial V}{\partial \tau}d\tau + \frac{\sigma^2}{2}S^2\frac{\partial^2 V}{\partial S^2}dt + \frac{\partial V}{\partial S}dS \\ &= \left(\frac{\partial V}{\partial t} + \frac{\partial V}{\partial \tau}\frac{d\tau}{dt} + \frac{\sigma^2}{2}S^2\frac{\partial^2 V}{\partial S^2}\right)dt + \frac{\partial V}{\partial S}dS, \end{aligned}$$

therefore we choose

$$\Delta = \frac{\partial V}{\partial S}.$$

Thus to satisfy

$$d\Pi = r\Pi dt,$$

there must be:
As $S > S_B$,

$$\frac{\partial V}{\partial t} + \frac{\sigma^2}{2}S^2\frac{\partial^2 V}{\partial S^2} + rS\frac{\partial V}{\partial S} - rV = 0; \tag{8.4.8}$$

As $S < S_B$,

$$\frac{\partial V}{\partial t} + \frac{\partial V}{\partial \tau} + \frac{\sigma^2}{2}S^2\frac{\partial^2 V}{\partial S^2} + rS\frac{\partial V}{\partial S} - rV = 0. \tag{8.4.9}$$

Next, let us analyze each of the three types of modified barrier options and find the mathematical model in each case (take the down-and-out option as example).
(1) **Step option**
Solution form : $V = V(S, t, \tau)$;
Domain: $\{0 \le S < \infty,\ 0 \le t \le T,\ 0 \le \tau \le T\}$;
PDE:

$$\begin{array}{lll} S > S_B & , & \text{Eq. (8.4.8)}, \\ S < S_B & , & \text{Eq. (8.4.9)}; \end{array}$$

Terminal condition:

$$V(S, T, \tau) = (S - K)^+ e^{-\rho\tau}; \tag{8.4.10}$$

Boundary conditions:

$$V(0, t, \tau) = 0, \tag{8.4.11}$$

$$V \sim S(\text{as } S \to \infty); \tag{8.4.12}$$

Continuity conditions:

$$V(S_B+0,t,\tau)=V(S_B-0,t,\tau), \tag{8.4.13}$$

$$\frac{\partial V}{\partial S}(S_B+0,t,\tau)=\frac{\partial V}{\partial S}(S_B-0,t,\tau). \tag{8.4.14}$$

By (8.4.13),(8.4.14), equations (8.4.8) and (8.4.9) can be combined into

$$\frac{\partial V}{\partial t}+H(S_B-S)\frac{\partial V}{\partial \tau}+\frac{\sigma^2}{2}S^2\frac{\partial^2 V}{\partial S^2}+rS\frac{\partial V}{\partial S}-rV=0. \tag{8.4.15}$$

(2)**Parasian option**
Solution form: $V=V(S,t,\tau)$;
Domain: $\{0\le S<\infty,\ 0\le t\le T,\ 0\le\tau\le D\}$;
PDE:

$$\begin{array}{lll} S>S_B & , & \text{Eq. (8.4.8)},\\ S<S_B & , & \text{Eq. (8.4.9)}; \end{array}$$

Terminal condition:

$$V(S,T,\tau)=(S-K)^+; \tag{8.4.16}$$

Boundary conditions:

$$V(S,t,D)=0, \tag{8.4.17}$$

$$(8.4.11),\ (8.4.12);$$

Continuity conditions:

$$(8.4.13),\ (8.4.14);$$

By (8.4.13),(8.4.14), equations (8.4.8) and (8.4.9) can be combined into (8.4.15).

(3) **Parisian option**
Solution form

$$V=\begin{cases} V(S,t,\tau), & 0<S\le S_B,\\ V(S,t), & S_B<S<\infty; \end{cases}$$

(This is the difference between Parisian option and Parasian option in view of the different definitions of the **occupation time** τ: when the asset price enters the region $S>S_B$ after crossing S_B from below, for Parasian option, the occupation time retains its current value, but for Parisian option, the occupation time is reset to zero. Imagine the occupation time be measured by a stopwatch. When S crosses S_B from below, for Parasian option, the stopwatch is paused, and for Parisian option, the stopwatch is not only stopped, but also reset to zero. Therefore when $S>S_B$, the Parasian option's price V depends on τ, but Parisian option's price V does not depend on τ).

Domain: $\{0\le S<\infty,\ 0\le t\le T,\ 0\le\tau<D\}$;

PDE:

$$S > S_B, \qquad \text{Eq. (8.4.8)},$$
$$S < S_B, \qquad \text{Eq. (8.4.9)};$$

Terminal condition: Eq. (8.4.16);
Boundary conditions: Eqs. (8.4.17), (8.4.11) and (8.4.12);
Continuity conditions:

$$V(S_B, t) = V(S_B, \tau, t) = V(S_B, 0, t), \tag{8.4.18}$$

$$\frac{\partial V}{\partial S}(S_B, t) = \frac{\partial V}{\partial S}(S_B, 0, t); \tag{8.4.19}$$

Here we see again the difference between Parisian option and Parasian option. Equation $V(S_B, \tau, t) = V(S_B, 0, t)$ shows: when S returns to S_B, the occupation time is reset to zero. In addition, only for $\tau = 0$, $\Delta = \frac{\partial V}{\partial S}$ is continuous at $S = S_B$. If $\tau > 0$, Δ is discontinuous in general.

Now let us discuss how to find solution for each type of the barrier options. For step options, closed form expression can be obtained but in a rather complex form. Therefore we will discuss the numerical solution.

Since step option and Parasian option both satisfy the same PDE (8.4.15), their numerical solution procedures are quite similar. Therefore we only need to study Parasian option's numerical calculation procedure.

(A)**Splitting method**

Partition the option's lifetime $[0, T]$ into N equal intervals:

$$0 = t_0 < t_1 < \cdots < t_N = T,$$

where $t_n = n\Delta t,\ \Delta t = \frac{T}{N}$.

Parasian option

In each interval $[t_n, t_{n+1}]$, $(0 \le n \le N-1)$, suppose $V(S, t_{n+1}, \tau)$ is known, we want to find $V(S, t_n, \tau)$. First, solve the first order PDE terminal-boundary value problem(S is a parameter, $0 \le S < \infty$) in the domain $\{t_n \le t \le t_{n+1},\ 0 \le \tau \le D\}$:

$$\begin{cases} \dfrac{\partial \hat{V}}{\partial t} + H(S_B - S)\dfrac{\partial \hat{V}}{\partial \tau} = 0, & (t_n \le t \le t_{n+1},\ 0 \le \tau \le D) \\ \hat{V}(S, t_{n+1}, \tau) = V(S, t_{n+1}, \tau), & (0 \le \tau \le D) \\ \hat{V}(S, t, D) = 0. & (t_n \le t \le t_{n+1}) \end{cases}$$

The characteristic line of this equation is

$$\tau = H(S_B - S)(t - t_{n+1}) + \tau^*.$$

For $S < S_B$, the characteristic line is shown in the figure below:

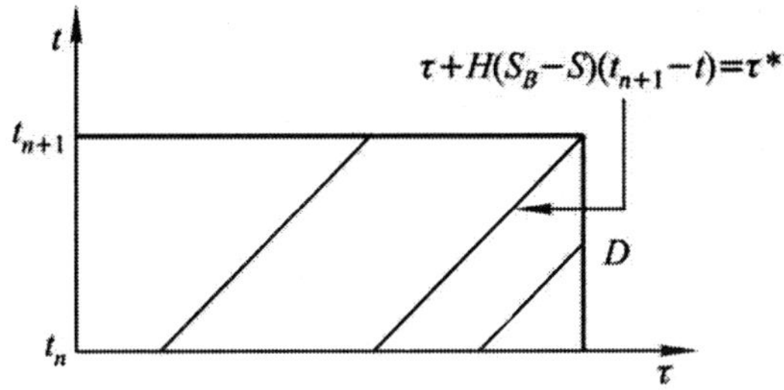

Thus the solution of the above problem is :
if $\tau + H(S_B - S)(t_{n+1} - t) < D$,

$$\hat{V}(S, t, \tau) = V(S, t_{n+1}, \tau + H(S_B - S)(t_{n+1} - t)),$$

if $\tau + H(S_B - S)(t_{n+1} - t) > D$,

$$\hat{V}(S, t, \tau) = 0.$$

Next, take $\hat{V}(x, t, \tau)$ as the initial value. In the domain $\{0 \le S < \infty,\ t_n \le t \le t_{n+1}\}$, solve the Black-Scholes equation(τ is a parameter):

$$\begin{cases} \dfrac{\partial V}{\partial t} + \dfrac{\sigma^2}{2} S^2 \dfrac{\partial^2 V}{\partial S^2} + rS\dfrac{\partial V}{\partial S} - rV = 0, \\ V(S, t_{n+1}, \tau) = \hat{V}(S, t_n, \tau), \end{cases}$$

Here

$$\hat{V}(S, t_n, \tau) = \begin{cases} V(S, t_{n+1}, \tau + H(S_B - S)\Delta t), & (0 \le \tau \le D - H(S_B - S)\Delta t) \\ 0. & (D - H(S_B - S)\Delta t \le \tau \le D) \end{cases}$$

Thus we have found the solution in the domain $\{0 \le S < \infty,\ t_n \le t \le t_{n+1},\ 0 \le \tau \le D\}$

$$V = V(S, t, \tau),$$

and in particular,

$$V|_{t=t_n} = V(S, t_n, \tau).$$

Since

$$V(S, t_N, \tau) = V(S, T, \tau) = (S - K)^+,$$

by the backward induction, we can find the price of Parasian option in the whole domain $\{0 \le S < \infty,\ 0 \le t \le T,\ 0 \le \tau \le D\}$.

Parisian option

For Parisian option, V and $\Delta = \frac{\partial V}{\partial S}$ are discontinuous at the barrier $S = S_B$ for $\tau > 0$. Therefore the equations (8.4.8) and (8.4.9) cannot be combined into (8.4.15). So there will be a difference when using the splitting method.

In each interval $[t_n, t_{n+1}]$, suppose $V(S, t_{n+1})(0 < S \leq S_B)$ and $V(S, t_{n+1}, \tau)(S_B < S < \infty)$ are given. We can rewrite it as $V(S, t_{n+1}, \tilde{H}(S_B - S)\tau)$, where

$$\tilde{H}(S) = \begin{cases} 1, & S > 0, \\ 0, & S \leq 0. \end{cases}$$

(Note the difference between $\tilde{H}(S)$ and $H(S)$ at $S = 0$.)

First, solve the first order differential equation (S is a parameter, $0 \leq S < S_B$) in the domain $\{t_n \leq t \leq t_{n+1},\ 0 \leq \tau \leq D\}$:

$$\begin{cases} \frac{\partial \hat{V}}{\partial t} + \frac{\partial \hat{V}}{\partial \tau} = 0, \\ \hat{V}(S, t_{n+1}, \tilde{H}(S_B - S)\tau) = V(S, t_{n+1}, \tilde{H}(S_B - S)\tau), \\ \hat{V}(S, t, \tilde{H}(S_B - S)D) = 0. \end{cases}$$

The characteristic curve of the equation is

$$\tau = (t - t_{n+1}) + \tau^*. \qquad (0 < S < S_B)$$

Thus if $\tau + (t_{n+1} - t) < D$,

$$\hat{V}(S, t, \tilde{H}(S_B - S)\tau) = V(S, t_{n+1}, \tilde{H}(S_B - S)[\tau + (t_{n+1} - t)]),$$

if $\tau + (t_{n+1} - t) > D$,

$$\hat{V}(S, t, \tilde{H}(S_B - S)\tau) = 0. \qquad (t_n \leq t \leq t_{n+1})$$

Thus we have

$$\hat{V}(S, t_n, \tilde{H}(S_B - S)\tau) = \begin{cases} V(S, t_{n+1}, \tilde{H}(S_B - S)(\Delta t + \tau)), & (0 \leq \tau \leq D - \Delta t) \\ 0. & (D - \Delta t \leq \tau \leq D) \end{cases}$$

Next, solve the Black-Scholes equation (here τ is a parameter) in the domain $\{0 \leq S < \infty,\ t_n \leq t \leq t_{n+1}\}$:

$$\begin{cases} \frac{\partial V}{\partial t} + \frac{\sigma^2}{2} S^2 \frac{\partial^2 V}{\partial S^2} + rS\frac{\partial V}{\partial S} - rV = 0, \\ V\big|_{t=t_{n+1}} = \hat{V}(S, t_n, \tilde{H}(S_B - S)\tau). \end{cases}$$

Thus we have found the solution in the domain $\{0 \leq S < \infty,\ t_n \leq t \leq t_{n+1},\ 0 \leq \tau \leq D\}$:

$$V = V(S, t, \tilde{H}(S_B - S)\tau). \qquad (t_n \leq t \leq t_{n+1})$$

In particular

$$V\mid_{t=t_n} = V(S, t_n, \tilde{H}(S_B - S)\tau).$$

Since

$$V(S, t_N, \tilde{H}(S_B - S)\tau) = (S - K)^+,$$

thus using the backward induction, we can find the price of Parisian option in the whole domain $\{0 \le S < \infty,\ 0 \le t \le T,\ 0 \le \tau \le D\}$.

(B)**Finite Difference Method with Characteristic line**

Under the transformation

$$x = \ln \frac{S}{S_B}, \qquad S_B u(x, t, \tau) = V(S, t, \tau).$$

(8.4.8) becomes

$$\frac{\partial u}{\partial t} + \frac{\sigma^2}{2}\frac{\partial^2 u}{\partial x^2} + (r - \frac{\sigma^2}{2})\frac{\partial u}{\partial x} - ru = 0, \tag{8.4.20}$$

as $x < 0$, and (8.4.9) becomes

$$\frac{\partial u}{\partial t} + \frac{\partial u}{\partial \tau} + \frac{\sigma^2}{2}\frac{\partial^2 u}{\partial x^2} + (r - \frac{\sigma^2}{2})\frac{\partial u}{\partial x} - ru = 0, \tag{8.4.21}$$

as $x < 0$. Partition the domain $\{x \in \mathbf{R}, 0 \le t \le T, 0 \le \tau \le D\}$ as follows:

$$x_i = i\Delta x, \qquad (i = 0, \pm 1, \pm 2, \dots)$$

$$t_n = n\Delta t, \qquad (n = 0, 1, \dots, N)$$

$$\tau_\ell = \ell \Delta \tau, \qquad (\ell = 0, 1, \dots, L)$$

where

$$\Delta t = \Delta \tau = \frac{T}{N} = \frac{D}{L}.$$

Parasian option

Since when crossing the barrier ($x = 0$, i.e. $S = S_B$), both u and $\frac{\partial u}{\partial x}$ are continuous, therefore (8.4.20),(8.4.21) can be combined into

$$\frac{\partial u}{\partial t} + H(-x)\frac{\partial u}{\partial \tau} + \frac{\sigma^2}{2}\frac{\partial^2 u}{\partial x^2} + (r - \frac{\sigma^2}{2})\frac{\partial u}{\partial x} - ru = 0. \tag{8.4.22}$$

In order to discretize it , we use the finite difference scheme with characteristic line, draw a characteristic line in (t_{n+1}, τ_ℓ)

$$\tau = H(-x)(t - t_{n+1}) + \tau_\ell,$$

then write the equation (8.4.22) as

$$\frac{d}{dt}u(x,t,H(-x)(t-t_{n+1})+\tau_\ell) + \left[\frac{\sigma^2}{2}\frac{\partial^2 u}{\partial x^2} + (r-\frac{\sigma^2}{2})\frac{\partial u}{\partial x} - ru\right]_{\tau=H(-x)(t-t_{n+1})+\tau_\ell} = 0. \tag{8.4.23}$$

Discretize (8.4.23), denote $u_{i,\ell}^n = u(x_i, t_n, \tau_\ell)$, then for $x > 0$(i.e. $i > 0$),

$$\frac{u_{i,\ell}^{n+1} - u_{i,\ell}^n}{\Delta t} + \frac{\sigma^2}{2}[\frac{u_{i+1,\ell}^{n+1} - 2u_{i,\ell}^{n+1} + u_{i-1,\ell}^{n+1}}{\Delta x^2}]$$

$$+(r-\frac{\sigma^2}{2})[\frac{u_{i+1,\ell}^{n+1} - u_{i-1,\ell}^{n+1}}{2\Delta x}] - ru_{i,\ell}^n = 0,$$

For $x \le 0 (i \le 0)$,

$$\frac{u_{i,\ell}^{n+1} - u_{i,\ell-1}^n}{\Delta t} + \frac{\sigma^2}{2}[\frac{u_{i+1,\ell}^{n+1} - 2u_{i,\ell}^{n+1} + u_{i-1,\ell}^{n+1}}{\Delta x^2}]$$

$$+(r-\frac{\sigma^2}{2})[\frac{u_{i+1,\ell}^{n+1} - u_{i-1,\ell}^{n+1}}{2\Delta x}] - ru_{i,\ell-1}^n = 0,$$

and

$$u_{i,\ell}^N = (e^{i\Delta x} - K_B)^+, \qquad (i = 0, \pm 1, \ldots; \ell = 0, 1, \ldots, L)$$

where $K_B = \dfrac{K}{S_B}$;

$$u_{i,L}^n = 0. \qquad (i = 0, \pm 1, \ldots;\ n = 0, 1, \ldots, N)$$

Parisian option

Denote $u_{i,0}^n = u(x_i, t_n, 0) = u(x_i, t_n)$. Then for $x \ge 0$ ($i \ge 0$),

$$\frac{u_{i,0}^{n+1} - u_{i,0}^n}{\Delta t} + \frac{\sigma^2}{2}\left[\frac{u_{i+1,0}^{n+1} - 2u_{i,0}^{n+1} + u_{i-1,0}^{n+1}}{\Delta x^2}\right] + \left(r-\frac{\sigma^2}{2}\right)\left[\frac{u_{i+1,0}^{n+1} - u_{i-1,0}^{n+1}}{2\Delta x}\right] - ru_{i,0}^n = 0, \tag{8.4.24}$$

for $x < 0$ ($i < 0$),

$$\frac{u_{i,\ell}^{n+1} - u_{i,\ell-1}^n}{\Delta t} + \frac{\sigma^2}{2}\left[\frac{u_{i+1,\ell}^{n+1} - 2u_{i,\ell}^{n+1} + u_{i-1,\ell}^{n+1}}{\Delta x^2}\right] + \left(r-\frac{\sigma^2}{2}\right)\left[\frac{u_{i+1,\ell}^{n+1} - u_{i-1,\ell}^{n+1}}{2\Delta x}\right] - ru_{i,\ell-1}^n = 0, \tag{8.4.25}$$

and

$$u_{i,\ell}^N = (e^{i\Delta x} - K_B)^+, \quad (i = 0, \pm 1, \ldots;\ \ell = 0, 1, \ldots, L) \tag{8.2.26}$$

$$u_{i,L}^n = 0, \quad (i = 0, \pm 1, \ldots;\ n = 0, 1, \ldots, N) \tag{8.4.27}$$

$$u_{0,\ell}^n = u_{0,0}^n. \qquad (\ell = 0, 1, \ldots, D-1;\ n = 0, 1, \ldots, N) \tag{8.4.28}$$

Parisian option price can be calculated as follows: If $u_{i,\ell}^{n+1}$ is given, we can solve (8.4.24) to get $u_{i,0}^n$ $(i \geq 0)$. Then by the continuity condition (8.4.28) at $x = 0$, we can find $u_{0,\ell}^n$. Finally, solve the equation (8.4.25), and with the boundary condition (8.4.27), we can find $u_{i,\ell}^n$, $(i < 0)$.

Summary:

(1) Unlike vanilla options, the mathematical model of the European barrier options is a terminal-boundary value problem for a parabolic PDE, where the barriers form the domain boundaries. The boundary conditions are imposed according to the knock-out or knock-in terms.

(2) A knock-out barrier option extinguishes when the asset price hits the barrier. To avoid this abrupt change, an occupation time $\tau_t(\hat{\tau}_t)$ is introduced in the modified barrier options, and the Black-Scholes equation is replaced by different types of hyperparabolic equations in three variables S, t and τ. Since these equations contain only the first derivative of the solution with respect to τ, thus it is natural to use the splitting method (to "split" the equation into a first order PDE and a second order equation) and the finite difference method with characteristic line (to form a finite difference scheme along the characteristics line of the first order PDE).

Exercises

1. A financial institute sells a callable European call option. That is, when the stock price reaches $S = S_c$ ($S_c > K, K$ is the strike price), the seller has the right to repurchase the option at $S_c - K$. Valuate this option.

2. A financial institute sells a callable European down-and-out call option, with the barrier at $S = S_B$ and repurchase price $S = S_c$, and

$$S_B < K < S_c \qquad (K \text{ is the strike price})$$

Model this barrier option, and find the expression of the option price for the case $r = \frac{\sigma^2}{2}$, $q = 0$.

3. Let $V(S, t; S_B)$ be the price of a down-and-out call option with barrier level S_B. Show that if $S_B < K$, then $V(S, t; S_B)$ is a monotone decreasing function of S_B. Explain its financial meaning.

4. Formulate the call-put parity for the up-and-in options, and prove it.

5. Let $V_\infty(S; S_B)$ be the price of a perpetual American up-and-out put option, and assume $S_B > K$. Valuate the option and find the optimal exercise boundary $S = \gamma(S_B)$. Show that If $S_{B_1} > S_{B_2} (> K)$, then

$$V_\infty(S; S_{B_1}) \geq V_\infty(S; S_{B_2}),$$

$$\gamma(S_{B_1}) < \gamma(S_{B_2}).$$

6. Let $V(S,t;S_B)$ be the price of an American up-and-out put option, and assume $S_B > K$. Set up its price model, and show that

$$V(S,t;S_B) \leq V_\infty(S;S_B);$$

And show that if $S(t;S_B)$ is the optimal exercise boundary, then

$$S(t;S_B) > \gamma(S_B).$$

7. Take an American up-and-out put option as example, describe the BTM for American barrier options.

Chapter 9

Path-Dependent Options (II) —— Strongly Path-Dependent Options

The payoff of strongly path-dependent options depends not only on the underlying asset price on the expiration day, but also on the path of the asset price over the entire or part of the option's lifetime. There are two kinds of strong path-dependence: the option payoff may depend on the average or the maximum (minimum) of the asset price over some certain periods in the option's lifetime. For strongly path-dependent options, in addition to time t and the asset price S_t, the option price depends also on a path variable J_t, which can be either the path average of the price or the maximum (minimum) price up to time t. That is, $V = V(S, J, t)$.

This chapter is organized as follows: 1. Model PDE problems for the strongly path-dependent options; 2. Investigate whether the PDE problem can be reduce to a 1-D problem by a transformation $\xi = \xi(S, J, t)$ so that the option price only depends on t and the new variable ξ: $V = V(\xi, t)$; 3. Find solutions: analytical solutions if it is possible, and approximate solutions by using the BTM.

9.1 Asian Options

Asian option is an option whose payoff at maturity depends on the average price of the underlying asset over the option's lifetime. Here the average can be either arithmetic average or geometric average. Let J_t, the path variable, denote the average asset price for the period up to t, then

	arithmetic average	geometric average
discrete case	$J_n = \frac{1}{n}\sum_{i=1}^{n} S_{t_i}$	$J_n = (\Pi_{i=1}^{n} S_{t_i})^{\frac{1}{n}} = e^{\frac{1}{n}\sum_{i=1}^{n}\ln S_{t_i}}$
continuous case	$J_t = \frac{1}{t}\int_0^t S_\tau d\tau$	$J_t = e^{\frac{1}{t}\int_0^t \ln S_\tau d\tau}$

Correspondingly, there are two kinds of Asian options: **arithmetic average Asian options** and **geometric average Asian options**.

Furthermore, there are two types of payoffs for the Asian options:

(1) **Fixed strike price**(take the call options as example):

$$\text{payoff} = (J_T - K)^+.$$

(2) **Floating strike price** (take the call options as example):

$$\text{payoff} = (S_T - J_T)^+.$$

Then we have: Asian options with fixed strike price and Asian options with floating strike price accordingly. Thus without distinguishing call and put, there are four types of Asian options:

arithmetic average Asian options with fixed strike price.
geometric average Asian options with fixed strike price.
arithmetic average Asian options with floating strike price.
geometric average Asian options with floating strike price.

Since the volatility of the average price is always less than the volatility of the individual price series that make up the average, the premium of an Asian option is usually less than that of the corresponding vanilla option.

Example Consider a six-month call option of stock. If $S_0 = K = \$145, r = 6\%, q = 3\%, \sigma = 29.5\%$, then the premiums according to the Black-Scholes theory are

	Average period	Premium
European vanilla option		\$12.87
Asian option (arithmetic/geometric)	30days	\$12.16/12.03
	60days	\$11.30/11.23
	180days	\$7.31/7.13

The above table shows:

(1) An Asian option costs less than its vanilla counterpart, and its premium tends to decrease with increasing average period.

(2) The price of a geometric Asian option is always lower than its arithmetic counterpart. This is due to the inequality

$$(\prod_{i=1}^{n} S(t_i))^{\frac{1}{n}} \leq \frac{1}{n}\sum_{i=1}^{n} S(t_i).$$

Asian options are widely used in the international trading. Consider an import company that imports goods from a foreign country and selling them in domestic market. Suppose the company pays bills in foreign currency monthly, and calculates the earnings in home currency annually. Then the company faces a foreign exchange rate risk. It can choose either of the following plans to avoid the risk:

(A) Buy 12 options, each pays one month's bill, at a predetermined currency exchange rate.

(B) Buy a 12-month arithmetic average Asian option according to the whole year's need.

We will use the following example to compare the premiums (calculated by the Black-Scholes theory):

Example A US company imports Japanese products. It pays 1 million Yen to the Japanese company every month. Suppose the US company decides to lock at the current exchange rate 1USD = 85Yen. Assume $r = 6\%, q = 3\%, \sigma = 18\%$. Then for Plan (A), the premiums for the 12 options are \$258, \$372, \$463, \$540, \$610, \$674, \$733, \$789, \$842, \$892, \$940, \$987, adding up to \$8100. For Plan (B), the premium of the 12-month Asian option is \$5795.

Both plans can help the US company to accomplish its goal, but at different costs. Plan (B) costs \$2305 less than Plan (A), a 28.46% saving.

For a foreign trade company, if cost in the home country's currency is known, then to avoid currency exchange risk, it usually chooses Asian options with fixed strike price to secure earnings. On the other hand, if cost and earning are both settled in foreign currency, and the concern is in the currency exchange risk at the end of the year when payments are sent to the home country, then it should choose Asian options with floating strike price. In general, Asian options with fixed strike price are more popular than Asian options with floating strike price.

Since arithmetic average is simpler than geometric average, arithmetic Asian options are more favored than geometric Asian options in financial markets. However, since the asset price movement is described by the geometric Brownian motion in our price model, from the Black-Scholes theoretical viewpoint, the pricing problems of geometric average Asian options are simpler than those of arithmetic average Asian options.

9.2 Model and Simplification

The price of an Asian option is

$$V = V(S_t, J_t, t).$$

Construct a portfolio

$$\Pi = V(S, J, t) - \Delta S,$$

where Δ can be chosen such that Π is risk-free in $(t, t + dt)$, i.e.,

$$d\Pi = r\Pi dt = r(V - \Delta S)dt. \tag{9.2.1}$$

By the Itô formula,

$$\begin{aligned} d\Pi &= dV - \Delta dS - q\Delta S dt \\ &= (\frac{\partial V}{\partial t} + \frac{1}{2}\sigma^2 S^2 \frac{\partial^2 V}{\partial S^2} - q\Delta S)dt + \frac{\partial V}{\partial S}dS + \frac{\partial V}{\partial J}dJ - \Delta dS \\ &= (\frac{\partial V}{\partial t} + \frac{1}{2}\sigma^2 S^2 \frac{\partial^2 V}{\partial S^2} - q\Delta S + \frac{\partial V}{\partial J}\frac{dJ}{dt})dt + (\frac{\partial V}{\partial S} - \Delta)dS. \end{aligned} \tag{9.2.2}$$

We can choose

$$\Delta = \frac{\partial V}{\partial S},$$

then combining (9.2.1) and (9.2.2), we get

$$\frac{\partial V}{\partial t} + \frac{\partial V}{\partial J}\frac{dJ}{dt} + \frac{1}{2}\sigma^2 S^2 \frac{\partial^2 V}{\partial S^2} + (r-q)S\frac{\partial V}{\partial S} - rV = 0, \tag{9.2.3}$$

where

$$J_t = \begin{cases} \frac{1}{t}\int_0^t S_\tau d\tau, & \text{(arithmetic average)} \\ e^{\frac{1}{t}\int_0^t \ln S_\tau d\tau}. & \text{(geometric average)} \end{cases} \tag{9.2.4}$$

Therefore

$$\frac{dJ_t}{dt} = \begin{cases} \frac{1}{t}[S_t - J_t], & \text{(arithmetic average)} \\ J_t[\frac{\ln S_t - \ln J_t}{t}]. & \text{(geometric average)} \end{cases} \tag{9.2.5}$$

Substituting (9.2.5) into (9.2.3), we get the model for the Asian option pricing:

Arithmetic average Asian option pricing model: a terminal-boundary problem in the domain $\{0 \le S < \infty, 0 \le J < \infty, 0 \le t \le T\}$:

$$\begin{cases} \frac{\partial V}{\partial t} + \frac{S-J}{t}\frac{\partial V}{\partial J} + \frac{\sigma^2}{2}S^2\frac{\partial^2 V}{\partial S^2} + (r-q)S\frac{\partial V}{\partial S} - rV = 0, & (9.2.6) \\ V(S,J,T) = \begin{cases} (J-K)^+, & \text{(call option with fixed strike price)} \\ (K-J)^+, & \text{(put option with fixed strike price)} \\ (S-J)^+, & \text{(call option with floating strike price)} \\ (J-S)^+. & \text{(put option with floating strike price)} \end{cases} & (9.2.7) \end{cases}$$

Geometric average Asian option pricing model : a terminal-boundary problem in the domain $\{0 \le S < \infty, 0 \le J < \infty,\ 0 \le t \le T\}$:

$$\begin{cases} \frac{\partial V}{\partial t} + J\frac{\ln S - \ln J}{t}\frac{\partial V}{\partial J} + \frac{\sigma^2}{2}S^2\frac{\partial^2 V}{\partial S^2} + (r-q)S\frac{\partial V}{\partial S} - rV = 0, & (9.2.8) \\ V(S,J,T) = \begin{cases} (J-K)^+, & \text{(call option with fixed strike price)} \\ (K-J)^+, & \text{(put option with fixed strike price)} \\ (S-J)^+, & \text{(call option with floating strike price)} \\ (J-S)^+. & \text{(put option with floating strike price)} \end{cases} & (9.2.9) \end{cases}$$

Equations (9.2.6),(9.2.8) are 2-D hyperparobolic equations. To solve the terminal-boundary problem (9.2.6),(9.2.7) and (9.2.8),(9.2.9), we will reduce them into a 1-D problem by suitable transformation. Fortunately, all Asian option pricing problems can be reduced to 1-D problems. However, only for the geometric Asian options the price has closed-form expressions. For simplicity, we will discuss the call option only.

(A) Arithmetic average Asian option with fixed strike price

Define

$$\xi = \frac{TK - tJ}{S}, \tag{9.2.10}$$

$$V = \frac{SU}{T}. \tag{9.2.11}$$

By straightforward calculation, we have

$$\begin{aligned} \frac{\partial V}{\partial t} &= \frac{S}{T}\left[\frac{\partial U}{\partial t} + \frac{\partial U}{\partial \xi}\left(-\frac{J}{S}\right)\right], \\ \frac{\partial V}{\partial J} &= \frac{S}{T}\frac{\partial U}{\partial \xi}\left(-\frac{t}{S}\right), \\ \frac{\partial V}{\partial S} &= \frac{U}{T} + \frac{S}{T}\frac{\partial U}{\partial \xi}\left(\frac{tJ - TK}{S^2}\right), \\ \frac{\partial^2 V}{\partial S^2} &= \frac{2}{T}\frac{\partial U}{\partial \xi}\left(\frac{tJ-TK}{S^2}\right) + \frac{S}{T}\frac{\partial^2 U}{\partial \xi^2}\left(\frac{tJ-TK}{S^2}\right)^2 - \frac{2S}{T}\frac{\partial U}{\partial \xi}\left(\frac{tJ-TK}{S^3}\right), \end{aligned}$$

Substituting these into (9.2.6), we get

$$\frac{\partial U}{\partial t} + \frac{\sigma^2}{2}\xi^2\frac{\partial^2 U}{\partial \xi^2} - [(r-q)\xi + 1]\frac{\partial U}{\partial \xi} - qU = 0. \tag{9.2.12}$$

And by (9.2.7), we have the terminal condition:

$$U|_{t=T} = \frac{T}{S}V\bigg|_{t=T} = \frac{T}{S}(J-K)^+ = (-\xi)^+. \tag{9.2.13}$$

Thus, under the transformation (9.2.10), (9.2.11), the arithmetic average Asian option with fixed strike price is reduced to a Cauchy problem (9.2.12),(9.2.13) for a 1-D parabolic equation in the domain $\{\xi \in R, 0 \le t \le T\}$.

(B) Arithmetic average Asian option with floating strike price
Define

$$\xi = \frac{tJ}{S}, \tag{9.2.14}$$

$$V = SU. \tag{9.2.15}$$

By straightforward calculation, we have

$$\begin{aligned}
\frac{\partial V}{\partial t} &= S\left[\frac{\partial U}{\partial t} + \frac{\partial U}{\partial \xi}\left(\frac{J}{S}\right)\right], \\
\frac{\partial V}{\partial J} &= t\frac{\partial U}{\partial \xi}, \\
\frac{\partial V}{\partial S} &= U + S\frac{\partial U}{\partial \xi}\left(-\frac{tJ}{S^2}\right), \\
\frac{\partial^2 V}{\partial S^2} &= S\frac{\partial^2 U}{\partial \xi^2}\left(\frac{tJ}{S^2}\right)^2.
\end{aligned}$$

Substituting them into (9.2.6), we get

$$\frac{\partial U}{\partial t} + \frac{\sigma^2}{2}\xi^2\frac{\partial^2 U}{\partial \xi^2} + [1 - (r-q)\xi]\frac{\partial U}{\partial \xi} - qU = 0, \tag{9.2.16}$$

and by (9.2.7), we have

$$U|_{t=T} = \frac{1}{S}V|_{t=T} = \left(1 - \frac{tJ}{ST}\right)^+ |_{t=T} = \left(1 - \frac{\xi}{T}\right)^+. \tag{9.2.17}$$

Thus under the transformation (9.2.14),(9.2.15), the arithmetic average Asian option with floating strike price is reduced to a boundary-terminal value problem (9.2.16),(9.2.17) for a degenerate parabolic equation in the domain $\{0 \le \xi \le \infty, 0 \le t \le T\}$.

(C) Geometric average Asian option with fixed strike price
Define

$$\xi = \frac{t \ln J + (T-t)\ln S}{T}, \tag{9.2.18}$$

$$V = U(\xi, t). \tag{9.2.19}$$

By straightforward calculation, we have

$$\begin{aligned}
\frac{\partial V}{\partial t} &= \frac{\partial U}{\partial t} + \frac{\partial U}{\partial \xi}\left[\frac{\ln J}{T} - \frac{\ln S}{T}\right], \\
\frac{\partial V}{\partial J} &= \frac{\partial U}{\partial \xi}\frac{t}{TJ}, \\
\frac{\partial V}{\partial S} &= \frac{T-t}{TS}\frac{\partial U}{\partial \xi}, \\
\frac{\partial^2 V}{\partial S^2} &= \left(\frac{T-t}{TS}\right)^2\frac{\partial^2 U}{\partial \xi^2} - \frac{T-t}{TS^2}\frac{\partial U}{\partial \xi}.
\end{aligned}$$

Substituting them into (9.2.8), we get

$$\frac{\partial U}{\partial t}+\frac{\sigma^2}{2}\left(\frac{T-t}{T}\right)^2\frac{\partial^2 U}{\partial \xi^2}+\left(r-q-\frac{\sigma^2}{2}\right)\left(\frac{T-t}{T}\right)\frac{\partial U}{\partial \xi}-rU=0, \qquad (9.2.20)$$

and by (9.2.9), we have

$$U|_{t=T}=V|_{t=T}=(J-K)^+|_{t=T}=(e^{\xi}-K)^+. \qquad (9.2.21)$$

Thus by the transformation (9.2.18),(9.2.19), the geometric average Asian option with fixed strike price is reduced to a Cauchy problem (9.2.20),(9.2.21) in the domain $\{\xi \in \mathbf{R}, 0 \le t \le T\}$.

(D) Geometric average Asian option with floating strike price

Define

$$\xi=\frac{1}{t}\ln\frac{J}{S}, \qquad (9.2.22)$$

$$V=SU. \qquad (9.2.23)$$

By straightforward calculation, we have

$$\begin{aligned}
\frac{\partial V}{\partial t}&=S\frac{\partial U}{\partial t}+S\frac{\partial U}{\partial \xi}\left(-\frac{\xi}{t}\right),\\
\frac{\partial V}{\partial J}&=S\frac{\partial U}{\partial \xi}\left(\frac{1}{tJ}\right),\\
\frac{\partial V}{\partial S}&=U+S\frac{\partial U}{\partial \xi}\left(-\frac{1}{tS}\right),\\
\frac{\partial^2 V}{\partial S^2}&=S\frac{\partial^2 U}{\partial \xi^2}\left(\frac{1}{tS}\right)^2-\frac{1}{tS}\frac{\partial U}{\partial \xi}.
\end{aligned}$$

Substituting them into (9.2.8), we get

$$\frac{\partial U}{\partial t}+\frac{\sigma^2}{2}\frac{1}{t^2}\frac{\partial^2 U}{\partial \xi^2}-\left[\left(r-q+\frac{\sigma^2}{2}\right)+2\xi\right]\frac{1}{t}\frac{\partial U}{\partial \xi}-qU=0, \qquad (9.2.24)$$

and by (9.2.9), we have

$$U|_{t=T}=\frac{1}{S}V|_{t=T}=\left(1-\frac{J}{S}\right)^+|_{t=T}=(1-e^{T\xi})^+. \qquad (9.2.25)$$

Thus by the transformation (9.2.22),(9.2.23), the geometric average Asian option with floating strike price is reduced to the Cauchy problem (9.2.24),(9.2.25) in the domain $\{\xi \in \mathbf{R}, 0 \le t \le T\}$.

Remark For geometric average Asian options with floating strike price, although under the transformation (9.2.22),(9.2.23), the original boundary-terminal value problem is reduced to a 1-D problem, yet it is not easy to get a closed form solution for the Cauchy problem (9.2.24),(9.2.25), because the coefficients of the first order term in the equation (9.2.24) contains not only variable t, but also variable ξ. Therefore, sometimes we still prefer using the transformation (9.2.18),

(9.2.19), even though this transformation cannot reduce the geometric average Asian option with floating strike price (9.2.8),(9.2.9) to a 1-D problem (due to the condition (9.2.9), $V(S, J, t) = (S - J)^+$ cannot be transformed to a function of ξ only), but since the equation has a special structure analogous to a 1-D problem, there is a closed form solution.

For a geometric average Asian option with floating strike price, let

$$x = \ln S, \tag{9.2.26}$$

$$y = \frac{t \ln J + (T-t)\ln S}{T}, \tag{9.2.27}$$

$$V = U(x, y, t). \tag{9.2.28}$$

By straightforward calculation, the equation (9.2.8) is reduced to

$$\begin{aligned}&\frac{\partial U}{\partial t} + \frac{\sigma^2}{2}\left(\frac{T-t}{T}\right)^2 \frac{\partial^2 U}{\partial y^2} + \sigma^2\left(\frac{T-t}{T}\right)\frac{\partial^2 U}{\partial x \partial y}\\ &\quad+\frac{\sigma^2}{2}\frac{\partial^2 U}{\partial x^2} + \left(r - q - \frac{\sigma^2}{2}\right)\left[\frac{T-t}{T}\frac{\partial U}{\partial y} + \frac{\partial U}{\partial x}\right] - rU = 0,\end{aligned}$$

or

$$\begin{aligned}&\frac{\partial U}{\partial t} + \frac{\sigma^2}{2}\left[\left(\frac{T-t}{T}\right)\frac{\partial}{\partial y} + \frac{\partial}{\partial x}\right]^2 U\\ &\quad+\left(r - q - \frac{\sigma^2}{2}\right)\left[\left(\frac{T-t}{T}\right)\frac{\partial}{\partial y} + \frac{\partial}{\partial x}\right] U - rU = 0,\end{aligned} \tag{9.2.29}$$

and by (9.2.9), we get

$$U|_{t=T} = (e^x - e^y)^+. \tag{9.2.30}$$

Thus under the transformation (9.2.26)—(9.2.28), the geometric average Asian option with floating strike price is reduced to a Cauchy problem (9.2.29),(9.2.30) in the domain $\{(x, y) \in \mathbf{R}^2, 0 \le t \le T\}$.

(E) **American–style Asian options with floating strike price**

Any American-style Asian option with floating strike price, whether arithmetic average or geometric average, can be transformed to a 1-D free boundary problem.

(1)**Arithmetic average case**

Consider the dividend paying American-style Asian options with floating strike price. The pricing model is (take the call option as example) an obstacle problem in the domain $\{0 \le S < \infty, 0 \le J < \infty, 0 \le t \le T\}$:

$$\begin{cases}\min\{-\hat{\mathcal{L}}V, V - (S-J)^+\} = 0, & (9.2.31)\\ V|_{t=T} = (S-J)^+, & (9.2.32)\end{cases}$$

where

$$\hat{\mathcal{L}}V = \frac{\partial V}{\partial t} + \frac{S-J}{t}\frac{\partial V}{\partial J} + \frac{\sigma^2}{2}S^2\frac{\partial^2 V}{\partial S^2} + (r-q)S\frac{\partial V}{\partial S} - rV.$$

Let

$$\xi = \frac{tJ}{S}, \tag{9.2.33}$$

$$V = SU. \tag{9.2.34}$$

Under the above transformation, the obstacle problem (9.2.31), (9.2.32) becomes a 1-D free boundary problem in the domain $\{\xi \in \mathbf{R}_+, 0 \le t \le T\}$:

$$\begin{cases} \min\left\{-\hat{\mathcal{L}}_1 U, U - \left(1 - \frac{\xi}{t}\right)^+\right\} = 0, & (9.2.35) \\ U|_{t=T}\left(1 - \frac{\xi}{T}\right)^+, & (9.2.36) \end{cases}$$

where

$$\hat{\mathcal{L}}_1 U = \frac{\partial U}{\partial t} + \frac{\sigma^2}{2}\xi^2\frac{\partial^2 U}{\partial \xi^2} + [1-(r-q)\xi]\frac{\partial u}{\partial \xi} - qU.$$

(2) **Geometric average case**

Consider the dividend paying American-style Asian options with floating strike price, the model is (take the call option as example) an obstacle problem in the domain $\{0 \le S < \infty, 0 \le J < \infty, 0 \le t \le T\}$:

$$\begin{cases} \min\{-\tilde{\mathcal{L}}V, V - (S-J)^+\} = 0, & (9.2.37) \\ V|_{t=T} = (S-J)^+, & (9.2.38) \end{cases}$$

where

$$\tilde{\mathcal{L}}V = \frac{\partial V}{\partial t} + J\frac{\ln S - \ln J}{t}\frac{\partial V}{\partial J} + \frac{\sigma^2}{2}S^2\frac{\partial^2 V}{\partial S^2} + (r-q)S\frac{\partial V}{\partial S} - rV.$$

Let

$$\xi = \frac{1}{t}\ln\frac{J}{S}, \tag{9.2.39}$$

$$V = SU. \tag{9.2.40}$$

Under the above transformation, the obstacle problem (9.2.37),(9.2.38) becomes a 1-D free boundary problem in the domain $\{\xi \in \mathbf{R}, 0 \le t \le T\}$:

$$\begin{cases} \min\{-\tilde{\mathcal{L}}_1 U, U - (1-e^{t\xi})^+\} = 0, \\ U|_{t=T} = (1-e^{T\xi})^+, \end{cases}$$

where

$$\tilde{\mathcal{L}}_1 U = \frac{\partial U}{\partial t} + \frac{\sigma^2}{2}\frac{1}{t^2}\frac{\partial^2 U}{\partial \xi^2} - \left[\left(r - q + \frac{\sigma^2}{2}\right) + 2\xi\right]\frac{1}{t}\frac{\partial U}{\partial \xi} - qU.$$

For American-style Asian options with fixed strike price, it is not known whether it can be transformed into to a 1-D problem. But this is known: American-style Asian options with fixed strike price cannot be reduced to a 1-D free boundary problem under the transformation (9.2.10),(9.2.11) and (9.2.18),(9.2.19).

9.3 Valuation Formula for European-Style Geometric Average Asian Option

Closed form valuation formulas exist for the European-style geometric average Asian options.

(A) **Asian option with fixed strike price**

Under the transformation (9.2.18),(9.2.19), the pricing problem becomes a Cauchy problem

$$\begin{cases} \frac{\partial U}{\partial t} + \frac{\sigma^2}{2}(\frac{T-t}{T})^2\frac{\partial^2 U}{\partial \xi^2} + (r - q - \frac{\sigma^2}{2})(\frac{T-t}{T})\frac{\partial U}{\partial \xi} - rU = 0, & (9.3.1) \\ U|_{t=T} = (e^{\xi} - K)^+. & (9.3.2) \end{cases}$$

Let

$$W = Ue^{\beta(t)}, \quad (9.3.3)$$

$$\eta = \xi + \alpha(t), \quad (9.3.4)$$

$$\tau = \gamma(t). \quad (9.3.5)$$

Substituting them into (9.3.1), we get

$$\gamma'(t)\frac{\partial W}{\partial \tau} + \frac{\sigma^2}{2}(\frac{T-t}{T})^2\frac{\partial^2 W}{\partial \eta^2} + [(r-q-\frac{\sigma^2}{2})(\frac{T-t}{T}) + \alpha'(t)]\frac{\partial W}{\partial \eta} - (r+\beta'(t))W = 0.$$

Choose

$$\alpha'(t) + (r - q - \frac{\sigma^2}{2})(\frac{T-t}{T}) = 0,$$
$$\beta'(t) + r = 0,$$
$$\gamma'(t) = -(\frac{T-t}{T})^2,$$

and impose the terminal conditions:

$$\alpha(T) = \beta(T) = \gamma(T) = 0.$$

The solutions are

$$\alpha(t) = \frac{1}{2T}\left(r - q - \frac{\sigma^2}{2}\right)(T-t)^2,$$
$$\beta(t) = r(T-t),$$
$$\gamma(t) = \frac{1}{3T^2}(T-t)^3.$$

Under the transformation (9.3.3)—(9.3.5), the terminal-boundary value problem (9.3.1),(9.3.2) is turned into a Cauchy problem for the heat equation:

$$\begin{cases} \dfrac{\partial W}{\partial \tau} - \dfrac{\sigma^2}{2}\dfrac{\partial^2 W}{\partial \eta^2} = 0, \\ W(\eta, 0) = (e^\eta - K)^+. \end{cases}$$

Its solution can be written in the form of the Poisson formula:

$$W(\eta, \tau) = \frac{1}{\sigma\sqrt{2\pi\tau}}\int_{-\infty}^{\infty}(e^y - K)^+ e^{-\frac{(y-\eta)^2}{2\sigma^2\tau}}dy.$$

Back to the original variables (S, J, t) and function V by the transformation (9.3.3)—(9.3.5) and (9.2.18),(9.2.19), we get

$$V(S, J, t) = [J^t S^{T-t}]^{\frac{1}{T}} e^{(r^* + \frac{\sigma^*}{2})(T-t)} N(d_1^*) - KN(d_2^*),$$

where

$$d_1^* = \frac{\dfrac{1}{T}\ln\dfrac{J^t S^{T-t}}{K^T} + (r^* + \dfrac{\sigma^{*2}}{2})(T-t)}{\sigma^*\sqrt{T-t}},$$
$$d_2^* = d_1^* - \sigma^*\sqrt{T-t},$$
$$r^* = (r - \frac{\sigma^2}{2})\frac{T-t}{2T},$$
$$\sigma^* = \frac{\sigma(T-t)}{\sqrt{3T}}.$$

(B) **Asian option with floating strike price**

Under the transformation (9.2.26)—(9.2.28), the problem (9.2.8),(9.2.9) is reduced to a Cauchy problem (9.2.29),(9.2.30) in the domain $\{(x, y) \in \mathbf{R}^2, 0 \leq t \leq T\}$:

$$\begin{cases} \dfrac{\partial U}{\partial t} + \dfrac{\sigma^2}{2}\left[\dfrac{\partial}{\partial x} + \dfrac{T-t}{T}\dfrac{\partial}{\partial y}\right]^2 U + \left(r - q - \dfrac{\sigma^2}{2}\right)\left[\dfrac{\partial}{\partial x} + \dfrac{T-t}{T}\dfrac{\partial}{\partial y}\right]U - rU = 0, & (9.3.6) \\ U|_{t=T} = (e^x - e^y)^+ \hat{=} U_0(x, y). & (9.3.7) \end{cases}$$

The Cauchy problem (9.3.6),(9.3.7) can be solved by the Fourier transform ([43])

as follows. Let

$$\hat{U}(\xi,\eta,t) = \int_{-\infty}^{\infty}\int_{-\infty}^{\infty} U(x,y,t)e^{-i(\xi x+\eta y)}dxdy,$$

Applying the Fourier transform on both sides of (9.3.6), we get an ordinary differential equation for $\hat{U}$ as a function of t (ξ,η are parameters):

$$\frac{d\hat{U}}{dt} - \frac{\sigma^2}{2}\left(\xi + \frac{T-t}{T}\eta\right)^2 \hat{U} + i\left(r - q - \frac{\sigma^2}{2}\right)\left(\xi + \frac{T-t}{T}\eta\right)\hat{U} - r\hat{U} = 0, \quad (9.3.8)$$

Under the Fourier transform, the initial condition (9.3.7) becomes

$$\hat{U}(T) = \hat{U}_0(\xi,\eta). \quad (9.3.9)$$

The solution of the ordinary differential equation (9.3.8) with the initial value (9.3.9) is

$$\hat{U}(\xi,\eta,t) = \hat{U}_0(\xi,\eta)\exp\{-(d_1\xi^2 + 2d_2\xi\eta + d_3\eta^2) + i(d_4\xi + d_5\eta) - d_6\}, \quad (9.3.10)$$

where

$$\begin{aligned}
d_1 &= \frac{\sigma^2}{2}(T-t),\\
d_2 &= \frac{\sigma^2}{2}\frac{(T-t)^2}{2T},\\
d_3 &= \frac{\sigma^2}{2}\frac{(T-t)^3}{3T^3},\\
d_4 &= \left(r - q - \frac{\sigma^2}{2}\right)(T-t),\\
d_5 &= \left(r - q - \frac{\sigma^2}{2}\right)\frac{(T-t)^2}{2T},\\
d_6 &= r(T-t).
\end{aligned}$$

Performing the inverse Fourier transform to (9.3.10), we get

$$U(x,y,t) = \int_{-\infty}^{\infty}\int_{-\infty}^{\infty} U_0(\alpha,\beta)G(x-\alpha, y-\beta)d\alpha d\beta, \quad (9.3.11)$$

where

$$U_0(\alpha,\beta) = (e^{\alpha} - e^{\beta})^+, \quad (9.3.12)$$

$$G(x,y) = \frac{1}{(2\pi)^2}\int_{-\infty}^{\infty}\int_{-\infty}^{\infty} \exp\{-(d_1\xi^2 + 2d_2\xi\eta + d_3\eta^2) + i(d_4\xi + d_5\eta) - d_6\} \cdot e^{i(x\xi+y\eta)}d\xi d\eta. \quad (9.3.13)$$

To evaluate the integral (9.3.13), change the integration variables as follows

$$\xi = \frac{1}{\sqrt{2d_1}}(\hat{\xi} + \hat{\eta}),$$
$$\eta = \frac{1}{\sqrt{2d_3}}(\hat{\xi} - \hat{\eta}).$$

Since

$$\begin{aligned} & d_1\xi^2 + 2d_2\xi\eta + d_3\eta^2 \\ &= \frac{1}{2}\left[(\hat{\xi}+\hat{\eta})^2 + (\hat{\xi}-\hat{\eta})^2 + \frac{2d_2}{\sqrt{d_1 d_3}}(\hat{\xi}^2 - \hat{\eta}^2)\right] \\ &= \left(1 + \frac{d_2}{\sqrt{d_1 d_3}}\right)\hat{\xi}^2 + \left(1 - \frac{d_2}{\sqrt{d_1 d_3}}\right)\hat{\eta}^2, \end{aligned}$$

thus the integral (9.3.13) can be written as

$$\begin{aligned} G(x,y) &= \frac{1}{4\pi^2\sqrt{d_1 d_3}} e^{-d_6} \int_{-\infty}^{\infty} e^{-\left(1+\frac{d_2}{\sqrt{d_1 d_3}}\right)\hat{\xi}^2 + i\left(\frac{d_4+x}{\sqrt{2d_1}} + \frac{d_5+y}{\sqrt{2d_3}}\right)\hat{\xi}} d\hat{\xi} \\ &\quad \cdot \int_{-\infty}^{\infty} e^{-\left(1-\frac{d_2}{\sqrt{d_1 d_3}}\right)\hat{\eta}^2 + i\left(\frac{d_4+x}{\sqrt{2d_1}} - \frac{d_5+y}{\sqrt{2d_3}}\right)\hat{\eta}} d\hat{\eta} \\ &= \frac{e^{-d_6}}{4\pi^2\sqrt{d_1 d_3 - d_2^2}} \exp\left[-\frac{\left(\frac{d_4+x}{\sqrt{d_1}} + \frac{d_5+y}{\sqrt{d_3}}\right)^2}{8\left(1+\frac{d_2}{\sqrt{d_1 d_3}}\right)} - \frac{\left(\frac{d_4+x}{\sqrt{d_1}} - \frac{d_5+y}{\sqrt{d_3}}\right)^2}{8\left(1-\frac{d_2}{\sqrt{d_1 d_3}}\right)}\right]. \end{aligned}$$

Substituting it into (9.3.11), and back to the original variables (S, J, t) and the function $V(S, J, t)$ by the transformation (9.2.26),(9.2.28), we find

$$V(S,J,t) = S[e^{-r(T-t)}N(-g_2) - J^{\frac{t}{T}} S^{\frac{T-t}{T}} e^{g_0} N(-g_1)],$$

where

$$\begin{aligned} g_0 &= q(T-t) + (r - q + \tfrac{\sigma^2}{2})\frac{T^2-t^2}{2T} - \frac{\sigma^2}{6}\frac{T^3-t^3}{T^2} \\ g_1 &= \frac{\sqrt{3}}{\sigma(T^3-t^3)^{1/2}}[t\ln\tfrac{J}{S} - (r-q+\tfrac{\sigma^2}{2})(T^2-t^2) + \tfrac{\sigma^2}{6}\frac{T^3-t^3}{T}] \\ g_2 &= \frac{\sqrt{3}}{\sigma(T^3-t^3)^{1/2}}[t\ln\tfrac{J}{S} - (r-q+\tfrac{\sigma^2}{2})(T^2-t^2)]. \end{aligned}$$

9.4 Call-Put Parities for Asian Options

Based on the pricing models of Asian options, we can find the call-put parities for them.

(A) **Call-put parity for arithmetic average Asian option with fixed strike price**

Let $C(S, J, t)$ and $P(S, J, t)$ denote the price of an Asian call and put option, respectively. Define

$$W(S, J, t) = C(S, J, t) - P(S, J, t),$$

Then in $\{0 \le S < \infty,\ 0 \le J < \infty,\ 0 \le t \le T\}$, W satisfies

$$\begin{cases} \dfrac{\partial W}{\partial t} + \dfrac{S-J}{t}\dfrac{\partial W}{\partial J} + \dfrac{\sigma^2}{2}S^2\dfrac{\partial^2 W}{\partial S^2} + (r-q)S\dfrac{\partial W}{\partial S} - rW = 0, & (9.4.1) \\ W\,|_{t=T} = (J-K)^+ - (K-J)^+ = J - K. & (9.4.2) \end{cases}$$

Under the transformation (9.2.10), the function

$$\hat{W} = \frac{T}{S}W \tag{9.4.3}$$

satisfies the Cauchy problem in the domain $\{\xi \in \mathbf{R},\ 0 \le t \le T\}$:

$$\begin{cases} \dfrac{\partial \hat{W}}{\partial t} + \dfrac{\sigma^2}{2}\xi^2\dfrac{\partial^2 \hat{W}}{\partial \xi^2} - [(r-q)\xi + 1]\dfrac{\partial \hat{W}}{\partial \xi} - q\hat{W} = 0 & (9.4.4) \\ \hat{W}(\xi, T) = -\xi. \qquad (\xi \in \mathbf{R}) & (9.4.5) \end{cases}$$

Let

$$\hat{W}(\xi, t) = a(t)\xi + b(t). \tag{9.4.6}$$

Substituting it into (9.4.4), (9.4.5), and comparing the coefficients, we get:

$$\begin{cases} a'(t) - ra(t) = 0, \\ b'(t) - a(t) - qb(t) = 0, \\ a(T) = -1, \\ b(T) = 0. \end{cases}$$

The solutions are $(r \ne q)$

$$a(t) = -e^{-r(T-t)},$$
$$b(t) = \frac{-1}{r-q}[e^{-r(T-t)} - e^{-q(T-t)}].$$

Substituting them into (9.4.6), and by (9.2.10) and (9.4.3), we get ($r \neq q$):

$$C(S,J,t) - P(S,J,t) = \frac{S}{T}[a(t)\frac{TK - tJ}{S} + b(t)]$$
$$= [\frac{t}{T}J - \frac{S}{(r-q)T} - K]e^{-r(T-t)} - \frac{S}{(r-q)T}e^{-q(T-t)}. \quad (9.4.7)$$

(B) **Call-put parity for arithmetic average Asian option with floating strike price**

Define

$$W(S,J,t) = C(S,J,t) - P(S,J,t).$$

Then in $\{0 \leq S < \infty,\ 0 \leq J < \infty,\ 0 \leq t \leq T\}$, W satisfies (9.4.1) and the terminal condition

$$W\mid_{t=T} = (S-J)^+ - (J-S)^+ = S - J. \quad (9.4.8)$$

By the transformation (9.2.14), the function

$$\hat{W} = \frac{1}{S}W \quad (9.4.9)$$

satisfies the Cauchy problem in $\{0 \leq \xi < \infty,\ 0 \leq t \leq T\}$:

$$\begin{cases} \frac{\partial \hat{W}}{\partial t} + \frac{\sigma^2}{2}\xi^2\frac{\partial^2 \hat{W}}{\partial \xi^2} + [1 - (r-q)\xi]\frac{\partial \hat{W}}{\partial \xi} - q\hat{W} = 0, & (9.4.10) \\ \hat{W}\mid_{t=T} = 1 - \frac{\xi}{T}. & (9.4.11) \end{cases}$$

Let

$$\hat{W} = a(t)\xi + b(t), \quad (9.4.12)$$

Substituting into (9.4.10),(9.4.11), and comparing the coefficients, we get

$$\begin{cases} a'(t) - ra(t) = 0, \\ b'(t) + a(t) - qb(t) = 0, \\ a(T) = -\frac{1}{T}, \\ b(T) = 1. \end{cases}$$

Solve them to get ($r \neq q$)

$$a(t) = -\frac{1}{T}e^{-r(T-t)},$$
$$b(t) = \frac{1}{T(r-q)}e^{-r(T-t)} + \left[1 - \frac{1}{T(r-q)}\right]e^{-q(T-t)}.$$

Substituting them into (9.4.12), and by (9.2.14) and (9.4.9), we get ($r \neq q$):

$$C(S,J,t) - P(S,J,t) = S\left[a(t)\frac{tJ}{S} + b(t)\right]$$
$$= -\frac{t}{T}Je^{-r(T-t)} + \frac{S}{T(r-q)}e^{-r(T-t)} + \left[1 - \frac{1}{T(r-q)}\right]Se^{-q(T-t)}. \qquad (9.4.13)$$

(C) **Call-put parity for geometric average Asian option with fixed strike price**

Let

$$W(S,J,t) = C(S,J,t) - P(S,J,t).$$

Thus in $\{0 \leq S < \infty,\ 0 \leq J < \infty,\ 0 \leq t \leq T\}$, W satisfies the initial value problem:

$$\begin{cases} \dfrac{\partial W}{\partial t} + J\dfrac{\ln S - \ln J}{t}\dfrac{\partial W}{\partial J} + \dfrac{\sigma^2}{2}S^2\dfrac{\partial^2 W}{\partial S^2} + (r-q)S\dfrac{\partial W}{\partial S} - rW = 0, & (9.4.14) \\ W\mid_{t=T} = (J-K)^+ - (K-J)^+ = J - K. & (9.4.15) \end{cases}$$

By the transformation (9.2.18), in $\{\xi \in \mathbf{R},\ 0 \leq t \leq T\}$ W satisfies :

$$\begin{cases} \dfrac{\partial W}{\partial t} + \dfrac{\sigma^2}{2}\left(\dfrac{T-t}{T}\right)^2\dfrac{\partial^2 W}{\partial \xi^2} + \left(r - q - \dfrac{\sigma^2}{2}\right)\left(\dfrac{T-t}{T}\right)\dfrac{\partial W}{\partial \xi} - rW = 0, & (9.4.16) \\ W\mid_{t=T} = e^{\xi} - K. & (9.4.17) \end{cases}$$

Let

$$W = a(t)e^{\xi} + b(t). \qquad (9.4.18)$$

Substituting them into (9.4.16),(9.4.17), comparing the coefficients, we get

$$\begin{cases} a'(t) + \dfrac{\sigma^2}{2}\left(\dfrac{T-t}{T}\right)^2 a(t) + \left(r - q - \dfrac{\sigma^2}{2}\right)\left(\dfrac{T-t}{T}\right)a(t) - ra(t) = 0, \\ b'(t) - rb(t) = 0, \\ a(T) = 1, \\ b(T) = -K. \end{cases}$$

Solve them to get:

$$a(t) = e^{(T-t)\left[\frac{\sigma^2}{6}\left(\frac{T-t}{T}\right)^2 + \frac{r-q-\frac{\sigma^2}{2}}{2}\frac{T-t}{T} - r\right]},$$
$$b(t) = -Ke^{-r(T-t)}.$$

Substituting into (9.4.18), and by (9.2.18), we get

$$\begin{aligned} C(S,J,t) - P(S,J,t) &= a(t) J^{\frac{t}{T}} S^{\frac{T-t}{T}} + b(t) \\ &= \left\{ e^{(T-t)\left[\frac{\sigma^2}{6}\left(\frac{T-t}{T}\right)^2 + \frac{r-q-\frac{\sigma^2}{2}}{2}\frac{T-t}{T}\right]} J^{\frac{t}{T}} S^{\frac{T-t}{T}} - K \right\} e^{-r(T-t)}. \end{aligned} \tag{9.4.19}$$

(D) **Call-put parity for geometric average Asian option with floating strike price**

Let

$$W(S,J,t) = C(S,J,t) - P(S,J,t),$$

Thus in $\{0 \le S < \infty,\ 0 \le J < \infty,\ 0 \le t \le T\}$, W satisfies

$$\begin{cases} \dfrac{\partial W}{\partial t} + J\dfrac{\ln S - \ln J}{t}\dfrac{\partial W}{\partial J} + \dfrac{\sigma^2}{2}S^2\dfrac{\partial^2 W}{\partial S^2} + (r-q)S\dfrac{\partial W}{\partial S} - rW = 0, & (9.4.20) \\ W\,|_{t=T} = (S-J)^+ - (J-S)^+ = S - J. & (9.4.21) \end{cases}$$

Under the transformation (9.2.26)—(9.2.28), the function W satisfies the Cauchy problem in the domain $\{(x,y) \in \mathbf{R}^2,\ 0 \le t \le T\}$:

$$\begin{aligned} &\frac{\partial W}{\partial t} + \frac{\sigma^2}{2}\left(\frac{T-t}{T}\right)^2 \frac{\partial^2 W}{\partial y^2} + \sigma^2\left(\frac{T-t}{T}\right)\frac{\partial^2 W}{\partial x \partial y} \\ &\quad + \frac{\sigma^2}{2}\frac{\partial^2 W}{\partial x^2} + \left(r - q - \frac{\sigma^2}{2}\right)\left[\frac{T-t}{T}\frac{\partial W}{\partial y} + \frac{\partial W}{\partial x}\right] - rW = 0, \end{aligned} \tag{9.4.22}$$

and by (9.2.9),

$$W|_{t=T} = e^x - e^y. \tag{9.4.23}$$

Let

$$W(x,y) = a(t)e^x - b(t)e^y. \tag{9.4.24}$$

Substituting it into (9.4.22),(9.4.23), by comparing the coefficients we get

$$\begin{cases} a'(t) - qa(t) = 0, \\ b'(t) + \dfrac{\sigma^2}{2}\left(\dfrac{T-t}{T}\right)^2 b(t) + \left(r - q - \dfrac{\sigma^2}{2}\right)\left(\dfrac{T-t}{T}\right) b(t) - rb(t) = 0, \\ a(T) = 1, \\ b(T) = 1. \end{cases}$$

Solve them to get

$$a(t) = e^{-q(T-t)},$$

$$b(t) = e^{\frac{\sigma^2(T-t)^3}{6T^2} + \frac{(r-q-\frac{\sigma^2}{2})(T-t)^2}{2T} - r(T-t)}.$$

Substituting it into (9.4.24), and by (9.2.26),(9.2.27), we get

$$C(S,J,t) - P(S,J,t) = Se^{-q(T-t)} - J^{\frac{t}{T}} S^{\frac{T-t}{T}} e^{\frac{\sigma^2(T-t)^3}{6T^2} + \frac{(r-q-\frac{\sigma^2}{2})(T-t)^2}{2T} - r(T-t)}.$$

9.5 Lookback Option

A lookback option allows its holder to "look back" at the underlying asset price history on the expiration day, then choose the lowest(highest) price as the strike price to buy(sell) the underlying asset. Thus its payoff on the expiration date $(t = T)$ is

$$\text{payoff} = S_T - \min_{0 \le t \le T} S_t \text{ (call option)} \tag{9.5.1}$$

$$= \max_{0 \le t \le T} S_t - S_T \text{ (put option)} \tag{9.5.2}$$

Therefore lookback options are called "buy at the low, sell at the high" options, or standard lookback options. According to our classification of the path-dependent options, they should be called "lookback call(put) option with floating strike price". Options of this type are expensive because of high payoffs. However, the lookback call option is worthless if the asset price hits the minimum at expiration. In this case, the option holder has paid a dear premium for nothing.

Example Consider a 6-month stock call option. Suppose $S_0 = K = \$145, r = 6\%, q = 3\%, \sigma = 29.5\%$, the premiums calculated by the Black-Scholes theory are:

	premium
European vanilla option	\$12.87
lookback option	\$23.12

In this example, the premium of the lookback option is nearly twice that of its vanilla counterpart!

The payoff of lookback options, which is a typical type of the strongly path-dependent options, depends strongly on the underlying asset's price history in the option's lifetime. The path dependency variable J is

$$J_t = \min_{0 \le \tau \le t} S_\tau \text{ or } J_t = \max_{0 \le \tau \le t} S_\tau. \tag{9.5.3}$$

It follows from the definition of the path variable that, for the lookback call option, there is

$$S_t \geq J_t = \min_{0 \leq \tau \leq t} S_\tau, \tag{9.5.4}$$

whereas for the lookback put options, there is

$$S_t \leq J_t = \max_{0 \leq \tau \leq t} S_\tau. \tag{9.5.5}$$

Pricing model(take the put option as example)
Let V denote the price of a lookback put option,

$$V = V(S, J, t),$$

where J is defined in (9.5.3).

To apply the Δ-hedging technique, construct a portfolio Π:

$$\Pi = V - \Delta S,$$

Choose Δ, such that Π is risk-free in $(t, t + dt)$, i.e.:

$$d\Pi = r\Pi dt. \tag{9.5.6}$$

By the Itô formula:

$$\begin{aligned} d\Pi &= dV - \Delta dS - qS\Delta dt \\ &= \left(\frac{\partial V}{\partial t} + \frac{1}{2}\sigma^2 S^2 \frac{\partial^2 V}{\partial S^2} - qS\Delta\right) dt + \frac{\partial V}{\partial J} dJ \\ &\quad + \left(\frac{\partial V}{\partial S} - \Delta\right) dS. \end{aligned} \tag{9.5.7}$$

As the path dependency variable J_t defined in (9.5.3) is not differentiable with respect to t, in order to find dJ_t, we need to approximate J_t by $J_n(t)$ as follows:

$$J_n(t) = \left[\frac{1}{t}\int_0^t (S_\tau)^n d\tau\right]^{\frac{1}{n}}.$$

Obviously $J_n(t)$ is differentiable with respect to t,

$$nJ_n^{n-1}(t)\frac{dJ_n}{dt} = \frac{S_t^n - J_n^n(t)}{t}. \tag{9.5.8}$$

Moreover, as $n \to \infty$, since S_t is a continuous function of t, thus there is

$$\lim_{n\to\infty} J_n(t) = \max_{0 \leq \tau \leq t} S_\tau = J_t. \tag{9.5.9}$$

Using $J_n(t)$ in place of the path variable J_t, assuming $S \leq J_n$, thus by (9.5.8), the equation (9.5.7) can be written as

$$d\Pi = \left(\frac{\partial V}{\partial t} + \frac{1}{2}\sigma^2 S^2 \frac{\partial^2 V}{\partial S^2} + \frac{\partial V}{\partial J_n}\frac{dJ_n}{dt} - qS\Delta\right) dt + \left(\frac{\partial V}{\partial S} - \Delta\right) dS. \tag{9.5.10}$$

Choose

$$\Delta = \frac{\partial V}{\partial S},$$

Then by (9.5.10),(9.5.6), we get

$$\frac{\partial V}{\partial t} + \frac{\left(\frac{S}{J_n}\right)^{n-1} S - J_n}{nt}\frac{\partial V}{\partial J_n} + \frac{1}{2}\sigma^2 S^2 \frac{\partial^2 V}{\partial S^2} + (r-q)S\frac{\partial V}{\partial S} - rV = 0.$$

$$(S \leq J_n) \tag{9.5.11}$$

For a given (J, t), let $n \to \infty$, then by (9.5.9), the coefficient of $\frac{\partial V}{\partial J_n}$ in equation (9.5.11) approaches 0. Thus we have

$$\frac{\partial V}{\partial t} + \frac{1}{2}\sigma^2 S^2 \frac{\partial^2 V}{\partial S^2} + (r-q)S\frac{\partial V}{\partial S} - rV = 0. \tag{9.5.12}$$

$$(0 \leq S \leq J < \infty,\ 0 \leq t \leq T)$$

By (9.5.1), we get

$$V(S, J, T) = J - S, \tag{9.5.13}$$

Since $\{S = J,\ 0 \leq J < \infty, 0 \leq t \leq T\}$ is the boundary of the domain, we need a boundary condition:

$$\frac{\partial V}{\partial J}\mid_{S=J}= 0. \tag{9.5.14}$$

Its financial meaning is clear: the option price is not sensitive to the level of the maximum of the asset price.

Therefore the price model for the lookback put option is the terminal-boundary problem (9.5.12)—(9.5.14) in the domain $\{0 \leq S \leq J < \infty,\ \ 0 \leq t \leq T\}$. Notice that the path variable J does not show up in (9.5.12). But J appears in the boundary condition (9.5.14) and the terminal condition (9.5.13).

Similarly we can formulate the price model for the lookback call options, which is the following problem in the domain $\{0 \leq J \leq S < \infty,\ 0 \leq t \leq T\}$

$$\begin{cases} \frac{\partial V}{\partial t} + \frac{\sigma^2}{2} S^2 \frac{\partial^2 V}{\partial S^2} + (r-q)S\frac{\partial V}{\partial S} - rV = 0, & (9.5.15) \\ V(S, J, T) = S - J, \qquad (0 \leq J \leq S < \infty), & (9.5.16) \\ \frac{\partial V}{\partial J}\mid_{S=J}= 0. \qquad (0 < J < \infty) & (9.5.17) \end{cases}$$

For the European lookback options, the pricing problem can be reduced to a 1-D problem, and has a closed-form solution.

To be specific, let us consider the lookback put options.

Let

$$x = \ln \frac{J}{S}, \qquad V = Su(x,t). \tag{9.5.18}$$

By straightforward calculation, we get

$$\frac{\partial V}{\partial S} = u + S\frac{\partial u}{\partial x}\left(-\frac{1}{S}\right),$$
$$\frac{\partial^2 V}{\partial S^2} = \frac{1}{S}\left[-\frac{\partial u}{\partial x} + \frac{\partial^2 u}{\partial x^2}\right],$$

Substituting them into (9.5.12), we get

$$\begin{cases} \dfrac{\partial u}{\partial t} + \dfrac{\sigma^2}{2}\dfrac{\partial^2 u}{\partial x^2} + \left(q - r - \dfrac{\sigma^2}{2}\right)\dfrac{\partial u}{\partial x} - qu = 0, & (9.5.19) \\ \qquad (0 < x < \infty,\ 0 \le t \le T) & \\ u\,|_{t=T} = e^x - 1, \qquad (0 \le x < \infty) & (9.5.20) \\ \dfrac{\partial u}{\partial x}\,|_{x=0} = 0. \qquad (0 \le t \le T) & (9.5.21) \end{cases}$$

Let

$$u = e^{\alpha x + \beta(T-t)} W, \tag{9.5.22}$$

where

$$\alpha = \frac{1}{2} + \frac{r-q}{\sigma^2},$$
$$\beta = -q - \frac{1}{8\sigma^2}[\sigma^2 - 2(q-r)]^2.$$

we get

$$\begin{cases} \dfrac{\partial W}{\partial t} + \dfrac{\sigma^2}{2}\dfrac{\partial^2 W}{\partial x^2} = 0, & (x \in \mathbf{R}^+,\ 0 \le t \le T) \\ W\,|_{t=T} = (e^x - 1)e^{-\alpha x}, & (x \in \mathbf{R}^+) \\ \left[\dfrac{\partial W}{\partial x} + \alpha W\right]\Big|_{x=0} = 0. & (0 \le t \le T) \end{cases}$$

We will solve it using the image method. However, straightforward continuation by symmetry (odd or even) does not work with the boundary condition (9.5.25). Therefore we define

$$\Phi(x) = \begin{cases} e^{-\alpha x}(e^x - 1), & x > 0, \\ \varphi(x), & x < 0. \end{cases} \tag{9.5.26}$$

and consider the Cauchy problem:

$$\begin{cases} \dfrac{\partial \hat{W}}{\partial t} + \dfrac{\sigma^2}{2}\dfrac{\partial^2 \hat{W}}{\partial x^2} = 0, & (x \in \mathbf{R}, \quad 0 \le t \le T) \quad (9.5.27) \\ \hat{W}\Big|_{t=T} = \Phi(x). & (x \in \mathbf{R}) \quad (9.5.28) \end{cases}$$

We need to choose $\varphi(x)$, such that the solution $\hat{W}(x,t)$ to the Cauchy problem (9.5.27),(9.5.28) satisfies the boundary condition (9.5.25) at $x = 0$

$$\left[\frac{\partial \hat{W}}{\partial x} + \alpha \hat{W}\right]\Bigg|_{x=0} = 0. \tag{9.5.29}$$

If this can be accomplished, then by the uniqueness of the solution of the problem (9.5.23)—(9.5.25), we can assert

$$W(x,t) \equiv \hat{W}(x,t). \qquad (x \ge 0,\ 0 \le t \le T) \tag{9.5.30}$$

By the Poisson formula, the solution to (9.2.27),(9.2.28) can be written as

$$\hat{W}(x,t) = \int_{-\infty}^{+\infty} \Gamma(x-\xi,t)\Phi(\xi)d\xi, \tag{9.5.31}$$

where $\Gamma(x-\xi,t)$ is the fundamental solution of the equation (9.5.27):

$$\Gamma(x-\xi,t) = \frac{1}{\sigma\sqrt{2\pi(T-t)}} e^{-\frac{(x-\xi)^2}{2\sigma^2(T-t)}}. \qquad (0 \le t < T)$$

Thus we have

$$\begin{aligned} \frac{\partial \hat{W}}{\partial x} &= \int_{-\infty}^{\infty} \Gamma_x(x-\xi,t)\Phi(\xi)d\xi \\ &= -\int_{-\infty}^{\infty} \Gamma_\xi(x-\xi,t)\Phi(\xi)d\xi \\ &= -\Gamma(x,t)\varphi(0) + \int_{-\infty}^{\infty} \Gamma(x-\xi,t)\Phi'(\xi)d\xi. \end{aligned}$$

Then (9.5.29) can be expressed as follows:

$$\begin{aligned}
0 &= \left[\frac{\partial \hat{W}}{\partial x} + \alpha \hat{W}\right]\Bigg|_{x=0} \\
&= -\Gamma(0,t)\varphi(0) + \int_{-\infty}^{\infty} \Gamma(\xi,t)[\Phi'(\xi) + \alpha\Phi(\xi)]d\xi \\
&= -\Gamma(0,t)\varphi(0) + \int_{-\infty}^{0} \Gamma(\xi,t)[\varphi'(\xi) + \alpha\varphi(\xi)]d\xi \\
&\quad + \int_{0}^{\infty} \Gamma(\xi,t)[(1-\alpha)e^{(1-\alpha)\xi} + \alpha e^{-\alpha\xi} + \alpha e^{(1-\alpha\xi)} - \alpha e^{-\alpha\xi}]d\xi \\
&= -\Gamma(0,t)\varphi(0) + \int_{-\infty}^{0} \Gamma(\xi,t)[\varphi'(\xi) + \alpha\varphi(\xi) + e^{(\alpha-1)\xi}]d\xi.
\end{aligned}$$

Choose $\varphi(x)$ that satisfies the following equation and boundary condition:

$$\begin{cases} \varphi'(\xi) + \alpha\varphi(\xi) = -e^{(\alpha-1)\xi}, \\ \varphi(0) = 0. \end{cases}$$

If $2\alpha - 1 \neq 0$, i.e. $r \neq q$, then the solution is

$$\varphi(x) = \frac{-1}{2\alpha - 1}[e^{(\alpha-1)x} - e^{-\alpha x}].$$

Substituting it into (9.5.31),(9.5.30), we get

$$\begin{aligned}
W(x,t) = &\int_{-\infty}^{0} \Gamma(x-\xi,t)\left[\frac{1}{2\alpha-1}(e^{-\alpha\xi} - e^{(\alpha-1)\xi})\right]d\xi \\
&+ \int_{0}^{\infty} \Gamma(x-\xi,t)[e^{(1-\alpha)\xi} - e^{-\alpha\xi}]d\xi.
\end{aligned}$$

In the case $r = q$,

$$\varphi(x) = -xe^{\alpha x},$$

$$\begin{aligned}
W(x,t) = &-\int_{-\infty}^{0} \Gamma(x-\xi,t)\xi e^{\alpha\xi}d\xi \\
&+ \int_{0}^{\infty} \Gamma(x-\xi,t)[e^{(1-\alpha)\xi} - e^{-\alpha\xi}]d\xi.
\end{aligned}$$

Back to the original variables (S, J, t) and function V by (9.5.22),(9.5.18), we get the valuation formula for the lookback put options:

In the case $r \neq q$,

$$V(S,J,t) = Je^{-r(T-t)}\left[N(b_1) - \frac{1}{\theta}\left(\frac{J}{S}\right)^{\theta-1} N(-b_3)\right]$$
$$-Se^{-q(T-t)}\left[N(b_2) - \frac{1}{\theta}N(-b_2)\right];$$

In the case $r = q$,

$$V(S,J,t) = -Se^{-r(T-t)}\left[N(b_2) + \ln\left(\frac{J}{S}\right)N(-b_3) - \frac{\sigma^2}{2}(T-t)N(-b_2)\right.$$
$$\left.-\frac{\sigma\sqrt{T-t}}{\sqrt{2\pi}}e^{-\frac{b_3^2}{2}}\right] + Je^{-r(T-t)}N(b_1),$$

where

$$b_1 = \frac{\ln\frac{J}{S} + \left(-r+q+\frac{\sigma^2}{2}\right)(T-t)}{\sigma\sqrt{T-t}},$$

$$b_2 = b_1 - \sigma\sqrt{T-t},$$

$$b_3 = b_2 + \frac{2(r-q)(T-t)}{\sigma\sqrt{T-t}},$$

$$\theta = \frac{2(r-q)}{\sigma^2}.$$

Similarly, we can get the pricing formula for the lookback call options:
In the case $r \neq q$,

$$V(S,J,t) = -Je^{-r(T-t)}\left[N(a_2) - \frac{1}{\theta}\left(\frac{S}{J})^{1-\theta}N(-a_3)\right)\right]$$
$$+Se^{-q(T-t)}\left[N(a_1) - \frac{1}{\theta}N(-a_1)\right];$$

In the case $r = q$,

$$V(S,J,t) = Se^{-r(T-t)}\left[N(a_1) + \ln\left(\frac{S}{J}\right)N(-a_3) + \frac{\sigma^2}{2}(T-t)N(-a_1)\right.$$
$$\left.-\frac{\sigma\sqrt{T-t}}{\sqrt{2\pi}}e^{-\frac{a_3^2}{2}}\right] - Je^{-r(T-t)}N(a_2),$$

where

$$a_1 = \frac{\ln \frac{S}{J} + \left(r - q + \frac{\sigma^2}{2}\right)(T-t)}{\sigma\sqrt{T-t}},$$

$$a_2 = a_1 - \sigma\sqrt{T-t},$$

$$a_3 = -a_1 + \frac{2(r-q)\sqrt{T-t}}{\sigma},$$

$$\theta = \frac{2(r-q)}{\sigma^2}.$$

Remark Having studied the lookback options which belong to the path-dependent option with floating strike price, it is natural to ask a question, how to price lookback options with fixed strike price, whose payoff function at maturity is given by

$$\text{payoff} = (\max_{0 \le t \le T} S_t - K)^+ \quad \text{(call option)}$$

or

$$\text{payoff} = (K - \min_{0 \le t \le T} S_t)^+. \quad \text{(put option)}$$

Its pricing formula can be obtained by using PDE approach. However, since its derivation is rather complicated and this type of options is not popular in the financial market, we will not discuss it here.

Remark The lookback options are closely related to the reset options which we discussed in the previous chapter. In fact, it is obvious that if $0 = t_0 < t_1 < \cdots < t_N = T$ are the reset times, and $\Delta t = \max_{0 \le i \le N-1} |t_{i+1} - t_i|$, then as $\Delta t \to 0$, the reset option will become the lookback option. Therefore, the reset option pricing can be approximated by a lookback option pricing, as the valuation formula of lookback options is much simpler than that of reset options.

American lookback options

According to the arbitrage-free principle, the model for American lookback options is (take the put option as example) in the domain $\{0 \le S < \infty,\ S \le J,\ 0 \le t \le T\}$, $V = V(S, J, t)$ that satisfies

$$\begin{cases} \min\{-\mathcal{L}V, V - (J - S)\} = 0, & (0 \le S \le J < \infty, 0 \le t \le T) \\ \left.\frac{\partial V}{\partial J}\right|_{S=J} = 0, & (0 \le J < \infty, 0 \le t \le T) \\ V|_{t=T} = J - S, & (0 \le S \le J < \infty) \end{cases}$$

Here

$$\mathcal{L}V = \frac{\partial V}{\partial t} + \frac{1}{2}\sigma^2 S^2 \frac{\partial^2 V}{\partial S^2} + (r - q)S\frac{\partial V}{\partial S} - rV.$$

This is a 2-D problem. By the transformation (9.5.18), it can be reduced to a 1-D problem. That is, in the domain $\{0 \le x < \infty,\ 0 \le t \le T\}$, $u = u(x,t)$ satisfies:

$$\begin{cases} \min\{-\mathcal{L}_0 u, u - (e^x - 1)\} = 0, & (x \in \mathbf{R}^+, 0 \le t \le T) \\ \left.\dfrac{\partial u}{\partial x}\right|_{x=0} = 0, & (0 \le t \le T) \\ u(x,T) = e^x - 1, & (x \in \mathbf{R}^+) \end{cases}$$

where

$$\mathcal{L}_0 u = \frac{\partial u}{\partial t} + \frac{1}{2}\sigma^2 \frac{\partial^2 u}{\partial x^2} + \left(q - r - \frac{\sigma^2}{2}\right)\frac{\partial u}{\partial x} - qu.$$

Its equivalent free boundary problem is: find $\{u(x,t), X(t)\}$, such that in the domain $\{0 \le x \le X(t),\ 0 \le t \le T\}$, it satisfies:

$$\begin{cases} \mathcal{L}_0 u = 0, & (0 \le x \le X(t), 0 \le t \le T) \\ u(X(t),t) = e^{X(t)} - 1, & (0 \le t \le T) \\ \dfrac{\partial u}{\partial x}(X(t),t) = e^{X(t)}, & (0 \le t \le T) \\ \dfrac{\partial u}{\partial x}(0,t) = 0, & (0 \le t \le T) \\ u(x,T) = e^x - 1. & (0 \le x \le X(T)) \end{cases}$$

Since

$$\left.\left[\frac{1}{2}\sigma^2 \frac{\partial^2 u}{\partial x^2} + \left(q - r - \frac{\sigma^2}{2}\right)\frac{\partial u}{\partial x} - qu\right]\right|_{t=T} = q - re^x,$$

thus from the discussion of the properties of the free boundary in §6.5, we know that

$$X(T) = \max\left(\ln\frac{q}{r}, 0\right)$$

and

$$X(t) \text{monotone decreasing.}$$

Substituting it into the original variables (S, J, t), thus for the American look-back put options, the optimal exercise boundary Γ has the following properties:

(1) For any given t, Γ_t is a line: $J = Se^{X(t)}$;
(2) In the case $t = T$,
  if $r \ge q$, $\Gamma_T:\quad J = S$,
  if $r < q$, $\Gamma_T:\quad J = \frac{q}{r}S$;

(3) As $T - t$ increases, the continuation region $\{0 \le \frac{J}{S} \le e^{X(t)}\}$ expands (see the figure)

(4) As $T-t$ increases indefinitely, $e^{X(t)}$ has an upper limit, which is the optimal exercise boundary of the perpetual American lookback put option. The proof is analogous to what we did in §6.5.

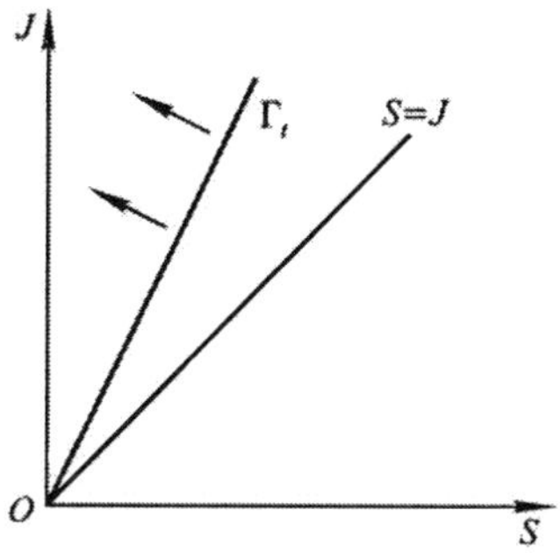

9.6 Numerical Methods

Although some types of the path-dependent option pricing problems (such as geometric average Asian options, lookback options) have closed form valuation formula, numerical methods are often prefered.

The most important and widely used numerical method is the binomial tree method (BTM).

In this section, we will first introduce the BTM, then the finite difference schemes with characteristic line, and finally establish the equivalence of the two methods.

A. **Binomial tree methods for the path-dependent options**

Partition the option lifetime $[0,T]$ into N equally spaced nodes a distance Δt apart:

$$0 = t_0 < t_1 < \cdots < t_N = T,$$

where $t_n = n\Delta t,\ (0 \le n \le N),\ \Delta t = \frac{T}{N}$.

Construct the BTM process for the random variables S (the underlying asset price) and J (the path variable) as follows:

Let $S_i^n = S_0 u^i d^{n-i}$ $(0 \le i \le n)$ denote the possible prices of the underlying asset at t_n, $J_{i,k}^n$, $(k \in I_i^n)$ denotes the possible values of the path variable at t_n when the underlying asset price is S_i^n, where I_i^n is the set of indices of the path variable corresponding to S_i^n.

Suppose at $t = t_n$,S_i^n, $J_{i,k}^n$ are known, what will be their possible values at $t = t_{n+1}$?

By the BTM process$(d < 1 < u)$:

$$S_i^n \begin{cases} \nearrow \; S_{i+1}^{n+1} = S_i^n u \\ \searrow \; S_i^{n+1} = S_i^n d. \end{cases}$$

To find out the corresponding changes in $J_{i,k}^n$, we consider the following three cases:

Suppose the path of the underlying asset price from S_0 at $t = 0$ to S_i^n at $t = t_n$ is $\{S_0, S_{i_1}^1, \ldots, S_{i_{n-1}}^{n-1}, S_i^n\}$.

In $[t_n, t_{n+1}]$, the asset price can change from S_i^n to either S_{i+1}^{n+1} or S_i^{n+1}, thus

(1) **corresponding arithmetic average**

$$J_{i,k}^n = \frac{1}{n}\sum_{\ell=1}^{n} S_{i_\ell}^\ell \qquad (S_{i_n}^n = S_i^n)$$

changes to

$$J_{i+1,k_u}^{n+1} = \frac{1}{n+1}\left\{\sum_{\ell=1}^{n} S_{i_\ell}^\ell + S_{i+1}^{n+1}\right\},$$

$$J_{i,k_d}^{n+1} = \frac{1}{n+1}\left\{\sum_{\ell=1}^{n} S_{i_\ell}^\ell + S_i^{n+1}\right\};$$

i.e.

$$J_{i,k}^n \begin{cases} J_{i+1,k_u}^{n+1} = \frac{n}{n+1} J_{i,k}^n + \frac{1}{n+1} S_{i+1}^{n+1} \\ J_{i,k_d}^{n+1} = \frac{n}{n+1} J_{i,k}^n + \frac{1}{n+1} S_i^{n+1}; \end{cases} \tag{9.6.1}$$

(2) **corresponding geometric average**

$$J_{i,k}^n = (\prod_{\ell=1}^{n} S_{i_\ell}^\ell)^{1/n}$$

changes to

$$J^n_{i,k} \begin{cases} J^{n+1}_{i+1,k_u} = (J^n_{i,k})^{\frac{n}{n+1}}(S^{n+1}_{i+1})^{\frac{1}{n+1}} \\ \\ J^{n+1}_{i,k_d} = (J^n_{i,k})^{\frac{n}{n+1}}(S^{n+1}_{i})^{\frac{1}{n+1}}; \end{cases} \tag{9.6.2}$$

(3) **corresponding maximum(minimum)**(to be specific, take the maximum as example)

$$J^n_{i,k} = \max_{1\le \ell \le n} S^{\ell}_{i_\ell}$$

changes to

$$J^n_{i,k} \begin{cases} J^{n+1}_{i+1,k_u} = \max\{J^n_{i,k}, S^{n+1}_{i+1}\} \\ \\ J^{n+1}_{i,k_d} = J^n_{i,k}. \end{cases} \tag{9.6.3}$$

Remark Notice that the BTM process of the variable $J^n_{i,k}$ is path-dependent. For each S^n_i, the corresponding path variable $\vec{J}^n_i = \{J^n_{i,\ell}\}_{\ell \in I^n_i}$ is a 2^{n-1} dimensional vector in general (there may be overlaps among its components).

Once the BTM process of the asset price and the path variable is established, we can derive the BTM algorithm for the path-dependent option pricing using the Δ-hedging technique, which is based on the arbitrage-free principle.

For each one-period and two-state process

$$S^n_i \begin{cases} \nearrow S^{n+1}_{i+1} \\ \searrow S^{n+1}_{i}, \end{cases} \qquad J^n_{i,k} \begin{cases} \nearrow J^{n+1}_{i+1,k_u} \\ \searrow J^{n+1}_{i,k_d}, \end{cases}$$

the corresponding process of the option price is

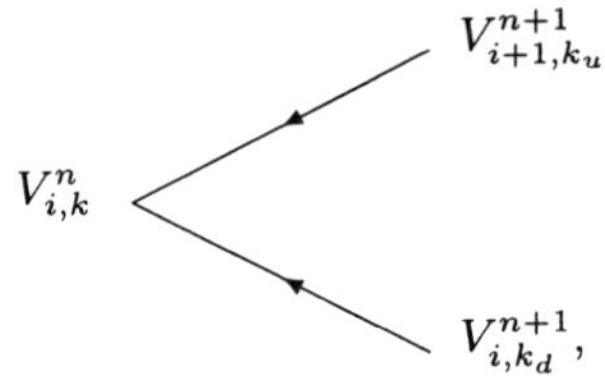

where

$$\begin{cases} V^{n+1}_{i+1,k_u} = V(S^{n+1}_{i+1}, J^{n+1}_{i+1,k_u}, t_{n+1}), \\ V^{n+1}_{i,k_d} = V(S^{n+1}_{i}, J^{n+1}_{i,k_d}, t_{n+1}), \\ V^{n}_{i,k} = V(S^{n}_{i}, J^{n}_{i,k}, t_{n}). \end{cases} \tag{9.6.4}$$

Construct a portfolio

$$\Pi = V - \Delta S,$$

and choose Δ, such that in $[t_i, t_{i+1}]$, Π is risk-free. Then we get

$$V^{n+1}_{i+1,k_u} - \Delta S^{n+1}_{i+1} = V^{n+1}_{i,k_d} - \Delta S^{n+1}_{i} = \rho(V^n_{i,k} - \Delta S^n_i).$$

The solution is

$$V^n_{i,k} = \frac{1}{\rho}[qV^{n+1}_{i+1,k_u} + (1-q)V^{n+1}_{i,k_d}], \tag{9.6.5}$$

where

$$q = \frac{\rho - d}{u - d}, \qquad 1 - q = \frac{u - \rho}{u - d}. \tag{9.6.6}$$

Algorithm Before we calculate the path-dependent option price, we first need to form the binomial tree of the asset price and the path variable. In particular, we need to input all of the information about each asset's price S^n_i and corresponding path vector $\vec{J}^n_i$, its components $J^n_{i,k}$ and their corresponding J^{n+1}_{i+1,k_u} and J^{n+1}_{i,k_d}.

At $t = t_N = T$, according to the given payoff function, $\{V^N_{i,k}\}_{k \in I^N_i}$, $(0 \leq i \leq N)$ is given. In order to obtain $\{V^{N-1}_{i,k}\}_{k \in I^{N-1}_i}$, $(0 \leq i \leq N-1)$:

Step 1 For each path dependent index $k \in I^{N-1}_i$ at $t = t_{N-1}, S = S^{N-1}_i$, find the indices $k_u \in I^N_{i+1}$ and $k_d \in I^N_i$ among the path vectors $\vec{J}^N_{i+1}$ and $\vec{J}^N_i$ corresponding to $S = S^N_i$ and $S = S^N_{i+1}$ at $t = t_N$.

Step 2 Among $\{V^N_{i+1,k}\}_{k \in I^N_{i+1}}$ and $\{V^N_{i,k}\}_{k \in I^N_i}$, find the components J^N_{i+1,k_u} and J^N_{i,k_d} corresponding to indices k_u, k_d, and calculate the corresponding prices V^N_{i+1,k_u} and V^N_{i,k_d}.

Step 3 Calculate $V^{N-1}_{i,k}$ by the formula (9.6.5)

Then by the backward induction, we get all prices of the path-dependent option, especially the premium on the initial date.

Remark Although the above algorithm is not very complex, it may require large amount of processor time and memory space. Note that there is a 2^{n-1} dimensional vector $\vec{J}_i^n$ at each node S_i^n, and for each vector $\vec{J}_i^n$ we must store its components and correspondence information between $\vec{J}_{i+1}^{n+1}$ and $\vec{J}_i^n$. When n is large, computation can be very costly. Therefore more efficient modified algorithms are needed, especially for arithmetic average Asian options. We will not discuss it here. Readers can refer to [22][23].

B. **Finite difference scheme with methods of characteristic line**

To be specific, we only consider the arithmetic average Asian options, i.e. the problem

$$\begin{cases} \dfrac{\partial V}{\partial t} + \dfrac{S-J}{t}\dfrac{\partial V}{\partial J} + \frac{1}{2}\sigma^2 S^2 \dfrac{\partial^2}{\partial S^2} + rS\dfrac{\partial V}{\partial S} - rV = 0, & (9.6.7) \\ \qquad (0 \le S < \infty,\ 0 \le J < \infty,\ 0 \le t \le T) & \\ V(S,J,T) = f(S,J). \qquad (0 \le S < \infty, 0 \le J < \infty) & (9.6.8) \end{cases}$$

Partition $[0,T]$ into N equally spaced nodes a distance Δt apart:

$$0 = t_0 < t_1 < \cdots < t_N = T,$$

where $t_n = n\Delta t, \quad \Delta t = \dfrac{T}{N}$.

In each interval $[t_n, t_{n+1}]$, consider the following first-order partial differential operator

$$\frac{\partial V}{\partial t} + \frac{S-J}{t}\frac{\partial V}{\partial J}.$$

We look for a characteristic line starting from (J_0, t_n), that satisfies the initial value problem:

$$\begin{cases} \dfrac{dt}{t} = \dfrac{dJ}{S-J}, \\ J(t_n) = J_0. \end{cases}$$

Its solution is

$$J = S - \frac{t_n}{t}(S - J_0). \tag{9.6.9}$$

As well-known, along this characteristic line, there is

$$\frac{\partial V}{\partial t} + \frac{S-J}{t}\frac{\partial V}{\partial J} = \frac{d}{dt}V(S, S - \frac{t_n}{t}(S-J_0), t),$$

(because $J_0 = S + \frac{t}{t_n}(J - S)$.) Thus the equation (9.6.7) can be rewritten as

$$\frac{d}{dt}V(S, S - \frac{t_n}{t}(S - J_0), t) + \left[\frac{1}{2}\sigma^2 S^2 \frac{\partial^2 V}{\partial S^2} + rS\frac{\partial V}{\partial S} - rV\right]_{J=S-\frac{t_n}{t}(S-J_0)} = 0. \tag{9.6.10}$$

We want to write the terms inside the above brackets in terms of derivatives along the characteristic line. Let $\frac{d}{dS}$ denote the derivative with respect to S along the characteristic line, then

$$\frac{d}{dS} = \frac{\partial}{\partial S} + \frac{t - t_n}{t}\frac{\partial}{\partial J}, \qquad \frac{d^2}{dS^2} = \left(\frac{\partial}{\partial S} + \frac{t - t_n}{t}\frac{\partial}{\partial J}\right)^2.$$

Thus the equation (9.6.10) can be written as

$$\begin{aligned}&\tfrac{d}{dt}V(S, S - \tfrac{t_n}{t}(S - J_0), t) + \tfrac{1}{2}\sigma^2 S^2 \frac{d^2V}{dS^2} + rS\frac{dV}{dS} - rV\\ &-\left[\frac{\sigma^2}{2}S^2\left(2\frac{t-t_n}{t}\frac{\partial^2 V}{\partial S \partial J} + \left(\frac{t-t_n}{t}\right)^2\frac{\partial^2 V}{\partial J^2}\right)\right.\\ &\left.-rS\frac{t-t_n}{t}\frac{\partial V}{\partial J}\right]_{J=S-\frac{t_n}{t}(S-J_0)} = 0.\end{aligned} \tag{9.6.11}$$

Since our goal is to derive the discrete form of the equation (9.6.7), we can assume $S^2\frac{\partial^2 V}{\partial S \partial J}$, $S^2\frac{\partial^2 V}{\partial J^2}$, $S\frac{\partial V}{\partial J}$ are bounded. Thus we have

$$\frac{dV}{dt} + \frac{\sigma^2}{2}S\frac{d}{dS}S\frac{dV}{dS} + \left(r - \frac{\sigma^2}{2}\right)S\frac{dV}{dS} - rV + \mathrm{O}(\Delta t) = 0, \tag{9.6.12}$$

where $\frac{d}{dt}$ and $\frac{d}{dS}$ denote respectively derivatives with respect to t and S along the characteristic line.

Further discretize S. For any given $\Delta x > 0$, let $u = e^{\Delta x}$, and denote $S_i = u^i = e^{i\Delta x}, (i = 0, \pm 1, \ldots)$. Thus we get a partition in $0 \le S < \infty$.

By the explicit FDS:

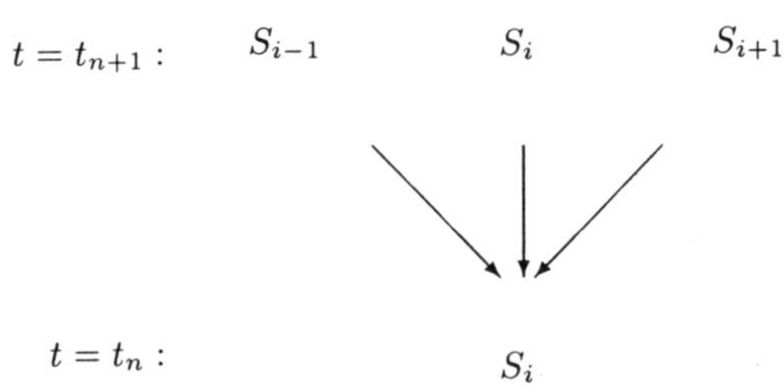

Let $J_0 = J_k$, the characteristic line starting from $t = t_n,\ J = J_k$ is

$$J = S - \frac{t_n}{t}(S - J_k). \tag{9.6.13}$$

Thus along this characteristic line, when $t = t_n,\ S = S_i$

$$V(t_n, S_i, J_k) = V_{i,k}^n$$

($V_{i,k}^n$ is defined in (9.6.4)); when $t = t_{n+1}, S = S_{i+1}, S_i$ and S_{i-1},

$$\begin{aligned}
V(t_{n+1}, S_{i+1}, J_{i+1,k_u}^{n+1}) &= V_{i+1,k_u}^{n+1},\\
V(t_{n+1}, S_i, J_{i,k_0}^{n+1}) &= V_{i,k_0}^{n+1},\\
V(t_{n+1}, S_{i-1}, J_{i-1,k_d}^{n+1}) &= V_{i-1,k_d}^{n+1},
\end{aligned}$$

where

$$\begin{aligned}
J_{i+1,k_u}^{n+1} &= \frac{1}{n+1}S_{i+1} + \frac{n}{n+1}J_k,\\
J_{i,k_0}^{n+1} &= \frac{1}{n+1}S_i + \frac{n}{n+1}J_k,\\
J_{i-1,k_d}^{n+1} &= \frac{1}{n+1}S_{i-1} + \frac{n}{n+1}J_k.
\end{aligned}$$

Consider the discrete form

$$\left(S\frac{dF}{dS}\right)_{S=S_i} = \frac{F_{i+1} - F_{i-1}}{\ln S_{i+1} - \ln S_{i-1}},$$

$$\begin{aligned}
\left(S\frac{d}{dS}S\frac{dF}{dS}\right)_{S=S_i} &= \frac{\left(S\frac{dF}{dS}\right)_{i+\frac{1}{2}} - \left(S\frac{dF}{dS}\right)_{i-\frac{1}{2}}}{\ln S_{i+\frac{1}{2}} - \ln S_{i-\frac{1}{2}}}\\
&= \frac{F_{i+1} - 2F_i + F_{i-1}}{(\ln S_{i+1} - \ln S_i)^2}.
\end{aligned}$$

Here, according to the assumption, we have

$$\ln\frac{S_{i+1}}{S_i} = \ln\frac{S_i}{S_{i-1}} = \ln\frac{S_{i+\frac{1}{2}}}{S_{i-\frac{1}{2}}}.$$

Since

$$S_i = e^{i\Delta x}, \qquad \ln\frac{S_{i+1}}{S_i} = \Delta x. \tag{9.6.14}$$

thus the explicit FDS for the equation (9.6.7) along this characteristic line can be written as

$$\begin{aligned}&\frac{V_{i,k_0}^{n+1}-V_{i,k}^{n}}{\Delta t}+\frac{\sigma^2}{2\Delta x^2}[V_{i+1,k_u}^{n+1}-2V_{i,k_0}^{n+1}+V_{i-1,k_d}^{n+1}]\\&+\frac{r-\sigma^2/2}{2\Delta x}[V_{i+1,k_u}^{n+1}-V_{i-1,k_d}^{n+1}]-rV_{i,k}^{n}+O(\Delta t)=0.\end{aligned} \tag{9.6.15}$$

After rearrangement, neglecting the higher orders, it can be written as

$$\begin{aligned}V_{i,k}^{n}=&(1+r\Delta t)^{-1}\left\{\left[\frac{1}{2}+\frac{\Delta t}{2\Delta x}\left(r-\frac{\sigma^2}{2}\right)\right]V_{i+1,k_u}^{n+1}\right.\\&\left.+\left[\frac{1}{2}-\frac{\Delta t}{2\Delta x}\left(r-\frac{\sigma^2}{2}\right)\right]V_{i-1,k_d}^{n+1}+\left(1-\frac{\sigma^2\Delta t}{\Delta x^2}\right)V_{i,k_0}^{n+1}\right\}\end{aligned} \tag{9.6.16}$$

This is the explicit FDS with characteristic line for the equation (9.6.7).

Since $V_{i,k}^N$ is known, we can find $V_{i,k}^n$, $(0\le n\le N)$ from the difference equation (9.6.16) by the backward induction.

It is easy to show that

1. *if*

$$\frac{\sigma^2\Delta t}{\Delta x^2}\le 1 \tag{9.6.17}$$

and

$$\frac{1}{2}-\frac{\Delta t}{2\Delta x}|r-\frac{\sigma^2}{2}|>0, \tag{9.6.18}$$

then the scheme (9.6.16) is stable.

2. As $\Delta x,\Delta t\to 0$, the limit of the difference scheme (9.6.15) is the equation (9.6.7), i.e.the scheme (9.6.16) is consistent with (9.6.7).

Then by the Lax's equivalence theorem we assert: *under the conditions (9.6.17),(9.6.18), as $\Delta t,\Delta x\to 0$, the solution by the FDS (9.6.16) converges to the solution of the original terminal-boundary problem (9.6.7),(9.6.8).*

Lemma *If*

$$\frac{\sigma^2\Delta t}{\Delta x^2}=1 \tag{9.6.19}$$

and

$$\frac{1}{2}-\frac{1}{2\sigma}|r-\frac{\sigma^2}{2}|\sqrt{\Delta t}>0, \tag{9.6.20}$$

then the FDS (9.6.16) is reduced to

$$V_{i,k}^{n}=\frac{1}{\rho}[qV_{i+1,k_u}^{n+1}+(1-q)V_{i-1,k_d}^{n+1}], \tag{9.6.21}$$

where

$$\begin{aligned}\rho&=1+r\Delta t,\\q&=\frac{1}{2}\left(1+\left(r-\frac{\sigma^2}{2}\right)\frac{\sqrt{\Delta t}}{\sigma}\right).\end{aligned} \tag{9.6.22}$$

As we have pointed out in §5.7:

$$
\begin{aligned}
&u = e^{\sigma\sqrt{\Delta t}}, \qquad d = e^{-\sigma\sqrt{\Delta t}}, \qquad \rho = e^{r\Delta t} \\
&q = \frac{1}{2}\left[1 + \frac{1}{\sigma}\left(r - \frac{\sigma^2}{2}\right)\right] = \frac{\rho - d}{u - d} + O(\Delta t^{3/2})
\end{aligned} \tag{9.6.23}
$$

By comparing (9.6.21) and (9.6.5), and by (9.6.23), we have proved: *When conditions (9.6.19), (9.6.20) hold, neglecting the higher orders of Δt, the BTM for the arithmetic average Asian option is equivalent to the explicit FDS with characteristic line for the equations (9.6.7),(9.6.8).*

Therefore by the convergence of the explicit FDS with characteristic line, we claim that the BTM for the arithmetic average Asian option is a well-posed algorithm.

Summery

(1) The model of the Asian option pricing is a terminal value problem for a 2-D hyperparabolic equation. All Asian option pricing problems can be reduced to a 1-D problem under suitable transformations. But only the geometric average Asian options have closed form valuation formula.

(2) BTM is the most popular numerical method for Asian option pricing. When neglecting the higher order terms, it is equivalent to the FDS with characteristic line (when $\frac{\sigma^2\Delta t}{\Delta x^2} = 1$). Notice that for the arithmetic average Asian options, since corresponding to each asset price S_i^n, its path variable $\vec{J}_k^n$ is a 2^{n-1} dimensional vector, its computation costs a lot of memory and processor time.

(3) The model for the lookback put options is a terminal-boundary problem for the Black-Scholes equation in the domain $\{0 \le S \le J < \infty, 0 \le t \le T\}$, where the boundary condition on $\{S = J, 0 \le t \le T\}$ is:

$$
\frac{\partial V}{\partial J}|_{S=J} = 0
$$

(where J is a parameter).

It can be reduced to a 1-D problem by suitable transformation, and a closed form solution can be obtained.

Exercises

1. Let V_t denote the price of an Asian option whose payoff at maturity $t = T$ is

$$
\text{payoff} = (J_T^\omega - K)^+,
$$

where

$$
J_T^\omega = \frac{1}{\omega}\int_{T-\omega}^{T} S_\tau d\tau \qquad \text{(arithmetic average)}
$$

or

$$J_T^\omega = e^{\frac{1}{\omega}\int_{T-\omega}^T \ln S_\tau d\tau}, \qquad \text{(geometric average)}$$

where ω is a given time period, $\omega < T$. Set up the pricing models for these two Asian options.

In the case $\omega = \frac{T}{2}$, find the valuation formula for the geometric average Asian options.

2. Let $S_1(t), S_2(t)$ be the prices of two risky assets. Their movement satisfies the stochastic differential equations (7.1.5)—(7.1.8). Let V_t denote the price of an Asian minimum call option on two risky assets, i.e., its payoff at maturity is given by

$$\text{payoff} = (\min(J_T^{(1)}, J_T^{(2)}) - K)^+,$$

where $J_t^{(i)}$ is the geometric average of the risky asset price $S_i(t)$

$$J_t^{(i)} = e^{\frac{1}{t}\int_0^t \ln S_i(\tau)d\tau}. \qquad (i = 1, 2)$$

(a) Set up the pricing model for the option.

(b) Transform the original 4-D problem to a 2-D problem.

3. Let S_t be the price of a continuous dividend-paying stock, with the dividend rate $q > 0$. A Russian option is such a perpetual American option that allows its holder to exercise it at any time $t > 0$, at the maximum value of the asset price in its path: $M_t = \max\limits_{0 \le \tau \le t} S_\tau$.

(a) Formulate the free boundary problem model for the Russian option pricing.

(b) Find the price and the optimal exercise boundary for the Russian option.

4. Show that: when neglecting the higher order terms of Δt, the BTM for the geometric average Asian option is equivalent to the FDS with characteristic line under certain conditions.

5. Formulate the explicit FDS for the lookback options, and show that: when neglecting the higher order terms of Δt, it is equivalent to the BTM under certain conditions.

Chapter 10

Implied Volatility

Volatility σ is a crutial parameter in the Black-Scholes formula. The option price is very sensitive to change in this parameter. In an underlying asset market, investors would definitely like to know how volatile the future price of the asset will be. Indeed, σ is in general unpredictable. However, the options market "knows" it. We can obtain and analyze prices of a number of options on a given underlying asset with various strike prices and expiration dates. If the Black-Scholes option pricing theory is correct, then the price quotes from the options market should reflect and reveal the price volatility of the underlying asset. The volatility derived from the quoted price of a single option is called the **implied volatility.**

In this chapter, we study how to recover the underlying asset price movement (under the risk-neutral measure) from the information of the options market using the Black-Scholes theory i.e. to infer the implied volatility of the underlying asset price.

10.1 Preliminaries

In deriving the Black-Scholes formula, we have assumed the volatility σ of the underlying asset to be constant throughout the option's entire lifetime. By the Black-Scholes formula, the option price is of the form:

$$V = V(S, t; \sigma, K, T).$$

Suppose we have learned from the market that at $t = t_0$, the price of an asset is $S = S_0$, and the price of its option with the strike price K_0 and expiration date T_0 is V_0. Then by the Black-Scholes formula we can get an equation for σ:

$$V_0 = V(S_0, t_0; \sigma, K_0, T_0). \tag{10.1.1}$$

Since

$$\frac{\partial V}{\partial \sigma} > 0,$$

σ can be uniquely determined from (10.1.1). Thus we have inferred the implied volatility $\sigma = \sigma_0$ of the underlying asset from the price of its option with the strike price K_0 and expiration T_0.

Since σ is a constant by assumption of the Black-Scholes formula, the implied volatility σ_0 thus derived should be independent of K_0 and T_0 of the option. That is, the implied volatility σ of a given underlying asset determined from options with different strike prices and expiration dates should all have the same value. But this cannot be true in general. In fact, *the implied volatility σ inferred from options with different strike prices and expiration dates is a function of K, T* $\sigma = \sigma(K, T)$.

For a given T, the implied volatility σ varies with the strike price K typically in one of the following ways:

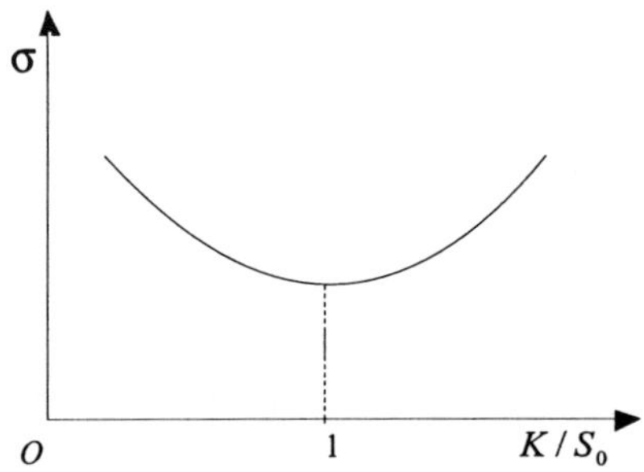

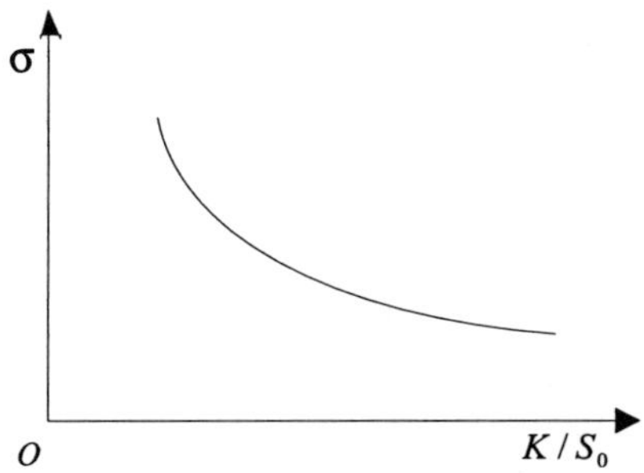

Here S_0 is the asset price at $t = t_0$. The first figure is called **volatility smile curve**, and the second figure is called **volatility skew curve**.

For a given strike price K, the implied volatility σ varies with the maturity T typically in one of the following ways:

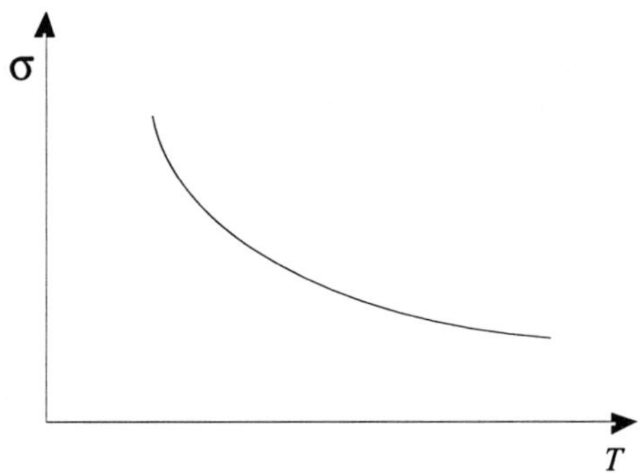

These pictures indicate, the constant volatility assumption in the Black-Scholes formula does not reflect the reality.

A more realistic model is: σ is a function of t and asset price S. Then the stochastic process of the asset price movement under the risk-neutral measure is

$$\frac{dS}{S} = (r-q)dt + \sigma(S,t)dW_t, \tag{10.1.2}$$

Correspondingly, the Black-Scholes equation becomes

$$\frac{\partial V}{\partial t} + \frac{1}{2}\sigma^2(S,t)S^2\frac{\partial^2 V}{\partial S^2} + (r-q)S\frac{\partial V}{\partial S} - rV = 0. \tag{10.1.3}$$

In general, this type of problem has no explicit solution. It must be solved by numerical methods.

With the improved price model of the underlying asset, we ask a question: *how can we determine the volatility of an underlying asset price from its option price quotes in the options market?* Mathematically, i.e. at $t = t_0, S = S_0$, if

$$V(S_0, t_0; \sigma, K_k, T_l) = V_{k,l} \qquad (k = 1, \ldots, m, l = 1, \ldots, n) \tag{10.1.4}$$

are given, find the volatility function

$$\sigma = \sigma(S,t).$$

We can either use the call options price quotes or the put options price quotes, since according to the call-put parity, the volatility $\sigma = \sigma(S,t)$ thus derived should be the same. To be specific, let us take call option as example.

Problem P *Let $V = V(S,t;\sigma,K,T)$ be a call option price, satisfying*

$$\begin{cases} \frac{\partial V}{\partial t} + \frac{1}{2}\sigma^2(S,t)S^2\frac{\partial^2 V}{\partial S^2} + (r-q)S\frac{\partial V}{\partial S} - rV = 0, & (10.1.5) \\ \qquad (0 \le S < \infty, 0 \le t < T) & \\ V(S,T) = (S-K)^+. \quad (0 \le S < \infty) & (10.1.6) \end{cases}$$

Suppose at $t = t^*, (0 \le t^* < T_1), S = S^*$,

$$V(S^*, t^*; \sigma, K, T) = F(K,T) \qquad (0 < K < \infty, T_1 \le T \le T_2)$$

is given, find $\sigma = \sigma(S,t), (0 \le S < \infty, T_1 \le t \le T_2)$

10.2 Dupire Method

Let

$$V = V(S,t;K,T)$$

be a European call option price. Define

$$\frac{\partial^2 V}{\partial K^2} = G(S, t; K, T). \tag{10.2.1}$$

By (10.1.5),(10.1.6), G satisfies

$$\begin{cases} \dfrac{\partial G}{\partial t} + \dfrac{1}{2}\sigma^2(S,t)S^2\dfrac{\partial^2 G}{\partial S^2} + (r-q)S\dfrac{\partial G}{\partial S} - rG = 0, & (10.2.2) \\ G(S,t) = \delta(K-S). & (10.2.3) \end{cases}$$

Since $\delta(x) = \delta(-x)$, thus $G(S,t;K,T)$ is the fundamental solution to equation (10.2.2). By Theorem 6.3: $G(S,t;K,T)$, as a function of $K,T(S,t$ are parameters), is the fundamental solution to the adjoint equation of the problem (10.2.2),(10.2.3), i.e.

$$\begin{cases} -\dfrac{\partial G}{\partial T} + \dfrac{1}{2}\dfrac{\partial^2}{\partial K^2}(\sigma^2(K,T)K^2G) - (r-q)\dfrac{\partial}{\partial K}(KG) - rG = 0, & \\ \qquad (0 \le K < \infty, t \le T) & (10.2.4) \\ G(S,t;K,t) = \delta(K-S). \quad (0 \le K < \infty) & (10.2.5) \end{cases}$$

Substitute (10.2.1) into (10.2.4),(10.2.5), then integrate twice with respect to K in $[K,\infty]$. Since

(1) for a given S, if $K \to \infty$,

$$V, K\frac{\partial V}{\partial K}, \sigma^2K^2G, K\frac{\partial G}{\partial K}, \frac{\partial}{\partial K}(\sigma^2K^2G) \to 0,$$

(2)
$$\int_K^\infty d\xi \int_\xi^\infty \delta(\eta - S)d\eta = \int_K^\infty (\eta - K)\delta(\eta - S)d\eta$$
$$= \int_0^\infty (\eta - K)^+\delta(\eta - S)d\eta = (S-K)^+,$$

(3)
$$\int_K^\infty G(S,t;\xi,T)d\xi = \int_K^\infty \frac{\partial^2 V}{\partial \xi^2}d\xi = -\frac{\partial V}{\partial K},$$

(4)
$$\int_K^\infty \frac{\partial}{\partial \xi}V(S,t;\xi,T)d\xi = -V(S,t;K,T),$$

(5)
$$\int_K^\infty \xi G(x,t;\xi,T)d\xi = \int_K^\infty \xi\frac{\partial^2 V}{\partial \xi^2}d\xi = -K\frac{\partial V}{\partial K} + V,$$

(6)
$$\int_K^\infty d\xi \int_\xi^\infty \frac{\partial^2}{\partial \eta^2}(\sigma^2(\eta,T)\eta^2G)d\eta = \sigma^2(K,T)K^2\frac{\partial^2 V}{\partial K^2}.$$

Thus the problem (10.2.4),(10.2.5) becomes

$$\begin{cases} -\dfrac{\partial V}{\partial T}+\frac{1}{2}K^2\sigma^2(K,T)\dfrac{\partial^2 V}{\partial K^2}-(r-q)K\dfrac{\partial V}{\partial K}-qV=0, & (10.2.6)\\ \qquad (0\le K<\infty, t\le T) & \\ V|_{T=t}=(S-K)^+. \quad (0\le K<\infty) & (10.2.7)\end{cases}$$

From (10.2.6), we get ([14])

$$\sigma(K,T)=\sqrt{\frac{\dfrac{\partial V}{\partial T}+(r-q)K\dfrac{\partial V}{\partial K}+qV}{\dfrac{1}{2}K^2\dfrac{\partial^2 V}{\partial K^2}}}. \tag{10.2.8}$$

Therefore, at $t=t^*, S=S^*$, if we can get from the options market the option price quotes with various strike prices and expiration dates, i.e. if we know the function $F(K,T)$:

$$F(K,T)=V(S^*,t^*;K,T), \tag{10.2.9}$$

then we can calculate $\sigma(K,T)$ by (10.2.8).

However, this algorithm is not robust to the real data and is thus not reliable. In fact, for a given $F(K,T)$, in order to calculate $\sigma(K,T)$ by (10.2.8), we need to calculate the derivatives F_{KK}, F_K and F_T. But a small error in F can result in big changes in its derivatives, especially in its second derivatives. Therefore the algorithm to compute $\sigma(K,T)$ by (10.2.8) is **ill-posed**.

As we pointed out in (10.1.4), in general, $F(K,T)$ is given on a set of discrete points $\{(K_k,T_l)\}(k=1,\dots,m, l=1,\dots,n)$. Thus interpolation or extrapolation technique would be required to obtain a continuous function $F(K,T)$ in the domain $(0\le K<\infty, T_1\le T\le T_2)$ from the values at discrete points. However, naive interpolation and extrapolation tend to incur irregularity and instability in the solution $\sigma(K,T)$. A more robust calibration method is hence needed.

Although Dupire method is not practical, nevertheless, we can follow its idea in solving this ill-posed problem. That is, we still want to reduce the implied volatility determination problem to a terminal state observation problem for a parabolic equation. Since the latter is a typical inverse problem, we can always find a well-posed algorithm for it.

10.3 Optimal Control Method

As a first step, let us assume $\sigma(S,t)\equiv\sigma(S)$, i.e. σ depends on S only, independent of t. Problem P(see (10.1.5),(10.1.6)) is analogous to a terminal state observation problem: i.e. for a Cauchy problem to parabolic equations, if the terminal value is given, how to determine a coefficient in the equation. However, Problem P is not a typical terminal state observation problem, since at the terminal time $t=t^*$

the function $V(S,t^*)$ is not given in the entire domain $(0 \le S < \infty)$. Instead, $V(S^*,t^*;K)$ is given as a function of the parameter K $(0 \le K < \infty)$, at a single point of S ($S = S^*$).

Nevertheless, following Dupire's idea, we have reduced Problem P to a typical terminal state observation problem.

Problem $\mathrm{P_0}$ *Let $V = V(K,\tau;\sigma)$ be a solution to the Cauchy problem*

$$\begin{cases} \frac{\partial V}{\partial \tau} = \frac{1}{2}\sigma^2(K)K^2\frac{\partial^2 V}{\partial K^2} - (r-q)K\frac{\partial V}{\partial K} - qV, & (10.3.1) \\ V(K,0) = (S-K)^+, & (10.3.2) \end{cases}$$

where $\tau = T - t$.

And suppose at $\tau = \tau^* = T - t^*$, $V(K,\tau^*)$ is given by

$$V(K,\tau^*;\sigma) = F(K), \qquad (0 \le K < \infty) \tag{10.3.3}$$

find $\sigma = \sigma(K)$.

Problem $\mathrm{P_0}$ is a typical terminal state observation problem (here the terminal time is $\tau = \tau^*$).

By transformation

$$y = \ln\frac{K}{S}, v = \frac{1}{S}e^{q\tau}V, \tag{10.3.4}$$

problem (10.3.1),(10.3.2) becomes

$$\begin{cases} \frac{\partial v}{\partial \tau} = a(y)\left(\frac{\partial^2 v}{\partial y^2} - \frac{\partial v}{\partial y}\right) - (r-q)\frac{\partial v}{\partial y}, \quad (y \in R, 0 < \tau \le \tau^*) & (10.3.5) \\ v(y,0) = (1-e^y)^+, \quad (y \in \mathbf{R}) & (10.3.6) \end{cases}$$

where

$$a(y) = \frac{1}{2}\sigma^2(K). \tag{10.3.7}$$

ProblemQ$_0$ *Find $\bar{a}(y) \in \mathcal{A}$, such that*

$$J(\bar{a}) = \int_{a\in\mathcal{A}} J(a), \tag{10.3.8}$$

where $v = v(y,\tau;a)$ is the solution to the Cauchy problem (10.3.5),(10.3.6),

$$J(a) = \frac{1}{2}\int_R |v(y,\tau^*;a) - v^*(y)|^2 dy + \frac{N}{2}\int_R |\nabla a|^2 dy, \tag{10.3.9}$$

$$v^*(y) = \frac{1}{S^*}e^{q\tau^*}F(S^*e^y), \tag{10.3.10}$$

(Function $F(K)$ is defined in (10.3.3)).

$\mathcal{A}$ is the admissible set of the variational problem (10.3.8). In order that the problem (10.3.5), (10.3.6) has solution, we choose the set as

$$\mathcal{A} = \{a(y)|0 < a_0 \le a(y) \le a_1, \int_{\mathbf{R}} |\nabla a|^2 dy < \infty\}, \tag{10.3.11}$$

where a_0, a_1 and N are **constants.** Here $J(a)$ is called the cost functional, $a = a(y)$ is called the control variable, and $\bar{a}(y)$ is called the optimal control or minimizer. The variational problem Q_0 is called the optimal control problem.

By the parabolic equations theory, it can be shown (see[24])

Theorem 10.1 *The variational problem* Q_0 *has at least one minimizer* $\bar{a}(y) \in \mathcal{A}$.

Next we establish the necessary condition for the minimizer $\bar{a}(y)$.

Let $\bar{a}(y)$ be the minimizer, since A is a convex set, thus for arbitrary $h(y) \in \mathcal{A}$, $a_\lambda(y) = (1-\lambda)\bar{a} + \lambda h \in \mathcal{A}, (\lambda \in [0,1])$. Define a function $j(\lambda)$:

$$j(\lambda) = J((1-\lambda)\bar{a} + \lambda h),$$

which attains the minimum at $\lambda = 0$, thus

$$0 \le j'(0) = \left[\frac{d}{d\lambda}\int_R |v^\lambda(y,\tau^*) - v^*(y)|^2 dy \right.$$
$$\left. + \ N\frac{d}{d\lambda}\int_R |\nabla((1-\lambda)\bar{a} + \lambda h)|^2 dy\right]_{\lambda=0}, \tag{10.3.12}$$

where $v_\lambda(y,\tau)$ satisfies

$$\begin{cases} \dfrac{\partial v_\lambda}{\partial \tau} = a_\lambda(y)\left[\dfrac{\partial^2 v_\lambda}{\partial y^2} - \dfrac{\partial v_\lambda}{\partial y}\right] - (r-q)\dfrac{\partial v_\lambda}{\partial y}, & (10.3.13) \\ v_\lambda(y,0) = (1-e^y)^+. & (10.3.14) \end{cases}$$

Denote $\xi_\lambda(y,\tau) = \frac{dv_\lambda}{d\lambda}$, by straightforward computation, we get

$$\begin{cases} \dfrac{\partial \xi_\lambda}{\partial \tau} = a_\lambda(y)\left[\dfrac{\partial^2 \xi_\lambda}{\partial y^2} - \dfrac{\partial \xi_\lambda}{\partial y}\right] - (r-q)\dfrac{\partial \xi_\lambda}{\partial y} + \left[\dfrac{\partial^2 v_\lambda}{\partial y^2} - \dfrac{\partial v_\lambda}{\partial y}\right](h-\bar{a}), & (10.3.15) \\ \xi_\lambda(y,0) = 0. & (10.3.16) \end{cases}$$

Thus (10.3.12) can be written as

$$\int_R (\bar{v}(y,\tau^*) - v^*(y))\xi_0(y,\tau^*)dy + \ N\int_{\mathbf{R}} \nabla\bar{a}\cdot\nabla(h-\bar{a})dy \ge 0, \qquad \forall h \in A \tag{10.3.17}$$

where $\bar{v}(y,\tau)$ is a solution to the problem (10.3.5),(10.3.6), where $a(y) = \bar{a}(y)$. $\xi_0(y,\tau^*)$ is the solution to the problem (10.3.15),(10.3.16), where $\lambda = 0$, i.e.

$$\begin{cases} \bar{\mathcal{L}}\xi_0 = \frac{\partial \xi_0}{\partial \tau} - \bar{a}(y)\left[\frac{\partial^2 \xi_0}{\partial y^2} - \frac{\partial \xi_0}{\partial y}\right] + (r-q)\frac{\partial \xi_0}{\partial y} = \left[\frac{\partial^2 \bar{v}}{\partial y^2} - \frac{\partial \bar{v}}{\partial y}\right](h-\bar{a}), & (10.3.18) \\ \xi_0(y,0) = 0. & (10.3.19) \end{cases}$$

Let $\varphi(y,\tau)$ be the solution to the adjoint problem of the problem (10.3.18),(10.3.19), i.e.

$$\begin{cases} \bar{\mathcal{L}}^*\bar{\varphi} = 0, \quad (y \in \mathbf{R}, 0 \le \tau < \tau^*) & (10.3.20) \\ \bar{\varphi}(y,\tau^*) = \bar{v}(y,\tau^*) - v^*(y), \quad (y \in \mathbf{R}) & (10.3.21) \end{cases}$$

where the differential operator $\bar{\mathcal{L}}^*$ is the adjoint operator of $\bar{\mathcal{L}}$:

$$\bar{\mathcal{L}}^*\bar{\varphi} = -\frac{\partial \bar{\varphi}}{\partial \tau} - \frac{\partial^2}{\partial y^2}(\bar{a}\bar{\varphi}) - \frac{\partial}{\partial y}(\bar{a}\bar{\varphi}) - (r-q)\frac{\partial \bar{\varphi}}{\partial y}.$$

Thus by the Green formula

$$\begin{aligned} &\int_0^{\tau^*}\int_{\mathbf{R}} (\bar{\varphi}\bar{\mathcal{L}}\xi_0 - \xi_0\bar{\mathcal{L}}^*\bar{\varphi})dyd\tau \\ &= \int_0^{\tau^*}\int_{\mathbf{R}} \left\{\frac{\partial(\bar{\varphi}\xi_0)}{\partial \tau} - \frac{\partial}{\partial y}(\bar{a}(y)\bar{\varphi}\frac{\partial \xi_0}{\partial y}) + \frac{\partial}{\partial y}(\xi_0\frac{\partial}{\partial y}(\bar{a}(y)\bar{\varphi}))\right. \\ &\quad \left. + \frac{\partial}{\partial y}(\xi_0\bar{a}(y)\bar{\varphi}) + (r-q)\frac{\partial(\xi_0\bar{\varphi})}{\partial y}\right\} dyd\tau \\ &= \int_{\mathbf{R}} \left[(\bar{\varphi}\xi_0)_{\tau=\tau^*} - (\bar{\varphi}\xi_0)_{\tau=0}\right] dy. \end{aligned}$$

By equation (10.3.18),(10.3.20) and the conditions (10.3.19),(10.3.21), we get

$$\int_0^{\tau^*}\int_{\mathbf{R}} \bar{\varphi}\left[\frac{\partial^2 \bar{v}}{\partial y^2} - \frac{\partial \bar{v}}{\partial y}\right](h-\bar{a})dyd\tau = \int_{\mathbf{R}} \xi_0(y,\tau^*)[\bar{v}(y,\tau^*) - v^*(y)]dy. \quad (10.3.22)$$

Substituting (10.3.22) into (10.3.17), we get

$$\int_0^{\tau^*}\int_{\mathbf{R}} \bar{\varphi}\left[\frac{\partial^2 \bar{v}}{\partial y^2} - \frac{\partial \bar{v}}{\partial y}\right](h-\bar{a})dyd\tau + N\int_{\mathbf{R}} \nabla\bar{a}\cdot\nabla(h-\bar{a})dy \ge 0. \qquad \forall h \in \mathcal{A}$$

Denote

$$f(y;\bar{v},\bar{\varphi}) = \frac{1}{N}\int_0^{\tau^*} \bar{\varphi}(\frac{\partial^2\bar{v}}{\partial y^2} - \frac{\partial \bar{v}}{\partial y})d\tau, \tag{10.3.23}$$

then the above inequality can be written as

$$\int_{\mathbf{R}} [\nabla\bar{a}\cdot\nabla(h-\bar{a}) + f(y;\bar{v},\bar{\varphi})(h-\bar{a})]dy \geq 0, \qquad \forall h\in\mathcal{A} \tag{10.3.24}$$

Choose a sufficiently smooth $\lambda(y)$, and let

$$0 \leq \lambda(y) \leq 1, \tag{10.3.25}$$

and let

$$h(y) = [(1-\lambda(y))]\bar{a}(y) + \lambda(y)a_i. \qquad (i=0,1)$$

By the definition of the admissible set $\mathcal{A}$ (10.3.11), for any $\lambda(y)$ satisfying (10.3.25), $h(y)\in\mathcal{A}$.

Thus from (10.3.24), for all $\lambda(y)$ satisfying condition (10.3.25), there must be

$$\int_{\mathbf{R}} \{\nabla\bar{a}\nabla[\lambda(y)(a_i-\bar{a})] + f(y;\bar{v},\bar{\varphi})[\lambda(y)(a_i-\bar{a})]\}dy \geq 0,$$

i.e.

$$\int_{\mathbf{R}} \{[-\bar{a}''(y) + f(y;\bar{v},\bar{\varphi})](a_i-\bar{a})\}\lambda(y)dy \geq 0 \qquad \text{for all } \lambda(y),$$

then there must be

$$[-a''(y) + f(y;\bar{v},\bar{\varphi})](a_i-\bar{a}) \geq 0, \qquad (i=0,1) \tag{10.3.26}$$

Since

$$a_0 \leq \bar{a} \leq a_1, \tag{10.3.27}$$

thus by (10.3.26) we get

$$[-a''(y) + f(y;\bar{v},\bar{\varphi})](\bar{a}-a_0) \leq 0, \tag{10.3.28}$$

$$[-a''(y) + f(y;\bar{v},\bar{\varphi})](a_1-\bar{a}) \geq 0. \tag{10.3.29}$$

Thus we have shown the variational inequality (10.3.24) and (10.3.27)-(10.3.29) are equivalent. This is a double obstacle variational inequality problem.

Thus we have established the necessary condition of the variational problem Q_0.

Theorem 10.2 *If $\bar{a}(y) \in A$ is the minimizer of the variational problem Q_0 (10.3.8), then there exists a triplet $\{\bar{a}(y), \bar{v}(y,\tau), \bar{\varphi}(y,\tau)\}$, which in domain $\{y\in R, 0\leq\tau\leq\tau^*\}$ is a solution to the following PDE problem:*

$$\begin{cases} \dfrac{\partial\bar{v}}{\partial\tau} - \bar{a}(y)\dfrac{\partial^2\bar{v}}{\partial y^2} + \bar{a}(y)\dfrac{\partial\bar{v}}{\partial y} + (r-q)\dfrac{\partial\bar{v}}{\partial y} = 0, & (10.3.30)\\ \bar{v}(y,0) = (1-e^y)^+, & (10.3.31)\end{cases}$$

$$\begin{cases} -\frac{\partial \bar{\varphi}}{\partial \tau} - \frac{\partial^2}{\partial y^2}(\bar{a}(y)\bar{\varphi}) - \frac{\partial}{\partial y}(\bar{a}(y)\bar{\varphi}) - (r-q)\frac{\partial \bar{\varphi}}{\partial y} = 0, & (10.3.32) \\ \bar{\varphi}(y,\tau^*) = \bar{v}(y,\tau^*) - v^*(y), & (10.3.33) \end{cases}$$

and (10.3.27)—(10.3.29). Here $v^*(y)$ and $f(y;\bar{v},\bar{\varphi})$ are defined in (10.3.4) and (10.3.23).

Remark Equation (10.3.30) with the initial condition (10.3.31) is a Cauchy problem to a forward parabolic equation; Equation (10.3.32) with the terminal condition (10.3.33) is a Cauchy problem to a backward parabolic equation; Equation (10.3.27)—(10.3.29) is a variational inequality to a second order ODE. Therefore this is a system of forward-backward parabolic equations coupled with an elliptic variational inequality.

The uniqueness of the solution to the above system of equations is investigated in [24].

10.4 Numerical Method

In order to find the numerical solution to the problem P_0, there are two approaches: (1) starting from the variational problem Q_0(10.3.8), discretize it, convert it to a convex constraint optimization problem, then find its approximate solution; (2) Starting from the necessary condition of the variational problem, i.e. to find the triplet $\{\bar{a}(y), \bar{v}(y,\tau), \bar{\varphi}(y,\tau)\}$, such that it satisfies the forward-backward PDE problem coupled with an elliptic variational inequality (10.3.27)—(10.3.33). In the following we explain the procedure for solving the problem (10.3.27)—(10.3.33).

We use iterative procedure as follows: ([26])

(1) Suppose at $t = t^*$, $S = S^*$, the option price quotes with different strike price K and the same expiration date, $V(S^*, t^*; K) = F(K)$, are obtained from the options market.

By (10.3.4) define function

$$v^*(y) = \frac{1}{S^*} e^{q\tau^*} F(S^* e^y), \tag{10.4.1}$$

where $\tau^* = T - t^*, y = \ln \frac{K}{S^*}$.

(2) Choose initial value $\sigma = \sigma_0(K)$ for iteration. It can be the implied volatility determined by the Black-Scholes formula, i.e. *to find $\sigma = \sigma_0(K)$ so that it satisfies the following transcendental equation:*

$$e^{-q(T-t^*)} S^* N\left(\frac{\ln \frac{S^*}{K} + (r - q + \frac{\sigma_0^2(K)}{2})(T-t^*)}{\sigma_0(K)\sqrt{T-t^*}}\right)$$

$$+ K e^{-r(T-t^*)} N\left(\frac{\ln \frac{S^*}{K} + (r - q - \frac{\sigma_0^2(K)}{2})(T-t^*)}{\sigma_0(K)\sqrt{T-t^*}}\right) = F(K). \tag{10.4.2}$$

Due to the strict monotonicity of the option price with respect to σ, equation (10.4.2) has a unique solution $\sigma = \sigma_0(K)$.

By (10.3.7) define function

$$a_0(y) = \frac{1}{2}\sigma_0^2(S^* e^y). \tag{10.4.3}$$

(3) Solve the Cauchy problem (10.3.30), (10.3.31), where $\bar{a}(y)$ is chosen as:

$$\bar{a}(y) = a_0(y),$$

where $a_0(y)$ is defined in (10.4.3). Thus we obtain a solution $v_0(y, \tau)$.

(4) Solve the backward Cauchy problem (10.3.32), (10.3.33), where

$$\bar{a}(y) = a_0(y),$$

$$\bar{\varphi}(y, \tau^*) = v_0(y, \tau) - v^*(y),$$

here $v^*(y)$ is defined in (10.4.1). Thus we get a solution $\varphi_0(y, \tau)$.

(5) By definition (10.3.23), compute $f(y; v_0, \varphi_0)$:

$$f(y; v_0, \varphi_0) = \frac{1}{N}\int_0^{\tau^*} \varphi_0(y, \tau)\left[\frac{\partial^2 v_0}{\partial y^2} - \frac{\partial v_0}{\partial y}\right] d\tau. \tag{10.4.4}$$

(6) Solve the variational inequality (10.3.27)—(10.3.29), where $f(y; \bar{v}, \bar{\varphi})$ is defined in (10.4.4). Thus we get $a = a_1(y), (y \in \mathbf{R})$. Then by induction we get the sequence $a = a_n(y), (n = 0, 1, 2, ...)$.

(7) Back to the original variables, calculate $\sigma_n(K)$:

$$\sigma_n(K) = \sqrt{2a_n(\ln \frac{K}{S^*})}.$$

In steps (3),(4),(6), we can use the difference method or other numerical methods to solve the Cauchy problem to parabolic equations and the boundary problem to an ordinary differential equation.

Remark The information obtained from the options market is usually in the form of finite discrete points. Thus in order to define the function $F(K) = V(S^*, t^*; K)$ in $0 \leq K < \infty$, we need to use interpolation and extrapolation to convert the discrete data to a continuous function in $0 \leq K < \infty$. This conversion introduces errors and sufficient care must be given when performing the calculation.

Summary

1. Since the implied volatility obtained by the Black-Scholes formula shows "smile" and "skew", we must modify the price movement model of the underlying asset, i.e., assume the volatility σ *is a function of* S, t.

2. Following Dupire's idea, we convert the implied volatility (function) $\sigma(S, t)$ *determination problem to a terminal state observation problem to a parabolic equation. Then in the framework of the optimal control theory, we have given a well-posed algorithm for seeking the implied volatility (function).*

Bibliography

[1] Bachelier, L. (1900) Théorie de la spéculation, Ann. Sci. École Norm. Sup., **17**, 21-86.

[2] Barles, G., Burdean, J., Romano, M. & Samsoen, N.(1995) Critical stock price near expiration, Math. Finan. , **5**, 77-95.

[3] Black, F.& Scholes, M.(1973) The pricing of options and corporate liabilities.J.polit.Econ., **81**, 637-654.

[4] Brennan, M. & Schwartz, E.(1977) The valuation of American put options, J.Finan., **32**, 449-462.

[5] Broadie, M.&Deltemple, J.(1997) The valuation of American options on multiple assets, Math. Finan., **7**, 241-286.

[6] Carr, P.&Faguet, D.(1994) Fast accurate valuation of American options, Working paper, Cornell University.

[7] Carr, P., Jarrow, R. & Myneni, R.(1992) Alternative charaterization of American put options, Math. Finan., **2**, 87-106.

[8] Chen, X., Chadam, J., Jiang, L.&Zheng W.(2001) Convexity of exercise boundary of the American put option for no dividend asset, Working paper, Tongji University.

[9] Cheng, W.&Zhang, S.(2000) The analysis of reset options, The Journal of Derivatives, 59-71.

[10] Chesney, M., Cornwall, J., Jeanhlanc-Picque, M., Kentwell, G. & Yor, M.(1997) Parisian pricing, Risk, **10**, (January) , 77-79.

[11] Cox, J.&Ross, S.(1976) The valuation of options for alternative stochastic processes. J.Finan.Econ., **3**, 145-166.

[12] Cox, J., Ross, S.&Rubinstein, M.(1979) Option pricing: A simplified approach, J. Finan. Econ.**7**, 229-263.

[13] Dewynne, J.N., Howison, S.D., Rupf, I.&Wilmott, P.(1993) Some mathematical results in the pricing of American options , Europ. J. Appl. Math., **4**, 381-398.

[14] Dupire, B.(1994) Pricing with a smile, Risk, **7**, (January) , 18-20.

[15] Friedman, Avner.(1982) Variational Principles and Free Broundary Problems, John Wiley& Sons, New York.

[16] Goldman, M.B., Sozin, H.B.&Gatto, M.A.(1979) Path dependent options:buy

at the low, sell at the high, J.Finan., **34**, 1111-1128.

[17] Hull, J. (2000) Options, Furtures and Other Derivatives, Fourth Edition, Prentice-Hall.

[18] Jacka, S.D. (1991) Optimal stopping and the American put, Math. Finan., **1**, 1-14.

[19] Jaillet, P., Lamberton, D.&Lapeyre, B.(1990) Variatinal inequalities and pricing of American options, Acta Appl. Math., **21**, 263-289.

[20] Jiang, L.(2002) Analysis of pricing American options on the maximum(minimum) of two risk assets , Interface &Free Boundaries, **4**, 27-46.

[21] Jiang, L.& Dai, M.(2004) Convergence of the explicit difference scheme and the binomial tree method for American options, J.Comp.Math., **22**, 371-380.

[22] Jiang, L.&Dai, M.(2000) On path-dependent options, Mathematical Finance-Theory &Applications, Higher Education Press, Beijing, 290-317.

[23] Jiang, L.&Dai, M.(2004) Convergence of binomial tree method for European/American path-dependent options, SIAM J. Numer. Anal., **42**, 1094-1109.

[24] Jiang, L.&Tao Y.(2001) Identifying the volatility of underlying assets from option prices, Inverse Problems, **17**, 137-155.

[25] Jiang, L., Yang D.& Zhang, S.(2004) On pricing model of reset option with N predetermined levels, J. System Sci. & Complexity, **17**, 137-142.

[26] Jiang, L., Chen, Q., Wang, L. &Zhang, J.E.(2003) A new well-posed algorithm to recover implied volatility, Quant. Finan., **3** 451-457.

[27] Karatzas, I.&Shreve, S.(1998) Methods of Mathematical Finance , Springer Verlag, Berlin, Heidelberg, New York.

[28] Kwok, Y.-K.(1998) Mathematical Models of Financial Derivatives, Springer Verlag, Berlin, Heidelberg, New York.

[29] Linetsky, V.(1999) Step options, Math.Finan.**9**, 55-96.

[30] Margrale, W.(1978) The value of an option to exchange one asset for another, J.Finan., **33**, 177-186.

[31] McDonald, R.L., Schroder, M.D.(1998) A parity result for American options, J.Comp.Finan., **3**, 5-13.

[32] Merton, R.C.(1973) Theory of rational option pricing, Bell J.Econ.Manag. Sci., **4**, 141-183.

[33] Merton, R.C.(1990) Continuous Time Finance, Basil Blackwell, Oxford.

[34] Musiela, M.&Rutkowski, M.(1998) Martingale Methods in Financial Modelling, Springer Verlag, Berlin, Heidelberg, New York.

[35] Richtmyer, R.D.(1957) Difference Methods for Initial-Value Problems, Interscience Publishers, Inc., New York.

[36] Rogers, L.C.G.&Shi, Z.(1995) The value of an Asian option, J.Appl.Prob., **32**, 1077-1088.

[37] Robinstein, M.(1991) One for another, Risk, **4**, (December) , 30-32.

[38] Stulz, R.M.(1982) Options on the minimum or the maximum of two risky assets, J.Finan.Econ., **10** , 161-185.

[39] Wan, N., (2003) The asymptotic expression of optimal exercise boundary near expiry for American options when $r = q$, Working paper, Tongji University.

[40] Wilmott, P., Dewynne, J.N. Howison, S.D.(1993) Option Pricing: Mathematical Models and Computation, Oxford Financial Press, Oxford.

[41] Wilmott, P.(1998) Derivatives: The Theory and Practice of Financial Engineering, John Wiley &Sons, Inc., New York.

[42] Zhang, P.G.(1997) Exotic Options, World Scientific Publishing Co.Pte. Ltd., Singapore.

[43] Zhang, Q.(1998) A theory study of path-dependent options with general payoff, Working paper, City Univ. of Hong Kong.

Index